THE AGE OF
CONSTANTINE THE GREAT

The Swiss historian, Jacob Christoph Burckhardt was born in Basel in 1818. He studied under Ranke at the University of Berlin and in 1844 returned to his native city to teach. Except for a brief period, Burckhardt remained at the University of Basel until a few years before his death in 1897.

Among his works are *Cicerone* (1855) and *The Civilization of the Renaissance in Italy* (1860). *Force and Freedom: Reflections on History* and *Griechische Kulturgeschichte* (*A History of Greek Culture*) were published posthumously.

The Age of Constantine the Great was published in 1852. The English translation, which appeared in 1949, was published by Pantheon Books.

THE AGE OF CONSTANTINE THE GREAT

Jacob Burckhardt

TRANSLATED BY MOSES HADAS

Doubleday Anchor Books

Doubleday & Company, Inc., Garden City, New York

1956

COVER BY ANTONIO FRASCONI

TYPOGRAPHY BY EDWARD GOREY

Copyright, 1949, by Pantheon Books, Inc.

TRANSLATOR'S FOREWORD

No EPOCH of remote history can be so relevant to modern interests as the period of transition between the ancient and the medieval world, when a familiar order of things visibly died and was supplanted by a new. Other transitions become apparent only in retrospect; that of the age of Constantine, like our own, was patent to contemporaries. Old institutions, in the sphere of culture as of government, had grown senile; economic balances were altered; peoples hitherto on the peripheries of civilization demanded attention, and a new and revolutionary social doctrine with an enormous emotional appeal was spread abroad by men with a religious zeal for a new and authoritarian cosmopolitanism and with a religious certainty that their end justified their means. For us, contemporary developments have made the analogy inescapable, but Jacob Burckhardt's insight led him to a singularly clear apprehension of the meaning of the transition almost a century ago, and the analogy implicit in his book is the more impressive as it was unpremeditated.

That is not to imply that Burckhardt conceived history's utility as providing a blueprint for future conduct. "We study history not to be clever for another time," he wrote, in obvious echo of Thucydides, "but to be wise for always." Burckhardt was indeed a pioneer in the humanist reaction against the microscopic but unimaginative history of the "scientific" historians, though his wide and deep erudition, aside from his imagination and taste, entitle him to a distinguished place even among the scientific historians. He would have subscribed heartily to the dictum of George Macaulay Trevelyan, the foremost modern exponent of humanist historiography: "Let the science and research of the historian find the fact, and let his imagination and art make clear its significance." Fifty years ago, when Burckhardt's great work on Greek civilization appeared posthumously, professional scholars expressed regret that the work had been published, on the ground that its material was already obsolete. It is true that many aspects of Burckhardt's subjects have received new illumination by detailed researches into administration, economics, and religion that have been carried out in the interval, but it is also true not only that Burckhardt has survived his critics of half a century ago but that his insight and his skill may still afford the lay reader a truer and more meaningful picture than can the production of contemporary professional historians. Surely *Constantine* communicates not only a more intelligible but also a more valid picture of events, their nexus, and their relevance than does the parallel twelfth volume of the sober *Cambridge Ancient History* (1939), which represents the latest technical knowledge, presented by a panel of the world's best specialists.

Burckhardt's own prefaces disclaim any intention to present a complete and systematic history of the period. For that kind of treatment such works as the *Cambridge Ancient History* and the *Cambridge Mediaeval History* with their excellent bibliographies are available, and will surely be consulted by the student who requires fuller information.

To print Burckhardt's notes without extensive modernization and discussion seemed inadvisable; scholars will recognize the sources for Burckhardt's statements and know where to find full documentation, and an elaborate apparatus would distort the book unduly, both physically and by making it appear a dull, systematic history rather than a penetrating and informed essay.

Concerning two general criticisms of Burckhardt's use of sources the reader must be apprised. The chief literary source for the Emperors from Hadrian to Numerianus (omitting those from 245 to 253) is the collection of biographies, ostensibly by six authors, known as the *Historia Augusta*. Burckhardt accepts the book's own statements that it was written under Diocletian and Constantine; most (but not all) scholars now hold that the book was written in the second half of the fourth century, under Julian and

Theodosius. If that is the case, incidents told of various Emperors and the occasional anti-Christian bias may be fictive retrojections. The other point concerns Burckhardt's attitude toward the Church writers Lactantius and especially Eusebius, whose good faith he impugns and whose portrait of Constantine as a Christian hero he rejects. Scholars jealous for the fair name of Church figures have criticized Burckhardt severely on this point. All that may be said is that Burckhardt knew his authors thoroughly (he was a student of Protestant theology before he became a historian and art critic) and also knew men and affairs; it is tolerably certain that none of the objections which were subsequently adduced to his views would have persuaded him to alter them essentially.

MOSES HADAS

Columbia University
December, 1948

PREFACE TO THE FIRST EDITION (1852)

In THE PRESENT work it has been the author's design to describe the remarkable half century from the accession of Diocletian to the death of Constantine in its quality as a period of transition. What was intended was not a history of the life and reign of Constantine, nor yet an encyclopedia of all worth-while information pertaining to his period. Rather were the significant and essential characteristics of the contemporary world to be outlined and shaped into a perspicuous sketch of the whole.

This goal the book has achieved in only a limited sense, and the reader may well deny it any title other than "Studies in the Age of Constantine." Those aspects of the life of the age which cannot be adequately recovered and hence could not be woven as a living element into the texture of the whole have been omitted; this applies to questions of property and wealth, industry and trade, state finance, and much else of the sort. The writer has not wished to carry scholarly controversies a single step further by adducing new details, only to leave the controversies essentially unresolved. In general he has addressed himself primarily not to scholars but to thoughtful readers of all classes, who are apt to follow an account only as it is able to present a definite and well-rounded picture. But if the new conclusions which he believes he has reached in the area here treated meet with the approval of specialists, he will value such approval highly. Apart from the choice of materials, which is not wholly free, the principles of arrangement and exposition here followed doubtless leave much to be desired, and the author is not convinced that he has hit upon either the best or the only correct principles. In works of general history there is room for differences of opinion on fundamental premises and aims, so that the same fact may seem essential and important to one writer, for example, and to another mere rubbish utterly without interest. Hence the writer is well aware that his treatment may be impugned as being subjective. It would have been safer, for example, to compose a new history of Constantine by means of subjecting existing accounts to critical examination and providing the whole with an appropriate quantity of citations of sources; but for the writer such an enterprise could not have exerted the inward attraction which is alone capable of repaying every effort. This is not to imply any adverse judgment whatever on the various methods by which the material has hitherto been treated; it will be enough for us if our offering is allowed its little place in the sun.

In the matter of citations the writer has set himself a definite limit. Readers acquainted with the subject will easily recognize how much he owes to Gibbon, Manso, Schlosser, Tzschirner, Clinton, and other predecessors, but also how much he was compelled throughout to resort to his own study of the sources. From the excellent work of Tzschirner, it may be noted in passing, he feels constrained to differ completely in one respect. The influence of Christianity on declining paganism seems to him to be rated much too high in that work, and he has preferred to explain the relevant phenomena as due to an internal development in paganism itself; the reasons for this preference cannot be elaborated here.

The sections of our book devoted to this subject (Chapters 5 and 6), it will be seen, lack virtually any reduction to system. The author was convinced that it was better to venture too little than too much. In general observations on spiritual matters, and especially in the field of the history of religion, he would liefer be reproached for hesitancy than for boldness.

PREFACE TO THE SECOND EDITION (1880)

WHEN the material for this book was assembled, nearly three decades ago, and its writing was taken in hand, the objective in the mind of the author was not so much a complete historical account as an integrated description, from the viewpoint of cultural history, of the important transition period named in the title. He was conscious that such a design involved highly subjective selection among the component elements which comprise the complete picture of the period, but the welcome which the book has received leads him to believe that his method has met the wishes of many readers. Since the book was written the epoch has been the object of much specialized research; in particular the political aspects and those involving Church history have received fresh literary treatment. This second edition will show evidence of great indebtedness for new and important matter to such scholars as Vogel, Hunziker, von Görres, and many others, and in particular to Preuss's excellent work on Diocletian. It has not been necessary, however, to increase the size of the book greatly, nor to change or abandon the scale of emphasis on cultural history by enlarging on political and biographical detail; it has been deemed sufficient to correct numerous errors of fact and to clarify the most essential historical connections where these have been more accurately determined. This is the best recommendation for the work in its new dress that can be offered to a predominantly new generation of readers.

CONTENTS

The
ROMAN EMPIRE
A.D. 297

THE GENEALOGY OF CONSTANTINE

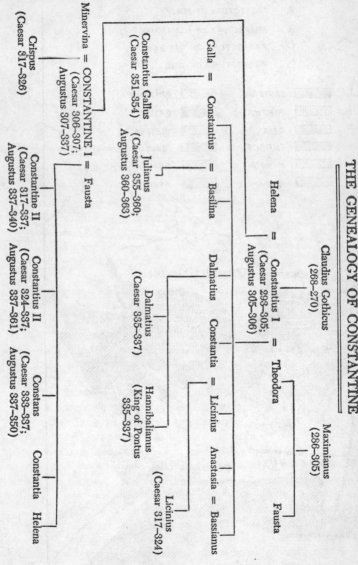

I

THE IMPERIAL POWER IN THE THIRD CENTURY

IN THE account of the period from the accession of the Emperor Diocletian to the death of Constantine the Great which lies before us, each section might well demand its own introduction, for events will be narrated not chronologically and by reigns but according to prevailing movements. But if a general introduction to the entire work be wanted, its principal content must be a history of the changing concepts of the character and function of the Emperor during the decline of the Roman Empire in the third century A.D. And this not because all other aspects of history may be derived from the character of the imperial office; but changes in that character do provide a basis for judging a multitude of events, external as well as spiritual, in the period following. Every form and degree which a rule based on force may assume, from the most frightful to the most beneficent, is here to be met with in remarkable alternation. Under the good Emperors of the second century, from Nerva to Marcus Aurelius (96–180 A.D.), the Roman Empire enjoyed an era of peace, which might have been an era of happiness as well if the profound malaise common to aging nations could have been reached by the benevolence and wisdom of even the best of rulers. The great stature, as men and as rulers, of a Trajan, a Hadrian, an Antoninus, or a Marcus Aurelius must not blind us to situations and conditions which had become patent to all. It was inevitable that the three great forces—Emperor, Senate, and Army—must again eventually confound one another and lose the harmony which had been painstakingly preserved. In the sequel the confusion seemed wholly irremediable when barbarian incursions, stirrings in the provinces, and natural catastrophes combined to contribute to it.

A prelude is offered by the reign of Marcus Aurelius himself. To speak of that Emperor's personality is superfluous; among the imperishable ideal figures of antiquity the Stoic philosopher seated upon the throne of the world is not the fairest or most youthful, but surely one of the most admirable. And yet he was not spared the menacing sound of harbingers of doom, pounding at the gates of the Empire. First, with regard to the imperial office itself, it became clearly apparent that, despite the system of adoptions which had linked the four great Emperors to one another, that office might be usurped by a coup. Avidius Cassius, the most important general of the realm, ventured such a coup, though unsuccessfully, after the Empire had enjoyed almost three generations of excellent or at least benevolent rule. As regards the army, Marcus Aurelius was reputed "never to have flattered the soldiers in speech and never to have done aught out of fear of them"; nevertheless Marcus acquiesced in the traditional abuse of bestowing a huge donative upon the army at his accession, and to such a degree that each soldier (at least those of the Guard) acquired a fortune, and that the soldiers thereafter regarded that amount as a norm. Of external misfortunes there must be reckoned the first violent incursion of a Germanic-Sarmatian tribal federation into the Empire, and a fearful pestilence. The Emperor's last years were filled with perilous war and deep anxiety. But even in his tent on the Danube he sought to raise himself above the cares and threats of the moment by the quiet cultivation of virtue and of the divine in the life of man.

For his son Commodus (180–192) Marcus is said to have instituted a kind of regency, "the best of the Senate"; at least during his first weeks the young ruler accepted the guidance of his father's friends. But very quickly he developed that repulsive imperial madness to which men had grown unaccustomed since the days of Domitian. Consciousness of dominion over the world and fear of all who might covet his rule begot an urge to quick enjoyment of what was his and to drown anxiety that gave no respite. In a character wanting native firmness such pressures soon evoked a combination of bloodthirstiness and voluptuousness. Occasion was provided by an attempt upon his life, of which his own family was not innocent but which was blamed upon the Senate. It was small wonder that the Prefect of the Guard soon became the first personage in the state and responsible for the life of the Emperor, as had been the case under Tiberius and Claudius, and that the few thousands which he commanded shared his feeling of being masters of the realm. One of these prefects indeed, the energetic Perennis, Commodus made a victim to a deputation of the disaffected Britannic army which, fifteen hundred strong, had made their way to Rome without hindrance. His successor, the Prefect Cleander, Commodus yielded to a hunger riot of the Roman populace; not, to be sure, without cause, for Cleander in his prodigious greed had not only antagonized the upper classes by confiscations and sale of public offices but had incurred the anger of the poor by a monopoly of grain.

When the cowardly and cruel ruler, dressed as a god, appeared in the amphitheater to be admired by the Senate which lived in constant peril of death, one might well ask whether this "Commodian Senate" deserved the old title, even though it still participated to some degree in provincial administration and the nomination of officials, and still possessed its own treasury and its external distinctions. Indeed it could hardly longer be called Roman, in the stricter sense, for the majority of its members were perhaps not even Italians, but provincials in whose families the dignity had sometimes become hereditary. From an ideal point of view it is easy to condemn this degenerate assembly in the severest terms, particularly since it is difficult to conceive clearly the effect of the deadly peril which hovered constantly over families and groups. Contemporaries judged more leniently. When Clodius Albinus refused to accept the dignity of Caesar at the bloody hands of Commodus he still regarded the Senate as sufficiently vital to favor the restoration of a republican constitution in a public harangue to his troops. Whether he was sincere is not to the point; it is enough that the Senate (as we shall see) still contained many of the noblest characters of the period and in times of stress displayed energy and decision in administration. Even the illusions under which we shall see it labor are not altogether to its discredit. Despite the intrusion of unworthy individuals, then, it is easy to understand that the Senate continued to be looked upon as the representative if not of the Empire at least of Roman society, and that it regarded itself as the natural sponsor of the so-called Senates or Curias of the provincial cities. It was still impossible to conceive of Rome without the Senate, even if its effectiveness seemed to be destroyed over long periods by violence from without.

After Commodus had further pillaged the senators in order to assuage the murmuring populace of the capital by monstrous gifts, he succumbed to an ordinary palace conspiracy.

The alarming aspect of imperial succession at Rome was the fact that no one knew precisely where the responsibility for raising a new Emperor lay. No dynasty could be established because the imperial madness—the fate of all the incumbents who were not especially gifted—compelled periodic revolution. Even aside from revolution, the childlessness of the dissolute Emperors and even of some among the better ones made a regular succession impossible. The practice of adoption went back to the house of Augustus, but adoptions could hope for recognition only if the adoptive father as well as the new son possessed the qualities requisite to make them effective.

Historically, the right to nominate the new Emperor obviously resided in the Senate, which had decreed one title of power after another to the divine Augustus. But when the Emperors came to hate the Senate and to rely exclusively upon the Guard, the latter assumed the right of election; and it was not long before the armies in the provinces competed with the barracks of the Praetorian camp at Rome. Soon the advantage of short reigns came to be appreciated, because the donative to the camp became more frequent. Another element was the shady intrigue of determined men whose interest might at times induce them to support a pretender whose early fall they both foresaw and desired.

Thus the murderers of Commodus put forward Helvius Pertinax, a sound man, as if to justify their deed; and Pertinax was acknowledged first by the soldiers and then by the Senate (193). By a show of favor to a certain Triarius Maternus the Guards extorted an enormous donative from Pertinax, to meet which Commodus' valuables had to be disposed of. The natural consequence was a second attempt, in favor of the Consul Falco. The third time the Guards began straightway with the murder of the Emperor. And now there ensued in the camp that unexampled auction of the imperial dignity. There was found a rich fool, Didius Julianus, who, for a sum in excess of one thousand dollars paid to each soldier, purchased for himself a few weeks of debauchery and terror. But this was the last and highest pinnacle of Praetorian presumption. Simultaneously three provincial armies gave themselves the pleasure of proclaiming their leaders Emperor, and among them was the gloomy African, Septimius Severus. Feckless Julian's first recourse was to dispatch assassins; there was an officer named Aquilius who had often been employed for murder in high places and who enjoyed a reputation like Locusta's in Nero's day. Then, because he had paid good money for the realm, Julian tried to negotiate a business deal with Severus. When Severus drew nearer Julianus declared him co-regent; but he was deserted and scorned and at the instance of the Senate executed while Severus was still several days' march from Rome.

Septimius Severus (193–211) is the first representative of thorough military rule. There is something un-Roman, something modern, in the pride of military profession and rank which he displayed even as a legate. The slight appreciation and esteem he would show the ancient majesty of the Senate might be apprehended by the deputation of a hundred senators which went to greet him at Terni, and whom he caused to be searched straightway to see whether they carried daggers. But his clearest manifestation of

military logic was his disarming and disgracing of the
Praetorians and his banishing them from Rome. His system
had no room for a privileged and corrupted Guard with
political pretensions. His own army, which he had brought
with him, he gave only a fifth of the requested donative.
Severus was equally consistent in his campaign against his
rivals, Pescennius Niger and Clodius Albinus, and extirpated all their following. It was inconceivable to him that
a number of senators could have been in correspondence
with them and even that the Senate as a whole could have
been neutral. "It was I who gave the city grain, I who
waged many wars for the state, I who gave oil to the people of Rome," he wrote to the Senate; "a fine requital truly
you have made me, a fine expression of thanks!" The
Senate, he continued, had greatly degenerated since the
time of Trajan and Marcus Aurelius.

Despite its importance and its indispensable military
significance as a stronghold against the barbarians of
Pontus, Byzantium, where Pescennius' followers had defended themselves for a year, was razed to the ground,
and its garrison, along with many of its inhabitants, was
put to death. The world must be given an example of the
fate of cities and factions which could not immediately
choose among a number of rival usurpers that one who deserved enduring obedience.

Albinus' followers fared no better. Severus had come into
possession of their correspondence; he might have burned
the letters unread, as Caesar had burned the letters of the
Pompeians. That would have been a generous gesture, but
altogether unsuitable to the times; the question was no
longer one of divergent principles and their amalgamation
through reconciliation and persuasion, but simply of sub-
jection. A crowd of senators and other notables in and out
of Rome were executed; the Emperor delivered eulogies
of Commodus before the Senate, people, and army, surely
not out of conviction but in mockery of the Senate. In Rome
itself, during this struggle for dominion, a spontaneous
lamenting and wailing once broke out at the Circus games;
an eyewitness could find no explanation for the phenomenon other than divine inspiration. "O Rome, Queen, Im-

mortal," the multitudes shouted with a single voice, "how long shall we suffer these things, how long will war be waged over us?" Ignorance of their future was the happier lot.

When peace was restored at home it became apparent that the military rule, with its necessary corollary of foreign war, had become an end in itself. The center of this rule was Severus, with his family, of whom he wished to form a dynasty, distributed over the highest offices; only his brother, who would very willingly have shared the rule, did Severus carefully keep at a distance. The first step for asserting power was the organization of a new Guard, which was more than four times the strength of the old. With such a personal force constantly available, quite a different posture could be assumed toward the provincial armies. With such a force, as events proved, one might travel about in the Empire and murder and pillage everywhere. The former Guard had consisted of Italians, and preferably of men from the region of Rome; now Severus filled Rome with the faces of rude and frightening barbarians. If his donative was meager, Severus raised the regular pay of the soldier higher than any other Emperor had done; instead of flinging away several millions at once, now there was a constant drain on the Empire for the benefit of the soldiers. The fatherly advice which Severus is said to have offered his sons seems to be rather a contemporary comment on Severus' administration than an actual utterance of the Emperor, but it is significant nevertheless: "Be united, enrich the soldiers, despise all others."

One might expect that a professional soldiery so highly esteemed and kept constantly on the alert by an active general would be a credit to the glorious military past of Rome. But this was not the case. Severus himself complained loudly concerning the deterioration of discipline, and in his great Asiatic campaign there were cases of insubordination which he was able to meet only by leniency and additional gifts. Could Severus have blinded himself to the fact that his innovations secured only himself and his own reign, and that they must inevitably bring destruction upon a weak and evil successor who was not (as

Severus was) his own Prefect of the Guard? Or was he indifferent regarding the person of his successor if only the military rule as such was maintained?

Here and during the last centuries of paganism in general one must not forget that even the mightiest figures had no complete freedom of action, because they yielded to astrology and portents. There is no other way to explain, to cite one example, why Severus, who loved strict justice, should so stubbornly have retained in the prefecture of the Guard and in the closest association with his own house so frivolous a wastrel as Plautianus. Numerous superstitions encompassed the life of Severus, from his childhood to the grave. Since the imperial throne had come to be the first prize in a lottery, there were parents in all classes of society who scrupulously observed the daily life of their more gifted children for signs of future dominion. The fact was noticed if a boy recited odd verses, if turtles or eaglets or even a purple pigeon's egg was brought into the house, if snakes moved into the house or a laurel sprouted, or similar events took place. But if a child was born with a welt forming a crown on his head, or if a bit of purple cloth was inadvertently used to cover a newborn infant, then his future as an Emperor was regarded as fixed. Many an Emperor was attended by such delusions throughout his reign, and these delusions affected his acts in a manner to us incalculable. Compassion is our only reaction when the aged Severus grows restless and irascible after his last victories in Britain because a Moor bearing a cypress wreath had encountered him, or because he was taken to the wrong temple for sacrifice, or because he was given dark-colored victims to offer up, which then followed him to his quarters.

But there was no need for omens at the imperial headquarters at York; Severus' own son Caracalla desired his life, persistently and almost openly. Severus had consciously raised pitilessness to a principle, in order to suppress any thought of usurpation; but high treason on the part of the heir apparent had not entered his calculations, nor the possibility that his Guard would so brazenly support the treachery. When he whispered to his dehumanized son, "Do not let them see you kill me!" the cry sounds like an agonized assertion of a principle of rule. Another remark he seems to have repeated several times: "I have been everything, and to no avail."

And now the repulsive monster called Caracalla ascended the imperial throne (211–217). From early youth he displayed an evil arrogance. He boasted that Alexander the Great was his model, and he praised Tiberius and Sulla. Later, perhaps after the murder of his brother Geta, came that authentic imperial madness, which employed the resources and the power of the entire Empire for its own sure destruction. His sole measure for security, which he regarded as adequate, was his camaraderie with the soldiery, whose exertions at least on occasion he shared. His similar easy familiarity with prize fighters and racing jockeys endeared him to the Roman mob. There was no need to please the respectable and the educated. After his fratricide, which the soldiers at first regarded with disapproval, Caracalla devoted himself entirely to such flattery of the mob. His requirements for his soldiers necessitated vast confiscations, and he put twenty thousand persons to death as adherents of Geta, among them a son of Pertinax; one of the more humane aspects of usurpations at Rome was that the relatives of fallen Emperors were generally spared. For his soldiers' sake also Caracalla embarked on a campaign in his own perfectly peaceful realm; the attacks of neighboring peoples he met with payments of money. The mass murders in Alexandria illustrate the attitude which despotism thought proper to meet the sophisticated mockery of the Alexandrians. The real penalty for such misdeeds (aside from the qualms of conscience of which our authors speak) was the tyrant's growing distrust of the privileged soldiery itself; at the end he came to rely entirely, as regards his immediate surroundings, upon a quite barbaric bodyguard composed of Celts and Sarmatians who could have no opinion on Roman matters, and he wore their own costume in order to retain their favor. To embassies from such peoples he used to say that if he should be murdered it would be well for them to invade Italy, for Rome would be easy to take. And yet he was struck down, in the very midst of these Guards, upon the instigation of men who were constrained to dispose of him in order that they might not themselves fall at his hands.

The nomination of his successors fell perforce into the hands of the all-powerful army. The army first named Macrinus, one of the two Prefects of the Guard, without being aware that Macrinus had contrived the death of their beloved Caracalla. Macrinus assumed Caracalla's name and gave him a splendid funeral in order to distract suspicion from himself. With dissembled impudence he greeted the Senate for his confirmation, and received the several titles of imperial power with seemly hesitancy. Nevertheless his first severe measure toward bridling an army which had grown unaccustomed to restraint hastened his destruction. Two young Syrians, collateral relations of the Antonines and Severus, suddenly rose to be heads of the Empire. These were the dissimilar cousins Elagabalus and Alexander Severus, together with their mothers Soaemias and Mammaea and their common grandmother Julia Maesa.

With all its loathsomeness and madness the reign of Elagabalus (218–222) is not without interest for the history of Roman rule. The incredible voluptuousness, the Asiatic pomp of idolatry, the thoughtless surrender to the pleasures of the moment, constituted in fact a reaction against the regime of Septimius Severus, which was by intention a soldier's regime. Elagabalus' war upon all Roman usages, his induction of his mother and grandmother into the Senate, his appointment of dancers, professional athletes, and barbers to high positions in the state, and his sale of public offices—these need not have caused his overthrow. Even his negligence in provisioning the capital might long have been condoned. His destruction arose from an awakened sense of shame in the soldiers, which was abetted by a conspiracy in favor of Alexander among the Emperor's own kindred. The soldiers knew that Alexander's life was in peril, and forced the trembling Emperor to purge his court. Elagabalus took his revenge by expelling the Senate from the city, a measure much to the credit of the Senate, as it proves that that body was not composed wholly of "slaves dressed in togas," as Elagabalus had thought. Finally the Guards murdered Elagabalus and raised Alexander Severus to the throne.

Of the many Emperors, none so evokes the sympathy of posterity as this man, a true St. Louis of antiquity, a man quite incomprehensible when considered in relation to his environment. His fall was the result of his efforts to turn from the debased abuses of military despotism into a path of justice and moderation. This need not imply any diminution of the reputation of his excellent mother, Mammaea; but his merit is still the greater, because, the course once set, he persevered in it with independent spirit and, motivated purely by virtue, was able to resist the many temptations of despotism. Above all we find a high regard for the Senate, such as had not been known since the time of Marcus Aurelius, and even the equestrian order, long fallen into oblivion politically, was spoken of as "nursery of the Senate." A commission of senators and an inner council of sixteen participated in government, and no effort was spared to train good and conscientious men for administration and to exercise diligent supervision. Unjust or venal officials alone could disrupt Alexander's even temper. With regard to the soldiers, he made no secret of the fact that the fate of the state rested upon them; he equipped them magnificently and treated them well. Yet just as he could boast that he reduced taxes, so he ventured to dismiss a mutinous legion. But things are reported of Alexander which are hard to reconcile with the brighter aspects of the picture. In the army we sense a continuous ferment. The Prefects of the Guard were changed under the most violent circumstances, and when Ulpian, the most eminent of their number, was murdered in the course of serious disturbances, the Emperor could only let the crime go unpunished. On this occasion we learn that the populace and the Guards engaged in bloody battle for three days in the streets of Rome and that the Guard reduced the citizenry to peace only by setting fire to their houses. The most absurd characters ventured to rise as usurpers against their excellent prince. One of them, Ovinius by name, he is said actually to have accepted as co-regent with ironic leniency; but Ovinius was wearied of his throne by being made to share in the hardships of a campaign. Another, whom the soldiers raised, simply decamped. A third, the slave Uranius, the Emperor seems to have been constrained to punish. Furthermore, since Alexander was fated, as his model Marcus Aurelius had been, to suffer special visitations of misfortune, a new and warlike Persian kingdom, that of the Sassanids, arose on the Eastern borders. Alexander's war against them met with only equivocal success. On the Rhine border there were threatening movements among the Germans. The temper of the youthful ruler is said to have grown melancholy; it is reported that he showed a tendency to miserliness, but this need only mean that some of his entourage could no longer control their greed for the war chest. On the campaign at the Rhine, not far from Mainz, the soldiers murdered him and his mother. It is futile to examine the motives of this deed as they are alleged. If the successor of a Severus, a Caracalla, and an Elagabalus wished to dismiss all brutal officials, to show austerity to the soldiers, and yet to practice leniency at dangerous junctures, he was predestined to a violent end. Conspiracy was a disease of the age; it was in the very air. Alexander strove in vain for respect in a century which recognized only fear.

Maximinus, who is conjectured to have been Alexander's murderer, mounted the throne (235–238). He was a Thracian shepherd, son of a Goth and an Alan woman, hence a thorough barbarian by descent and, moreover, by education. But the army was indifferent to such considerations; it consisted of utter barbarians from the Eastern marches to whom it was of no consequence whether or not their candidate was descended from the Antonines, had been trained in high office, or had served as Senator. Instead, Maximinus was over eight feet tall and of gigantic strength, a subaltern perhaps without peer in the entire Roman army.

In principle if not in actuality his rule was more frightful than that of any Emperor. The ancient world with its monuments filled with beauty and its life filled with culture incited a venomous rage in this barbarian, who was ashamed of his origin. Indeed, a gentle soul could not have maintained the usurpation. He required confiscations for the sake of his soldiers, and so a Roman Emperor proceeds to the systematic destruction of the very essence of Rome. He himself refused to be seen in the hated capital; at first he intended to have his son reside there, but ended by keeping him in his encampments on the Rhine and the Danube, whence he ruled the Empire. Terror-stricken Rome was apprehensive that a border army of barbarians might become the headquarters of world empire, an army that was thought of somewhat like that of Spartacus or of Athenion in the slave war. Maximinus' rage was directed against everything that was distinguished or rich or cultivated, and especially against the Senate, which he believed despised him. He caused large pictures of his German victories to be set up before the Senate House. But even the populace of the capital, which might have remained tranquil even if the entire Senate were executed, was embittered to the extreme by the reduction of supplies and the confiscation of funds for public spectacles. The provincial cities fared no better; their municipal resources, like those of their wealthy citizens, were pillaged to enrich the army. So bare and unadulterated a military rule has never reappeared in the West.

There followed a time of indescribable confusion. Of greatest interest is the vigorous and determined attitude of the much misunderstood Senate. Despair drove peasants and soldiers in Africa to revolt, and two respectable Romans, the Gordians, father and son, were forcibly put at the head of the insurrection. Upon report of this insurrection, the Senate declared against Maximinus. It was to be expected that unworthy members of that body would betray the secret resolution to the tyrant. Equally bold were the written invitations to defection which the Senate sent to the provinces. The possibility that others besides the Gordians would be proclaimed Emperor in other provinces and by other armies had to be reckoned with. Danger became critical when a commander in Africa named Capelianus (who secretly desired the Empire for himself) defeated the younger Gordian in the name of Maximinus; Gordian perished and his father hanged himself. Now the

Senate named a commission of twenty members who had experience of war, and of its own right proclaimed two Emperors, Pupienus and Balbinus (238). The situation was tense, pregnant with danger and terror. The people, which first had assisted in the proclamation of the Emperors, now again took sides with the Guards, who, irate at the independent choice of the Senate, demanded and forced the choice of a third Emperor or Crown Prince, the youngest Gordian to wit, a near relative of the first two. Our sources are confused and fragmentary; a battle to the death, for example, between Guards, gladiators, and recruits in Rome itself is dismissed with a word. It is hence impossible to pronounce a definitive judgment concerning this crisis; nevertheless, the Senate seems to have displayed singular resolution and fortitude, for it was able to uphold its two Emperors by the side of the Guards' protégé, and at the same time it bore the entire burden of defense against the oncoming Maximinus, and its commissioners directed warlike preparations throughout the provinces. At least they were assisted by the bitterness of the provincials against the cruel tyrant, so that he found Carinthia bare of people and provisions and his march through deserted Haemona (Ljubljana) was accompanied by hundreds of wolves. This experience had disheartened his Mauretanians and Celts when he arrived before Aquileia. And when that city, under the leadership of two senators, offered a long and desperate defense, his starving army struck him down in order to make its peace with the new Emperors.

Whether it was prudent to lead all or most of these troops to Rome we can no longer decide; they would have constituted a peril even in the provinces. But in Rome serious friction was to be expected, because of *esprit de corps*, between the predominantly Germanic army of the Senate's Emperors and Maximinus' troops. In any case the latter, as is the way of vanquished armies and defeated parties, sought an outlet for its ill humor. The victims were the two senatorial Emperors, and after they were dispatched soldiers and populace alike in wild tumult hailed the youthful Gordian (238–244) as Augustus. The Senate was overpowered but apparently by no means crushed; soldiers who forced their way into its session (held, at that time, on the Capitoline) were cut down by senators at the altar of Victory.

The next reign was a regime of eunuchs and cabals which surrounded the inexperienced youth. After a time a great and earnest man, the orator Misitheus, found his way to him and aroused his nobler nature. He became, we know not how, guardian, regent, even father-in-law to Gordian, and Gordian bestowed upon him both prefectures, that of the Guards and that of the capital. Misitheus' position, even the title "Father of the Prince" which the Senate bestowed upon him, recalls the Atabegs of the Seljuk Sultans in the twelfth century. Whether he established an understanding with the Senate cannot be determined; in any case this excellent reign did not long endure. On a campaign against the Persians which was otherwise successful the guardian succumbed to the poison of Philip called the Arab. Then Philip rendered the soldiers unruly by a contrived famine, thrust himself into the position of co-regent to the helpless Gordian through suborned officers, and gradually deprived Gordian of all authority and finally of his life.

Upon the report of Gordian's death the Senate intervened quickly, but the philosopher Marcus whom it named Emperor soon died, as did also a certain Severus Hostilianus who somehow next got possession of the throne. Philip, who had meanwhile arrived in Rome and had won over the most important of the senators by supple talk, was now acknowledged Emperor (244–249). To call Philip an Arab sheik is to do him too much honor; he derived from the disreputable tribe of southern Syrians east of the Jordan.

If the attraction of imperial power were not so utterly blinding it would be hard to conceive how this man could expect, with his negligible military capacity, to master the Roman Empire, which he had obtained by fraud, by distributing its principal offices to relatives and friends. While he was celebrating the Secular Games, which marked the city's thousandth anniversary, in Rome, barbarians were crashing into the Empire from several directions, and at least two armies were setting up new Emperors. In Syria there arose against Philip's brother Priscus the adventurer

Jotapian, who claimed descent from Alexander the Great, a name which still received almost superstitious reverence. In Moesia Marinus arose against Philip's son-in-law Severian, while near by the Goths were marching into the Empire.

The Empire's great and obvious peril once more aroused the genius of Rome. The second half of the third century is an era which would surely gain in esteem if we had fuller knowledge of its personalities and the motivation of their measures than our sources afford. Although the leading figures are not for the most part Roman in the strict sense, but rather Illyrian, that is to say, from the regions between the Adriatic and the Black Seas, nevertheless it was Roman culture and tradition, specifically in matters of war, that enabled them to become the new saviors of the ancient world. To be a Roman Emperor was no longer a pleasure but a fateful obligation. Men unworthy of it assumed the purple only under constraint; better men no longer pressed forward to the office but recognized in it duty or destiny. There is an unmistakable atmosphere of moral exaltation.

The great dangers soon put an end to Philip's reign. He turned to the Senate in terror and offered his abdication. There was silence, until the gallant Decius offered his services to subdue Marinus. He was successful, but asked to be recalled, for he saw that because of the general contempt for Philip the army would wish to make him Emperor. Philip refused his request, and the inevitable came to pass. In or after a battle against Decius, Philip was put to death by soldiers at Verona. The fact that Philip's brother Priscus could subsequently be governor of Macedonia proves that Decius need have no shame for what had transpired. In the sequel Priscus repaid him with treason.

Decius (249–251) was primarily an idealist, with the idealist's illusions. To employ his very great military capacity in the service of a refined senatorial regime, to restore ancient Roman virtue and religion and hence the power of the Roman name, and to establish it forever—these were doubtless his designs. It was in keeping with this design that he persecuted the Christians; sixty years later he might have employed similar zeal to guide the Christian spirit of self-sacrifice to the salvation of the Empire.

But he was not fated to attain his life's goal. Besides incursions of barbarians on all sides, famine and pestilence raged abroad; these must have induced permanent alterations in all of Roman life, for an aging people cannot abide the blows a youthful people may disdain. Decius' reward was a glorious death in battle against the Goths.

Again the Senate asserted its right. Besides Gallus, whom the soldiers raised, it named (251) its own Emperor, Hostilian, who soon died of an illness. While Gallus was buying the Goths off with tribute, there was a general with the troops on the Danube, the Mauretanian Aemilian, who spoke to his men of "Roman honor," and in the event of victory promised them the tribute which was being paid to the Goths. The victory was won, and the soldiers made Aemilian Emperor (253). But Decius' ideas were so far effective that Aemilian wished only to be called the Senate's general and to leave the government of the Empire to the Senate itself.

A perceptible lacuna in the *Historia Augusta* prevents valid conclusions concerning the events following. Aemilian marched toward Italy; Gallus, who marched against him, was murdered, together with his sons, by his own troops. But Valerian, one of Gallus' generals, marching down from the Alps, succeeded in some mysterious fashion in winning over the victorious army of Aemilian, which murdered its Emperor "because he was a soldier but no ruler, because Valerian was better suited to be Emperor, or because the Romans must be spared another civil war." The truth glimmers through this justification. Clearly these are not the doings of mutinous bands of soldiers. What is involved is undoubtedly an understanding among the higher officers of the three armies. Only an understanding of such a nature can explain the rise of Valerian (253), who was perhaps the most outstanding of all Romans, in civil offices as in war; left to themselves, the soldiers would either have insisted on their Aemilian or have raised to the throne some tall, handsome figure with the talents of a petty officer.

Henceforward imperial elections generally assume a new

form. In the barbarian wars which had persisted since the time of Alexander Severus there must have developed an excellent corps of generals, among whom competence was properly assessed and esteemed. Valerian, at least as Emperor, seems to be the very soul of this corps. His military correspondence, part of which was deliberately preserved in the *Historia Augusta*, demonstrates precise knowledge of men and their capacities and gives us a high opinion of the man who could recognize and promote Posthumus, Claudius Gothicus, Aurelian, and Probus. If there had been peace on the frontiers, perhaps the Senate would have had a regular share in government, as Decius and Aemilian designed. But since simultaneous barbaric incursions from all directions threatened to overwhelm the Empire entirely and since the true Rome had long abandoned the seven hills by the Tiber and was now to be found in the brave camps of Roman military leaders, it was only natural that the power of the state should also gravitate into the hands of the generals. These now constituted a kind of Senate in arms, which was scattered over all the border provinces. For short periods, to be sure, the Empire was quite out of joint, and here and there thoughtless caprice of the soldiers or despair in the provinces clothed the first available man with the purple; but when the initial shock was over, the generals occupied the throne with one of their own number. We can only surmise how prudence and calculation were reconciled with ambition and violence in individual cases, and the nature of the secret oaths that bound the group firmly together. No hostility was shown to the Senate; indeed it was generally treated with respect, and there was one occasion when the Senate could delude itself into believing that it had once more become the master of the Empire.

This remarkable transition merits examination in detail. Even under Valerian the defection of individual regions had begun, and when Valerian himself was treacherously made captive by the Sassanid King Shapur (260), contrary to all international law, while his son Gallienus was occupied with the war against the Germans, utter confusion set in. While Rome itself was threatened with invasion by nameless hordes and the Senate was constrained to organize a hasty civil guard, the Eastern countries one after the other renounced their allegiance. First the worthless parricide Cyriades allowed himself to be put forward by Shapur as pretender to the Roman throne, until Macrianus with his sons and his brave Prefect Balista rose to be savior of the Roman East (260). Shapur was forced to flee, and his harem was taken captive. The magnificent defense of Caesarea in Cappadocia must at least be mentioned. But the disintegration of the Empire proceeded. Generals and higher officials were constantly constrained to proclaim themselves Emperors only to protect themselves against other usurpers, and perished notwithstanding. So it befell Valens, surnamed Thessalonicus, in Greece, and so it befell Piso, whom Macrianus sent against Valens. So presently it befell Macrianus himself (261) when he marched against Aureolus, who was Gallienus' general on the Danube; and when he proved victorious Aureolus too may have turned against Gallienus. In the East Macrianus and his house were supplanted by Odenathus (262), a rich provincial. Several such usurped the imperial title at this time, but none possessed the talent and enjoyed the success of this Palmyrene patrician, who, with his heroic wife Zenobia, was able to establish a great Oriental kingdom. Descended from the Egyptian Ptolemies, including the famous Cleopatra, Zenobia with her colorful court of Asiatic generals later (267–273) ruled, on her sons' behalf, a realm extending to Galatia and into Egypt. It was in this territory that Gallienus' generals had successfully disposed of lesser usurpers—in southeast Asia Minor the pirate Trebellian, whom the incorrigible Isaurians had raised to be their lord; in Egypt Aemilianus, the former commandant of Alexandria, who, when a rioting mob threatened him with death, had assumed the imperial title (262–265) in order to evade rendering an account to Gallienus.

For a time Gallienus was forced to recognize Aureolus, who was mentioned above, as ruler of the Danube region. But long before (258), the troops on the Danube had raised the Governor Ingenuus, the better to protect the country against incursions. Gallienus had suppressed Ingenuus, and had visited fearful punishments on the region. The provincials thirsted for vengeance, and named as Emperor the heroic Dacian Regillianus (260), who claimed descent from the Dacian King Decebalus, Trajan's famous enemy; but they soon gave him up, out of fear of new punishment at the hands of Gallienus, whom events had made merciless. Bithynia had a usurper, but not even his name is known; Sicily too was ruled by nameless robbers (*latrones*).

The most remarkable series of usurpers appears in the West, specifically Gaul, to which Spain and Britain occasionally submitted. Here, because of indescribable distress caused by the barbarians, there arose (after 259) first against Valerian and then against Gallienus' son and generals a series of mighty protectors—Posthumus, Lollianus (or Laelianus), and Victorinus. These were not merely soldier Emperors, but governed with the enthusiastic and almost regular participation of the provincials. A true transalpine realm was in the making, and its notables formed a Senate for the Emperor, who generally resided at Treves. Far from raising the standard of half-forgotten Gallic, Britannic, or Iberian nationality, these countries wished only to be a Western Roman Empire and to protect Roman culture and institutions from barbarian incursions. As much cannot be said of Zenobia's realm. Remarkably enough, however, in the West, too, it was a woman, Victoria, the mother of Victorinus, who instituted adoptions and successions among the Emperors, was called "Mother of the Camps," and like some superhuman being held sway over the armies. Her son and grandson were cut down before her eyes by angry soldiers, but contrition was so great that the nomination of a new Emperor was left to her will. Her first choice, for the soldiers' sake, was a strong armorer, Marius (267); and after Marius was murdered she ventured to name her relative Tetricus, who was unknown to the army but whose unmilitary regime (after 267) the soldiers accepted, at least until Victoria's death.

The last place in this series of usurpations clearly belongs to Celsus in Africa, because his was least justified and least successful. Without the ground or pretext of barbarian attack, the Africans (apparently only the Carthaginians), upon the instigation of the proconsul and a general, proclaimed the Tribune Celsus Emperor. The deficiency in divine right was supplied by the cloak of the Heavenly Goddess, which was fetched from the famous oracular temple at Carthage for investing the pretender. Here, too, a woman played the leading role. An aunt of Gallienus caused Celsus to be murdered after seven days and his corpse to be torn by dogs; the inhabitants of Sicca insisted on this treatment out of loyalty to the Emperor. Then in addition Celsus was crucified in effigy.

In these unexampled and for the most part unmerited situations Gallienus' own conduct seems not to have been as indifferent or cowardly as the *Historia Augusta* would have us believe. Upon some of the so-called Thirty Tyrants, it is true, he bestowed the title of Caesar or Augustus; but others he fought with great energy. The indolence for which he was notorious must have seized him by spells, but have left him as suddenly. It was probably expected of him that he should march to Persia to liberate his father, but under the circumstances such an enterprise was quite unthinkable. His relation to the provincial Emperors whom he recognized is comparable to that of the Caliphs to the dynasties which declared their independence, except that he received no honorary gifts and no mention in public prayer. On the other hand, he asserted his own sway over Italy with great energy; and several of his father's more important generals remained loyal to him. He purposely kept the Senate from service in his army, indeed from visiting it, because even in this unparliamentary age he was haunted by fear of a senatorial military regime. When Aureolus carried his attacks into Italy, Gallienus, moving vigorously, compelled him to concentrate his forces in Milan, and there besieged him. Aureolus' situation had grown desperate when Gallienus was murdered (268). The perpetrator was a colonel of Dalmatian cavalry, the immediate instigators a Prefect of the Guard and a general of the Danube troops. But the prime movers were Aurelian (subsequently Emperor), who had joined the beleaguerers with cavalry, and the Illyrian Claudius, a favorite of the

Senate and at the same time one of the greatest generals of the day. Claudius had made no secret of it whenever he was displeased with Gallienus' laxity, and it was probably for this reason that he was stationed apart in Pavia. These generals are said to have held a formal council on the life and death of Gallienus, and it was at this council that the decision concerning Claudius' succession must have been reached.

All things considered, such a complot may be partially exculpated in view of the extraordinary circumstances. The men who pronounced judgment were not irresponsible. If the Empire was to regain its unity, Gallienus had to be eliminated as a factor; and this could not be achieved with Gallienus' consent, for he was unable to live without his imperial pleasures. Claudius may also have foreseen the looming Gothic invasion, which was the most frightful of the century, and this was a necessity that knew no law. Apart from this imminent invasion, even while Gallienus was encamped before Milan, the Alemanni were already in Italy, and it was Claudius' most pressing business, after he had quickly disposed of Aureolus in the battle at Pontirolo, to deal decisively with the Alemanni. In his grave inscription Claudius declares that he would have suffered Aureolus to live if consideration for his excellent army had permitted such leniency. We have no grounds to doubt the sincerity of these words.

Claudius (268–270) could only begin the gigantic task of restoring the Empire, and his first measures involved leaving his party in Gaul in the lurch. But his victory over the Goths at Nissa gave the ancient world reprieve. His other talents for government could hardly benefit the Empire, for he survived but a year; nevertheless it is unjust to doubt that these talents were real, simply because Claudius had the misfortune of falling into the hands of panegyrists. His true eulogy is the pride which the Illyrian cavalry took in being his compatriots and the spirited confidence with which his victory inspired individual weak cities and provincial populations to defend themselves against the barbarians. Spain deserted Tetricus to fall into Claudius' arms.

Claudius had an excellent brother, Quintillus, whom the Senate named Emperor out of respect for Claudius. But on his deathbed Claudius himself, in the presence of the assembled generals, had designated Aurelian as his successor, and the army immediately recognized the election. It was only consonant with the times that Quintillus should forthwith open his veins.

Aurelian, who was a native of the Belgrade region, seems a degree more barbarian than his predecessor, but in essentials hardly less worthy of the throne. In a brilliant campaign (272) he subjugated Zenobia and the East, and this immediately enhanced his reputation for invincibility to a wonderful degree. Marcellinus, governor of Mesopotamia, who was instigated by part of his army to usurp the imperial title, himself laid information of the matter before Aurelian. Antiochus, whom the foolish Palmyrenes raised to the office, Aurelian let go, after he had punished the Palmyrenes. But the rich Firmus, a pretender in Egypt, Aurelian ordered crucified as a robber, apparently only to use the opportunity of making a display of the profound and traditional Roman contempt of Egyptian character. To Tetricus, who was under intolerable constraint as a result of his false position with regard to the soldiers and who betrayed his own army in the battle at Châlons (272), Aurelian gave a remunerative office. If we add to these campaigns for restoring the Empire the persistent and victorious wars against the barbarians, we may conceive what an incomparable school of war the reign of Aurelian provided. The most important of his successors on the throne were trained by him and Probus.

Aurelian's relation to the Senate appears in a far less favorable light, and is pictured for us in the same colors as that of Septimius Severus. The Emperor made the Senate responsible for conspiracies and unrest of all sorts in the capital, and a number of its members were even executed. The miserable records of the time, study them as we will, nowhere suffice for definitive conclusions. We cannot say whether Aurelian sought to extend the iron discipline of the camps to civil life, or whether the Senate was blind to the times and wished to compete with the reconqueror of the

Empire for its government. That Aurelian was not personally cruel and that he was eager to avoid bloodshed is
demonstrated by decisive passages in his life. Nor was he
called the "murderer" but only "the pedagogue of the
Senate." But a situation like Aurelian's required a strong
spirit indeed not to suffer contempt of mankind to depress
him into gloom, or cowardice and convenience into bloodthirstiness. It is not easy to imagine the position of an Emperor of the period; it is quite impossible to say how even
the most equable temper might endure it over a long period. Of Aurelian's sun-worship, which was the prevalent
religion among soldiers at the end of paganism, we shall
speak in the sequel.

Aurelian was murdered by conspirators among his immediate entourage on an expedition against the Persians,
not far from Byzantium. It may be assumed that not more
than one of the more respected generals, Mucapor, was
involved in the deed; the others were men of the Guard,
whom a confidential secretary—himself implicated and ex-
pecting punishment—was able to alarm by a forged signature.

The generals then jointly dispatched the following communication to the Senate: "The courageous and successful
armies to the Senate and people of Rome: Our Emperor
Aurelian has been murdered by the craft of one man and
the delusion of good and bad men. Honorable and sovereign Fathers! Raise him to the gods and send us an Emperor out of your midst, one whom you deem worthy to
be Emperor; for we will not suffer it that one of those who
has done evil, out of error or malice, should rule over us."
This letter does honor to all concerned—to Aurelian, who
is so handsomely justified; to the Senate; and to the armies,
in whose name it is clear that the generals entered upon
the negotiations. On the part of men who had helped Aurelian subdue the world, this action cannot have been merely
an emotional *beau geste*.

But the Senate, whose ancient and august authority was
here so splendidly and unexpectedly recognized, rejected
the honor. After soldier regimes, such as those immediately
preceding must have been, the nomination of an Emperor

by the Senate would have been a grievous error. In Rome, furthermore, the possibility that, during the two months which must elapse while communications were going to and fro, the mood of the Eastern armies might have altered, either of itself or through intrigues, must have entered into calculations. But the army did abide by its resolution. There were three exchanges of letters, until the Senate finally resolved to make the choice. During the half year that elapsed all higher officials remained at their posts; no other army ventured to anticipate the action of the Eastern army; fear or respect maintained a remarkable balance among the existing forces.

If after a millennium and a half, in view of exceedingly fragmentary knowledge of the records, an expression of opinion were allowed us, we should have approved the Senate's final decision to name an Emperor but should have thought that the candidate must be one of the better-known generals who had not participated in the murder—Probus, for example. Instead it raised Tacitus, an elderly and respected senator who possessed knowledge of military affairs, and let loose jubilant rejoicing over this masterpiece of constitutionalism. Exultant letters went out to all the provinces: the Senate again possessed its ancient right of imperial nomination, and in future would issue laws, receive the homage of barbarian princes, decide on war and peace. The senators sacrificed white victims, went about in white togas, and in their palace halls opened wide the cabinets which held the *imagines* of their forebears. Tacitus, however, regarded himself as a doomed man, bestowed his enormous wealth on the state, and went to join the army. Out of a purely legalistic vagary the Senate inconsiderately refused Tacitus permission to name his brother Florian consul. This mark of renewed constitutional awareness is said to have pleased the Emperor; comment is idle.

In the East Tacitus waged a successful war against the Goths and Alans. But a faction of officers, reinforced by the threatened murderers of Aurelian, first murdered Maximin, the strict commandant of Syria and a relative of the Emperor, and then, out of fear of punishment, the Emperor himself, in the Pontus region. His brother Florian in Tarsus committed the imprudence of assuming the posture of successor, without consulting Senate or army, as if the imperial office were hereditary; even if it were, Tacitus' sons would take natural precedence over Florian. After a few weeks he, too, was killed by the soldiers.

In the meanwhile a purely military election had raised the mighty Probus to the throne. Probus was a compatriot of Aurelian, and Aurelian had designated him, at least by inference, as his successor. The Senate recognized him without demur, and Probus was tactful enough to reconcile the somewhat constrained mood of the Senate by bestowing certain honorary privileges upon it. The murderers of Aurelian and Tacitus he had brought before him, manifested his abhorrence and contempt of them, and caused them to be executed. Immediately upon his election he had told the soldiers that they would not find him indulgent, and he kept his word. His discipline was severe, but he led his men to those stunning victories which rid Gaul of Germans and cost the lives of four hundred thousand barbarians. If these victories did no more than preserve the *status quo*, if the subjugation of all Germany which was prerequisite to Rome's continued security, as Probus clearly appreciated, was not achieved, the fault was surely not his.

From the Rhine and the Neckar he moved to the East, and his generals were victorious in the distant Southeast. Usurpers did indeed rise against him—Saturninus, Proculus, Bonosus—but this was not due to the soldiers' ill will because of his severity, but rather to the desperate petulance of the Egyptians, fear of the Lyonnaise and their party of the Emperor's punishment, and a drunkard's terror because of a serious dereliction in border duty. In each case the usurper's sway was very brief. The great ruler, who is regarded as a soldier Emperor exclusively, cherished an ideal of a quite different character. He wished to bring it about —and he made no secret of his designs—that the complete defeat or weakening of the barbarian peoples should make soldiers unnecessary for the Roman state, and that an era of peace and recovery might be introduced. The *Historia Augusta* presents his wistful delineation of a Saturnian utopia. Such talk penetrated to the soldiers, who were already irked that their Emperor employed them, aside from the needs of war, on vineyards, canals, and roads. At a drainage project in Sirmium in his home country the soldiers killed him, apparently without premeditation, and immediately rued the deed. His family, like those of several of the fallen Emperors, left Rome and settled in upper Italy.

This time the army took no thought of the Senate. That the higher officers themselves elected or guided the election is a natural inference from the fact that an old martinet, the Illyrian Carus, was invested with the purple. With his younger and better son Numerianus he marched immediately to the completion of the Sarmatian and the resumption of the Persian wars. The wastrel Carinus he made co-regent, and gave him the supreme command against the Germans. He appears to have regretted this appointment and to have intended to replace his disappointing son by the energetic and noble Constantius Chlorus, father of Constantine; this would constitute a remarkable emancipation from dynastic ideas if the fact could be established.

In the East Carus and shortly thereafter Numerianus died (284) under mysterious circumstances. Numerianus' death was caused by Aper, Prefect of the Guard. Aper was not counted among the generals of the inner group, and apparently boldness was his only asset for making his usurpation successful. But when the death of the Caesar became known, Aper appears to have lost his composure, suffered himself to be overcome, and was bound for trial at court-martial before the entire army. Here, "by the election of the generals and officers," Diocletian, a distinguished commander, was proclaimed Emperor; Diocletian at once sprang upon Aper, who was still awaiting trial at the foot of the tribunal, and pierced him through. It is probably unjust to deduce that Diocletian was privy to Aper's crime; the simple explanation of the startling occurrence is that a Druid priestess in Gaul had once foretold that Diocletian would become Emperor if he dispatched a boar (*aper*). Ever since, whenever Diocletian went hunting, he looked for boars; now he was carried away by impatience when he saw the right boar before him.

It remained for Diocletian to dispute the rule of the world with Carinus. Carinus was not without military talent; he appears to have worsted the usurper Julianus en route in upper Italy (285) without difficulty. His war with Diocletian lasted for half a year, and even in the battle at Margus (not far from Semendria), which is usually regarded as the decisive engagement, it is possible that Carinus was the victor. But personal enmities which he had aroused by his excesses cost Carinus his life. Diocletian was immediately acknowledged by both armies. This and the fact that he dismissed no officers, made no confiscations, and even retained the Prefect of the Guard Aristobulus in his post, might suggest that a preliminary understanding had been reached with the army of Carinus; but we would rather agree with the elder Aurelius Victor in attributing this course to the singular leniency and deep insight of the new Emperor and his retinue. According to his own protestations he desired the death of Carinus not out of ambition but out of concern for the common weal. This may well be credited to a man who showed such unexampled forbearance in other cases.

II

DIOCLETIAN: HIS SYSTEM OF ADOPTIONS
AND HIS REIGN

OMENS WERE FULFILLED and oracles justified when the son
of Dalmatian slaves who had belonged to the Roman Senator Anulinus, being then some thirty-nine years of age,
ascended the throne of the world. Mother and son received
their name from their native place, tiny Dioclea near Cat-
taro; now for the Romans' sake Diocles, "famed of Zeus,"
added a proper Latin ending and made his name Di-
ocletianus. The allusion to the ruler of the gods in *Dio*-
he retained; his Latin cognomen Jovius is a reminiscence
of it.

Of his military achievements, his regime, and his character (which is a much disputed subject) we shall have to
speak in the sequel. What concerns us now is his peculiar
concept of the Emperor's authority, and the methods by
which he sought to secure, to share, and to bequeath that
authority.

Of the preceding Emperors, some had been prevented
by violent death from making any dispositions concerning
the crown; others had consciously delegated the decision
to their generals. The fact that Carus had summarily set
his sons up as his successors was perhaps the prime cause
of their fall. Diocletian's wife Prisca apparently bore him
only a daughter, Valeria, and he was hence constrained to
seek another answer to the problem of succession. If conditions in the Empire were peaceful, he might have postponed decision; but violent storms were brewing without,
and within there were, after Carus, crowds of usurpers—

Diocletian's own rule was in fact essentially a usurpation, even if it received the recognition of the Senate. What remedy offered?

What Diocletian did reveals nobility and insight in one aspect; in another it seems curious and enigmatic.

Experience of recent decades had shown that even the most energetic of rulers, the saviors of the Empire, must succumb to treachery and the aroused passions of the soldiery. The great generals who surrounded the Emperor could not prevent it; some would not, for ambition pointed, however timorously, to the throne. Eventually a situation like that under Gallienus and the Thirty Tyrants must inevitably recur, and in 285 all indications pointed to its being at hand; the Empire would again have disintegrated, perhaps forever.

Diocletian applied the correct antidote: he surrounded himself with successors and colleagues. Ambition's target was thus made more remote for the usurper, and probability of successful barracks insurrections diminished. For if only one of the Emperors or Caesars should fall, if a conspiracy could not succeed in removing and murdering two or four rulers in a single day, perhaps in Nicomedia, Alexandria, Milan, and Treves, then inexorable avengers would await the individual deed of violence. All good men knew at once what party they must follow; they need no longer throw themselves in unthinking terror into the arms of the soldiers' first chance choice. Another very great advantage of Diocletian's measure was the distribution of the tasks of government. Now these could be confronted calmly and thoughtfully and in accordance with a determined common plan and be carried out brilliantly.

But the artificial system of Diocletian's adoptions presents an enigma. The simplest and obvious solution, superficially considered, would have been for Diocletian to adopt a gifted family of several brothers and to distribute them in the provinces and in other governmental assignments. What the house of Carus had failed to achieve, partly by Carinus' fault, might now have succeeded; a discontinuous Caesarism might have been transformed into a hereditary dynasty, to which of necessity any monarchical government must eventually tend. Was it that Diocletian feared that a family thus exalted might supplant him? So imposing a personage as Diocletian could not easily have been brushed aside. Was it that he lacked confidence in the moral effectiveness of blood relationship in his degenerate age? He himself subsequently made the Caesars sons-in-law to the Emperors. Did he find it necessary to satisfy as many ambitions as possible by adoption or the hope of adoption? He knew better than anyone that it is precisely the most dangerous men who are never satisfied; nor was it in his nature to trouble about giving universal satisfaction or winning universal approval. If we examine the individual cases and their demonstrable or probable motives more closely, we may find the right path, though gaps in our tradition must leave many questions unanswered.

As early as 285, in view of the peasant war in Gaul, Diocletian raised his companion-in-arms Maximian to be Caesar, and in the year following to Augustus. The adoptive relationship was expressed in Maximian's cognomen Herculius, borrowed from the son of Zeus. After both had waged six years of unceasing war against barbarians, rebellious provinces, and usurpers in all parts of the Empire, without formally dividing the Empire among themselves, they raised (292) to the position of Caesars the Generals Galerius and Constantius Chlorus. On this occasion Diocletian expressly stated that "there shall hereafter be two greater in the state as rulers and two lesser as helpers." Maximian's son Maxentius was unceremoniously passed over; instead, an artificial bond of filial piety was contrived, by making the Caesars marry daughters of the Emperors. Galerius married Valeria, and Constantius, Theodora; Theodora was strictly speaking Maximian's stepdaughter. The Caesars had been trained in the school of Aurelian and Probus. Constantius was of noble birth, on his mother's side a great-nephew of Claudius Gothicus. Galerius was a burly shepherd's son, and therefore fond of saying that his mother had conceived him by a divine being in the form of a serpent or, like Rhea Silvia, by Mars himself. Now there were four courts, administrations, and armies. Constantius ruled Gaul and Britain; Galerius the Danube country and Greece; Maximian Italy, Spain, and Africa; and for Diocletian himself, the source of all their authority, Thrace, Asia, and Egypt were reserved. For over twelve years there obtained among men so diverse and in part so crude a most remarkable harmony, a harmony which becomes completely inexplicable when we observe one of the rulers sharing in the government of another's province and commanding armies there, or when we see how little Diocletian's tongue spared the passionate Galerius in the presence of whole armies. All that came from Diocletian—the most difficult plans of battle, the most questionable orders—was invariably carried out with filial obedience; there was never a doubt that he was the guiding spirit of the whole. "They looked up to him," says Aurelius Victor, "as to a father or a supreme god; what this signifies will become clear if we think of all the parricides committed from Romulus to our own day."

The crucial test of obedience was withstood by the associate Emperor Maximian when after twenty years of dual rule Diocletian required him (in 305) to join in the common abdication they had long before agreed upon. Maximian yielded, but with great reluctance. He patiently accepted the fact that when two new Caesars were named (Galerius and Constantius were promoted to be Emperors) his own son Maxentius was again passed over and that he himself, the veteran conqueror of the Bagaudae, the Germans, and the Moors, had no voice in the selection of Caesars. This privilege Diocletian had reserved exclusively for his adoptive son Galerius; Galerius appointed a loyal officer, Severus, to be Caesar of the West, and his nephew, Maximinus Daia, to be Caesar of the East. Constantius Chlorus received treatment similar to Maximian's; although he was advanced to the dignity of Emperor he must needs be content to accept Severus, instead of one of his own sons, as future Caesar. Christian authors praise his discreet moderation, quite needlessly.

In Lactantius' *De Mortibus Persecutorum*, composed not long after these events, a colorful and dramatic account is given of personal motivations for these statesmanlike measures. Gibbon realized that this report was not factual but the account of an embittered enemy; specifically, it is wrong in representing the retiring veteran Emperors as having been terrorized by Galerius. But one very remarkable detail probably has a basis in fact: Galerius is credited with the intention of retiring, like Diocletian, after twenty years of rule if the future succession should have been provided for. The author regards this as a voluntary decision, and his ardent hatred of Galerius apparently makes him loath to report it. But unless we are wholly deceived we have here a prescribed and essential principle of the Diocletianic system, which contemporaries could only partially divine. The establishment of a twenty-year period for the incumbency of the imperial office constitutes the capstone and safety control of the whole. The limitation was intended to stamp adoptions and successions with the seal of necessity and inevitability. But in the following year (306) the whole system was irremediably shattered by the usurpation of the Emperors' sons who felt they had been passed over. Constantine (the Great), with the help of his soldiers, claimed the inheritance of his father's rule, Maxentius wrested Italy for his own, and even the old Maximian forsook his unwelcome retirement in order to support his son's efforts. This disruption of his plans for the succession shattered Diocletian's solemn arrangements, and with them, he believed, the Empire itself was doomed. Deep sorrow surely filled his last years, which he spent, sick and weary of life, at home in the halls of his palace at Salonae, which was designed like a Roman camp.

In fact his ideal of government for the Empire was a curious and remarkable thing. And in view of the possible consequences of government by generals, as all the Emperors of the time were, we must be prepared for the curious; we cannot now be certain what experiences Europe of our own late day holds in store for our descendants. A dual twenty-year tenure with mandatory retirement; nomination of Caesars; the exclusive prerogative of the elder Emperors; the individual rulers (even if they should be heroes of abnegation) continuously irked and injured by the exclusion of their sons—all this to build an artificial dynasty. Granted that for the sake of imperial defense a division of power was essential, and that usurpation from without was infinitely more difficult against four rulers than against one—but how could usurpation be prevented in the imperial houses themselves? These are but a few of the puzzles for which Diocletian provides us no answers.

Political and psychological motives alone are not sufficient for a solution. The missing element is provided by the assumption of a religious superstition which pervaded and controlled all of these arrangements.

The importance of omens and soothsaying in the life of Diocletian has been mentioned above. He is spoken of as "an investigator of things to come," "always devoted to holy usages." We find him, surrounded by priests, zealously examining the entrails of sacrificial victims, filled with anxiety because of ominous lightning bolts. He was attentive to omens even in the matter of proper names. Galerius must take the name of Maximianus in order to effect a magic bond with the proven loyalty of the elder Maximian; for a similar reason the youthful Daia subsequently received the kindred name of Maximinus. Apparently the Emperor sought to attain a special relationship with the deity whose name he bore; Jupiter occurs very frequently on the obverse of his coins. It was under a pillar bearing the statue of Zeus in an open field near Nicomedia that his act of abdication took place, and the octagonal temple of Jupiter is still a striking feature in the palace at Salonae. His public proclamations also reveal a noticeable religious tendency; the preamble to the marriage law of 295 reads like a sermon, and the law against the Manichees of 296 breathes a personal fervor.

His colleagues in the Empire are almost equally devoted to superstition, without which, indeed, their long obedience is hardly explicable. They must have known that even their elevation was due to superstitious considerations. What strange anxieties, to us quite unintelligible, preceded Diocletian's adoptions! A figure appeared to him in a dream, for example, and peremptorily commanded that he choose as successor a certain man whose name was specified. He believed that magic was being employed against him and at length summoned the person named and said to him:

"Receive the rule which you demand from me each night, and do not begrudge your Emperor his rest!" We do not know to whom this palace anecdote refers, nor indeed whether it is correctly reported; it is surely significant nevertheless.

Maximian was a great, at least a capable, general, and Diocletian might have shown him consideration as an early confidant of his exalted plans; but it may well have been that the decisive factor in Maximian's elevation was the fact that he was born on the same day of the month as Diocletian. Of Constantius we can assume with some certainty that it was essentially because of the prophecy of Druid priestesses that Diocletian named him Caesar.

Constantius, as has been said, was a Dalmatian; Maximian a peasant's son from Sirmium (Mitrovica on the Sava), the home of the bravest Emperors of the third century; Galerius was a shepherd, either from Dacia or from Sardica (modern Sofia, in Bulgaria); Maximinus Daia was apparently from the same region; Constantius Chlorus was living in Nissa in Serbia when his son Constantine was born; Licinius, who later appeared as the friend of Galerius, was a peasant from the lower Danube; the home of Severus is unknown. There is a possibility (but no external evidence) that some local religion or superstition was a special bond among these rulers. Of Maximian's abdication we know only the formula which he pronounced in the temple of the Capitoline God (apparently in Milan): "Take back, O Jupiter, what thou has granted." Oaths, sacrifices, and dedications may have been Diocletian's substitute for what his political arrangements lacked in strength and permanence.

The reader who is unwilling to accept our explanation may assume that at his elevation of Maximian Diocletian could not forgo Maximian's co-operation and military talents, but that he passed over Maximian's son Maxentius because Galerius had long been his enemy. But it is questionable whether such a course of action can be reconciled with the character of Diocletian and his indisputable stature as a ruler. There is a deep seriousness in his regulations, particularly in his reduction of the imperial office to a fixed

term. If others regarded this office as a matter of pleasure,
that was not Diocletian's fault; he regarded it as an awesome and responsible obligation which children and gray-
beards must be spared for their own and the Empire's happiness. At the same time the just ambition of the current
Caesars was taken into the reckoning; they could now calculate the day and the hour by which at latest (if nothing
transpired in the interval) they would ascend the throne.
It was with the feeling of a man who knew the day of his
death that the Emperor celebrated at five-year intervals
the quinquennalia, and then the decennalia, and then the
quindecennalia; inexorably there approached the vicennalia, upon which he must divest himself of the purple.
Such was the will of the "All-powerful Goddesses of Fate"
who are celebrated on a coin of the year of abdication.
That successors could not remain forever bound, Diocletian
knew well enough; but he wished, it would seem, to provide an example. Furthermore, only the stipulation of a
twenty-year term could guarantee the exclusion of the Emperors' sons, which would not have been the case if the
term were for life. It may be asked whether it was wise
to provide hostile and subversive elements in the state with
a fixed term upon which insurrection might be successful;
but means of resistance could also be made ready. During
the illness which preceded Diocletian's abdication, for a
month and a half, the people were uncertain whether he
was still alive; nevertheless not a hand was raised in the
well-ordered state.

Remarkably enough, the same questions and the same
events were afoot in the kingdom of the Sassanids, the Empire's hostile neighbor on the east. Of Bahram III, who
ruled for only a few months in 293, our authorities tell us
for the first time that the King of Persia had made a certain
son or brother, whom he designated as his successor,
provisionally prince of a province, with the title Shah;
Bahram himself, as long as his father Bahram II was alive,
was called merely Shah of Segan or Sistan. After his short
reign, which was apparently attended by violent disturbances, his younger brother Narsi succeeded; and Narsi
himself then crowned his son Hormuz as his successor, and

in 301 withdrew into the quiet of private life, "under the shadow of the goodness of God." According to Mirkhond he was moved to this step by thoughts of death, "whose season is recorded in eternal decrees and may not be evaded." Possibly the Magi foretold the precise hour of his death, and thus banished his joy in life. But it is also suggested that Narsi wished to avoid the vicissitudes of a royal destiny, of which his wars with the Romans had given him abundant experience. "The way is long," he says, "often one must ascend, and often descend again." It is not impossible that Narsi's example may have had its effect upon the mind of Diocletian.

Closely related to the solemn pomp and circumstance arising from superstitious considerations which surrounded Diocletian's life is the sudden and striking growth of elaborate court ceremonial. The elder Aurelius Victor would explain this development by the fact that Diocletian was an upstart, and as such naturally insatiable of outward show. But in that case it is strange that none of the great soldier Emperors of the third century, virtually all of whom rose to the throne from humble origins, preceded him in this affectation. For example, we see the mighty Aurelian associating quite simply with his old friends, whose wants, indeed, he supplied so that they could no longer be called needy. Silken clothes were too dear for him, and he wished to eliminate the use of gold for ornamenting buildings and garments. He was willing enough to permit others costly baubles, which might be melted down again, but he denied them to himself. His servants he dressed no more magnificently than he had done before he became Emperor. He was not at ease in the splendid palace on the Palatine whose colored marble walls were stained with the blood of so many Emperors; like Vespasian before him, he preferred the Gardens of Sallust, and in its spacious courts he might be seen daily exercising himself and putting his horses through their paces. All of this was now changed. Diocletian had friends from his early days, but confidence was vanished, perhaps on either side; Diocletian had cause to fear that intimacy with third parties might disrupt the artfully contrived harmony with his colleagues. Instead

of the simple purple with which almost all his predecessors
(excepting only the mad Emperors) had been content, Diocletian wore, after 293, silk and gold embroidered garments, and even his shoes were decorated with precious
stones and pearls; upon his head he wore a diadem, a
white band set with pearls. Naturally, these were the official vestments in which he appeared only on ceremonial
occasions. On his flying journeys and campaigns he and
his colleague Maximian adopted a different style, as did
also the Caesars, who were quick to follow their every hint;
Constantius in particular was devoted to simplicity. But in
Nicomedia Diocletian insisted upon pomp. Access to his
sacred person was daily rendered more difficult by elabora-
tions of ceremonial. In the halls and forecourts of the palace, officers, court officials, and guards were posted; in the
inner chambers influential eunuchs held sway. If a man's
business or rank made access to the Emperor possible, he
must follow Oriental usage and prostrate himself to make
his address. Even upon the occasion of the meeting of Diocletian with Maximian in Milan (291) the panegyrist
Mamertinus designates the ceremonial "a reverence en-
shrined in the sanctuary's innermost chamber, which might
delight and astonish only such natures whose rank and degree granted access to your person."

Nor was the change confined to mute forms: the critical
word too was pronounced. The Emperor no longer called
himself by the titles of republican Rome, now grown empty,
such as the consulship, the tribunician power, and the like;
he was now called *Dominus,* Lord. Roman feeling had stubbornly resisted the title *Rex* because of the word's disagreeable associations. The Greeks had always been used to the
royal title in Sparta and the semi-civilized neighboring
countries and had themselves employed it for centuries for
the successors of Alexander; from the very beginning they
called the Roman Emperors Βασιλεῖς, "Kings," because
the maintenance of the republican fiction was to them
meaningless. But now the royal title was not enough; another was introduced to express the relationship between
full domination and servitude. Now a true apotheosis need
occasion no surprise. The Senate had long exercised the

right of canonization of deceased Emperors; in point of
fact the same honor was shown living Emperors in sacrifices
and oaths before their statues, upon which occasion the
ambiguous and hence untranslatable expression *numen
imperatoris* might be used. Maximian, indeed, had himself
represented on coins in the lion-skin of his divine patron,
a weakness which he shared with Commodus and similar
predecessors in the imperial office.

A man of Diocletian's importance and experience does
not assume the burden of so exalted a representation without a sufficient cause. We know, moreover, that he frequently complained of the disadvantages of seclusion. He
was aware of the great advantages which might accrue to
a ruler from personal contact with his subjects, from higher
officials to the humblest petitioner. "Four or five band
together," he says, "to deceive the Emperor; they set a
decision before him; shut up in his chambers, he cannot
know the true situation; he can only know what they tell
him. He nominates officials who had better not been appointed, and removes officials who had better remained at
their post; thus even the best and cleverest Emperor is
taken in."

One reason may be suggested which may have moved
him to these restrictive measures despite his clear insight
into their disadvantages. After the wars of Aurelian and
Probus the court and especially the General Staff may have
been filled with a large number of barbarian officers who
because of their diverse origin and un-Roman education
could not enter into the easy atmosphere of camaraderie
which had formerly prevailed in the imperial court. Until
the period of the great persecution there was also a great
number of Christians at the various courts; and the solemn
usages of court ceremonial prevented disagreeable incidents with pagans. To be sure, there was a certain fondness
for the grandiloquent, revealed even in edicts; but how
little the Emperor was moved by mere vanity and love of
pomp is shown by the fact that he postponed to the end
of his reign (303) his one triumph after so mighty a succession of victories, and that the celebration of that triumph
was on a modest scale.

Diocletian's break with Roman tradition was patent in more than one respect. At the beginning of his reign, for one thing, he showed no special interest in the city of Rome itself. As late as the third century the Emperors had as a rule lived on the Palatine, perhaps less out of piety for its hallowed memories and the sanctuaries of the world capital than because its central situation, and its magnificence, and the wealth of pleasure it offered made it especially suitable for the imperial residence, and because, besides its ancient claims, it still retained a vestige of actual power. For Rome was the seat of the Senate, which had but recently deposed and nominated and recognized Emperors. Only Elagabalus ventured to banish the Senate from the city, but no other Emperor before or after him. Others trod upon its dignity and sought to demoralize it; cleverer Emperors established a *rapprochement* with it. Apprehension of the restless populace and the remnants of the Praetorian cohorts was only a minor motive in the consideration shown the Senate, at least on the part of the more capable rulers; for a weak prince there was fully as much danger within Rome as outside it.

But when requirements of border defense necessitated the division of imperial authority, it was impossible that Rome should remain the residence of one of the two or four rulers. Preservation of the Empire's boundaries took precedence over cordial relations with the Senate, which could in any case be maintained by a prince with true Roman sentiments. Maximian made his residence in Milan, which the pressure of the Alemanni, resumed after the death of Probus, had well-nigh made a border post. It was as well calculated to secure Gaul as any position south of the Alps could be, and at the same time it enabled its occupant to observe Italy or intervene in Africa. The Caesar Constantius, who waged continual war, is most frequently encountered in Treves, and later in York. Diocletian settled in Bithynia at Nicomedia, at the head of a deep gulf in the Sea of Marmora. Thence he could keep under surveillance the movements of the Goths and of other Pontic tribes which threatened the lower Danube, and at the same time be within reach of the plains of the upper Euphrates, where the struggles against the Persians were waged. In the early years of his reign, indeed, no fixed residence was possible; both Augusti hastened from battlefield to battlefield, and the Caesars soon did likewise. This did not affect Diocletian's somewhat morbid passion for building. He transformed a quarter of Nicomedia into a large and regular palace, whose design, like that of the palace he later constructed at Salonae, perhaps followed the lines of a military encampment. It included basilicas, a circus, a mint, an arsenal, and separate residences for his wife and his daughter. Naturally the city grew, as is the way of royal residences. At the beginning of the fourth century Nicomedia is said to have resembled a quarter (*regio*) of Rome. In Milan most of the buildings which the fourth-century poet Ausonius found to admire were perhaps built by Maximian.

Rome must have been highly sensitive to the changed position, even if it suffered no outward loss. A hostile source (Lactantius) reports that Maximian attacked wealthy senators who were falsely accused of aspiring to rule, so that the lights of the Senate were continually being extinguished and its eyes pierced. Attempts to blame or exculpate, on this side or on that, are futile. In the history of Zosimus, who alone approaches truth and completeness in describing and appraising the character of Diocletian, there is a gap of twenty years. Perhaps the account of the last great persecution seemed too favorable to the persecutor in the sight of zealous Christians, and they found it easier to maim the work than to refute it, just as contemporary pagans mutilated Cicero's books *On the Nature of the Gods*, to prevent Christians from finding in them weapons for their polemic against polytheism.

Tension between Senate and Emperors arose from the fact that Diocletian had become Emperor, and had nominated his colleagues, without the Senate's co-operation. All that was left for the Senate was to recognize them and for form's sake bestow the consulship upon them from time to time. That distinction Diocletian esteemed so lightly that on one occasion he left Rome only a few days before he was to make his ceremonial entry into the office. On the occasion of the Emperors' meeting in Milan in 291 a depu-

tation from the Senate was in attendance, apparently as a
gesture of loyalty. The panegyrist Mamertinus declared in
the presence of Maximian: "The Senate has bestowed a
similitude of its own majesty upon Milan, so that the city
might possess dignity as the seat of empire when both Emperors are there met together." The expression seems unfriendly, and we do not know how it was received; yet
it does imply that in the year in question relations between
Emperors and Senate were not yet openly hostile. When
and how they deteriorated remains a puzzle. Maximian
was by nature cruel and deceitful, and Diocletian may not
have been beyond transgressing when transgression was expedient. Both found the Romans' "free if not bold manner
of speech" highly distasteful. Particularly objectionable to
the new rulers were the prearranged slogans, shouted in
rhythm and with many repetitions, with which the senators
in their precincts and the populace in the Circus offered
homage or admonition to the Emperors. Surely without
sufficient grounds they would not have sacrificed the heads
of the Senate, if indeed things went so far and our author
has not expanded some insignificant detail, as is his wont,
into a monstrous crime.

But toward the population of Rome (to avoid using the
desecrated term "people of Rome") Diocletian and his colleague later showed marked favor. As if Rome wanted for
pleasure resorts, they built the most colossal of all Roman
baths upon the Viminal (299). Among the ten or so baths
erected by earlier Emperors and private philanthropists,
those of Caracalla with their gigantic halls were most impressive. The building art was grown too exhausted to vie
with the astonishing spans of Caracalla's arches, but Diocletian's baths surpassed Caracalla's in area. Their compass
was twelve hundred paces, and they contained three thousand rooms. The astonishing central structure, whose granite columns are fifteen feet in circumference, is now the
core of the Church of the Carthusians; other remains of the
baths are to be found in cloisters, vineyards, and lonely
avenues scattered about in a wide circle. In the same year
Maximian started construction of baths at Carthage, perhaps with a similar view to conciliating the populace. In

the past Carthage had been the chief stage for the debut of usurpers. Other constructions undertaken at Rome during this reign are mentioned by name: the Senate House, which had been burned in the reign of Carinus, the Forum of Caesar, the Basilica Julia, and the Theater of Pompey were restored. New buildings included, beside the baths, two porticoes called Jovia and Herculea, three nymphaea, temples of Isis and Serapis, and a triumphal arch. Perhaps the striking mass of splendid buildings with which Diocletian furnished the carping and dangerous Antiochenes was intended as a distraction from political preoccupations. Among the buildings in Antioch which are recorded by name are temples of Olympian Zeus, Hecate, Nemesis, and Apollo, a palace in the city and one in the suburb called Daphne, several baths and granaries, and a stadium; most of these were new buildings, some were restorations.

In Rome the public distributions and the games were not interrupted; it was only after the abdication of 305 that Galerius ventured to abolish all special consideration for the ancient mistress of the world. But Diocletian had offended Rome in another respect, as has already been indicated. Behind his baths, surrounded on three sides by the Wall of Aurelian, there is a large vineyard, later the property of the Jesuits, with dilapidated arched cells built against the wall. This had once been the Praetorian camp, the denizens of which had so often caused the imperial purple to flutter in the breeze upon their swords' points. Many previous attempts had been made to disband and supplant them; but in the third century the original practice seems to have been restored, namely, that a few thousand men were enlisted in the vicinity of Rome and in adjacent parts of Italy; these are to be regarded not as an Imperial Guard but rather as a garrison for the capital. Now Diocletian reduced their numbers considerably, surely not merely out of fear of the restless and demanding Italians in their midst, but also for reasons of economy and because the course of events had supplied a new corps in their place. The Empire had been saved by a great series of Illyrian Emperors beginning with Decius; small wonder that thirty years of war had surrounded them with a faithful band of com-

patriots who were closer to the Emperors than the Latins
and Sabines of the Praetorians. These Illyrians were further
recommended by their effective use of their national
weapon. They comprised two legions, each of six thousand
men, now honored by being called Jovians and Herculians,
after the supplementary names (*agnomina*) of the Emperors; previously they had been called Martiobarbuli,
after the leaden balls of which each man carried five (or
five pair) fastened to his shield and which they could sling
with the speed and force of an arrow. They now received
official preferment above all other legions, but this does not
necessarily imply that they were permanently quartered
near the Emperor's person. Though the sentiments which
the Praetorians had provoked in Rome were chiefly fear
and hatred of themselves, their dissolution was now looked
upon as an assault upon the majesty of the capital. Common
antipathy fashioned a bond, and the few Praetorians who
remained in the camp at Rome later participated in the
insurrection against Galerius, having reached an understanding with Senate and people.

The Romans might bewail and abhor this turn of events,
but in point of fact no injury had been done them. Eventually the great delusion that the Emperor still continued as
the magistrate and representative of the local Roman or
even Italian life and people and that he ruled the world in
their name must have been dissipated. If Diocletian had
not given outward confirmation of the extinction of Roman
primacy by removal of the imperial residence, introduction
of Oriental court ceremonial, depreciation of the Senate,
and diminution of the Praetorians, Christianity must soon
have performed the same office in its own manner, for
of necessity Christianity created new centers of gravity for
its power. Presently we shall have to recount under what
mighty and fearful circumstances Diocletian's innovations
were given effect—while he and his colleagues were forced
to defend the Empire upon all its frontiers and wrest it
from usurpers' hands bit by bit; these things should not be
forgotten in shaping our judgment of Diocletian.

As regards the higher pitch of court procedure and the
new ceremonial, there were doubtless people enough to

welcome it with enthusiasm. In periods of transition, such as Diocletian's was, the Emperor still felt the need of receiving public praise; a thorough military despotism may dispense with this species of recognition, despise it, or even resent it. But men had only just emerged from the ancient world, with the common and open participation or interest in public affairs which was the breath of its life. Education was still rhetorical and public discourses occupied a position of such importance in the lives of men as the modern world is incapable of imagining. Among these discourses were the panegyrics delivered at annual festivals or other solemn occasions by some distinguished rhetor of the city or vicinity in the presence of the Emperor or some high official. We have preserved the Younger Pliny's well-known *Panegyric* on Trajan; then, after a long gap, as it happens, a heap of eulogies of Diocletian's colleagues together with a few on later Emperors. As historical sources these speeches must naturally be used with caution; but they tell us much that is valuable, and they are by no means negligible as literature. Their flattery is doubtless a continuation of the style which characterized the lost panegyrics of the third century. With realism bordering on impertinence the rhetor identifies himself with the Emperor present in person, whom he conceives in the most exalted terms. One after the other he divines the Emperor's thoughts, plans, and sentiments; here the subtle courtier exercises restraint, because even idealizing fiction, let alone truth, may be indiscreet. But this is overweighed by a penetrating bouquet of direct and ecstatic praise calculated to delight the senses of a Maximian—though Maximian scarcely possessed sufficient learning to understand the flattering allusions and associations. Much play is made with Maximian's cognomen Herculius, and his history is constantly intertwined with and made parallel to that of Hercules; but even Hercules' prowess falls short, for his victory over Geryon was a petty thing compared to Maximian's over the Bagaudae. Comparison with Jupiter, usually reserved only for the elder Emperor, carries the panegyrist somewhat further; Jupiter's childhood, like that of Maximian, who grew up on the banks of the Danube, was filled with the alarums of war. Tirelessly the speaker heaps image upon image to celebrate the concord of the Emperors: their reign is common as is the light of day to a pair of eyes; forasmuch as they were born on the same day (see page 35), theirs is a twin rule like that of the Heraclids in Sparta; Rome is now happier than under Romulus and Remus, of whom the one slew the other; Rome may now style herself both Herculea and Jovia. Just as the history of Hercules was employed to glorify Maximian, so was the myth of Zeus applied to Diocletian, particularly with respect to Zeus' omnipresence, which the Emperor's rapid journeys seemed to emulate. But through the measured cadences of these periods there echoes a bold and shameless preference of Maximian, which that Emperor perhaps was pleased to hear, with a straight face. "By accepting coregency you have given Diocletian more than you have received from him. . . . You emulate Scipio Africanus; Diocletian emulates you." Mamertinus ventured to declaim such sentences as these before the whole court at the palace in Treves. Interspersed among such sentences, to be sure, there was an opulent flow of flowery adulation for both Emperors alike. "Just as the Rhine may confidently dry its stream after Maximian's victories beyond its banks, so the Euphrates need no longer protect Syria now that Diocletian has passed over it. . . . You both postpone your triumphs for the sake of ever new victories; always you hasten to greater things." Much lesser achievements were also boldly inflated. On the occasion of the meeting of 291, when Diocletian hurried to Milan from the East and Maximian crossed the Alps thither in midwinter, Mamertinus declaimed: "One who did not travel with you might well believe that Sun and Moon lent you their diurnal and nocturnal chariots. The might of your majesty shielded you from bitter frost. Gentle spring zephyrs and sunshine followed you where all else froze. Beshrew thee, Hannibal, with thy crossing of the Alps!" It is quite in keeping with this conceit that the reign of these Emperors marked a sudden increase in the earth's fertility. A few years earlier the poet Calpurnius Siculus had employed a similar and more pronounced bucolic tone (in his eighth or fourth Eclogue) to hymn the Caesar Numerian: in his presence forests fell silent for reverence, lambs frolicked gaily, fleeces and milk grew abundant, fields and orchards luxuriant, for within his mortal frame there lurked a god, perhaps supreme Jupiter himself.

The orator Eumenius' approach to the educated Caesar, Constantius Chlorus, was somewhat more delicate. For example, he speaks of escorting the youth of Gaul to the large map of the world which was painted upon the wall in the hall at Autun, between the temple of Apollo and the Capitol with its sanctuary of Minerva. "There let us see how Diocletian's clemency pacifies the wild insurrection of Egypt; how Maximian shatters the Moors; how under your hands, Lord Constantius, Batavians and Britons again raise their sorrowful countenances from their jungles and floods; or how you, Caesar Galerius, tread Persian bows and quivers down to earth. For now it is become a joy to behold the painted earth, for we can see upon it naught that is not ours." His spirited description of the new Golden Age wins our forgiveness for the playful symbolism which the orator contrives for the fourfold rule. He sees the number four as the fundamental principle in the cosmic order, expressed in the four elements, the four seasons, even the four continents. It is not for naught that a lustrum follows upon the passing of four years; in the heavens a four-horse team flies before the chariot of the sun; and the two great luminaries of heaven, sun and moon, are attended by two lesser lights, the morning star and the evening star. It would not be surprising if somewhere in Gaul a mosaic should be excavated in which these notions were worked into an artistic composition. Plastic art and rhetoric must frequently have resorted to similar means for tasks of this sort. Eumenius, by the way, is distinguished from the other panegyrists not only by his tact and his talent; we shall see in him a quite honest patriot who employed flattery not for personal advantage. Here as in a thousand other cases historical judgment must be careful to discern what the age and the environment impose upon the individual and what he does by virtue of his own resolution.

Whether language had grown several degrees more servile in Diocletian's court and had been infected by phrases of adulation we do not know. In any case ceremonial requirements, as far as they related to the person of the Emperor, were still quite simple and innocent. Certainly they are not to be compared with those of the later Byzantine court, where in the tenth century the Emperor Constantine Porphyrogenitus was himself constrained to act the court chamberlain and compose a systematic treatise to introduce contemporaries and posterity to the labyrinth of sacred usages, to whose bondage the Autocratores, all-holy and beloved of God, were gradually forced to submit after Church and court ceremonial had interpenetrated and augmented one another.

If from the throne downward a hierarchy of title and rank gradually overwhelmed Roman society, the fault is not necessarily Diocletian's. The ossification which now overtook ancient life made some such development inevitable. For a long while the regime had been almost purely military. Such a regime must always fashion the state mechanism after its own image; subordination is its very soul, and organization must be by ranks and grades, with strict and visible marks of gradation. Many institutions of this character, which tend to be attributed to Diocletian, may well have been introduced by his predecessors. The complete transformaion of the state took place only under Constantine.

Diocletian did considerably increase the number of officials. It was surely not so much the four courts as the four administrations that multiplied the burdens. According to Lactantius, Diocletian's reign is liable to the following fearful indictments: "Each of the four rulers kept for himself more soldiers than previous Emperors had had altogether. There was an unexampled rise in taxation. The number of those who received so far exceeded the number of those who paid that the exhausted peasants forsook their farms, and cultivated land reverted to forest. To make terror universal, the provinces were cut up into sections, and every region, every city, was overburdened with crowds of officials, with tax collectors, vice-gerents of prefects, and the like. In consequence little was done for the common interest; nay, there were only condemnations, proscriptions, extortions without number or end, accompanied by intolerable violence." Diocletian is further charged with accumulating infinite treasure.

We now listen to a Christian who is in other respects no less partisan than Lactantius. This is what Eusebius says: "What words are adequate to describe the abundance and the blessed times before the persecution, when the Emperors showed us peace and friendship, when their vicennalia were celebrated in profound peace with festivals, spectacles, and banquets." Can any part of Lactantius' indictment be justified?

Diocletian's increase of the army was absolutely essential, for, as we shall see, he must needs wrest half the Empire from the hands of usurpers and barbarians who had taken possession of it. What strength was necessary for this purpose, none could judge better than he. Concerning the proportions of his increase we have no details; anyone who wishes may believe the fiction writer who says that Diocletian's army was more than four times the size of Aurelian's or Probus'.

Next we glance at the charge of hoarding wealth, a charge which no prince can escape. Many rulers have in fact accumulated great treasures of precious metal, taking a false view of its absolute worth, and have been unable to bring themselves to spend it usefully at the suitable moment. Oriental despotism generally is afflicted with this fault, and its subjects follow their despot's example and bury every piece of silver in the ground. But miserliness can hardly be the explanation in the case of Diocletian. Expenditures for regaining and reconstituting the shattered Empire must have been too enormous for any disproportionately large surplus to have remained in the treasury. The requirements of border security alone, the fortresses which stretched from the Netherlands to the Red Sea, together with their garrisons, would make any surplus impossible even in the later and more peaceful period of his reign.

It was necessary for the Empire to strain every effort, and when objectives are as great and as successfully achieved as Diocletian's generally were, the ruler must at

least be absolved of the vulgar charge that he afflicted people only to devour their gold and silver himself. His numerous buildings, indeed, might raise a suspicion of extravagance, but far the greater number appear to have
been political gifts to specific cities, by means of which the
need for garrisons was reduced. Compared to the extravagant building of Constantine, Diocletian's expenditures
are inconsiderable. The palace at Salonae covered a large
area, it is true, but its individual rooms were distinguished
neither in height nor in size and were not to be compared
with the colossal halls of the baths in Rome. In the reconstruction of Nicomedia some expropriations may have been
made, as had been done in the city foundations of the
Hellenistic kings and was to be done in the refounding of
Byzantium; but to believe that Diocletian leveled capital
charges against the owner of any fair estate and any handsome dwelling that he saw is possible only to the credulous.
It is sad enough that many prosperous people were ruined
because of the pressing need for money; but this was
doubtless the work of cruel officials, with whom the administration had been cursed long before Diocletian's day.

The new division of the Empire into one hundred and
one provinces and twelve dioceses was certainly not introduced by a regime like Diocletian's without good and sufficient grounds; nor was the number of officials increased
without need. Diocletian himself was the most industrious
official of his Empire. Besides his military campaigns, he
was constantly traveling hither and yon on hurried journeys, always governing and making decisions. His itinerary
for 293 and 294, for example, can be established almost
week by week and day by day by the dating of his rescripts. The lawbooks contain more than twelve hundred of
his rescripts on matters of private law. If we are to name a
specific ground for the new division of the Empire into
smaller provinces and for the increase in the number of
officials, it would be that the existing machinery seemed
inadequate to the Emperor and that he regarded stricter
supervision and better execution of orders as essential. He
could only work with the material that he found ready to
hand, and none could know better than he how unsatis-

factory that material was. In any case, distinctions between
the provinces were now finally abolished in favor of a uniform administration. What Diocletian began Constantine
completed and perfected.

All are agreed that the Roman system of finance was on
the whole bad and oppressive, and there is no ground for
assuming that Diocletian had a superior insight for improv-
ing the national economy; the most efficient of the Emperors had none. Modern conditions in the great European
nations demonstrate how great the interval can be between
thorough understanding of these matters and actual abolition of what is bad. But what the elder Aurelius Victor, one
of Diocletian's fairest critics, makes as a special charge
against him can easily be interpreted to his credit. In a
passage unfortunately corrupt and ambiguous the charge
is made that "a portion of Italy" was drawn upon for certain
general taxes and duties (*pensiones*); "under the restrictions then obtaining" this situation was tolerable, but in the
course of the fourth century its effect was to ruin the country. Of whatever nature these taxes may have been, it was
in any case just that Italy should help carry the Empire's
burdens, since it was no longer able to save the Empire
and to rule it.

For criticism of the Roman financial system in general,
reference must be made to specialist researches in that subject; but one particular point must be touched upon here.
For the year 302, various annals record that "the Emperors
at that time commanded that there should be cheapness"—
that is, Diocletian established maximum prices for foodstuffs. According to views prevalent today, no measure is
to be more severely condemned than the establishment of
ceiling prices; their maintenance premises the ceaseless
rhythm of the guillotine, as the instructive example of the
French National Convention demonstrates. The measure
presumes either the most extreme and desperate need, or a
total disregard of the true concepts of value and price. The
inevitable consequences ensued. Goods were hidden, despite the prohibition they grew dearer than ever, and countless sellers were made liable to the death penalty, until
the law was rescinded.

An exact record of this measure is preserved in the famous inscription of Stratonicea, which reproduces the entire edict along with several hundred prescribed prices (in part illegible and difficult to interpret). In the preamble the Emperors express themselves somewhat as follows: "The price of things bought in the markets or brought daily into the cities has so far exceeded all bounds that measureless avarice is restrained neither by rich harvests nor by abundance of goods. . . . Unprincipled greed appears wherever our armies, following the commands of the public weal, march, not only in villages and cities but also upon all highways, with the result that prices of foodstuffs mount not only fourfold and eightfold, but transcend all measure. Frequently a single purchase robs the soldier of his pay and our gifts. . . . Our law shall fix a measure and a limit to this greed." There follow threats of severe penalties for such as transgress the law.

The considerations which led to this measure are as enigmatic as the provisions of the measure itself. The readiest explanation is that some cabal of speculators in the East had caused a rapid rise in prices of indispensable foodstuffs, that everyone suffered from the rise, and that the suffering of the army threatened far the greatest and most immediate danger. The preponderant portion of the Empire's income was in kind, but it may not have been possible to make sufficient stocks available to individual garrisons at the moment of need. When the resolution was taken to correct the situation, perhaps in haste or under emotional stress, the measure was extended to cover all classes of people and all kinds of goods and to afford particular assistance to urban populations.

The tables of the inscription constitute a document of the first importance, for they provide an official indication of the contemporary value of goods and services in relation to one another. The reduction of individual values to terms of modern currency is much more difficult.* Scholars are

* A text, translation, and interpretation of Diocletian's edict on prices may be found in an appendix to Volume 5 of Tenney Frank's *Economic Survey of Ancient Rome* (Baltimore, 1940). The real value of the prices listed is impos-

not yet agreed on the value of the unit which is indicated in the edict merely by an asterisk; some understand it to be the silver denarius, others the copper denarius. If the coin is silver, the prices seem monstrous; if copper, they are not very different from our own. Hence copper has the greater probability, provided that our assumptions regarding weights and measures are correct. On the basis of a copper denarius the chief results are as follows: Fixed wages seem somewhat lower than the average which obtained in France three decades ago (1820), calculated at 1.25 francs. Farm laborers received 65 centimes daily; masons, carpenters, blacksmiths, bakers, lime-burners, 1.25 francs; muleteers, shepherds, water-carriers, sewer-cleaners, and the like, board and 50 to 65 centimes. Among teachers the *paedagogus* (in the strict sense) received 1.25 francs for each ward monthly, as did also the teacher of reading and the teacher of writing; the arithmetic teacher, on the other hand, and the stenography teacher received 1.90 francs; the teacher of Greek language and literature 5 francs, and the teachers of Latin and of geometry the same. The prices of shoes were as follows: for peasants and drivers, 3 francs; for soldiers, 2.50 francs; for patricians, 3.75; for women, 1.50. Naturally, there were variations in quality and workmanship. Prices of meat, in Roman pounds of 12 ounces, were: beef and mutton, about 28 centimes; lamb and pork, about 35 centimes, not to mention the various sausages described and listed in detail, and the special delicacies. Ordinary wine, reckoning the *sextarius* at half a liter, was somewhat cheaper than at present, namely, 20 centimes. Aged and better quality wine was 60 centimes; the noble Italian wines, including Sabine and Falernian, were 75 centimes. Beer (*cervesia cami?*) was 10 centimes, and a cheaper variety (*zythum*) 5 centimes.

sible to determine, for we have no fixed gauge like the price of wheat, which is elsewhere used to determine values. It has therefore been thought best to let Burckhardt's estimates in terms of French francs of his own day stand; these give the correct relationship of the prices of commodities to one another, which is essentially all that the edict can tell us.—Translator.

These figures, adopted from the calculations of Dureau de la Malle, are doubtless too low, but they serve to demonstrate proportional relationships in values. Unfortunately, no price is given for wheat, which is a reliable index. In the edict itself the prices are doubtless set at a high level, for to set low prices would have been futile from the start; we must not be deceived by the statement of the Idatian chronicles that "the Emperors . . . commanded that there should be cheapness."

Of all Diocletian's measures, his introduction of maximum prices can perhaps be most sharply criticized. For once the absolute state in its reliance upon its means of enforcement was guilty of a miscalculation; nevertheless we must not overlook the Emperor's good intentions. These are apparent in the new tax registers which he caused to be made throughout the Empire in the last year of his reign (305). Our source tells us, indeed, that "he caused the land to be measured and burdened it with levies"; but the intention was clearly not merely to raise the tax but to apportion it more justly.

Considered all in all, Diocletian's reign may be regarded as one of the best and most beneficent which the Empire had ever enjoyed. If we are not prejudiced by the dreadful pictures of the Christian persecutions and by the distortions and exaggerations of Lactantius, the traits of the great ruler assume a quite different aspect. A contemporary who dedicated a work to him may not be rated a competent witness; nevertheless it may be mentioned that according to the biographer of Marcus Aurelius in the *Historia Augusta* (19), Marcus was Diocletian's model for morality, for social behavior, and for clemency, and occupied a principal place in Diocletian's household cult. A later author also merits citation. The elder Aurelius Victor, who was by no means blind to the darker side of Diocletian and is even hostile in questions of the Italian policy, says of him: "He suffered himself to be called Lord, but behaved like a father; doubtless he wished to show, in his wisdom, that not evil names but evil deeds are what matter." And a little further, after enumerating Diocletian's wars: "The institutions of peace also were strengthened by just laws. . . . Diligent zeal was shown for provisioning, for the city of Rome, for the welfare of the officials; and incentives to improvement were given by promoting the efficient and penalizing malefactors." And finally, in connection with the abdication, Victor concludes: "In the conflict of opinions perception of the true situation has been obscured. In our judgment it wanted a lofty character to despise all pomp and to step down to ordinary life."

Furthermore this absolute ruler, who was forced to win his realm back from usurpers step by step, was large-spirited enough to do away with political espionage. Apparently he found that his authority was so fully secured by its division that he no longer required such service. In any case political intelligence had fallen into the hands of a corporation which might have constituted a danger to the regime itself. Originally, the *frumentarii* were supply officers who were sent ahead of the armies; later they were ordnance officers; and finally they came to be used for transmitting and carrying out various questionable orders. They degenerated into a clique which employed false charges and the dread of false charges, especially in remote provinces, for blackmailing respectable citizens. Not much more is known of them, but we may imagine that their abuses were frightful. They were a band of wicked men, enjoying high protection, conniving with and supporting one another, eavesdropping upon and exploiting every suspicious mood of the Emperors; and they used their position to terrify old and respected families in Gaul, Spain, or Syria and to force them to sacrifice their all for fear of being denounced as participants in an imaginary conspiracy. With Constantine, though he generally showed his hatred of informers, the thing came up again, but under another name. Again it was the managers of the Emperor's transport who undertook the despicable role, under the title of *agentes in rebus* or *veredarii*.

In other respects the despotism of the Roman Emperors did not show so much concern with the painstaking supervision of trifles, with regulations for each and every detail of life, specifically with the dictation and control of cultural tendencies, as is likely to infect the modern state. The rule of the Emperors, which has won such ill repute for attending so little to the life of the individual, for exacting such oppressive taxes, for providing for public security so badly, was content to confine itself to its most essential purposes and to make no restrictions on the local life of the provinces which had once been subdued with streams of blood. On the other hand, the government failed to intervene when it might well have done so. Thus it suffered not only local but also class distinctions to persist and to develop. An aristocracy of freedom from taxation was formed, for example, of senatorial families, of teachers and physicians appointed by the state, and of several other categories, among which Christian priests were eventually included. There could no longer be any thought of a new and vital organization of the state; the most that even a ruler like Diocletian could hope to attain was the preservation of the extent of the Empire and a moderate improvement of corruptions within it.

III

INDIVIDUAL PROVINCES
AND NEIGHBORING COUNTRIES: THE WEST

No SECRET was made, in the preceding chapter, of the inadequacy of generalizations concerning many of the most important issues in the later Roman Empire. What is lacking is the essential basis—knowledge of conditions in the individual provinces. Scattered notices in the historians, the mass of inscriptions which have been collected, and monumental remains yield many certain and valuable facts, some directly and some by inference; but the large intervening gaps which cannot be supplied are all the more distressing. Here we can only assemble, in the manner of a digression, the essential facts concerning those provinces which, as the gaping wounds in the ailing body politic, would in any case claim careful attention. First we shall glance at contemporary Gaul, with whose fate that of Britain was closely bound.

The great tyrants of Gaul had once vigorously defended the west against the invading Germans. But the violence of their successions, their continual warfare against foreign enemies, and finally civil strife between the party of Tetricus and that of the Italian Emperors, which was ended by Aurelian's campaign in Gaul and his battle at Châlons-sur-Marne—all resulted in an intolerable increase of general misery and the dissolution of all political and moral restraints. Now the campaign against the Franks and the Alemanni was renewed; the latter were defeated at Windisch by the general Constantius Chlorus under Aurelian (274), and indeed on the same day that his son Constantine was born. But victories seemed only to summon new hosts of these inexhaustible and youthful peoples across the Rhine. It no longer availed for capacious colonels to drink their envoys under the table and then draw their secrets out. They were no longer impressed when the Emperor received their deputations with calculated pomp before his crescent-shaped lines, himself clad in purple upon a lofty pulpit, before him the golden eagles of the legions, the imperial images, and the banners of the armies inscribed in gold and borne upon silver lances. Under Probus the war again assumed huge proportions, and without that great Emperor's skill and courage Gaul would definitely have been lost. Even so there arose a new party, chiefly in Lyons and its vicinity, which openly strove for a continuation of a Gallic empire after the model of Posthumus and Victorina. When Diocletian subsequently divided the imperial authority, he may have had to take these circumstances into consideration. But before that happened Probus' conquests in southern Germany were again lost, and unhappy Gaul was again traversed by German hordes. Carinus did defeat them, and left an army in Gaul; this army, however, he had to recall for his war against the usurper Julian and against the approaching Diocletian. Thereupon the entire social structure of Gaul went awry.

Now, and repeatedly thereafter in the great crises in ancient France, it was the peasants who suddenly rose with terrifying power. At the time they lived in forms of slavery which had been handed down from ancient days, though the relationship was not always called by that name. A number of peasants were actual farm slaves; others were serfs, bound to the soil; still others were called *coloni*, that is, tenants who yielded half their produce to their lords. There were also better situated lessees, who paid their rent in money; and finally there was a mass of so-called free workers and wage earners. But all were now united by a common misfortune. The landlords, drained by confiscatory levies for the requirements of the divided state, wished to recoup their losses from the peasants, just as the French nobility did after the Battle of Poitiers, when they required ransom money for the knights who had been taken captive

with John the Good. The result in the first instance is styled
the Bagauda, in the second the Jacquerie (1358). Peasants and shepherds left their huts in crowds, and wandered
about as beggars. Turned away on all sides and driven out
by the city garrisons, they gathered into *bagaudae,* which
is to say, "bands." They slaughtered their cattle and devoured their flesh; they armed themselves with their farm
tools, mounted their farm horses, and rode through the
plain country, not only to satisfy their hunger but to dev-
astate it in their unreasoning despair. Then they threatened
the cities, where an impoverished proletariat eager for
plunder would frequently open the city gates to them. General despair and the native Gallic craving for adventure
shortly so increased their army that they could venture to
raise two of their number, Aelianus and Amandus, to be
Emperors, and so to renew the claim for a Gallic imperium.
The court of these rustic Emperors must have been motley
and peculiar; the third century had set many stout peasants and sons of slaves upon the throne of the world, but
generally such as had served an apprenticeship to royal
authority in the armies and then in the imperial General
Staff. Aelianus and Amandus could make no such claim,
but perhaps they could make another which outweighed
their other shortcomings. Christian tradition, documented
from the seventh century, made Christians of them and
thus justified their stand against the idolatrous Emperors. It
can certainly be assumed that there were numbers of Christians among the poor and wretched folk who joined the
Bagaudae, and also persecuted men of every sort, even
criminals.

It appears that southern and western Gaul was less affected by the movement than the north and east, where
pressure must have been much greater because of the barbarians. An hour beyond Vincennes the strong current of
the Marne, shortly before it flows into the Seine, forms a
peninsula, upon whose ridge the Benedictine abbey of
Saint-Maur-des-Fossés was later built. The ancient Celts
had shown special preferences for such points in choosing
their fortresses (*oppida*), and certainly the peninsula already had rampart, moat, and walls when Aelianus and

Amandus made it the Bagaudae Fortress; it bore this name for centuries, though very little can have been built upon it in the year 285–286. From this impregnable point, which could be approached by no ford or shoal, they carried their raids near and far, and to this fortress they brought their booty. In time they grew bold enough not only to impose their confiscations upon weaker cities without more ado, but also to beleaguer stronger cities. They succeeded in taking the ancient and spacious city of Augustodunum (Autun), and they showed no mercy either to its temples or to its basilicas or baths; everything was plundered and destroyed, and the inhabitants were driven into exile.

The Bagaudae had to be got rid of before they should similarly destroy one city after another and with them every stronghold against the barbarians. This was the task of the then Caesar, Maximianus Herculius, and his success earned him the title of Augustus. We learn only that he accomplished the task quickly and easily, crushing some of the bands by direct attack and forcing others to surrender by starvation, assisted by a plague. Whether any direct relief of the oppressive burdens which had provoked the uprising ensued is more than doubtful, for complaints of excessive taxes rather increased than otherwise. But indirectly the situation of the country in general improved, for the Germans remained humbled for some decades and usurpations ceased. But in the fifth century and perhaps even in the fourth similar causes produced similar effects. Bagauda again raised its head, and we may almost surmise that it had never wholly ceased.

But we return to the period of Diocletian. Many regions of Gaul continued prostrate. The landlords of Autun, for example, who were deep in debt, had not so far recovered by the time of Constantine that they could set their old irrigation and reclamation works in progress. Their soil degenerated to marshes and briers; the Burgundy vines withered, and the wooded hills became the haunts of wild beasts. "Once the plain as far as the Saône was happy and rich, as long as the waters were kept under control; now the lowlands have become river bed or sloughs. The mighty vines are run to wood, and new ones cannot be planted.

. . . From the point where the road turns toward Belgian
Gaul [that is, from Autun] all is desolate, mute, and
gloomy wilderness. Even the military road is rough and
uneven, and makes the transportation of produce as well
as courier service difficult." Once more during the Middle
Ages, about the time of the Maid of Orléans, things had
so degenerated that it could be said that from Picardy to
Lorraine no peasant's hut stood erect. But in twenty years
a vital nation may recover from what would be a death-
blow to a declining people.

What price Maximian's and Constantius' strenuous and
constant exertions? The protection of the Rhine, to which
they devoted the highest skill and courage, afforded the
possibility of recovery for the interior, but not recovery itself. Nevertheless the efforts of the two princes produced
substantial results, and the Germans felt their blows over a
long period. Several times Maximian forced his way across
the Rhine, like Probus, and subdued (287–288) Burgundians, Alemanni, Heruli, and Franks. Constantius liberated the country of the Batavii from the Franks (294)
and defeated the Alemanni, who had again broken in, in
the frightful battle of Langres (298; according to some,
300) where sixty thousand of their number perished. The
Romans, indeed, were aided by an internal crisis among
the Germans, of which we unfortunately know little. "The
East Goths," we are told, "destroyed the Burgundians, but
the Alemanni took up arms for the vanquished. The West
Goths, with a host of Taifales, campaigned against the
Vandals and the Gepidi. . . . The Burgundians seized the
territory of the Alemanni, but paid for it with heavy losses,
and now the Alemanni wish to regain what they lost." Here,
obviously, is the explanation of the singular truce, broken
only for short periods, between Romans and Germans under Constantine the Great. The profoundly significant
changes which he was to introduce could be carried out
without too great interruption from abroad. Simultaneously, in the far East the peace of 297 and the minority
of the Sassanid Shapur II must have served the same end.

Meanwhile Maximian and Constantius had completed
the fortification of the Rhine as a boundary. It was to these

"fortresses with troops of cavalry and cohorts" near the
river that the reputed restoration of "cities sunk in the for-
est-night and haunted by wild beasts" must have been limited, although the panegyrist to whom we owe these words
makes them the text for a general eulogy of the returning
Golden Age. Where there had been cities, the fourth century knew only fortresses, and even so there were significant gaps.

Perhaps only Treves, the imperial residence of the North,
was restored with any magnificence. From the ruins which
the visit of the Franks, perhaps also of the Bagaudae, left
behind, there arose a great circus, several basilicas, a new
forum, a huge palace, and several other luxurious structures. Unhappy Autun found a warm advocate in
Eumenius, who here shows his better side. He was secretary (*magister sacrae memoriae*) to Constantius and received a pension, probably in reward for important services, of more than twenty-six thousand francs along with a
sinecure as president of the schools of Autun, where his
grandfather, a native of Athens, had occupied a professor-
ship. Now he made it his ambition to devote his entire
income, though he had a family, to the benefit of these
schools, and moreover to direct the gracious attention first
of Constantius and then of Constantine to these badly disrupted institutions and to the ruined city. It is such local
patriotism after the ancient manner that reconciles us to
and engages our sympathy for so many of the Greek and
Asiatic Sophists of the first and second centuries of the
Christian era who appear in the *Lives* of Philostratus. We
must learn to understand the singular mixture of nobleness
and flattery which that period produced. "With humble
adoration I receive this reward," says Eumenius, "for the
honor it confers upon me, but I wish to grant it as a gift.
. . . For who can now be of so lowly a spirit, and so dis-
inclined toward striving for glory, that he would not wish
to create a memorial and to leave behind him a goodly
reputation?" The restored schools would teach men how to
praise their princes worthily; eloquence could be put to no
fairer use. Old Maximian himself is made to stand, quite
undeservedly, as parallel to Hercules Musagetes, the

leader of the Muses; for nominating a scholarch for Autun was to him as important a matter as dealing with a troop of cavalry or a Praetorian cohort. But the restoration of the city as a whole had to wait a long while; only Constantine, with a significant exemption from taxation and with direct subsidies, was able to give it appreciable help. Eumenius' description of Constantine's entry (311) is almost moving: "For you we have decorated the streets that lead to the Palatium as our poor resources afford. Nevertheless we bear at least the symbols of all our guilds and corporations, and the images of all our gods. Our few musical instruments you have met several times because by byways we hastened to overtake you time and again. You have probably noticed the well-intentioned vanity of poverty."

In the desolate northern and eastern regions of Gaul the system introduced under Claudius and Probus could only be continued for better or worse: German war captives were settled as farm slaves, some even as free peasants, and some, indeed, as border guards. The panegyrists find it a matter for praise that all market halls were filled with captives who sat awaiting their fate; that the Chamavian and the Friesian, once such nimble thieves, were now cultivating the fields in the sweat of their brow and bringing cattle and corn to market; that these erstwhile barbarians were now subjected to Roman conscription and military discipline; that Constantius had brought the Franks from the remotest barbarian shores to educate them to agriculture and military service in the wildernesses of Gaul; and so on. In point of fact these were experiments under constraint of necessity, and indeed pregnant with danger; northern Gaul was already half Germanized. As soon as the kindred of these captives should again invade Gaul they would find faithful allies in the settlers, unless a considerable period should intervene.

Constantine's good fortune, talent, and cruelty succeeded in preventing this eventuality. In the first year after his father's death (306) it fell to his lot to defeat an alliance of several Frankish peoples who belonged to the later so-called Ripuarian Franks (apparently the Chatti

and Ampsivarii, along with the Bructerii). During his father's lifetime they had crossed the Rhine; now he crushed
them and took their princes Ascarich and Regais (or
Merogais) captive. Both were thrown to the beasts in the
amphitheater at Treves, whose impressive ruins may yet
be visited in the vineyards. The same fate befell crowds of
captive Bructerii "who were too unreliable to serve as soldiers, too willful to serve as slaves"; "the wild beasts were
wearied because of the large number of their victims."

Twice again, in 313 and about 319, short campaigns
against the Franks are briefly mentioned by the historians;
their importance must therefore have been slight. Constantine even regained possession of a section of the right
bank of the Rhine, and at Cologne he built a great stone
bridge, which stood until the middle of the tenth century,
but in so dilapidated and dangerous a condition that Archbishop Bruno, brother of Otto the Great, had it pulled
down. The bridgehead was Castra Divitensia, modern
Deutz. These successes were commemorated by a periodic
festival, the Frankish Games (*ludi Francici*). At the triumphal celebration of 313 the Franks devoted to death rushed
to meet the wild animals with impatient longing.

Attempts to construct a complete picture of ancient Gaul
as it may have been under Diocletian and Constantine are
futile, for our more abundant sources begin only with
Valentinian I. What has been said above yields an approxi-
mate notion of the lot of the rural population. But the Gaul
felt his poverty more keenly than many other peoples of the
Empire. Of a superior physique, tall and strong, he was
careful of his person, loved cleanliness, and disliked going
about in rags. He was a great guzzler, especially of wine
and other intoxicating beverages, but he had the temperament
of the born soldier who knew no fear and shunned no
hardship until advanced old age. It was thought that this
was attributable to his copious supply of strong blood, and
he was compared to the lean and emaciated southerner,
who could indeed still hunger with an onion a day, but in
battle was parsimonious of his blood, of which he had so
little to spare. Neither did the Gallic women, fair and robust as they were, shun battle; they were terrible when

they raised their white arms and distributed blows and kicks "like catapult-shots." Such a peasantry cannot be pushed too far, and a certain degree of misery will inevitably provoke an outbreak—as indeed then came to pass.

But in the cities, too, poverty and need prevailed. The most important possession of the city dweller in this almost exclusively agricultural country was land let to tenants or cultivated by slaves; hence the urban dweller shared the misery of the rustics to the full. Furthermore here, as in the Empire as a whole, the state oppressed the rich by the institution of decurions, inasmuch as it made the owners of more than twenty-five acres of land responsible for the assessed, and often capriciously increased, taxes of the district. Individuals occasionally sought to evade this responsibility by desperate measures, later even by flight to the barbarians. If we nevertheless find examples of extraordinarily wealthy people and great luxury, the readiest explanation is the persistence of so-called senatorial families whose status was hereditary and who, besides their title of *clarissimi* and other distinctions of honor, also enjoyed exemption from the decurionate which was the ruin of other city dwellers. Another explanation is implied in a remarkable trait of the ancient Gallic national character: they were partial to factions of all sorts, and these tended, especially in times of need, to a client relationship, the protection of the weak by the strong. This relationship had assumed a hypertrophied form by the time of Julius Caesar, who found the masses in bondage to the nobility. Half a millennium later the same plaint recurs practically unaltered. Salvian laments the lot of the smallholder who, reduced to despair by oppressive officials and unjust judges, delivered himself and his property to the great of the land. "Then their plots of land become highways, and they the *coloni* of the rich. The son inherits nothing because the father once required protection." In this way it became possible for an individual grandee, the single lessee of public lands and the like, to join endless *latifundia* together and then, after the ancient manner, display generosity to his city or province, for example by erecting splendid public buildings, while all about him languished or lived at his mercy. If this cannot be demonstrated for Gaul in individual cases, it is still the only explanation for the contrast between the outward magnificence of the cities (in so far as this was not the result of imperial munificence) and the notorious poverty. In temples, amphitheaters, theaters, triumphal arches, fountains, baths, monumental gates, the cities of southern Gaul especially can compare with most of those of Italy, as their ruins testify. Even today they are the ornaments of their localities, just as once when they were yet intact they delighted the poet Ausonius. Aside from gifts, the decurions doubtless often helped defray the necessary expenditures from their own or the city's resources.

Of Gaul's educational institutions we shall speak presently; they secured the country its significant position with reference to the Roman culture of which it was so proud. There was no longer any desire to return to the old Celtic ways; every effort was directed toward becoming Roman. The people must have made special efforts, for example, to forget their own language; Roman colonization and administration alone would never have suppressed it so thoroughly. Perhaps the language situation in Alsace may offer a certain analogy to that in ancient Gaul; the old language continues in daily life, but in all matters of higher education or official procedure the new assumes its place and everyone prides himself on it, however faulty his command of the new language may be. The ancient religion of the Gauls also had to adapt itself to Roman dress and the gods not only submitted (where such a thing was feasible) to the Roman style in names, but also in plastic representation; that style seemed not a little provincial and rank once it ventured out of the ancient cities of the South which understood art. But in one case at least the classical sculptor was required to represent a purely Celtic ideal, to wit, that of the mysterious Matrons, who were customarily enthroned in triads, with marvelous headdress and with bowls of fruit in their laps. A whole crowd of local divinities, whose names could for that reason not be translated into Latin, are represented only by dedicatory inscriptions without images.

But what of the Druids, that once so mighty priesthood which administered the Gallic religion? Of old, together with the nobility, they had constituted the ruling class. The nobles controlled government and war, the Druids the judiciary and the care of occult sciences and powerful superstitions, whereby they enveloped the entire life of the people as with a great web. Their ban was a fearful punishment; a man excluded from sacrifice was accounted unclean and outside the law. Being dedicated to the deity, the Druids were free of imposts and military service. Perhaps their sanctuaries (or temples, if they may be so called) possessed broad domains; certainly they had treasures of precious metals, so abundant that they became proverbial.

From this lofty estate the Druids had long been reduced, but we cannot say when or how. The enormous extortions of Julius Caesar had certainly affected the temple treasures and hence the power of the Druids. That power was reduced, moreover, by the intermingling of Roman worship with their own and by the introduction of Roman priesthoods. Tremors of discontent became evident under Augustus and Tiberius; the latter, at least, is said to have found himself constrained "to abolish the Gallic Druids and similar soothsayers and physicians." But they persisted even after Claudius, according to Suetonius, "completely abolished their fearfully cruel religion, whose practice Augustus had already forbidden to Roman citizens." The reference is to human sacrifice; Claudius also took exception to the dangerous amulets of which the Druids made use—for example, the eggs of certain serpents, which were believed to guarantee victory in disputes and access to princes. The class as such must now have lost its cohesion; the Druid convocations between Dreux and Chartres gradually diminished, and the migration of Druid disciples to Britain, which had been recognized from time immemorial as the highest school of Druid wisdom but had now also become Roman, ceased. But Druids continued to function even in Christian times, doubtless because the people in their daily life could not forgo the superstitious rites which the Druids practiced. Their situation in the third century can easily be imagined. The educated class had long since adopted

Roman ways and had given up any connection with the old national priesthood. In consequence the priests lost their higher spiritual significance and became conjurers, quacks, and soothsayers—a transformation analogous to that of the priests in Egypt. The Druid priestesses in particular strike us as the gypsies of the declining ancient world. Aurelian inquired of a number of them—perhaps a corporation of priestesses—concerning the succession in the Empire, and surely not in jest, for in such a matter jesting was dangerous. Sometimes they uttered their prophecies unsolicited. One bold woman, indifferent to consequences, called to Alexander Severus in the Gallic tongue: "Depart, hope for no victory, do not trust your soldiers!" A Druid landlady in the country of the Tungrii (near Liége) with whom the subaltern Diocles, later Diocletian, was reckoning his daily board, said to him: "You are too greedy, too stingy." "I will be generous if I ever become Emperor," he replied. "Do not mock," the hostess answered, "you will become Emperor when you have slain a boar."

The Druid religion must have maintained itself longest in the regions which still retain traces of Celtic character and language, that is in Brittany and the western part of Normandy. We know of one Druid family of the fourth century who derived from this region and whose members were among the most learned rhetors of the school of Bordeaux. They enjoyed a certain prestige by reason of the fact that the priesthood of the Celtic sun-god Belenus was hereditary in their house. But, significantly enough, they found it advantageous to Grecize this connection and to call themselves Phoebicius and Delphidius.

Where they continued to exist, the Druids presumably kept the cult as active as they could, until late in the Christian centuries the common people dedicated this worship to the huge and shapeless stone monuments characteristic of the ancient Celts, those pillars, flagstones, columns, benches, fairy-walks and the like, where lights and sacrifices burned bright by night and revels were celebrated. But deep darkness covers the decline of Celtic paganism. In later times, magnified by distance, the Druids live on as giants, the Druid priestesses as fairies, and over the stone

monuments, which were deemed uncanny, the Church pronounced its exorcism in vain.

While Maximian was bringing Gaul to obedience, there
was defection in Britain. This was a postlude to the con-
serving usurpation of the Thirty Tyrants under Gallienus
on the one hand, and on the other the prelude to the final
loss of Britain, which took place some hundred and forty
years later.

Since the time of Probus the waters of the island, as of
the coast of Gaul, swarmed with pirates, who are called
now Franks (later Salii), now Saxons. To cope with them
there was need of a fleet, which was in fact equipped at
Boulogne (Gessoriacum). The command of this fleet Maximian entrusted to Carausius, a brave soldier familiar with
the sea, who had proved his mettle in the Bagaudae war.
Carausius was a Menapian (Brabant) of mysterious, possibly un-Roman origin. He soon began to use his position
to play a remarkable game: he allowed the pirates to go
on their raids uninterrupted, and then intercepted them on
their return, in order to retain their booty for himself. His
wealth aroused attention, and Maximian, who had discovered all, issued orders for his death; but Carausius was
able to circumvent him. He bound his soldiers, as well as
the Franks and Saxons, to himself by rich gifts, so that he
could put himself forward as Emperor while still in Gaul
(286), but with no intention of remaining there. He moved
his entire fleet to Britain, where the Roman soldiers at once
declared for him, so that the entire country came into his
power; Maximian lacked the most essential means to pursue
him. He ruled the island, rich at the time, for seven years,
and defended the northern border against its hereditary
enemies, the Caledonians. Boulogne and its surroundings
he retained as a bridgehead for shelter and for freeboot-
ing—a role taken by Calais at the end of the Middle Ages.
As ruler of Britain, Carausius sought to retain Roman education and art, but for the sake of his alliance with the
Franks in the Low Countries he and his Romans assumed
their dress, and he accepted their young men into his army
and navy, where they could learn all the Roman art of war.
If England had continued isolated under Carausius and

similar successors for a longer period, there is no question
but that it would have been barbarized before it could
have adopted and assimilated itself to the Roman-Christian
education which was the most important legacy of the
ancient world. On the other hand, the island's sudden
realization of its future role as ruler of the seas makes an
impressive spectacle; based upon it, a bold upstart rules
the mouth of Seine and Rhine and spreads his terror over
the entire seacoast. But the only basis of his popularity
was that the pirates, now in his service, should no more
trouble the coasts, and that he should defend the northern
frontier.

Maximian was forced to equip a new fleet (289), but
his efforts appear to have been unsuccessful; all the experienced seamen were in the usurper's service. Anxious
lest Carausius extend his rule farther, the Emperors decided to come to terms with him (290). He received the
island and the title of Augustus; he could in any case not
have been prevented from continuing to use that title. But
the Emperors were determined not to allow him to keep his
gains for long. As soon as the two Caesars were adopted,
some pretext, perhaps the situation at Boulogne, was used
to effect a breach (293). Constantius Chlorus besieged the
city. Carausius' naval station patiently allowed the harbor
where it was situated to be blocked by a mole and fell into
the hands of the besieger. Perhaps these events affected
sentiment in England and gave Allectus, a trusted comrade of the usurper, courage to murder him; people and
soldiery at once acknowledged Allectus. Now Constantius
took time to provide a broad and reliable base for the future conquest of Britain, and above all to secure his right
flank by subjugating those Franks who occupied Batavia.
He defeated them (294) and transplanted a large part of
them in Roman territory, near Treves and Luxembourg. At
the same time a new fleet was equipped, and two years
later (296) all was in readiness for the main attack. Allectus posted a fleet at the Isle of Wight to observe enemy
movements, but the imperial Admiral Asclepiodotus, who
was under sail at the mouth of the Seine, was able to elude
it under cover of a thick mist and to land somewhere on

the west coast. Here he burned his boats, apparently because his forces were too slight to admit of division into an attacking arm and a garrison for the fleet. Allectus, who had expected Constantius' principal attack with the Boulogne fleet near London, lost his bearing and had to hasten westward with no preparation. He met Asclepiodotus en route. It was probably a quite insignificant engagement between a few thousand men, in which Allectus himself fell, that decided the fate of England. When Constantius landed in Kent he found the island subdued. The panegyrist takes comfort for the blood spent in this war from the thought that it was the blood of hireling barbarians.

It was necessary for Constantius to bestow upon the island the same advantages it had enjoyed under Carausius, particularly in the matter of guarding the frontiers and of residing in the country for considerable periods. With the Franks now humbled, the first of these requirements was not difficult; as for the second, in times of peace he divided his time between Treves and York, which was the scene of his death (306).

And so was saved the considerable Roman culture which made a distinction, perceptible to this day, between England and Scotland, beyond Hadrian's wall, and Ireland, across the strait. The doom of the fifth century came too late to destroy its mighty traces entirely.

Our chief task should now be to describe the contemporary situation of the Germans, not only on the frontiers of the Empire, but as far to the north and east as they can be traced. As future heirs of the Empire, they merit the closest attention, even though, as it happened, the age of Constantine was for them a period of recession and internal disruption. Even the most fleeting notices and suggestions must be treasured in order to restore, as far as possible, the tattered and evanescent likeness of that great roll of peoples.

But the writer's spirit sinks before the task, in view of the scientific discussion which has been devoted to the principal questions of ancient German history for many years—discussion to which he is in no way competent to contribute. The conclusions of Jakob Grimm's *History of the German*

Language would not only alter hitherto prevalent assumptions concerning the western Germans in many respects, but would also assign to the Germans in closer or remoter degree the ancient peoples of the Danube and Pontus, in particular the Dacians and Getae and even the Scythians, and would identify the Getae with the later Goths. This would completely alter views hitherto held concerning the power and extent of the Germans, and to no less degree transform the ancient history of the Slavs, who, as the Sarmatae of antiquity, would be thought of as living between and among the above-named Germanic peoples.

But even if we could demonstrate with precision the situations, migrations, and mixtures at least of the frontier peoples, from the Netherlands to the Black Sea, during the half-century from Diocletian to the death of Constantine, their internal conditions would still present a great riddle. Where shall we find information concerning the ferment and transformation of Germanic character from the time of Tacitus, concerning the causes of the great tribal alliances, concerning the sudden drive of Pontic Goths to conquest in the third century, concerning their no less striking repose in the first half of the fourth? Where shall we find a gauge to measure the degree of penetration of Roman ways into the Germanic frontier regions? Little is known even of the customs and condition of the Germans who were accepted in the Roman Empire, soldiers as well as *coloni*. We must therefore be content with brief mention of the remaining wars at the northern hem of the Empire, as we were with those on the Rhine. Those northern wars cannot have been very significant, to judge from the laconic remarks recorded concerning them; virtually all attendant circumstances, even of place and position, are passed over in silence.

"The Marcomanni were defeated thoroughly"—that is our only notice (299) during a long stretch of time concerning the people which constituted the center of a great alliance under Marcus Aurelius and threatened the very existence of the Empire.

The Bastarnae and Carpi, apparently Gothic peoples of the lower Danube, were defeated by Diocletian and Galerius (291–295) and the entire folk of the Carpi were settled upon Roman soil, after one hundred thousand Bastarnae had experienced the same fate under Probus.

The Sarmatae, apparently a Slavic Danube people, caused recurrent anxiety. Diocletian campaigned against them, first alone (289), then with Galerius (294), and also transplanted many of them in the Empire. Later incursions were punished by Constantine in an expedition (319) which cost their King Rausimod his life. But toward the end of his life (334) Constantine is said to have accepted into the Empire no fewer than three hundred thousand Sarmatae after they had been ejected from their homeland by an insurrection of their slaves (obviously a people they had previously subjugated). Unfortunately, virtually all explanatory circumstances that would afford ground for judging such mass acceptance of whole peoples are wanting; we cannot distinguish the boundary between coercion and voluntary migration, nor can we surmise the military or economic calculations which led the Roman rulers to such measures. A single treaty, if it were preserved, would throw greater light upon these conditions than all our conjectures, to which we must resort for reconstructing the course of events through analogy.

A Gothic incursion is also mentioned (323), apparently of different character than earlier and later invasions, perhaps the work of a single tribe which secret Roman connivance enticed across the badly guarded borders. Constantine is said to have terrified the enemy by his approach and then to have defeated and forced them to restore the captives they had carried off. An equivocal light is thrown over this whole war by its connection with the attack against Licinius (which will be treated below). Some years later (332) Constantine and his son and namesake marched, upon the petition of the harassed Sarmatae, into the country of the Goths, approximately Moldavia and Wallachia. It is said that one hundred thousand men (apparently of both parties) perished of hunger and cold. The son of King Ariaric was received among the hostages. There followed the intervention into the affairs of the Sarmatae, which has been mentioned above, and their transplanting.

The question always arises, What Goths and what Sarmatae are intended? These names embrace entire series of tribes, originally one but long since separated, whose level of education perhaps represented all degrees and shades between a virtually Roman urban culture and the life of savage hunters. The existence and the character of the Gothic Bible of Ulfilas (shortly after Constantine) justify *a posteriori* a very high estimate of the education of the tribes concerned even in the age of Constantine. But other remains betray barbaric crudeness. To work available individual traits into a single picture transcends the writer's purpose as it does his powers.

Nor can adequate attention be given the pendant of the Gothic picture, the Roman or sometime Roman Danube countries of Dacia (Transylvania, Lower Hungary, Moldavia, and Wallachia), Pannonia (Upper Hungary, including the neighboring regions to the west and south), and Moesia (Serbia and Bulgaria), because the writer does not possess control of the considerable new discoveries in these regions. In the period with which we are here dealing these regions were a military frontier, as they are in a measure today, except that the defense was then against the north instead of against the south. After Philip the Arab the alarums of war were never silent in this region, and Aurelian was forced practically to yield Dacia, Trajan's dangerous conquest, to the Goths. But previously, and in the less threatened areas also subsequently, a very significant Roman culture must have obtained; even in a soil rooted up by repeated migrations the effects of this culture were not to be totally effaced, and still persist recognizably, for example in the Romance language of the Wallachs. Cities like Vindobona (Vienna), Carnuntum (St. Petronell), Mursa (Osijek), Taurunum (Semlin), and above all Sirmium (Mitrovica), and then southward Naissus (Nissa), Sardica (Sofia), Nicopolis on the Haemus, and the whole rich itinerary of the Danube imply conditions which possibly considerably surpassed the Rhine border in wealth and importance. If modern hands might sometime remove the Slavic and Turkish debris from the old cities of the Danube, the Roman life of those regions would again come to the light of day. World history might have taken another direction if in these countries a Germanic people capable of culture had succeeded, by intermixture with the vigorous inhabitants of northern Illyria, in establishing a powerful and enduring realm.

On the Black Sea, finally, the Germans along with other barbarians encountered Greek, mostly Milesian, colonies which, as the northernmost outposts of Hellenism for more than eight hundred years, had made the Pontus a "Hospitable Sea" (*Euxeinos*). Part of them had long since amalgamated with certain barbaric tribes to form the so-called Bosporan Kingdom, which embraced more than half of Crimea and the lower slopes of the Caucasus beyond the Strait of Kerch, and so controlled the entrance to the Sea of Azov and perhaps considerable stretches of its coast also. Coins and inscriptions testify a royal succession without interruption until Alexander Severus; then there follow at intervals the names Ininthimeuos, Teiranes, Thothorses, Phareanzes, and under Constantine, from 317 to 320, a King Rhadamsadis is attested.

When Rome made one after the other of the small kingdoms on its eastern boundary into a province, only Armenia and Bosporus remained, and these detached themselves more and more from Rome and were doubtless barbarized. Under Diocletian the Bosporans in alliance with the Sarmatae waged an unsuccessful war against their neighbors along the entire east side of the Pontus. Constantius Chlorus, who took the field against them in northern Asia Minor, called upon the Chersonesites to invade the Bosporan country from the west, and his maneuver was very successful. The Bosporans were forced to come to terms, whereby they lost almost all of Crimea as far as the region of Kerch (Panticapaeum, the ancient capital of Mithridates the Great) to the Chersonesites. The Greek colony had luckily recognized its obligation as vassal of the Roman Empire, whereas the Prince of Bosporus thought the general crisis of the Empire absolved him from every duty. In relation to the Greek cities of the coast these kings continued to be styled only archons, which was the title of the principal city magistrates in Hellas; in relation with non-Greeks, however, they did not hesitate to assume the style "King of Kings," as the rulers of Persia had once done.

But we turn from this small kingdom back to the West. In the rich garland of ancient Greek colonies whose finds are beginning to fill the museums of southern Russia, two arouse our special sympathy by their zealous efforts to preserve Greek life pure and complete despite their environment. Victorious Chersonesus, modern Sevastopol, was a colony of Heraclea on the Pontus, and thus indirectly of Megara. The near-by promontory of Parthenium bore sacred memories; here there still stood the temple of the importunate Artemis of the Taurians, who until Iphigenia's priesthood required to be conciliated by human sacrifice. The coins of the city bore the figure of the goddess. Under Roman rule Chersonesus again flourished, and under Diocletian, as has been mentioned, it even extended its territory; internally it retained all its Greek institutions and for its victory obtained complete exemption from taxation. The citizens still formed a *demos;* among the archons who were at the head of the council was one for whom the year was named, as at Athens. There followed officials of every kind, strategoi, agoranomoi, gymnasiarchs—usually honorary appointees for services to the state which must often have cost the incumbents dear. An inscription from the end of the pagan period, for example, celebrates Democrates, son of Aristogenes, not only for his legislative proposals, orations, and his two terms as archon, but also because, at his own expense, he journeyed several times as ambassador to the Emperors (Diocletian and Constantius?), because he defrayed the costs of festivals and public services of all sorts out of his own means, and conscientiously administered all matters. The inscription ends, "to the preserver, the incomparable, the friend of his country, from the noble council, the august people." His reward was this inscribed stone and the annual ceremonial reading of a special honorary decree. Like the free cities of the Empire in the later Middle Ages, Chersonesus possessed excellent artillery. In the war with the Bosporans its war chariots bearing catapults were at once put in action; its artillerymen were famous.

Ancient and once powerful Olbia (near modern

Ochakov), a Milesian foundation, was no less concerned to preserve its Greek character. The Olbians proclaimed their Ionian descent in language and customs. They knew the *Iliad* by heart, and neglected non-Ionian poets; a number of respectable later Greek authors were natives of Olbia. Internal institutions and offices were not inferior to those of Chersonesus. The city was able to keep quite free of the barbarians who dwelt around it, but at times paid them tribute. Antoninus Pius sent it help against the Tauro-Scythians; we have yet to discover how it fared later when the great Gothic power which surrounded it began to stir.

As if in defiance of the continuous menace of their situation, the Greeks, as far as their settlements reached to the north of Pontus, paid special reverence to Achilles, the ancient embodiment of the heroic ideal of their people. He is the true ruler of the Pontus, the Ποντάρχης, as he is styled in many inscriptions. In Olbia, as in all the cities of the coast, he had splendid temples. Sacrifices were offered to him "for peace, for fertility, and for gallantry in the city." Festive contests in music of the double-flute and in throwing the discus were celebrated in his honor; especially famous was the foot race of boys on a near-by dune which was called the "course of Achilles," because the hero himself was believed to have once held a foot race on the spot. If barbarians of Asiatic origin (the small race of Sinds) inhabited the dune, the island of Leuke in the Pontus, not far from the mouth of the Danube, belonged entirely to the shade of Achilles. A white cliff (so the descriptions have it*) towered from the sea, partly surrounded by overhanging crags. There was no dwelling, no human sound, either on the shore or in the secluded vales; only coveys of white birds hovered over the cliffs. Reverent awe inspired

---

* If ancient descriptions are to be taken literally, Leuke would be as difficult to locate today as the Isles of the Blessed or the Isles of the Hesperides. But if it is merely a matter of a general locality with which the myth and its imaginative imagery can be associated, any of the small islands at the mouth of the Danube, or perhaps a point on its present sand dunes, would do. An author like Ammianus, who insists upon Leuke, must surely have had some definite information.

those who sailed by. None who stepped upon the island ventured to spend the night there; after they had visited the temple and grave of Achilles and inspected the votive offerings deposited by earlier callers from ancient times, voyagers embarked again at evening. This was the place which Poseidon had once promised divine Thetis for her son, not only for his burial but for his continued existence in blessedness. But Achilles was not the sole occupant; gradually legend gave him as comrades other heroes and blessed spirits who had led a blameless life on earth and whom Zeus was unwilling to leave in the gloom of Orcus. Those white birds, which resembled halcyons in appearance, were regarded with devotion. Perhaps they were the visible manifestations of those happy souls for whose lot latest paganism most yearned.

IV

INDIVIDUAL PROVINCES
AND NEIGHBORING COUNTRIES: THE EAST

WE TURN to the Eastern frontiers; here too the Empire struggled for its very existence. Diocletian inherited insurrections and bloody wars; at the cost of endless toil he and his co-rulers had to defend and in part reconquer the East.

The enemy which was destined to prove worst was, indeed, still slumbering. The Arabs who would one day spread over the East with sword and Koran still lived back of Syria and Palestine, divided into hundreds of tribes, devoted to their astrology and idolatry, their soothsaying and sacrifices. Some had gone over to Judaism, and in the following century there were even a few Christian tribes. The nation's central point was the Kaaba at Mecca, which had been founded by Ishmael. Near by, at Ocadh, an annual twenty-day fair was held, where in addition to trade and worship there took place poetic contests, whose remains— seven poems, the *Mu'allaqāt*—have come down to our time. Occasional contacts with Rome were friendly. Arab horsemen served in the Roman army, and not infrequently Arabs visited ancient holy sites in Palestine which were at the same time markets, as for example the oak of Abraham at Mamre; but for the most part they were dangerous neighbors to that country. We are told that Diocletian took defeated Saracens captive, but with no specific details. In the struggles of the Emperors for Mesopotamia and Egypt they are first mentioned only at the end of the fourth century; their hour was not yet struck.

Greater by far and nearer was the danger which, from

the time of Alexander Severus, threatened from the Kingdom of the Sassanids. If one considers that Kingdom's moderate extent and the probable sparsity of its population,
every advantage seems clearly to be on the side of the
Romans. Could not the Empire easily withstand the peoples from the upper Euphrates to the Caspian Sea and the
Persian Gulf, eastward as far as the Strait of Hormuz? In
point of fact the attacks of the Sassanids were rather in
the nature of predatory incursions than wars of conquest;
but the danger was and remained great and troublesome
because the Emperors were always simultaneously threatened by the Germans and frequently by defection and
usurpation in addition, and so could employ only limited
resources against the East. Because it was the persistent
enemy of the Roman Empire, and for the sake of its own
remarkable internal situation, the Sassanid kingdom merits
a short treatment at this point.

In the first place that kingdom was an artificial creation
claiming to be the restoration of a condition long vanished.
The ancient Kingdom of the Persians, conquered by Alexander, fell for the most part into the hands of the Seleucids;
the defection of Mesopotamia and the eastern hill country
gave rise to the Parthian Kingdom of the Arsacids, which
was quickly barbarized. As heirs to Asia Minor, the Romans were compelled to wage strenuous wars against the
Arsacids, difficult not so much because of any special internal strength of the loosely confederated state whose supreme king was hampered by the willfulness of the greater
vassals, as because of the nature of the country, which was
altogether unfavorable for an attacking army. After the last
king, Artabanus, had forced Caracalla's successor Macrinus
to an ignominious peace and withdrawal, he fell by the
usurpation of Ardeshir Babecan (Artaxerxes Sassan), who
claimed descent from the old rulers of Persia and at once
gathered the Persians of Farsistan about himself in order,
after the Oriental fashion, to replace the ruling Parthians
by a new ruling people. He not only intended to restore
the state of the ancient Achaemenids, of Darius and Xerxes,
with its institutions, but the ancient teaching of Zoroaster
was to displace Parthian astrology and idolatry. The Magi,

many thousands in number, assembled at a council; by a miracle the pure fire-worship, said to have been forgotten, was restored; the King became the first of the Magi; and the counsel and soothtelling of the Magi assumed equal authority with the King. In return the Magi granted him the title of a god, and indeed of a *yazata*, the servant of Ormuzd; he was of equal birth with the stars, and could call himself brother to sun and moon. Christians recognized no claim of this sort, and consequently fared worse than in the Roman Empire; there was no such dogmatic fanaticism as prevailed here in the Roman requirement to offer sacrifice to the Emperors. It appears that many Christians had fled to these regions during the Parthian period and that the Arsacids had tolerated them, perhaps on political grounds; these all now fell into the hands of the Magi. Later, under Shapur II (310–382), the Jews, who were very influential in Persia and had the support of the Queen, are said to have participated in the great persecution in which no fewer than twenty-two bishops, among others, succumbed.

Upon a sheer cliff not far from Persepolis the graves of the ancient Kings of Persia are to be seen, chiseled in the austere style of ancient Persia and on a colossal scale. The Sassanids were unwilling to give up this hallowed site; a series of reliefs added below represents scenes of war, ceremonial, and the chase, in all of which the King appears as the principal personage. The hostile Roman Empire seems to have provided the artists (perhaps captives of war) for this work; at least the sculptures, like the little surviving architecture generally, show the influence of senescent Roman art. The principal remains are some entrances to mountain grottoes vaulted with round arches, and the palaces of Firuz-Abad and Sarbistan, designed in the style of Roman baths with great niche-like openings and vaulted chambers, but much barbarized in execution. There were no temples, properly speaking; the central hearth of the cult was the pyreum or fire-altar, and it is on the steps of this altar that we regularly find the King, surrounded by Magi.

Orthodoxy had become an essential principle of the

state. It was in vain that the reformer Mani, who wished
to construct a new and loftier whole out of elements of
Christian, Parsee, and Buddhist religions, appeared in
Persia with his tablet of painted symbols. Bahram I had
his doctors defeat him in disputation and then flay him;
his skin was stretched over the gate of Djondishapur as a
general warning. On one occasion, however, we find that a
King sought to liberate his race from the oppressive rule of
the Magi. Yezdegerd I Alathim (400–421) had his son
Bahram-gur brought up far from his court by an idolatrous
Arab chieftain, Noman of Hira, later a convert to Christianity. But in the end the prince was not recognized, "because he had adopted Arab ways," and had literally to
fight for his crown with a rival King, Kesra or Khosru, who
had been set up by the nobles. Not far from the royal
residence at Madain the tiara of the Sassanids was laid
down between two hungry lions, to see which of the two
suitors for the throne would reach for it first. Kesra willingly allowed Bahram-gur to make the first approach, and
Bahram-gur slew the two lions and at once set the crown
upon his head. But orthodoxy continued in its full splendor.
When King Cobad later (491–498) followed the heretical
teacher Mazdak, who preached communism and community of wives, there was a general uprising against him,
and he was forced to spend some time in the "castle of
oblivion." It is only in the last days of the kingdom that
large-scale religious exhaustion can be sensed.

In political matters the picture is the usual one of Asiatic
despotism. The people could only offer adoration. When a
new King had delivered his first allocution, all prostrated
themselves with their faces to the ground and remained
in this posture until the King issued his order to arise. It
was long before humility developed so far even in the Eastern Roman Empire; under Diocletian prostration still was
limited to the interior of the palace. The Oriental's joy in
striking acts of mercy or justice, which offer the consolation
of equality before despotism, is also involved. Yet the King
was surrounded by an aristocracy of uncertain origin, perhaps the families of the grandees whom Ardeshir brought
from Farsistan. This nobility seems to have shared influ-

ence at court with the Magi, and to have attempted more than one revolution upon its own account. It was this aristocracy which forced Bahram II (296–301), in conjunction with the Great Magus (the Mobed of Mobeds), to submission, which raised the unwilling Bahram III to the throne (301), and which cut through the ropes of Shapur III's tent, so that he was suffocated when the tent collapsed. But in many questions of the succession the nobility exercised its decisive power in so prudent a manner that the Roman Empire might well envy the Persians this element of their political life. It was natural for the nobility to be concerned for the continuance of the dynasty, because its own position depended on hereditary right. What a contrast with the kaleidoscopic change of Emperors when, after the death of Hormuz II (310), the Persian grandees placed the tiara upon the pregnant body of one of his wives! She insisted that she knew the child would be a boy, and Hormuz himself had long before received a response from the astrologers that a great and victorious King would be born to him. The boy was born; the grandees named him Shapur II, and administered the realm until he attained his majority. He received ceremonial attendance in the palace ten times daily. Fortunately, he was a powerful man, who developed and grew independent very early; his life and reign lasted for seventy-two years, his reign being exactly the length of Louis XIV's. Another incidental similarity to Louis is the fact that he compelled the nobility to leave their country castles and settle in his sight in the capital Madain (ancient Ctesiphon and Seleucia).

But the succession, as has been remarked, was not without violence, although the Kings sought to avert it by crowning a prince during their lifetimes (see page 36). The grandees and perhaps the Magi also frequently favored individual princes within the house of the Sassanids; even acknowledged Kings feared usurpation on the part of their kin. To remove such suspicions from his father Shapur I, Hormuz I sent him (with characteristic Oriental transfer of the symbolic to the real) his right hand, which he had amputated; but the father refused to accept this noble declaration of incapacity to rule.

Internally the regime obviously proceeded with higher means toward higher ends than the Parthians, who had always remained crude, had done. Of several Sassanid Kings such benefactions are reported as have always been the ideal of an Oriental prince: protection of agriculture, irrigation works, the prosecution of justice, codification of laws, buildings useful and ornamental (at least on the great royal roads), new city foundations, patronage of scholars and artists from far and near. Of all the Kings, not only their outward appearance but also their manner of thought have been transmitted, after the Asiatic manner, in significant proverbial verses.

The saying of the founder, Ardeshir I, sounds like a motto for the fate of his kingdom in general: "There is no kingdom without soldiers, no soldiers without money, no money without population, no population without justice." It was by such a circuitous route that the King had to achieve insight into the moral end of the state. In any event, military security was the prime task. For this kingdom, which caused the Romans so much anxiety, itself suffered from the same external dangers as did the Empire. From the south the Arabs began to press forward; the Magi are said to have known even then that they would one day conquer Persia. Shapur II, during whose minority they had wrested large stretches from the Persian realm, undertook a terrible campaign of vengeance against the Arabs in his sixteenth year (326). He built a fleet on the Persian Gulf and sailed across to Arabia. After a general massacre on Bahrein Island and among the tribes of Temin, Bekr-ben-Waiel, Abdolkais, and others, he had the shoulders of the survivors bored and ropes passed through by which to drive them; Constantine only threw his German captives to the wild beasts in the arena at Treves.

Another dangerous enemy threatened from the north, from the region of the Caspian Sea—the Ephthalites or White Huns, as they are wrongly named, one of those Turkish tribes which seem to have been born specifically to bring doom to the Near East in the various centuries.

The victorious war which Bahram-gur (420–438) waged against them belongs to the adventures, told in many forms, of which the romance of his life is composed; but his driving of the nomads back over the Oxus is probably fact. Nevertheless, not long thereafter they found opportunity to intervene in the war of succession (456) of the two sons of Yezdegerd II; Firuz, the elder of the sons, who had been deposed and had taken refuge with them, they supported with a large army and restored to the Persian throne. Thenceforward their influence, even their intervention, was no longer to be evaded, and the Sassanids often paid them annual tribute.

The later vicissitudes of the realm and its final period of splendor under Koshru Nushirwan do not require to be dealt with here. We turn to special events which fall in the epoch of Diocletian and Constantine.

At the time of Gallienus and the Thirty Tyrants the Kingdom of Palmyra was Rome's champion against the Persians. Odenathus defeated Shapur I, the proud victor over Valerian, and pursued him to Ctesiphon. But when Aurelian later attacked the Palmyrenes, Sassanid policy turned to their support, in order to preserve a weaker neighbor. Bahram I sent an army to help Zenobia, and this army, like the Queen's own, was defeated by the Roman Emperor. Aurelian and then Probus had to be conciliated with gifts. Probus nevertheless prepared for a Persian war, which was actually undertaken by his successor Carus. Brilliant successes again took the Roman army beyond the Tigris, but lost their value by the sudden death of Carus and the return of his son Numerian to Rome (283). As was to be expected, Bahram II, after some hesitation, eagerly exploited the great confusion in the entire Roman Empire at the accession of Diocletian, in order to secure himself and expand to the west. For a time the Emperors could only allow him his way, for nearer troubles occupied their attention. Their struggle was taken over for them by Armenia.

This country, under a collateral branch of the fallen Parthian royal houses of the Arsacids, had formerly enjoyed Roman protection. But when the Roman Empire began to disintegrate under Valerian and Gallienus, Shapur I subdued Armenia with the help of native factions. Tiridates, son of the murdered King Chosroes, was saved only by the loyalty of the royal servants, and was brought up under the protection of the Roman Emperors. Endowed with prodigious strength and high spirit, honored even for victories at the Olympian Games, he seemed peculiarly suited to step forth as a claimant of the lost kingdom of his fathers. As Nero had once invested his like-named ancestor with Armenia, so Diocletian is now said to have invested Tiridates (286). Tiridates found his country suffering from systematic oppression, even religious. The intolerant Parseeism of the foreign rule had broken the statues of the deified Kings of Armenia and the sacred images of sun and moon, and instead had erected a pyreum to Sacred Fire on Mount Bagavan. Quickly nobles and commoners rallied about the prince; the Persians were ejected, and rescued treasures, even a rescued princess, were brought to light. Mamgo, an allegedly Scythian but probably Turkoman chieftain who had been banished to Armenia by Shapur, went over to the new ruler with his followers. But Narses I mustered his forces, conquered Armenia anew, and forced Tiridates again to seek the protection of the Romans.

Meanwhile Diocletian and his colleagues had mastered most of their enemies and were now able to turn their attention to the East. While the senior Emperor marched to subdue Egypt, which had been rebellious for some time, he entrusted the campaign against Narses to his Caesar, Galerius; their joint headquarters was Antioch. But two indecisive battles and a third which Galerius lost through excessive boldness again drenched with Roman blood the desolate plain between Carrhae and the Euphrates where Crassus had once led ten legions to their death. Diocletian, who had meanwhile subjugated Egypt, while Maximian's Caesar, Constantius Chlorus, was simultaneously returning rebellious Britain to the Empire, was doubly incensed that on the Euphrates alone Roman arms should prove inferior. On his return the defeated Caesar met him in Syria; Diocletian suffered him, dressed in his purple cloak as he was, to run beside his chariot for a mile, in full view of the soldiers and the court. More clearly than anything else, this incident indicates the true tone of Diocletian's rule. Galerius' devotion was not in the least diminished; his only request was permission to erase the disgrace by victory. Now instead of the less able Asiatics the irresistible Illyrians marched out, together with an auxiliary army of mercenary Goths; all together they were only twenty-five thousand, but first-class fighting men. This time (297) Galerius moved beyond the Euphrates to the hill country of Armenia, where he found the people favorable to the Roman cause and where the Persian army, consisting chiefly of cavalry, would be less terrifying than in a battle on the plains. (Among the Persians, according to Ammianus, the infantry was regarded only as camp-followers.) Galerius himself, with only two men accompanying him, spied out the careless Persian camp, and then suddenly attacked it. His success was complete. After a general carnage King Narses fled wounded to Media; his and his grandees' tents, filled with rich booty, fell into the hands of the victors, and his wives and a number of his kinsmen were taken captive. Galerius understood the value of such pledges, and treated his captives with kindness and care.

If surviving accounts of the war are brief and scant, those of the peace negotiations which followed go into minute details. In the first overtures, which Apharban, a confidant of Narses, made to Galerius alone, the high-flown Asiatic flattery is quite amusing. Rome and Persia are for him the two lamps, the two eyes of the world, and must not irritate one another. It was only by so great a prince as Galerius that Narses could have been conquered; even so human affairs are changeable. How critical the situation of Persia must have been is indicated by the fact that the King left all political terms to the discretion of the Romans' "philanthropy" and asked only for the return of his family. Galerius first spoke to the envoy harshly and reminded him of the Emperor Valerian, whom the Persians had tortured to death, but then addressed a few kinder words to him. Then the Emperor and the Caesar met at Nisibis on the Euphrates. This time as victor Galerius was received with

the highest honor, but again he manifested selfless submission to Diocletian's superior judgment and declined the
easy and certain conquest of Hither Persia, of which only
the more valuable border districts were to be incorporated. A secretary, Sicorius Probus, was sent to Narses,
who had withdrawn to Media to gain time and gather
troops in order to impress the weary Roman envoy. Probus
received an audience on the river Asprudus and concluded
a treaty by which Narses ceded five provinces, including
the land of the Kurds and the entire region of the upper
Tigris as far as Lake Van. This secured their earlier possession, the upper Euphrates, to the Romans, and at the
same time erected a wall for their protectorate Armenia,
of material, to be sure, which had belonged to the Armenians before the Parthian conquest. Still, a considerable
stretch of land was ceded to them in the southeast, and
Tiridates was again installed as King. The King of Iberia
was also henceforward to be vassal of the Romans; this was
an important development, for this rough hill country
north of Armenia (corresponding more or less to modern
Georgia) with its warlike inhabitants could serve as an
outpost against the barbarians from beyond the Caucasus.
Upon the conclusion of these terms Narses' family, which
had been kept at Antioch, was restored to him.

The entire frontier was now provided with fortresses and
garrisons. The period of peace which now ensued for
Hither Asia lasted for almost forty years, to the end of Constantine's life. The victorious Emperors could hardly have
realized that their great successes substantially paved the
way for the peaceful spread of the Christianity they hated.
The contrary influence which Persia exerted upon the Roman Empire through its Manichaeism and its manifold superstitions will be touched upon later.

Despite later admixtures, even of Shiite Mohammedanism and the culture it involved, the Persian people and
their customs are still partly to be recognized from the
descriptions which Ammianus gave of them in the fourth
century and Agathias in the sixth. They have retained the
ambiguous glance, under arched eyebrows which run together over the nose, and the carefully tended beard. Cer-

tain rules of etiquette obtain now as then. Of their ancient reputation for moderation there is still a remnant. The singular mixture of effeminate luxury and high personal courage is still characteristic, as is bold braggadocio and self-seeking cunning. Their sweeping and colorful dress and tinsel ornaments were noticed by the Romans as they are by us. Usages dependent upon religion, as for example exposing corpses to dogs and carrion birds, could naturally survive only where Parseeism has persisted. Many of their superstitions Mohammedanism extirpated or transformed into fairy stories. To the Persian of the Sassanid period all his daily life, every step and turn, was filled with threatening or alluring magic, and the holy fire of the pyres issued oracles continuously. The great Shapur II was not content with these; among the Magi proper there were necromancers who had to conjure shades for him at critical junctures—even that of Pompey.

It has often been remarked how closely Sassanid usages correspond to those of the Middle Ages in the West, at least in certain aspects. For one thing there is the monastic abstinence of the Magi and their position as a sort of clergy alongside the nobility. It is to be regretted that we have no details of this matter and are even ignorant of the manner in which they perpetuated themselves as a class. The nobility itself, with its bluff chivalry, is quite Western. Its formal relationship to the King appears to have been feudal; its principal obligation was assistance in war. As represented in monuments, these Persian warriors in mail and plumed helmets, with lance and sword, and with the magnificent accouterments of their steeds, are quite like the knights of our own Middle Ages. As with the knights, the soul of their activity was adventure, whether in war or love. Legend early transformed a figure like Bahram-gur into a splendid pattern of this character, and heroes of the mythical period, a Rustem or a Feridun, were already held in high honor. Such romanticism, as indeed anything impractical, offers a stark contrast to Roman ways.

Let us glance back to Armenia. Hitherto this country with its brave and educatable people had always heeded influences and impressions from abroad; it had achieved only a relatively rudimentary culture, and was soon to be subject to new and lasting poverty and servitude. But the period of Tiridates, which was at the same time the period of its conversion to Christianity, constitutes a bright interval. Christianity, in the form of the Armenian Church, would one day be the chief support for Armenian nationality.

This is the account of Moses of Chorene (*fl.* 440), the chronicler of the Armenians: Gregory the Illuminator, deriving from a collateral branch of the royal house of the Arsacids, was brought as a child to Roman Cappadocia by a peculiar concatenation of circumstances, and there was raised by a Christian family, and later married to a Christian woman, Maria. After three years of marriage they separated, in order to serve God in voluntary abstinence. Of their two sons the younger became an anchorite, and the elder continued the family. Gregory then returned to Armenia with Tiridates, who was still a pagan, and began, with great danger, to convert the people.

From other sources we learn that a saintly woman, Ripsime, labored along with him and even suffered a martyr's death, but that the conversion proceeded with speed. Before the Diocletianic persecution of 302 Gregory baptized Tiridates himself and a large part of the people. He survived the period of the Nicene Council, which he was unwilling to attend because of humility, and spent his old age from 332 onwards as a recluse in the hills which are called Mania Caves. He himself installed his son Aristaces as his successor in the episcopacy or high-priesthood. He died unknown, and shepherds buried him; long afterwards his body was discovered and solemnly interred in Thordan.

Tiridates survived Constantine, and was posioned by the nobility in 342. Soon civil war and intervention from abroad brought the Arsacid kingship as well as the Arsacid priesthood, which was also hereditary, into great distress and confusion. But the impression of the conversion persisted through all the foreign regimes which followed. Christianity, through petrified in its Monophysite form, still unites the Armenians, who are dispersed as far as Austria, with the exception of the (Roman Catholic) Uniates, who at present include some of the best and most highly cultured elements of their people.

Such was the condition of Rome's friendly and hostile neighbors to the east. The Asiatic provinces of the Empire itself enjoyed peace in the time of Diocletian and Constantine, interrupted only for short periods by the great imperial wars. A portrait of Syria and Asia Minor at this period would require a special and considerable investigation. We shall limit ourselves to pointing to a sore spot which brought shame to the body of the Empire for centuries, the robber country of the Isaurians, which is a standard item in all histories of the Roman Empire.

The earlier piracy and slave trade of the Cilicians, which grew active when the successor kingdoms (of Alexander the Great) were in their decline, is much better known because it was suppressed in the memorable last years of the Republic by Pompey the Great after Cilicia had long furnished base and refuge to piracy of the entire Mediterranean. Even then hoary Isaura was cited as one of the robbers' nests of the interior, and after Isaura, all of the region back of Cilicia proper came to be called Isauria. It is a rough hill country of volcanic formation, with high peaks, and its cities were rather in the nature of fortresses. Whether a remnant of the robber character survived in this back country from the pirate war, or whether the populace newly adopted this manner of life in the Empire because of total lack of supervision, the Isaurians of the third century were the plague of southern Asia Minor. At the time of the Thirty Tyrants they found it expedient to raise one of their leaders, Trebellian, to Emperor, and he held court at Isaura, struck coins, and maintained himself in his wild hills for a considerable period. We do not know how Causisoleus, one of Gallienus' generals, succeeded in getting hold of his person; in any event his death did not mean the conquest of the country, for the Isaurians held together so much the more firmly out of fear of the further vengeance of the Roman Emperor. Under Claudius Gothicus a new attack was undertaken against them, and was so far successful that the Emperor could now form a

plan to transfer the Isaurians down to Cilicia and settle
them there while a loyal follower would receive their
empty country for his own; rebellion thus would have been
rendered impossible. But the early death of Claudius seems
to have prevented the execution of this project, and soon
the Isaurians were as bold and active as before. Under
Probus one of their robber chiefs, Lydius, made Lycia and
Pamphilia unsafe. He not only made himself secure against
all attacks in inaccessible Cremna (in Pisidia) but also assured himself against starvation by sowing and reaping.
The unhappy inhabitants whom he had ejected and whom
the Roman commandant wished to send back to him perforce, he hurled down from the city walls into the gorges.
An underground passage from Cremna passed under the
Roman camp to a distant secret spot in the open; this passage Lydius' men used to bring cattle and provisions into
the city from time to time, until the enemy discovered it.
Then Lydius felt compelled to reduce his company to the
indispensable minimum by murder; a few women were left
alive, and were held in common. At length his best artillery-
man, with whom he had quarreled, went over to the Romans and from their camp hurled his projectiles at an opening in the walls which Lydius used as lookout. The robber
chieftain was fatally wounded, but exacted an oath from
his men not to surrender the fortress; this did not prevent
them from breaking their pledge as soon as he had given
up the ghost. But the best that this victory achieved was
to secure Pisidia for some time; Isauria, adjacent on the
east, continued in the hands of the robbers as before. This
is stated as clearly as possible in a notice from the time
of Diocletian: "From the time of Trebellian the Isaurians
are regarded as barbarians, and since their land is situated
in the midst of Roman territory, they are hedged in with
a new species of border guards like an enemy frontier.
Their locale alone protects them, for they are themselves
neither impressive in stature nor dangerous by reason of
courage, nor remarkable by reason of weapons, nor particularly clever; their only strength is the inaccessibility of
their domicile in the hills."

That new species of border guards and the manner

of their warfare against the robber folk we become acquainted with in several instances in the course of the fourth century. The Empire employed no fewer than three legions, later at least two, for this single purpose. Staff headquarters were apparently at Tarsus in Cilicia and at Side in Pamphilia, supply dumps in Peleas, while the troops were either posted in the villages and fortresses of the interior or moved about in mobile columns. Nevertheless they did not venture far into the hills after experience taught them that the sheer ascents made any Roman tactic useless, as soon as boulders were rolled down upon them. The Isaurians had to be awaited in the plains, when they came to raid Cilicia, Pamphilia, Pisidia, and Lycaonia; here they were easily mastered, and either dispatched or delivered to the beast hunts in the amphitheaters of large pleasure-loving cities like Iconium. But even the Cilician shore could not always be protected; the old pirate nature of the hill folk occasionally broke out so violently that for long periods (for example, around 355) they held stretches of coast-land in their possession and obliged navigation to hug the shores of Cyprus, which lay opposite. The siege of the important Seleucia Tracheotis, Cilicia's second city, did not seem to them too bold an enterprise; only a large Roman relieving army moved them to raise the siege. Then they were again successfully contained in their hill country for several years by a system of redoubts and ramparts until they broke out in large bands in 359 and terrified the country by their robberies. Effective threats rather than punishment are said to have once more restored them to quiet. A new raid into Pamphilia and Cilicia, in which they murdered all who fell into their hands, is reported for the year 368. A company of light Roman troops with one of the highest imperial officials, the Neoplatonist Musonius, at their head, were attacked in a narrow gorge and annihilated. Thereupon the Isaurians were pressed and pursued from place to place until they sued for peace and obtained it upon surrender of hostages. One of their most important localities, Germanicopolis, which was their customary mouthpiece, represented them in these negotiations also; there is no mention of any specially powerful chieftain or prince. Eight years later, under Valens, the Isaurians come into view again; about 400 the general Tacitus was compelled to purge Cilicia of robbers; in 404 the general Arbazacius defeated the Isaurians, but was then bribed by them, and they continued in their ways for years on end. So it went until late in the Byzantine period, with attack, defense, and apparent submission. The people, whose number was small, must have been thoroughly barbarized. The Romans approached them only as enemies, and it is understandable but no less regrettable that we have no description of political, moral, and religious conditions as they developed among the Isaurians. In many respects their relation to Rome was like that of the Circassians to Russia, but in principle it was different. Isauria had been Hellenized at least superficially, and was later gradually barbarized. That such a process could take place unhindered is significant of the internal condition of the Roman Empire in more than one respect.

We now turn to the southern shore of the Mediterranean. Among the unhappiest lands of the Roman Empire we again find Egypt, where Diocletian was to make a sorry name for himself by the cruel suppression of one of those insurrections in which Egyptian history, after the conquest by the son of Cyrus, is so rich.

The attitude of the Roman to Egypt was a curious mixture: profound contempt and strict control of the natives (Egyptians as well as colonized Greeks and Jews) go hand in hand with traditional reverence for the records and monuments of the millennia-old Pharaonic period and its living remains—I refer to that occult priestly religion whose Isis cult, symbols, incantations, and magic arts the late Roman world could least do without. The same Roman prefect or *epistrategos* who held sway with robbery and cruelty would make a pilgrimage to hundred-gated Thebes and Philae, and have his name chiseled on the calf of the statue of Memnon, together with the statement that he heard its famous reverberation at dawn. The secular curiosity of the student of antiquity and the tourist, and the romantic longing of the educated were also directed largely to Egypt and its age-old civilization. Egypt was the scene of the romances of Xenophon of Ephesus and of Heliodorus; in the colorful stories of their lovers, Anthia and Habrocomes, Theagenes and Chariclea, Egyptian robber bands occupy the same role as modern novelists customarily assign to Italian *banditti*—to say nothing of the symbolic romance of Synesius which clothed events of the age of Arcadius in an ancient Egyptian dress. "Everything that is told of Egypt," says Heliodorus, "interests the Hellenic hearer exceedingly." In plastic art also Egyptian modes became fashionable, especially under Hadrian, and much later there was a fondness for Egyptian landscapes trimmed with marvelous animals, feluccas, the arbors and the shore casinos of the life-giving Nile, somewhat as our fashion has occasionally adopted Chinese motifs. The famous mosaic of Palestrina is of this character.

But the actual conditions were grim and terrible. Ancient civilizations, which after a brilliant past fall into the hands of alien and relatively barbaric conquerors and through long centuries are passed unconsulted from hand to hand, easily assume a character which strikes the foreign ruler as a sullen fractiousness, even though it only partially deserves such a name. The Persian conquest marked the beginning of this attitude; it embittered the Egyptians, and permanently, not only by subjugation and oppression itself, but also by flagrant contempt of their ancient religion. The simple light-worship of the Persians conflicted with the massive half-animal pantheon of their new subjects; to the one, precisely those things which the other regarded as sacred were unclean. Hence arose those endless insurrections which streams of blood could never quench.

The Greek rulers who succeeded the Persian brought no such cleavage with them; in the polytheism of the Near East and Egypt their Hellenic faith sought not the differences but, and very eagerly, kinships with itself. For Alexander the Great Ammon was equivalent to Zeus, whom he regarded as his own progenitor. Even before Alexander, the Greek had no doubt that his Apollo was the same as the Egyptian Horus, Dionysus as Osiris, Demeter as Isis; and now he found counterparts for half his Olympus on the Nile. Ptolemy son of Lagus, who had secured Egypt for himself when Alexander's great legacy was divided among his generals, was especially concerned, as were his immediate successors who organized the new kingdom, to conciliate the Egyptians in certain matters. It was not to their interest to follow the brutal Persian manner of needlessly treading every national characteristic underfoot and thus provoking desperate insurrection. Their interest was rather in the direction of a well-organized and self-contained military and official hierarchy, exercising only so much pressure as was necessary to bring the financial resources of the country into the royal treasury, where, despite one hundred and fifty thousand soldiers and four thousand ships, incredible sums were stored up. Egypt's ancient and original agrarian division into *nomes* was left undisturbed. Even the caste system held no danger, since there was no longer a native warrior caste. The priests and their rule of the temples were encouraged and their worship promoted by solemn royal participation, although at the same time considerable taxes were exacted from them. Ptolemy Euergetes built the magnificent temple of Esne in a style which is not noticeably different from the ancient Egyptian. The Kings of his line continued to have themselves embalmed and were worshiped as "savior gods" along with and even above Isis and Osiris. This was the most manifest symbol of an amalgamation which was more and more fully realized in the fact that the Greeks were no longer secluded in foreign settlements, but were scattered over the country and lived among the Egyptians. The new cosmopolis of Alexandria, however, continued predominantly Greek. Here the Greek character, which had become cosmopolitan and communicable in the form we call Hellenistic, shed its most brilliant light. For a time there was no city in the world which could compare with Alexandria in splendor and in material as well as spiritual activity; but neither was there anywhere so concentrated a measure of corruption as at Alexandria, where three peoples (counting the Jews) had all gone astray from their pristine national character and required policing rather than government.

When, after the victory of Actium, Augustus took over the country, which had declined somewhat in the interval, its only excuse for existence was suddenly reduced to the service of Rome, as source of profit and as granary. No province was watched as closely as this, both because of the dangerous spirit of the people and ominous prophecies, and because of its singular importance. Without imperial permission no Roman senator or knight might visit the country; the position of Prefect of Egypt was one of high importance and trust because nowhere else was such care necessary to prevent defection and usurpation. Naturally, the prefect had to be given broad plenipotentiary powers; his outward bearing was calculated to incarnate their old kingship to the Egyptians, and the impressive official journeys of the prefect, at least, did recall ancient Egyptian royalty. He could be seen with a large retinue, including priests, sailing up and down the Nile on one of those gilded floating confections which the luxury of the Ptolemies had introduced. The system of graded officials subordinate to the prefect was maintained virtually as it had been taken over from the Ptolemies. Least account was taken of the people; we do not know whether it could choose even its lowliest functionaries, or whether it might assemble for any other purpose than to signify homage to the Emperor. The occupation troops, which were to guard the country from enemies from within and without, were few, even for the sparing Roman system. Soon after Augustus there were at most twenty thousand troops, for eight million inhabitants (among them a million Jews). The region of Memphis, where the Nile begins to divide, was recognized by the Romans, as it was later by the Arabs, as one of the most important strategic points; a legion was therefore permanently posted at Babylon, modern Old Cairo. In times of peace the soldiers were required to dig Nile canals, drain swamps, and the like. Probus used them even for constructing temples and other monumental buildings. The outlay could not be too large if the country was to yield the expected profit. To realize this profit Rome made enormous demands. A fifth of the entire production of grain (as had been the requirement under the Pharaohs) or its partial equivalent in money as a ground tax, or perhaps even double tithe plus ground rent, had to be delivered to the state. Temple property was not free of this contribution. In addition to the more than million and a half hundredweight of grain annually thus realized, there were head taxes and high import and export duties. These yielded more than they had done under the Ptolemies because the entire Roman world had gradually grown accustomed to certain Indian wares which came chiefly through Egypt. Custom stations are mentioned from the mouths of the Nile to Upper Egypt and the Red Sea; the collectors were Egyptian, apparently because no others were suitable for the hateful business. Of the mines, perhaps only a small portion was directly useful to the state. Egypt's valuable minerals, the emeralds of Coptos, the red granite of Syene, the porphyry of the Claudian mountain, served luxury in dress and building. In addition to the Arabs, who were especially skillful in discovering deposits, thousands of condemned persons worked in the mines.

As regards the employment and the economic condition of the people, we can assume that Upper and Middle Egypt, as far as it is irrigated by the Nile, was entirely devoted to agriculture, and that the lively manufacture of textiles of all sorts, together with glassware and pottery, was limited to Lower Egypt, where the Delta and adjacent regions also offered great facilities for agriculture. In the upper country we may imagine that the great ancient cities were practically deserted and reduced to their indestructible temples and palaces; at least the later foundation of Ptolemais (near Girga) had surpassed them all and had come to equal Memphis—which need not mean a great deal. The population of the lower country, it may be conjectured with certainty, was composed predominantly of proletarian wage earners who possessed nothing and required little. Their industry, at least in Alexandria, had aroused the admiration of Hadrian: "Here no one is idle. Some make glass, others paper, still others are weavers; everyone belongs to a trade and makes it his vocation. Even rheumatics and the blind have their employment, and even those whose hands are lame are not idle." Whether this implies an extreme fragmentation of landed property, or, on the contrary, its centralization in a few hands, cannot be determined, for we do not know, for example, how large temple holdings and imperial domains may have been in Lower Egypt. But even freeholds were not in fact free, by reason of the enormous levies.

We have mention, incidentally, of a district called Bucolia, in the neighborhood of modern Damietta, where an ancient people, perhaps neglected for many centuries, developed into a kind of robber polity. In Italy itself the Empire at times permitted robber bands to grow out of hand. Under the very eyes of the mighty Septimius Severus and his victorious army the very capable Bulla Felix with a band of six hundred men was able to lay the entire Via Appia under contribution for two years. A few decades later there is incidental mention of a distinguished and wealthy robber family on the Genoese Riviera near Albenga which could employ two thousand armed slaves in its own affairs. We have already spoken of Isauria and the conditions which were tolerated there. But against the Egyptian Bucoles even Marcus Aurelius was constrained to wage war. "They rose up," says Dio Cassius, "and moved the other Egyptians also to revolt; a priest [and] Isidorus led them. First they trapped a Roman captain; they approached him, dressed as women, as if they would offer him money for the release of their men. Then they murdered him and his companion, swore a covenant over the entrails of the companion, and ate them. . . . They defeated the Romans in open battle, and would almost have taken Alexandria also had not Avidius Cassius, who marched against them from Syria, been able to subdue them by disrupting their unanimity and separating them, for battle could not be ventured against that mad mass."

The Bucoles proper numbered hardly a few thousand, and if number were the significant factor they might well be passed over in a history of the Roman Empire. We should find similar examples of ancient and oppressed peoples reduced to new barbarization elsewhere in the Empire if the history of the provinces were not so mute. The name Bucoles, "Cowherds," suggests a remnant of the old caste of that name; but these men apparently had nothing to do with cows, except perhaps those they stole. The flood of one of the middle arms of the Nile supplied a large lake near the sea, and the reedy marshes about the lake were the dwelling place or at least the hide-out of these pariahs; this was perhaps the most unsanitary spot in Egypt, and hence no one was likely to dispute its possession. Here the Bucoles lived partly on barges, partly in huts on small islands; young children were fastened by straps which were just long enough to prevent them from falling into the water. Passages for their peculiar canoes, where none but they could find the way, were cut through the sedge. We find mention of robber villages, but these are probably the same settlements by the lake. The Bucoles were joined by everyone who was at odds with ordinary organized society; the character which they developed is indicated by the uprising under Marcus Aurelius. Even the appearance of these people, with hair down to the eyes in front and hanging long behind, was terrifying. The contrasts offered by localities a few days' walk apart are very striking: rich, industrial Alexandria; the robber state in the marshes; westward on the Lake Mareotis the last Jewish hermits; in the near-by Nitric Desert the first Christian recluses. The Bucoles themselves proved unwilling to have anything to do with Christianity; even at the end of the fourth century there was no single Christian among these "wild barbarians."

But it is time to consider the character and special destiny of the Egyptians in the later Roman period. "The Egyptian is ashamed," says Ammianus, "if he cannot show his brown and lean body marked with welts upon welts received for refusal to pay his taxes. No physical torture has yet been discovered severe enough to make a hardened Egyptian robber acknowledge his name." This was the attitude of the lower classes toward their officials. In any general misfortune, whether war or crop failure, the first complaint was against the government. The permanent temper of the masses was insurrectionary, and would have been so even against better rulers. In ordinary times this was revealed by a venomous mockery, which knew no bounds when it emerged from servile flattery. A respectable Roman matron who was forced to live in Egypt as the wife of the prefect never appeared in public for thirteen years and allowed no Egyptian into her house, so that she might at least be ignored. Those who could not thus protect themselves were exposed to the most ribald comments and songs, "things which might seem to the Alexandrians very agreeable, but to the victim annoying." In the case of Caracalla, as we know, they found the wrong man; he paid them out with a massacre of many thousands, which had been contemplated for years. Augustus and Nero managed more cleverly; they paid no attention to the Alexandrians' mockery, and found amusement in their talent for flattery and applause.

The Egyptians showed an appetite for quarrel and strife and unparalleled deceit and litigiousness not only to their superiors but also among themselves. These otherwise gloomy people could then be seen aflame with fiery anger and wild insults, perhaps only because a greeting had not been returned, or place had not been yielded in the baths, or because their insane vanity had otherwise been injured. Since the slightest disturbance might serve embittered thousands as a signal for the eruption of their inner ferment, there was always general danger in such incidents; and the official responsible for order and obedience in Egypt could thus justify inhuman repression, at least to the Emperor. It was known that peace could be restored only after blood had flowed. It is characteristic of Alexandria that in that city earlier than elsewhere in the Empire, perhaps even in Ptolemaic times, ardent partisanship for the charioteers of the Hippodrome regularly led to violence and murder.

One thing in particular can inflame such ancient, misunderstood, and abused people to insane effort, and that is their religion, which, though degenerated and bereft of all moral vitality, still takes the place of the lost national bond. So for the Egyptians first their paganism and then even their Christianity served as the channel for an amorphous and suppressed fury. The need for fanatic outbreaks was present; time and destiny determined its object. Pagan

Rome was careful not to give offense in these matters. The Emperors, when they visited the country, participated in ritual and sacrifice; in the monuments they always appear as ancient Egyptian kings, with inscriptions reading, "the Ever-living, the Beloved of Isis, the Beloved of Phtha"; temples were built or completed by them or as votive offerings for them. But within Egypt itself there was always occasion for religious animosities because of jealousies between temple and temple, expressed in divergent partisanship for the sacred animals. Juvenal and Plutarch have left us genre-pictures of the subject, which might be read with unmixed pleasure if the shadowy outline of the oldest civilization on earth did not possess something of the venerable which we do not willingly see wholly trodden in the dust. Orthodoxy in one city took no exception to eating animals which were worshiped in another. "In my day," writes Plutarch (*Isis and Osiris*, 72), "the people of Oxyrhynchus ("Piketown") caught a dog and sacrificed it and ate it as if it had been sacrificial meat, because the people of Cynopolis ("Dogtown") were eating the fish known as the oxyrhynchus, or pike. As a result of this they became involved in war and inflicted much harm upon each other; and later they were both brought to order by chastisement of the Romans." Juvenal (15, 33 ff.) tells of the shameful attack of the Tentyrites against the people of Ombi, who were carefree and drunk at a festival they were celebrating; not only were mutilations and murder involved, but the devouring of a dismembered corpse, as was the case in the story of the Bucoles related above. It was easy for a legend to arise that an ancient King had once prudently prescribed various animal cults for various localities, because without the continuous rivalry thus engendered it would have been impossible to control the numerous and restless people of Egypt. In our summary view of paganism we shall have to return to this mighty religion, with its priests, its magicians, and its proud attitude to Greco-Roman paganism.

The Egyptian language, which survived and which persisted later in the so-called Coptic, was no longer the main vehicle of this religion. Men from all parts of the Empire were eager to submit to the fashionable superstition. Alex-

andria, which was predominantly Greek, had in its factories
and harbors a mob as fanatic as any other on the Nile, as
the Christians found to their distress. Here the persecution
of Decius was anticipated by a full year (251) when a
soothsayer aroused the people with his wild improvisations. Here too there appeared refinements in the execu-
tioner's art, as is natural among oppressed people. Those
persecuted had their faces and eyes pierced by pointed
reeds, were dragged on the pavements, had their teeth
knocked out, had their limbs broken separately, and the
like, to say nothing of the regular judicial tortures.

Socially, the entire character of this people was repulsive
to the Romans. Where traveling Egyptians were to be
dealt with anywhere in the wide Roman Empire, some
coarse gaucherie was to be expected, "for that is the way
they have been brought up." Their shouts and screams in
the presence of official personages, be it the Emperor himself, were intolerable. Hence there were few qualms when
the time came to bring Egypt to its senses by chastisement.
Beyond the general calamities in the shape of war and
pestilence which afflicted the Empire after the middle of
the third century and depopulated the earth, Egypt was
visited by its own special misfortunes.

Under Gallienus (254–268) it came to pass that the
slave of an Alexandrian official received a military scourg-
ing because he had said, with some Egyptian mockery,
that his sandals were better than those of the soldiers. The
crowd showed its sympathy and mobs congregated before
the residence of the Prefect Aemilianus, though it was not
at first known who was to be object of the agitation.
Soon stones were thrown, swords drawn, noise and fury
mounted; the Prefect must either have fallen victim to the
mob, or, if his exertions should succeed in mastering the
mob, he could only expect dismissal and punishment. In
this crisis he raised himself to Emperor, apparently on the
demand of the troops, who hated the indolent Gallienus
and required a leadership free of petty responsibilities
against the barbarians who were harassing the country.
He marched through Egypt, thrust the invading peoples
back, and retained the grain in the country; some such

deliverance might have been expected as the West found
at this period through Posthumus and his successors. But
when Aemilianus was preparing for an expedition across
the Red Sea, Egypt surrendered him to Theodotus, whom
Gallienus had sent as general, and Theodotus sent him as
prisoner to Gallienus. Perhaps he was strangled at the same
spot in the Tullian prison at Rome where Jugurtha had
once starved to death.

Whether Gallienus' vengeance visited any additional
special punishment upon the country is not known. In any
case it can have done him little good, for Egypt was soon
again lost to him (261), for a short time, it is true, but
under horrible circumstances, though they can only be surmised. We do not know what battles raged in Alexandria
and between whom, during the year in which Macrianus
was master of the East; but at the end of that period
Bishop Dionysius describes the city as having become unrecognizable by reason of the cruelties; the main thorough-
fare, perhaps the famous street of thirty stades, as desolate
as the wilderness of Sinai; the waters of the deserted harbor dyed red with blood, and the near-by canals of the
Nile floating with corpses.

Gallienus regained mastery of Egypt, but under his successors Claudius Gothicus and Aurelian, the great Queen
of Palmyra, granddaughter of the Ptolemies, caused Egypt,
or at least Alexandria, to be twice conquered in her name.
This was a manifestation (like similar movements in several
provinces) of the last national stirring of considerable scale
in an otherwise unwarlike and senile people; there was
strong partisanship both for and against Zenobia, and native
armies, as it appears, reinforced the troops on either side.
The Palmyrenes were victorious, but not long thereafter
their own kingdom fell through the great campaign of Aurelian (273). The Palmyrene party among the Egyptians
which had been hostile to Rome could expect nothing but
the severest chastisement; probably out of their despera-
tion a rich Seleucid settled in Egypt, Firmus by name,
arose as Emperor. Our only source for this incident as-
sures us that he will not confuse the three persons called
Firmus who figured in the contemporary history of Africa;

but his description of the usurper of Egypt who is here involved presents such extraordinary contradictions that it can hardly refer to a single individual. His Firmus rides upon ostriches and is also able to digest an entire ostrich and the flesh of hippopotamuses, to say nothing of his familiarity with crocodiles; he has an anvil placed upon his body and beaten upon with sledge hammers. The same man is the friend and companion of Zenobia and one of the greatest merchants and industrialists of Egypt. He boasted that he could maintain an army with the income of his paper factories alone; he had large contracts to supply the Arabs and the Blemmyes, who controlled the trade with the Red Sea and the interior of Africa; his vessels frequently sailed to India. Whereas elsewhere they were officers, provincial nobility, and adventurers who assumed the royal purple, it is significant of Egypt that here a great merchant ventures the attempt after incessant war had in any case threatened him with ruin.

Aurelian wished to dispose of the "throne thief" quickly; he defeated him in battle and then besieged him in Alexandria. Here Firmus and his party appear to have maintained themselves for some time in the area of the old royal fortress, Bruchion; at least, after Aurelian laid hands upon Firmus and slew him he thought it appropriate to raze that entire stately quarter of the city. Thus was reduced to ashes the palace of the Ptolemies, their magnificent tombs, the Museum to which was linked all spiritual associations of later Hellenism, and the gigantic columns of the propylaea upon which a lofty dome had been raised —to say nothing of the devastated theaters, basilicas, gardens, and the like. Was it vindictiveness, or did the victor follow only strategic considerations? We must not forget that certain areas of the Empire would be reduced to starvation if rebellious Egypt, as in fact happened under Firmus, restricted its exports. But it is a melancholy sign for rulers and ruled alike that such sacrifices had to be offered to render a city incapable of insurrection and defense.

To the Egyptians this destruction served only as an added goad. Under Probus (276–282), or perhaps earlier, one of the most energetic of the generals, the Gaul

Saturninus, came to Egypt, and the bold Alexandrians immediately hailed him Emperor. Terrified at the notion, Saturninus fled to Palestine. Since he did not know the magnanimous character of Probus, he concluded upon further reflection that he was lost, and tearfully wrapped himself in the purple peplum of a statue of Aphrodite, while those of his party paid him homage. His solace was that he would at least not perish alone. Probus was compelled to send an army, and the unhappy captive usurper was strangled against Probus' will. Later Probus was again forced to wage war in Egypt, because the Nubian race of the Blemmyes, which had long been dangerous, had taken possession of a portion of Upper Egypt, specifically Ptolemais on the Nile, of which we have already spoken. The irreconcilably rebellious inhabitants had connived with the Blemmyes. These Blemmyes, a lean, brown, elusive desert folk, had got control of transportation between the harbor cities of the Red Sea and the Nile; to subjugate or destroy them would have been equally impractical, and so from time to time it was necessary at least to curb them. This time, too, the Roman generals obtained the upper hand, and surely imposed severe penalties. But under Diocletian all of Egypt again rebelled, and indeed for a period of years, for from Gaul, which had scarcely been subdued, the Emperors had been compelled to reconquer Britain, overthrow a usurper at Carthage, repel invasions of Moorish tribes, and wage war almost along the entire frontier. While the Blemmyes were again in control of Upper Egypt, at Alexandria a man quite unknown otherwise, L. Elpidius Achilleus, proclaimed himself Augustus (286). It was only after ten years (296) that Diocletian was in a position to intervene. He marched to Egypt through Palestine accompanied by the twenty-two-year-old Constantine, whose large and majestic figure outshone the Emperor. Again there was a long siege of Alexandria which lasted for eight months, during which the aqueducts were destroyed; and after Achilleus was killed there was another frightful chastisement. The capital was turned over for plunder to the army, which was presumably extremely embittered, the followers of the usurper were proscribed, and large numbers were executed. When Diocletian rode into the city, legend tells, he ordered his army to murder until blood should reach his horse's knee; but not far from the gate the animal slipped upon a corpse and stained its knee in blood, whereupon the order to murder was straightway rescinded. The spot was long marked by a brazen horse.

In Middle Egypt the city Busiris was entirely destroyed. Upper Egypt fared no better; here the rich market Coptos, where the Blemmyes would naturally take their position, suffered the same fate as Busiris. Upon this occasion Diocletian (according to Eutropius; the Christian Orosius, who uses Eutropius, says nothing of the matter) issued many prudent regulations which continued in force. He abolished, doubtless on good grounds, the old regional divisions and the organization of the country which was instituted by Augustus, and divided the country into three provinces corresponding to the organization of the other parts of the Empire. The security of trade communications was provided by setting up as competitors to the Blemmyes another African tribe from the Great Oasis, the Nobates. The Nobates were retained permanently in the pay of the Empire, and an unproductive strip of Roman territory above Syene was ceded to them, where they were henceforward to live and guard the frontier.

It was not Diocletian's fault that exhaustion of army and treasury made such makeshifts necessary, and that a kind of tribute had to be paid to the Nobates and Blemmyes alike. But quite Diocletianic is the manner by which these people were pledged to their obligations. Upon the frontier island of Philae, which incidentally received new and strong fortification, temples and altars were newly built or extant ones newly dedicated for the common *sacra* of the Nobates and the Romans and provided with a common priesthood. Both desert peoples were of the Egyptian faith, the Blemmyes with special inclination to human sacrifice; they now received or retained the right to carry the image of Isis from Philae to their country at certain holy seasons and to keep it there for a fixed period. An extant inscription depicts the solemn progress of the sacred barge carrying the image of the goddess upon the Nile.

Meanwhile a new city had arisen in Upper Egypt near Coptos, which had been destroyed; this the Emperor named Maximianopolis in honor of his eldest colleague. This was perhaps only a garrison, or perhaps it was the old Apollinopolis rechristened.

Some comfort at least was given to Alexandria itself in its sorrow and depression; Diocletian again assigned the city definite distributions of grain, a favor which many cities outside Italy had come to enjoy. In return the Alexandrians now counted their years according to Diocletian's reign, and the Prefect Pompeius in 302 erected in his honor the pillar which has wrongly been called Pompey's. The pillar still bears the inscription: "To the all-holy Autocrator, the genius of the city of Alexandria, the unconquered Diocletian." The gigantic monolith, taken from an earlier public building or intended for one which was never completed, towers high above the scarcely recognizable remains of the Serapeum.

Finally we have a late and somewhat enigmatic notice to the effect that Diocletian at that time caused all of the writings of the ancient Egyptians concerning the production of gold and silver to be collected and burned so that the Egyptians should no longer draw wealth from such sources and in their consequent pride rise up against Rome. It has been shrewdly remarked that Diocletian would certainly have retained the books for his own and the Empire's use if he had believed in the possibility of alchemy. But it is hardly likely that Diocletian's measure proceeded, as Gibbon assumes, purely out of benevolent enlightenment. Perhaps transmutation into gold was linked with other revolting superstitions in Egypt which the ruler, who was a pious man in his own fashion, wished to discourage.

With Diocletian insurrections in Egypt ceased, and for a considerable period. Had he been able in his wisdom actually to help the country substantially, to improve the character of its inhabitants, or at least to keep them intimidated over a long period? Did the new general imperial regulations suffice to make insurrection unattractive or impossible? The most probable explanation has already been suggested. In the first place the division of imperial authority prevented the rise of native and local usurpers in the provinces. Furthermore, after Constantine Egyptian passions found an outlet in ecclesiastical disputes, which were more appropriate to the sinking energies of that unhappy nation than desperate rebellions against Roman officials and armies. The long series of theological disturbances was initiated by the Meletian and Arian quarrel as soon as Christianity was proclaimed. But in Egypt, as nowhere else in the Empire, the pagans also were zealous for their religion and defended it with bloody uprisings.

From one point of view Egypt, like all Africa, was the securest possession of the Roman Empire; aside from a number of half-savage tribes whose incursions could easily be repelled with moderate effort, the frontiers were only desert. While the frontiers on the Rhine, the Danube, and the Euphrates were menaced by strong and hostile peoples, here relatively slight garrisons, suitably distributed, were sufficient. For at that time none could dream that a religious and conquering fanaticism would one day arise in Arabia and irresistibly roll victorious over the entire southern and eastern portions of the Roman Empire and assimilate them to itself. In the third century the northern coast of Africa was certainly incomparably more populous than it has ever been since. The monuments of Algeria, the large number of bishoprics later recorded, the considerable cultural activity and its place in later Roman literature, imply conditions which cannot be fairly judged by the relative poverty of external events. Above all Carthage, which had been restored by Caesar, had by reason of its position become one of the first cities of the Empire, and also one of the most dangerous. The city's moral corruption, which later demoralized the brave Vandals as Capua's luxury had demoralized Hannibal's soldiers, was not the worst; the temple which Dido had founded to the celestial deity Astroarche was fatal to the Empire, less on account of its complaisant prostitutes than by reason of the subversive oracles which it issued and the support which it gave to more than one usurper. The purple robe, which hung from the image enthroned upon lions and wielding lightning and scepter, covered the shoulders of more than one anti-Emperor. Now too upon the accession of Diocletian a certain Julian rose in opposition to him. Of his origin and subsequent fate we know nothing; he must have been at the head of the so-called Quinquegentiani or Five Peoples against whom Maximian was forced to campaign and of whom we know little more. They were doubtless Mauretanians, that is, from the western half of North Africa, where the Atlas range must have sheltered, as it does today, a number of small peoples inaccessible to direct attack. No serious occupation on the part of these peoples was to be feared if the Roman officials did not willfully neglect their duty. Maximian undertook this war only after several years of relaxation (297), whence we may infer that the danger was not pressing and that corn shipments to Italy were not interrupted. With the defection of Egypt, which had lasted until the year preceding, the Empire could less than ever have forgone the grain from Africa.

V

PAGANISM: INTERMINGLING OF GODS

MARTYRDOM and the streams of Christian blood shed in the great persecutions have given a frightful reputation to the last period of the reign of Diocletian and Maximian. Efforts to determine the scope of the persecutions and the number of their victims, even approximately, have been in vain. There are no trustworthy data on the number of Christians in the Roman Empire at the time, and without such data calculation is impossible. According to Stäudlin, Christians comprised half the entire population; according to Matter, a fifth; according to Gibbon, only a twentieth; according to La Bastie, a twelfth, which is perhaps nearest the truth. More precisely, we may conjecture that for the West the proportion was a fifteenth, and for the East a tenth.

But let us ignore the numerical relationship for the moment and consider the contemporary internal conditions of the two great rival organizations, Christianity and paganism.

Christianity was brought to the world by high historical necessity, as a period to antiquity, as a break with it, and yet in part to preserve it and transmit it to new peoples who as pagans might well have utterly barbarized and destroyed a purely pagan Roman Empire. The time was come for men to enter into a new relationship with things of the senses and things beyond the senses, for love of God and neighbor and separation from things earthly to take the place of older views of the gods and the world.

Three centuries had stabilized the life and doctrine of the Christians into fixed forms. Constant threats and frequent persecutions had kept the community from early disintegration and enabled it to overcome serious internal cleavage. It had succeeded in separating out of its body ascetic fanatics (Montanist and others) as well as speculative enthusiasts (the Gnostics) who sought to make of Christianity a framework for Platonic and Oriental ideologies. With Manichaeism, the newest and strongest attempt of this character, the struggle had just begun. Forerunners of Arianism, in the shape of disputes concerning the Second Person of the Trinity, seemed effectively disposed of. Numerous quarrels concerning individual points of Church discipline did indeed appear, but in this period of persecution these differences did not prove as dangerous as they later did in the centuries of the Church triumphant when such matters became occasion for permanent cleavages.

Within Christianity itself many things were freely countenanced which were later found irreconcilable. In the fourth and fifth centuries people rightly wondered how it had been possible for the Church to tolerate the speculation and the symbolic interpretation of Scripture of an Origen. Many others who were esteemed as Fathers in the burgeoning and struggling Church were later recognized as half heretic. The catechumens of the old Church derived from too many origins, had received too diverse educations, and had joined the Church out of reasons too various, for complete uniformity of life and doctrine to be possible. As in all earthly concerns, those rare souls filled with spiritual profundity and practical devotion were surely a small minority; the great mass felt attracted by the forgiveness of sins which was made prominent, by the immortality of the soul which was promised, and by the mystery which surrounded the sacraments and which for many was surely only a parallel to the pagan mysteries. The slave was attracted by Christian freedom and brotherly love, and many an unworthy convert by the very considerable alms which were bestowed with true impartiality, particularly by the community in Rome.

The large number of heroic martyrs who from time to

time quickened the relaxed tension of the community and implanted contempt of death anew does not testify so much to the internal perfection of the Church as to the future victory which was inevitable to a cause cherished with such devotion. Firm belief in an immediate entry to heaven surely inspired many persons who were internally confused and even debased to voluntary immolation; in any case, the value set upon life in that age of suffering and despotism was slighter than in the centuries of Germano-Roman domination. At times there was a veritable epidemic of self-sacrifice; the Christians thrust forward to death and had to be admonished by their teachers to spare themselves. Soon the martyrs became shining ideals of all life; a literal cult became attached to their burial places, and their intercessions before God became one of the highest hopes of the Christian. Their superiority to other saints is easy to understand: no other religion has so glorified its individual blood witnesses as has Christianity, and none has so preserved its own struggles in memory. Scenes of martyrdom became classic ground, and the persecutions of the earlier Emperors, especially those of Decius, had provided that such ground should be found underfoot everywhere. In view of the usages of the martyr cult which had become traditional, the Diocletianic persecutions would seem to have been ill-advised from the outset.

About this time the organization of the Church already showed the beginnings of a regular hierarchy. To be sure, the choice of spiritual leaders or at least their confirmation remained in the hands of the communities, but these came more and more definitely to be distinguished from the *laity* as *clergy*. Distinctions arose among the bishops according to the position of their cities and with particular consideration for the apostolic foundation of certain congregations. The synods, which were convened for many various reasons, served to unite the bishops as a higher rank. Among the bishops themselves serious degeneration becomes apparent as early as the third century. We find many of them sunk in worldly pomp, as Roman officials, as merchants, even as usurers; the egregious example of Paul of Samosata is rightly thought to be by no means unique.

Naturally, by the side of the worldlings we find their extreme opposites, men who retired from temporal concerns, state, and society into solitude. We shall have to discuss the origin of the eremite movement along with other points here touched upon.

A large and widespread literature, which includes several of the best products of modern historiography, deals in detail with the matters mentioned above, each according to the point of view which the author adopts and his reader demands. No one can begrudge the present work because its viewpoint is not that of edification, which a scholar like Neander, for example, may properly adopt.

If we seek to realize in brief the true strength of the Christian community at the beginning of the last persecution we shall find that it lay neither in numbers, nor in a consistent superiority in its members' morality, nor in the excellence of its internal constitution, but in the firm belief in immortality of the soul which permeated each individual Christian. We shall show presently that later paganism directed all its efforts to the same goal, but by gloomy and labyrinthine bypaths and without Christianity's triumphant conviction; it could not maintain competition with Christianity in the long run because Christianity had so utterly simplified this problem. To the political needs of the ancient world, furthermore, which the Roman rule of force had brought to despair of politics, Christianity offered a new state, a new democracy, even a new civic society, if it could have been kept pure. Many an ancient ambition, finding itself without position in the Roman state, threatened and reduced to silence, was able to make its way to an episcopal see in the congregations and thus find some scope at least for self-assertion. On the other hand, the best and most humble must have found the congregations a sacred refuge from the pressure of Roman corruption, now grown rank.

Confronting these great advantages we find paganism in full process of dissolution, so that it can hardly be thought of as likely to endure even without the appearance of Christianity. If we imagine, for the sake of illustration, that Mohammed had straightway introduced his fanatic monotheism without any preparation on the part of Christianity, Mediterranean paganism would certainly have succumbed to his first attack as surely as did the paganisms of the Near East. Paganism had been mortally weakened by internal disintegration and willful intermixture from without.

The state religion of the Empire, which must form our point of departure, was in any case the Greco-Roman polytheism shaped by the prehistoric relationship of the two cults and their later amalgamation. Out of nature divinities and tutelary deities for every possible situation in life, a remarkable circle of superhuman figures had arisen, in whose myths, however, ancient man everywhere recognized his own likeness. The connection of morality with this religion was quite loose, and depended largely on the feeling of the individual. The gods indeed were believed to reward good and chastise evil, but they were thought of as givers and preservers of life and property rather than as superior moral forces. His various mysteries provided the Greek, in addition to popular beliefs, not a purer religion, even less a sage enlightenment in sacred matters, but only a secret rite of worship which would render the gods especially favorable to the initiate. A beneficial effect was involved, at least incidentally, in the specific requirement of purity and also in the quickening of national sentiment which was characteristic of the mysteries as well as of the festive games of the Greeks.

In opposition to this religion, philosophy, as soon as it was lifted above questions of cosmogony, proclaimed the unity of the divine being more or less clearly. Thus a way was opened to highest religiosity and to the fairest moral ideals, but also to pantheism and even to atheism, which could claim similar freedom with respect to popular beliefs. Those who did not deny the existence of gods explained them pantheistically as the basic forces of the universe, or, like the Epicureans, left them idle and indifferent to the world. "Enlightenment" too had its part in the mélange; Euhemerus and his followers had long ago made the gods out to be ancient rulers, warriors, or the like, and had explained miracles rationally as deception or misunderstanding. They were on the wrong trail, and later the

Church Fathers and apologetes were constantly being misguided by them in their evaluation of paganism.

All of this ferment the Romans had taken over along with Greek culture, and preoccupation with these problems became to the educated a matter of principle as well as of fashion. Along with superstition, disbelief grew among the higher classes of society, though genuine atheists may have been few. With the third century, however, as a result of the great dangers of the Empire, disbelief waned visibly, and a kind of faith came to the fore, though to the advantage of the foreign cults rather than of the old state religion. But in Rome the ancient native cult was so closely bound up with the state, and the relevant superstition so firmly rooted, that the unbeliever as well as the believer in foreign cults had to show official Roman piety in questions relating to the sacred fire of Vesta, to the secret pledges of rule, to the state auspices, for Rome's eternity depended on these sanctities. Not only were the Emperors themselves *Pontifices maximi,* with specific ritual obligations but their title of Augustus signified a supernatural consecration, justification, and immunity. It was no mere flattery when superstition finally accorded them the status of *daimones* after Christianity put an end to the apotheoses, temples, altars, and priesthoods which had been their prerogative for three hundred years.

There can be no doubt that even in the latest period of paganism's dominance the genuine Greek and Roman religion had not been supplanted in the hearts of many individuals by alien deities, not replaced by magic and incantation, not dispersed by philosophic abstractions. This cannot be demonstrated directly because worship of the old gods did not exclude worship of the new, and because in the interchange of deities, which will be noticed below, a new god might be worshiped under the name of an old, and vice versa. But the probability cannot be denied when we see the old and naïve relationship of the sound ancient man to gods and fate break out here and there with compelling force. "Thee I worship," Avienus addresses Nortia, the Etruscan equivalent to Fortuna, "I whom Vulsinii bore, who dwell at Rome, who was twice honored by the proconsulship, who am dedicated to poesy, innocent and without reproach, happy in my wife Placida and in my healthy and lively children. As for the rest, may it transpire according to the decree of destiny."

In other cases the old religion and its view of life asserts itself emphatically even though innovations have been added. Diocletian's own faith must have been of this character. At least he was faithful to the Etruscan haruspices, which were not yet at war, as later in Julian's court, with Neoplatonist conjurers; his tutelary deity continued to be Jupiter; and the oracle which he consulted in matters of greatest moment was that of the Milesian Apollo. His morality and religiosity, as expressed, for example, in his legislation, has closest affinity with that of Decius; in his cult of the good Emperors, especially of Marcus Aurelius, who was worshiped as a *daimon*, he also follows Alexander Severus. On the other hand, it may be assumed that many portions and implications of the old religion had long died and been forgotten. The crowd of petty Roman tutelary deities had perhaps come to be regarded as antiquarian trifles, though Christian writers inveigh against them as something still persisting. Men scarcely longer thought of the god Lateranus in connection with the hearth, of Unxia in connection with anointing, of Cinxia in connection with girdling, of Puta in connection with pruning, of Nodutis in connection with grain stalks, of Mellonia in connection with bee-keeping, of Limentinus in connection with the threshold, and the like. A quite different and generalized view of *genii* and *daimones* had long come to prevail in the minds of men. Much of the earlier belief was and remained quite local in character.

Greece especially retained in imperial times its affectionate esteem of local cults and mystery worship. Pausanias, who wrote a description of Greece in the second century, provides ample evidence for the special worship of gods and heroes in every city and locality and for the various priesthoods in charge of this worship. His silence concerning the mysteries was a pious duty; posterity would have been grateful to him for transgressing it.

Just as the Roman state required certain *sacra* for its

continued existence—with the result, for example, that the sacred fire was tended by Vestal Virgins far into Christian times—so the private life of the individual, from the cradle to the grave, was shot through with religious usages. At home, feasting and sacrifice were inseparable. On the city streets one encountered processions and spectacles, sometimes dignified and handsome, sometimes bacchanalian and orgiastic, which filled the Greek like the Roman calendar of feasts. In the country there were sacrifices without end at chapels, grottoes, crossroads, and under venerable trees. The newly converted Arnobius tells of the devotion he had felt as a pagan when he passed tree trunks decked with gay ribbons or boulders bearing traces of the oil which had been poured upon them. It is difficult to extract the moral content from a cult which seems so superficial and frequently altogether frivolous, and many will deny that such a content is to be found. Does not virtually the same question arise, after fifteen hundred years, concerning the festivals of the Mediterranean Catholic? The sound of thoroughly sensual music surrounds the High Mass and, interrupted by salvos of cannon, accompanies the sacrament; a lively market, abundant food, gaiety of all sorts, and the inevitable fireworks in the evening, constitute the second part of the festival. One who takes exception to all this cannot be prevented from so doing; but we must not forget that this outward conduct is not the whole religion and that in different people the highest feelings are aroused by different means. If we leave aside Christian feelings of sinfulness and humility, of which the ancient world was not capable, we shall be able to judge their worship more justly.

Details of mythology, which were never a matter of faith, were wholly abandoned long before Lucian made a delightful burlesque of them. Christian apologetes were somewhat disingenuous when they sought out a collection of disgraceful items from the most diverse myths and by misunderstanding and mixing elements of disparate character heaped ridicule upon the ancient beliefs. They must have known that attacks of this sort, which they drew from the ancient poets and mythographers, possessed only slight relevance to their own century. Protestantism, for example, might as justly be held responsible for the absurdities in many legends. The religious consciousness of the masses was little concerned with myth; it was satisfied with the existence of individual divinities as rulers and protectors of nature and of human life. How completely contemporary philosophy disposed of the myths we shall see in the sequel. But the pagans continued to put weapons into the hands of Christian polemicists by their dramatic representations of individual myths, and often of the most objectionable.

For in one province mythology reigned supreme until the latest period, the province of art and poetry. Homer, Phidias, and the tragedians had once helped create the gods and heroes, and now what had vanished from faith was preserved in stone, color, masks, writings, and terra cotta. But their life was more apparent than real. Of the fate of the plastic arts and the causes of their decline we shall deal presently; here we must observe that their ability to support the old mythology was nullified by the fact that they entered the service of mythicizing philosophy and even of the foreign cults. Drama was largely and perhaps completely supplanted by the local mime and by the silent pantomime with music and dance. All religious aspects, such as had once made Attic drama a form of worship, disappeared. The description of the elegant Corinthian ballet *Paris on Ida* in the tenth book of Apuleius shows that the theater in Greece itself during the age of the Antonines served only as an eye-filling spectacle. Here at least we may assume a refined and stylized work of art, whereas in the Latin parts of the Empire, especially in regions only half Romanized and only through military colonies, the exhibitions must have been crude indeed, if the theaters presented any dramatic performances at all and were not wholly given to gladiatorial games, wild beast hunts, and the like. The scurrilous aspects of mythology were intentionally made prominent. All the adulteries of Jupiter, even those which involved his transformation into an animal, all the scandals of Venus, were presented to ribald laughter. Similar epiphanies found place even in the mimes. An Aristophanic audience could tolerate such things without prejudice to faith, but in a sick age they were the *coup de grâce* for the old religion as a whole.

If we move from the sphere in which ballet master and stage mechanic were supreme to the realm of poetry, so far as we can follow it in the few survivals from the end of the third century, we still find scattered evidence of great talent for mythologic treatment, most brilliantly represented by Claudian a full century later; but the last trace of inner conviction had long been extinguished. The poem of a certain Reposianus, for example, who may have flourished about 300, depicts the dallying of Mars and Venus with the same purpose as we may assume in the pantomimes: sensually attractive images skirting the obscene. Venus while awaiting the god of war passes the time in dancing, and the poet describes her various postures with a well-developed sense for the coquetry of his time; then when Mars appears he calls upon Cupid, the Graces, and the maidens of Byblos to disrobe him. But what a Mars is this! He is intentionally represented as uncouth as the goddess is seductive. He falls into the bower of roses like a lump of lead, and in the description of his slumber the reader is not spared his lusty snores. When Rubens, for example, tackles ancient myth in his own manner, he may be absolved by the impression of mighty if errant energy he conveys; but here we are at the lowest rung of degradation of ancient saga without other recompense than pretty verses. A satirical Christian could not have effected his purpose better, and we might be prepared to accept some such explanation for this poem if the pretty picture of Cupid did not prevent it. Cupid curiously inspects the weapons which Mars has laid aside, decorates them with flowers, and then, when jealous Vulcan makes his rowdy entrance, creeps under the helmet to hide.

There were some poets who had grown wholly surfeited with mythology as a path trodden to shreds. "Who has not sung," cries Nemesianus, "the sorrows of Niobe bereft, of Semele, and . . . [here follow thirty hexameters of titles of myths]. All of this has been exhausted by a crowd of great poets; the saga of the ancient world is used up." The poet therefore turns to green forests and meadows, not, how-

ever, to compose landscape poetry, but to introduce his
own theme, the breeding of hunting dogs. Then when he
is done with this theme, he remembers to celebrate the
deeds of his patrons, the Caesars Carinus and Numerianus.

A similar feeling had long given didactic poetry, especially among the Romans, marked preference over epic;
but the preference had never been expressed so bluntly.
One charming poem of mythologic content, the *Bacchus*
of Calpurnius Siculus (*Eclogue* 3), may be cited here for
its remarkable dependence upon works of plastic art; it
recalls Philostratus' descriptions of pictures but surpasses
them in style. We even find the hoary Silenus, who rocks
the infant Bacchus in his arms as a nurse, makes him laugh,
amuses him with castanets, and good-naturedly allows him
to pluck at his ears, chin, and the hair of his chest. Then
the growing god teaches the satyrs the first vintage, until
they grow drunk with the new beverage, smear themselves
with wine lees, and abduct nymphs. This bacchanal, in
which the god even gives his panthers drink out of the mix-
ing-bowl, is one of the last ancient works of living beauty.

All this goes to prove that mythology was rather a burden
than a support for sinking classical religion. Of attempts to
maintain and justify myths by philosophic interpretation we
shall speak in the sequel.

But this classical religion was also disturbed and
breached by another factor, namely, admixture of the cults
of subjugated provinces and foreign countries. We are now
in a period of a consummated theocrasy (intermingling of
gods).

This came about not because of the mingling of peoples
in the Empire or because of caprice and fashion alone, but
because of the age-old urge of polytheistic religions to approach one another, to seek out similarities, and to transform them into identities. In all ages parallels of this sort
have suggested the intriguing idea of a common primitive
religion, which each man pictures according to his own
bent, the polytheist differently from the monotheist. And
so worshipers of similar deities sought and found themselves, some unwittingly and some with philosophic intent,

before the same altars. Hellenic Aphrodite was willingly recognized in the Astarte of the Near East, in the Hathor of the Egyptians, in the Celestial Goddess of the Carthaginians; and other divinities were similarly identified. This must be especially noticed, even for the later Roman period: the mixture of gods is at the same time a substitution of gods; the alien gods were not only propagated by the side of the native, but were substituted for the native according to their inward kinship.

A second cause of theocrasy is to be seen in the recognition, as it were, political, which the Greek and Roman and the polytheist generally paid to the gods of other peoples. He acknowledged them as gods, even if they were not his own. There was no strict dogmatic system to guard the frontiers of native belief. Rigidly as ancestral superstitions were preserved, there was rather friendliness than hate for the superstitions of others. Certain solemn transfers of divinities from one country to another were enjoined by oracles and other supernatural admonitions. Thus Serapis of Sinope was moved to Alexandria under the first Ptolemy, and the Great Mother of Pessinus to Rome during the Second Punic War. Among the Romans it became virtually a conscious principle, half political and half religious, not to offend the gods of the many subjugated peoples, but rather to show them reverence and even to accept them among their own gods. The attitude of the provinces was very diverse. Asia Minor willingly met the Roman halfway. Egypt was unyielding; it translated what it received from the Ptolemies and the Romans into its own ritual and art forms, whereas the Romans sought to please the Egyptians by worshiping the Egyptian gods in something approximating the Egyptian forms. The Jew, finally, would have nothing to do with Roman religion, whereas Romans of good taste observed his Sabbath and Emperors came to worship in the temple on Moriah. There took place, as we shall directly see, a partly active and partly passive mingling of gods.

A third cause for accepting foreign cults lay in the fear and anxiety which oppressed the pagan who had grown to disbelieve in his old gods. It is no longer a matter of "gods everywhere" in the pleasing sense of earlier centuries. Rather, the thoughtful man sought for new symbols daily, and the thoughtless for new fetishes, which were the more welcome the more distant and mysterious their origin seemed. A special factor multiplied confusion. The polytheism of ancient civilizations survived in all the stages of its development simultaneously. As fetishism it continued to worship aeroliths and amulets, as Sabaism stars and elements, as anthropomorphism partly nature gods and partly tutelary gods—while the educated had long since inwardly discarded these husks and wavered between pantheism and monotheism. And now all these stages of various paganisms interacted upon Greco-Roman paganism, and vice versa. We have reports of remarkable instances, and sometimes they make melancholy reading. Nero was brought up in the Roman religion, but he soon despised it, and adhered only to the Syrian goddess. Presently he deserted her, played knavish tricks with her image, and placed his sole faith in an amulet which a man of the people had given him and to which he now offered sacrifice thrice daily.

This example, one of many that might be cited, provides a hint of the nature of the cults of foreign gods in general. They were not approached in the same spirit as were the old Olympians; wrenched out of their natural environment and alien to Roman life, government, and climate, they could impress the Romans only as weird and daimonic powers which could be prevailed upon only by mysteries and magic rites, perhaps also by great material expenditures. It is not for nothing that Lucian assigns to foreign gods the superior rank when, in *Jupiter Tragoedus* (Ch. 8), he establishes a hierarchy of the gods based on the material they were made of; anxious superstition preferred to have its gods made of the most precious metal. "You see the peculiarity of the Greek contingent: they have grace and beauty and artistic workmanship, but they are all marble or bronze—the most costly of them only ivory with just an occasional gleam of gold, the merest surface plating; and even those are wood inside, harboring whole colonies of mice. Whereas Bendis here, Anubis there, Attis next door, and Mithras and Men, are all of solid gold, heavy and intrinsically precious."* But this sort of cult demoralized the attitude to the ancient national gods.

Let us now look at the active (from the Roman point of view) mixture of gods, in which the Romans were rather the givers than the receivers.

Such a relationship obtained, it is obvious, chiefly for those peoples which Rome took over in a semi-civilized state and in which it could give currency to its superior culture as well as to its religion; these were the peoples of Gaul, Spain, and Britain. Unfortunately, it is only in Gaul that we know something of the religious conditions, and that chiefly through dedicatory inscriptions and sculptures.

The later Romans in their truly universal superstition participated in the local cult in Gaul, as they did elsewhere, as long as it retained any vitality. They not only consulted the Druids concerning the future, as we have seen, but they took part in actual ritual. So the later Emperor Pescennius Niger solemnly participated in an occult rite in Gaul to which only continent people could be invited. But no Gallic deity was transferred to Italy, Africa, or Greece. (If we find the Celtic sun-god Belenus in Aquileia, other Celtic divinities in Salzburg and Styria, Apollo Grannus at Lauingen in Swabia, and the like, these are not to be understood as importations from the period of theocrasy but as the latest evidence of the presence of the aboriginal Celtic population of these regions before Germans, Slavs, and Avars penetrated the Alps.) In Gaul itself every effort was made to clothe the popular religion in a Roman dress. The gods assumed not only Roman names but also the art forms of classical anthropomorphism. Taran had to be called Jupiter, and was depicted as such; Teutates as Mercury; Hesus or Camulus as Mars. Other deities at least retained their names, either alone or along with a Roman name. Thus we have Belenus or Apollo Belenus, and frequently, Apollo Grannus, Mars Camulus, Minerva Belisana, and the like. Then the Romanized gods received special cognomens

---

* H. W. and F. G. Fowler, *The Works of Lucian of Samosata*, III, 84. Oxford 1905.—Translator.

in addition; some we can derive from localities, or explain by conjecture; some are frankly baffling. Thus we have Diana Abnoba (the designation of the Black Forest); Diana Ardoinna (perhaps Ardennes); Mars Vincius (Vence, in southern France); Hercules Magusanus and Saxanus (especially in the Netherlands); Mars Lacavus (at Nîmes); Apollo Toutiorix (at Wiesbaden). Or the Romanized god was associated with a non-Romanized, perhaps kindred, deity; so Veriogodumnus was associated with Apollo in Amiens; and Sirona, who is conceived somewhat as Diana or Minerva (as is Belisana), in Bordeaux and southern Germany. But Romanization went no further. A host of deities retained their Celtic names, mostly with the prefix Deus (or Dea) Sanctus (or Sancta), or even Augustus (or Augusta), which was here employed without reference to the title of the Emperors. At first glance one is tempted to regard all these deities as local, and many in fact are, as for example Vosegus in Bergzabern, Nemausus in Nîmes, Aventia in Aventicum, Vesontius in Besançon, Luxovius in Luxeuil, Celeia in Cilli; but others have no such signification, as for example Abellio in Convennes, Acionna in Orléans, Agho in Bagnères, Bemilucius in Paris, Hariasa in Cologne, Intarabus in Treves. Moreover, many appear in widely disparate localities: Taranucus in Heilbronn and in Dalmatia; the water-goddess Nehalennia in France and in the Netherlands. The eagerness with which the gods were Romanized wherever possible is also indicated by the Roman class names for the numerous minor collective deities: Matres, Matrones, Campestres (field spirits), Silvani (forest spirits), Bivia, Trivia, and Quadrivia (divinities of the crossroads), Proxumi and Vicani (geniuses of neighborhood), and the like. The Sulevi and the Comedovi, which belonged to the same category, must have defied translation. Such expressions as "Genius of the Place" and "Genius of the Region," strictly speaking, imply only Roman ritual practices, but it is probable that they here represent Celtic usages. In any case, until late in the fourth century the mightiest god continued to be Teutates-Mercury, who still offered vigorous resistance to St. Martin of Tours; Jupiter the saint regarded as stupid and dull, *brutus atque hebes*.

The reaction of these Occidental religions upon Rome itself was singularly slight, as we have remarked, or non-existent.

The situation with reference to the ancient civilizations of the East, Persia, Egypt, Asia Minor, and the Semites, was very different. To the latter the far-flung geographical distribution of their settlements was a great advantage, for the Romans did not first learn their idolatry in Syria; Semitic religion had for many centuries been spread abroad by Phoenicia and Carthage over the entire Mediterranean and even beyond the Pillars of Hercules. As Rome gradually incorporated Spain, Africa, and the islands, it took over broad stretches of Punic territory and Punic cult. The Roman hated Carthage but not its gods. Persian dualism, on the other hand, especially in its later orthodox renewal by the Sassanids, resisted any mixture and compromise with the Greco-Roman circle of gods as vigorously as did Jewish monotheism. But Persia offered an older metamorphosis of Parseeism, which had degenerated in the direction of superstition, and from this Rome borrowed Mithras.

The peoples of the Near East from the Euphrates to the Mediterranean, the Archipelago, and the Pontus, with which it is proper to begin, were by no means derived from the same racial strain, but their religions had so affected one another from high antiquity that for such a late epoch as we are here dealing with we may regard them as one. Determination of origins is not relevant in this place and would lead us far astray. Furthermore, long before the Roman victories over Antiochus the Great another mixture of gods had taken place involving the gods of the Near East and those of Greece, from the period of the Hellenization of Asia Minor and with accelerated speed under Alexander's successors. This mixture was parallel to the mingling of Greek and Oriental language and culture. The magnificent Greek cities, which sprang out of the earth everywhere in the lands of the successors in incredible number, retained, along with their Greek language, civic polity, and mores, their Greek gods. But in the country, particularly at a distance from the sea, the old language maintained itself more or less stubbornly, and at a later period, with the inward exhaustion of the formative force of Greece, its strength actually increased. In Palestine, under the protection of a rigidly exclusive religion and way of life, Aramaic survived despite terrible upheavals. In Syria, so soon as it was a question of popular effectiveness and no longer of classical elegance, writers reverted to the native language, as is shown in the second century in the Gnostic Bardesanes, in the fourth in St. Ephraem, and clearly enough by the Syriac versions of the Bible. We have no detailed information of the language situation in Asia Minor, but as long as the popular language was maintained, the popular gods were also.

The general basis for the religions in question is worship of the stars, but confused to the point of being unrecognizable by an idolatry which was partly an addition from without, partly a necessary internal development. An elaborate sacrificial service sought to conciliate the gods by offerings, chiefly of animal life, but also by regular and occasional human sacrifice. These persisted with singular stubbornness, particularly in regions of Phoenician culture; they survived long after the fall and reconstruction of Carthage, so that Tiberius was compelled to proceed against them with drastic penalties. The highest pair of deities, Baal and Astarte (sun and moon, morning star and evening star), survived in Roman times under the most diverse names and personifications and in numerous temples as Lord and Lady of all life. From the Old Testament we know Baalzebub, Baalpeor, Baalberith, and the like, whose names may have been long forgotten. In Palmyra Baal seems to have been divided into two divinities for sun and moon, as Aglibol and Malachbel, who are represented on a very late Palmyrene relief in the Capitoline Museum bearing the Greco-Roman name of the donor, Lucius Aurelius Heliodorus, son of Antiochus Hadrianus. In the magnificent and exceedingly large and lofty temple at Emesa lay the Black Stone, an aerolith, which was regarded as an image of the sun-god Elagabalus and was worshiped as such far and wide. Elagabalus' priests wore long purple tunics embroidered with gold and diadems of precious stones. In the temple at Hierapolis, beside the famous Syrian goddess (who will be mentioned below), there stood a golden image of Baal, represented as Zeus, seated on a chariot drawn by bulls. At Heliopolis (Baalbek) Baal was worshiped in a quite late half-Roman personification; his golden image bore not only the scourge of the Roman sun-god, but also the lightning of Jupiter. Antoninus Pius built a new temple on the huge foundations of the old; the ruins of this temple still justify its being accounted at the time one of the wonders of the world. After what has been said above, the name of Zeus, to whom Antoninus dedicated the sanctuary, should not mislead us, seeing that the ancient place name referred to Baal and the Greek to Helios. This temple, like that at Emesa, enjoyed a wide reputation for its oracle, which might be consulted by letter—an arrangement not unusual in Asiatic oracles. More dubious and less significant traces of Baal-worship under the Emperors may be passed over; suffice it that this cult, more or less transformed, continued to be the principal worship of the Near East, to which some of the most important temples were dedicated, and hence probably many others also, of which we have no information. Perhaps the god Carmel, who possessed an altar on the mountain of the same name and dispensed oracles, was also a transformation of Baal. As an outpost of this cult to the south was Marnas, the god of Gaza, if Marnas really was a form of the great god. It was Marnas who was the despair of the Christian teachers and settlers of that region throughout the fourth century, and who made the region about Gaza a virtually inexpugnable refuge of paganism. We shall meet him presently as the personal enemy of St. Hilarion.

This major Semite god now forced his way into Roman religion in more than one form. Romans who lived or had lived in the East probably worshiped him as Zeus or Jupiter. But the worship of the sun-god which became so prominent in the later period must have been shared principally by Baal and Mithras; less attention was paid to the ancient Sol-Helios. Elagabalus eventually received, at least for a number of years, a large and distinguished position in the Roman pantheon through the mad youth who had been and continued to be his priest and took the god's name when he sat upon the throne of the world. When this Antoninus Bassianus brought the Black Stone of Emesa to Rome (between 218 and 222) one could say that theocrasy had well-nigh reached its consummation. The new god received a great temple and colossal sacrifices, and soon a wife also. The Emperor fetched the image and treasures of the Celestial Goddess from Carthage and married her to Elagabalus; mythologically no exception could be taken to the match. Rome and Italy were required to celebrate the marriage in a festive manner. The palladium, the fire of Vesta, and other ancient Roman *sacra* were brought to the temple of the new god. After the murder of the imperial priest the stone is said to have been escorted back to Syria, apparently because of the loathsome memories connected with it.

But much more powerful than the worship of Baal in the Roman Empire was that represented by the Great Goddess of many names. In relation to the sun-god she is the moon; in a broader sense she is Nature, mother of all living things. From high antiquity onwards the Near East celebrated her with wild bacchanalian tumult, as was appropriate to a divinity devoid of all moral attributes. Joyous shouts and mourning wails, orgiastic dances and lugubrious flute music, prostitution of women and self-castration of men had always accompanied this cult of the sensual life of nature. A myth not very widely dispersed but varying in its forms according to place and time was woven about these celebrations and provided the Romans of a quite late period occasion for strange mysteries.

For the moment we shall disregard Egyptian Isis, who is a kindred collateral form of the Great Goddess, and follow the latter in the forms which are still recognizable in the third century.

The Old Testament knew and abhorred her as Ashtaroth, and there were still temples of Astarte in Phoenicia; Lucian knew one in Sidon. He mentions it in passing in his famous piece *On the Syrian Goddess;* this essay is our source for facts, but is of no less interest as illustrating the attitude of this frivolous, Greek-educated Syrian to his pagan cult. Nowhere has Lucian pushed his mockery so far; he assumes naïveté and imitates the style and Ionic dialect of respectable old Herodotus in order to make the ridiculous aspects of that particular idolatry more uproarious. But we also learn what scenes must have surrounded and influenced the mocker's youth before he broke with all cults and all religions. No Athenian could have written Lucian's books.

From Phoenicia this worship, under the title of the Celestial Goddess, spread far over the Mediterranean and mingled with the classical cult. The Greeks recognized the goddess as Aphrodite Urania, the Romans as Venus Coelestis, and these names later obtained currency even in Semitic countries. This Aphrodite was not thought of as the goddess of love and charm, but as a fertility goddess. The island of Cyprus, where Greek and Semitic culture met, was chiefly dedicated to this goddess; its cities of Paphos and Amathus were proverbial for her service. The island of Cythera and the sanctuary of Mount Eryx in Sicily also belonged to Urania. In Carthage, at least in her later transformation, she was the most important deity, and the name of the city Gades, Gadeira (Cadiz), perhaps signifies the location of a temple of Urania. These sanctuaries were designed quite differently from the temples of the Greek gods. The idol stood in the open, in a high and roofless niche, and frequently consisted only of a conic stone; railings, halls, and courts, in which doves were kept, surrounded the sanctuary. Free-standing pillars also occur in these precincts, and recall the pillars Jachin and Boaz before the temple in Jerusalem.

A transformation of the name Astarte is Atargatis, the goddess with human shape above and fish shape below. She doubtless still possessed her once famous temples at Askalon, near that of the Philistine fish-god Dagon, and also elsewhere. In a very late Hellenized form, she was enthroned in the famous temple of Hierapolis in northern Syria which Lucian describes and which may have survived intact until the fourth century. In a raised choir behind, to which only the priests had access, beside the Baal-Zeus which has been mentioned, there was the golden image of the goddess on a chariot harnessed with lions. Her attributes were borrowed from various Greek goddesses: in her hands were scepter and spindle, about her body the girdle of Urania, on her head the rays of the mural crown, and a stone which illuminated the entire temple area at night. In addition, space was found in the precinct for various other Greek or Grecized gods. There was a bearded and robed Apollo who stirred when an oracle was requested; on such occasions the priests lifted him and carried him about, as he directed. A forward motion signified an affirmative, a backward motion a negative reply; and the god is said to have sweated profusely the while. There were also an Atlas, a Hermes, and an Eileithyia in the interior, and outside, near or on the great altar which stood in the open air in front of the principal entrance to the temple, there was a large number of brazen figures representing kings and priests from highest antiquity until the Seleucid period; there was also a number of figures from the Homeric cycle of legends. But the most remarkable thing was not the statues but the cult, whose vastness and confusion can only here be apprehended. In the great court sacred bulls, horses, and tame lions and bears moved about freely; near by was a pool full of sacred fish, and at its center an altar, to which devotees swam daily, to crown it in accordance with vows. Around the temple lived a crowd of flautists, emasculated priests (*galli*), and raving women; these spent their time in noisy and spectacular processions, in sacrifices, and in every possible indecency. The spring festival, for which there was an enormous pilgrimage from all Syria to Hierapolis, appears to have been entirely devoted to madness. Not only was half a forest burned at this festival with sacrifices of all kinds (animals, clothing, valuable objects), but it was an occasion for recruiting the *galli*; many an unhappy man was carried away by the orgies, to the point of emasculating himself in honor of the goddess. And this temple was one of the most revered of the Near East; Cappadocia as well as Assyria, Cilicia as well as Phoenicia contributed to its treasures. Its Ionic colonnades resting upon masonry terraces with huge propylaea, upon a hill which towered over the city, made a brilliant and conspicuous spectacle. It is remarkable that this temple precinct, with its wild scenes, also supplied a model for the later stylites; from the propylaea there towered two enormous stone pillars representing phalluses, such as were found in Asia Minor wherever similar cults obtained, and upon these annually a man would climb, to pray for seven days and sleepless nights; those who wished his intercession brought an appropriate gift to the foot of the pillar. Could such an obscene cult better be atoned for in the Christian period than by a saintly penitent ascending the pillar to serve God after his own manner, not for weeks, but for decades on end?

An especially revolting service of this goddess, finally, who is here again designated as Aphrodite, was associated with the solitary temple in the grove of Aphaka in the Lebanon. Harlotry and the obscenities of the eunuchs laid all shame aside; nevertheless year after year worshipers came to throw precious gifts into the lake near the temple and to wait for the miracle, a ball of fire which appeared on the mountain height and then sank into the lake. It was believed that this was Urania herself.

Beside this great and many-formed Mother of Life there appears, also in diverse forms, the personification of that which she brings forth, which sprouts in spring and dies in winter. Sometimes this is her son or her daughter, sometimes her husband or, especially, her lover. After the wild joy of the spring festival there follows the mourning and wailing for the departed, celebrating the sorrow of the Great Goddess. As Isis mourned for slain Osiris in Egypt, so in Phoenicia the heavenly Aphrodite mourned for Adonis, the "Lord" who becomes completely acclimated in Cyprus and penetrates deep into Greek cult, so that Rome could receive him as a Greek divinity. But the most magnificent celebration of this service was in Alexandria, where it survived the introduction of Christianity by a century, though hardly with the exuberance which Theocritus shows (in *Idyll* 15) it possessed under the first Ptolemies. The festival closed with a procession of women to the seacoast, where an image of Adonis was sunk in the waves. In

Antioch too the festival of Adonis showed a stubborn vitality.

If this god can be regarded as Greco-Roman because of his immemorial position in the circle of classic deities, such was not the case with a special form which he assumed in Asia Minor. In Phrygia and neighboring countries we meet the Great Goddess as Cybele, Magna Mater, Acdestis, Dindymene, Berecynthia, Pessinuntis, and otherwise, and with her as her lover Atys or Attis, whose emasculation and death are mourned. The ancient temple of Pessinus, with its priests who ruled like princes, and its great revenues, had long bestowed its image and its cult on Rome, and even earlier the Greeks had adopted the goddess under various names, so that her image with its mural crown and lion team was familiar everywhere, and even the emasculated Phrygian priests were accepted in Rome. But Rome insisted, at least in the beginning, that the swarm of eunuchs, flautists, trumpeters, tambourine girls, and the rest must not recruit from the Roman population. When their license of mendicancy was later not withdrawn, this was perhaps calculated to separate the cult the more clearly from Roman life. It had been received at the bidding of the Sibylline Books and the Delphian Oracle; but republican Rome and for a long period imperial Rome was not inclined to propagate it in the provinces. Juvenal finds the drunken eunuch, his tambourine at his side, sleeping in a corner tavern among sailors, thieves, runaway slaves, and cutthroats. But by their mendicancy the priests of the Goddess Mother with their Phrygian caps gained access to the homes of wealthy Rome; they exploited the superstitions of women, and in return for gifts of eggs and worn clothing gave good advice against the threatening fevers of late summer. From attendance at the toilette of great ladies it was no great step to their being accepted into the household and to conversation. In that age superstitions prospered in the degree of their absurdity. Soon we find inscriptions of priests of the Great Mother, *archigalli* and arch-priestesses, bearing Roman names, and sanctuaries of the cult begin to spread over all Italy and Gaul. Itinerant priesthoods were formed which—the veritable scum of society—traveled from place to place and engaged in the most shameless beggary in the name of the small images which they carried about on the back of an ass. Dressed and bedizened in feminine fashion, they sang and danced to tambourine and flute, whipped and mutilated themselves till the blood flowed, only to compensate themselves by thefts and nameless excesses. So are the mendicant priests painted in Lucian and Apuleius in the age of the Antonines. Later, at least in Rome, the cult of the Great Mother must have shown a more respectable side and, specifically, have given up castration; otherwise the participation of distinguished citizens, openly acknowledged in monuments, would be inexplicable. Of the mysteries proper, which were connected with this worship at least by the third century, we shall speak presently.

The symbolic acts at the great annual festival in April, whose meanings had long since become unintelligible, gave Church writers special offense. The festival began at the vernal equinox. A pine—the tree under which Atys had mutilated himself—was felled in the forest and carried in procession to the temple of the goddess, in Rome on the Palatine hill. A special rank of Tree Bearers (*dendrophori*) is several times mentioned in later inscriptions. On this occasion the *galli* appeared with disheveled hair and smote themselves upon the breast as if in great anguish. On the second day there was a search for strayed Atys, accompanied by trumpet blasts. The third day was called the Day of Blood, because to honor Atys' memory the *galli* wounded themselves in the shade of a pine decorated with violet wreaths and an image of the unfortunate youth. These were days of gloomy and unrestrained mourning—even of a kind of penitential fast. On the fourth day, the so-called Hilaria, joy was unrestrained, and all Rome joined in, probably because an earlier spring festival had become amalgamated with this; otherwise the celebration signified the assumption of Atys among the immortals. The fifth day marked a pause. On the sixth the image of the goddess—a head of black stone set into a silver figure—along with sacred vessels was taken to the water (at Rome to the

Almo brook), rinsed, and then brought back to the temple in a barefoot, disorderly procession.

If the Westerner was incapable of appreciating this festival in its original mythologic sense, he abandoned himself fully to it as a habit and a welcome occasion for release. The ceremony proved to be one of those the pagans were most loath to give up, and despite the change of date, the erection of Maypoles before churches, in Italy *piantar il Maggio,* may have been a final echo of the festival of the Great Mother. Another consequence of this cult may be surmised in the retinues of eunuchs which became common in noble Roman houses. In the fourth century the presence of eunuchs among the domestics of even pious Christian families was accepted as natural; as a purely Oriental fashion the custom could not have gained headway in Rome if the swarms attending the goddess of Pessinus had not accustomed people to the unedifying sight of an unsexed crowd.

Another figure of the Great Goddess may be mentioned here, though very briefly—Anaïtis (Enyo) of Eastern Asia Minor, whose cult was no less dissolute. Hers was the powerful temple rule of Comana in Cappadocia, with its numerous sacred prostitutes of both sexes. Some think she is to be recognized in the ancient Roman war goddess Bellona, whose priests annually cut their arms in a wild revel. Later, in the third century, there were even mysteries of that name, in which the blood of the priest of Bellona was caught up on a shield and distributed to those seeking initiation.

Besides these two great divinities of the Semites, there is a third which must not be passed over, though its intermingling with Greco-Roman religion dates not from the Empire but from remote antiquity. This is Melcart of the Phoenicians, of whom the Greek Heracles is only one aspect. His cult, though now under a Roman name, extended from remote ages as far as Phoenicians and Carthaginians settled; one of his most famous temples was that at Gades (Cadiz). In Italy and Greece the classical concept of the son of Zeus and Alcmene was sufficient; but later theocrasy specifically received the so-called Tyrian

Hercules also into its great pantheon. A southern Italian inscription of the time of Gallienus is dedicated to him, somewhat as in modern times names and copies of widely dispersed miraculous images are repeated on many altars.

With all that has been said, we are still not in a position to sketch a true and lifelike picture of religious conditions in Asia Minor and Syria in the late Empire. In any case the mixture was extremely diverse, according as Greek life in general penetrated or was restricted. A melancholy spectacle is afforded by those magnificent temples of the Greco-Roman style erected to some amorphous Asiatic idol. The noblest and fairest was put to the service of the most repulsive, because some temple administration had accumulated enough lands, moneys, and contributions to undertake a monumental and luxurious building. Waxing superstition, indeed, impelled more and more Greeks and Romans of Asia Minor to these altars of Oriental gods, even to gods newly sprung up, if their interpreters and priests possessed sufficient effrontery. From Lucian we know that charlatan Alexander of the second century, who first gulled the simple Paphlagonians of Abonoteichos with his little snake-god, and then all Asia Minor, including the most distinguished Roman officials.

Adequate reports concerning the later history of the temple administrations generally, of which Strabo knew no inconsiderable number in the time of Augustus, are unfortunately wanting. Even at Palmyra the relationship in which the warrior and commercial aristocracy stood to the great Temple of the Sun and its treasures is not clear. How many ruins of the Near East of the Roman period stand mute! To begin with, there are the majestic Petra in Arabia and the pillar city of Gerasa, east of the Jordan, both places which would hardly have been known by name from the writers of the Empire, if their solitary splendor had not been discovered by astonished modern travelers.

Acceptance of Near-Eastern divinities involved only new superstition and an extension of worship; no new cultural element came to Rome with these cults. The impressive entry of Egypt's gods into the great mixture was quite different. They were accompanied by the ancient reverence of the Greek for the priestly wisdom of the Egyptian, in which it was expected that theology, astronomy, natural history, medicine, and prophecy would be found in equal perfection. Here it was not an affair of raving eunuchs but of a priestly caste which had once ruled the Pharaohs and their people, and had bequeathed mighty monuments.

This caste appears to have suffered significant degradation at the time of the Ptolemies, and temple holdings were made to contribute to the burdens of the state, without resistance. The old esteem for their occult wisdom disappeared after Alexander's city rose on the sands of the Delta and became the laboratory for Greek scholars and Greek-educated Egyptians who formed the greatest center for the newly discovered modes of scientific collecting and research. The Macedonian King, his officials, and his soldiers were no longer guided from the temples, and hence it was no longer worth the effort to maintain the old system of priestly knowledge intact. Upon the occasion of his visit to Heliopolis in Lower Egypt Strabo reports: "We also saw great houses in which the priests resided, who were once philosophers and astronomers; but now the sense of corporate obligation and tradition are vanished. At least we saw no representative of this sort, but only officials for sacrifice and custodians who explained objects of interest to foreigners." Among other points of attraction, the place was shown where Plato was said to have lived for thirteen years without being able to obtain the essence of their secrets from the priests. Now anyone who treated these matters seriously was laughed at among educated people. But in the realm of superstition Egypt soon regained the influence which it had lost in the realm of knowledge.

In the first place the old religion was strongly entrenched in the country itself (see p. 95). This was due partly to the native stubbornness of the Egyptian, who found no better way to preserve his national consciousness against foreign rulers, and partly to the traditional organization. No people of the ancient world made its entire life so completely dependent upon sacred doctrines and prescriptions as the Egyptian. For millennia the best energies of the nation were directed toward glorifying their relationship to the supernatural by symbols. Temple buildings, festivals, sacrifices, and burials occupied a position in comparison with which ordinary civic life, agriculture, and commerce could only claim subordinate importance. Such a situation, never completely abolished or supplanted by anything essentially different, must have continued to exert a very strong effect. Most of the temples still stood intact; a passionate repugnance kept the memory of the destruction perpetrated by Cambyses and the Persians fresh even in the Roman period. The priests who still possessed palaces near and at the temples doubtless did everything possible to preserve the oracles and sacrifices in all their brilliance and dignity and to celebrate the processions through the broad halls and courts and through the corridors of sphinxes and rams with all magnificence. If we may assume that the entire hierarchy persisted in the proportions it demonstrably had under the Ptolemies, it would comprise a whole army of consecrated priests. To be sure, the head was broken off this dangerous spear; the Ptolemies identified the chief priest of their own deified persons with the chief priest of all Egypt and assigned him a seat in Alexandria. The Romans too understood how to provide for the danger; at least under Hadrian the position of "chief priest of Alexandria and all Egypt" was occupied by a Roman, L. J. Vestinus, who was at the same time head of the Museum at Alexandria. But the mass of priests doubtless continued to be Egyptians. There were the *prophetes,* who issued oracles or carried out certain especially sacred sacrificial usages; the *hierostoli,* who cared for the wardrobe of the idols; the *pterophori,* who wore wings upon their heads; the *hierogrammateis,* who had once administered all sacred wisdom but were now probably degraded to be interpreters of dreams; the *horoscopi* or casters of nativities; the *pastophori,* who carried the receptacles with the images of the gods in the processions; the singers; the stampers of sacrificial animals; the keepers of sacred animals; the various grades of embalmers and funerary attendants; and finally numerous temple slaves who lived partly as monks in voluntary seclusion, and partly as itinerant mendicants. Around the temples of Serapis, especially that near Mem-

phis, there were to be found since the second century B.C.
the cells of those "immured ones" who hoped to become
pure by lifelong incarceration in the vicinity of the god—
obviously a close and undeniable pattern for Christian recluses; they received their food only through small win-
dows, and died in their holes. This entire great host,
whether it was maintained at full strength or not, had only
one interest: to preserve Egyptian superstition by every
means and to impress the Romans as much as possible.

In addition to a great number of more or less local divinities, the general Egyptian deities Isis, Osiris, and Anubis
had their temples everywhere. In Alexandria and several
other cities there was added the god Serapis, who had been
brought from Sinope and was thought to be connected with
Osiris as god of the dead. Serapis' temple was regarded
as one of the marvels of ancient architecture and was surrounded by structures which, after the destruction of the
Museum under Aurelian, contained the still highly important scientific institutions, among others one of the two
great libraries. It is worth while to hear Rufinus' remarks
concerning this remarkable structure, fabulous and vague
as they are, because we can apprehend here more clearly
than elsewhere how much Hellenism was able to accommodate itself to national character in this home of all superstition. The Serapeum, towering above the city upon a
foundation a hundred steps high, appears to have been a
gigantic domed structure surrounded upon all four sides by
chambers, stairs, and secret corridors, and above even by
quarters for the priests and cells for penitents. A fourfold
portico ran either about the building itself or surrounded
an open court. The most precious materials, including gold
and ivory, were not spared anywhere in the structure. In
the great central hall stood the image of the god, in proportions so colossal that its outstretched hands touched
either wall; it was fashioned, after the manner of chryselephantine statues, of various materials over a wooden core;
the uncovered portions were probably of some sort of sacred wood. The walls were plated with bronze, and Alexandrian fantasy imagined a second inner plating of silver,
and an innermost plating of gold. The entire great chamber

was dark, and intended to be illuminated artificially. Only on the festive day, when the image of the sun-god was brought to visit Serapis, was a small aperture to the east opened at a specific moment, when brilliant sunlight struck the lips of the image of Serapis; this was called the sun kiss. Other optical or mechanical devices, for which the temple must have been equipped like a theater, are not described in detail, or seem quite fanciful, like the story of the magnet in the ceiling which held the sun image, made of thin sheet iron, hovering in the air; the same story was later told of Mohammed's coffin. Like all temples of Serapis, this temple was also famous for so-called incubation. Sick persons slept there or sent others to sleep there in order to learn remedies through divinely sent dreams. The Greeks employed a similar method in their temples of Asclepius, and this was made the ground for identifying the two gods with one another.

Moreover, every wall and every doorpost throughout the city was marked with a symbol of the great god, and there were countless temples, chapels, and images of the other divinities in every street. It was believed that equipment for deceptive phantasmagoria was to be found or assumed in other temples also. Thus in the temple of a god who is designated Saturn in the Latin account, the great image was placed against the wall and its interior left hollow so that a priest might enter and speak through its open mouth; the temple candelabra were arranged so that they might be extinguished suddenly. But some devices of this character were perhaps not intentional deception, but machinery known and approved by everyone to enhance the great symbolic celebrations in which Egypt had been rich immemorially; if simple fanaticism caused anyone to regard them as miracles, the priests would naturally not disabuse him. We shall find the priests occupied also with theurgy and exorcism; but they themselves share in the delusion or at least do not stand completely outside it as deceivers. For superstition had here become the actual breath of life; at a quite late date the Egyptian divine family produced new shoots, as for example Serapis himself and the odious Canopus, who was worshiped in the shape of a pitcher with human head and extremities in the city of the Delta bearing his name. In Strabo's time the city of Canopus with its taverns was a favorite resort of the Alexandrians. Excursions were made on the Nile canal, which was alive day and night with barges filled with men and women who danced to the tune of flutes and indulged in all manner of excess. At that time a temple of Serapis, which was resorted to for curative dreams, was still the principal building in the city; later the sanctuary of Canopus himself occupied the foreground, and in the fourth century became an advanced school for all manner of magic.

Of the persistence and rivalry of animal cults we have spoken in the preceding section. Each nome or district worshiped its peculiar animal—sheep, wolf, baboon, eagle, lion, goat, shrew, and the like. The principal objects of universal worship were the two famous bulls: Mnevis, who was kept in a chapel near the Temple of Heliopolis as late as Strabo's time, and Apis, who was thought to incarnate the soul of Osiris, at Memphis. A black bull with a white mark upon its forehead and a crescent upon its flank was not always to be found; in the fourth century, upon one occasion, long search was necessary. When the bull was discovered he was conducted to Memphis in reverent procession together with the cow which had given him birth; a hundred priests welcomed him and escorted him to the temple which was to serve as his stall. There and in the court before the temple visitors inspected him and discovered omens in his every move. Once the bull refused to eat out of Germanicus' hand, and this was taken as ominous. At Arsinoë there were still priests who knew how to tame, or at least to feed, the crocodiles which were there worshiped. Among these countless natural beings which received worship mention must be made of the mightiest of all, to whom all Egypt owed its existence. The Nile possessed its own college of eunuch priests who "served and entertained" him with sacrifices so that he might vouchsafe his benison to the land. According to Eusebius, Constantine was to have abolished this priesthood, but his intention cannot have been carried out, for the priesthood long survived Con-

stantine's day. All that he was able to do, perhaps, was
to transfer the Nile gauge from the Serapeum to a Christian church.

Of the other Egyptian priests, as they existed at the time
of Trajan, Plutarch provides a somewhat excessively reverent description of the priests of Isis and wherever he can
do so interprets their usages and ceremonies as symbols.
Their distinguishing mark was their white linen dress and
shorn head. They practiced a kind of abstinence and
avoided many foods, both to prevent obesity and for a
variety of symbolic reasons. They also avoided the sea and
salt. With all its repetitious lamentations, their cult possessed no spiritual dignity; its place was taken by orgiastic
ululations and bacchanalian gesticulations. Here an ass was
flung down a cliff, there a gilded ox was led about covered with a black robe. A peculiar noise-making instrument, the sistrum, was supposed to restrain the wicked Ty-
phon (the destroying principle) by its din. Many aspects
of this cult bear the stamp of later meaningless contrivance
or borrowing. The Isis image was clothed in various colors,
some dark and some light, to represent day and night, fire
and water, life and death. Incense varied according to the
time of day: resin in the morning in order to banish the
mists of night, myrrh at noon, and at night *kyphi*, which
was compounded of sixteen ingredients to the accompani-
ment of constant prayer. *Kyphi* was also prepared in po-
table form; it was a specific whose constituents lent themselves to symbolic interpretation, but its effect must have
been narcotic.

Plutarch deals with his subject with complete seriousness; nevertheless he indicates that among the Egyptians
there were also people who found superstition and particularly the animal cult distasteful. "While the weak and the
simple fall into unqualified superstition," he says, "bolder
and prouder spirits necessarily succumb to unruly and athe-
ist thoughts."

We must now determine how much of this religion was
adopted by Rome in its bloom and later in its decline, and
in what spirit.

Aside from purely artistic borrowing which brought a

large number of Egyptian figures and ornamental motifs
to Rome, especially in the age of Hadrian, it is almost exclusively the circle of Isis which for centuries had found a
welcome in Greek and Roman religions.

Isis, the earth and indeed blessed Egypt itself, and
Osiris, the fertilizing stream of the Nile, were both conceived of by the Egyptians themselves as general symbols
of all life, and thus were made ready to enter into the
divine cult of other peoples. A collateral significance, which
the divine pair may have received from a Semitic source,
to wit as moon and sun, had virtually receded into the
background by the time of Herodotus. The Greeks unani-
mously regarded Isis as Demeter and Osiris as Dionysus,
but did not therefore completely disregard Isis' function
as moon-goddess. Indeed she shared, one after the other,
in the affairs of widely different deities; she was goddess
of the underworld, of dreams, of childbirth, even ruler of
the sea. When as a result of the conquest of Egypt by
Alexander that country was received into the great complex of Greco-Oriental life, the worship of Isis spread everywhere in the Greek world and eventually reached
Rome in the time of Sulla, though for a hundred years
thereafter it encountered vigorous public opposition.
Among the Romans Isis was accompanied sometimes by her
husband Osiris, but much more frequently by Serapis as
the Osiris of the underworld; by the dog-headed Anubis
(a bastard of Osiris who, as a messenger between the gods
and the underworld, was identified with Hermes); and
finally by Horus, Grecized as Harpocrates, to whom Isis
gave birth after the death of Osiris.

The original mythological significance of these beings,
even if we knew it for certain, does not suffice for an understanding of the meanings associated with them by the Romans. Besides his function as a god of healing, Serapis was
also a sun-god; a number of foreign gods and even some
native ones came to have that aspect. But this concept did
not detract from his rule over souls in life and in death.
Similarly, Isis and the other deities were transformed into
gods of salvation in a broad, and of healing in a specific,
sense, without thereby losing their connection with the un-

derworld. At this stage it is difficult to distinguish Isis from
Hecate, the three-formed goddess of the underworld who
rules in heaven as Luna, on earth as Diana, and in the underworld as Proserpina. To the elegiac poets, on the other
hand, she is the awesome and frequently conciliated mistress in the realm of love. As the number of aspects of life
subject to her dominion increased, it became less possible
to define her nature, as the Romans conceived it, in a common formula. She is found in widely disparate metamorphoses, even as Fortuna and Tyche, to say nothing of the
purely philosophic interpretation which subsequently discovered in her the great universal deity. The goddess had
long Romanized her figure and laid aside the familiar
Egyptian headdress. The costume of the priestess seems to
have supplanted that of the old goddess. The permanent
insignia of the goddess in pictures and statuary are now
the fringed mantle fastened to the tunic under the breasts
with a peculiar knot, and the sistrum in the hand.

Roman arms spread the worship of Isis to the frontiers
of the Empire, in the Netherlands as in Switzerland and
South Germany. It penetrated private life more thoroughly
and earlier than the cult of the great Semitic goddess. It
enjoyed imperial favor only after Vespasian, who had expressly shown Serapis reverence at Alexandria. His son
Domitian then built an Iseum and Serapeum in Rome;
previously the two deities had to content themselves with
unobtrusive chapels, at least within the city walls. Later
there were several considerable sanctuaries of the goddess
in Rome. At the temple discovered at Pompeii, which had
been restored sixteen years before the final catastrophe,
there is a secret stairway and an empty depression behind
the pedestal which bore the images and beside it a small
accessory structure with underground chamber. This arrangement gives ground for conjecture, but there is neither
room nor equipment for large and spectacular phantasmagoria such as the fancy of archaeologists and poets has associated with these slight structures.

The priests of Isis united into numerous colleges (as
pastophori and the like) in the larger cities had a consistently bad reputation as late as the first century. Among

other things they were said to arrange assignations, for which Isis in her temple, as has been remarked above, must have afforded protection. Juvenal shows profound contempt for the shorn swarm dressed in linen, which thrust its way with priestly cries of lamentation into the chambers of respectable Roman ladies, from which the eunuchs of the great Syrian goddess had just departed. The latter only begged; but the leader of the priests of Isis, who appeared in the costume of Anubis, could also utter threats and prescribe penances for certain agreeable sins. Even if the prescription involved a plunge in the Tiber in midwinter, it would be obeyed, for the lady's faith was firm and she believed that she heard Isis' own voice in her sleep.

From the second century onward the worship of Isis, like that of the Great Mother, was given a more elevated tone and probably greater dignity also by the participation of the Emperor and the higher classes. The difference as compared with earlier practice was so great that it gave rise to the theory that Commodus or Caracalla had first brought the cult to Rome. At the great processions there were henceforward *pausae,* that is, halting places, perhaps fitted with special structures. One such festive procession Commodus had represented in mosaic in a hall of his gardens. On these occasions he himself, shorn like a priest, would carry the image of Anubis, and with its snout strike the heads of the priests of Isis who walked beside him. But far the most circumstantial description of an Isis procession, which may serve as a general gauge for such processions at this time, is supplied by Apuleius in the last book of his *Metamorphoses.* The scene is laid in dissolute Corinth. The procession begins in the gayest carnival style with colorful masks of soldiers, hunters, gladiators, elegantly coiffured women, magistrates, philosophers (with robe, staff, slippers, and goatee), fowlers, and fishermen. There followed a tame bear on a sedan chair dressed as an old lady, an ape dressed as Ganymede with cap and orange-colored suit and with golden cup in hand, and even an ass with wings attached as a travesty on Pegasus, and running beside him a lame dwarf representing Bellerophon. Now the procession proper began. Garlanded women

dressed in white, the attendants of Isis' toilette, strewed
flowers and perfumes and gesticulated with mirrors and
combs. A crowd of both sexes followed with lamps, torches,
and tapers as if to do homage to the astral divinities. There
followed harpists, pipers, and a choir of singers dressed in
white; then the flautists of Serapis blowing a ritual temple
melody, and heralds to clear the way. Then came devotees
of all classes and ages dressed in white linen, the women
with anointed hair and transparent veils, the men with
hair cropped short; the sistrums which they swung noisily
were made of silver or even of gold according to their
means. Now the priests themselves appeared with the secret symbols of the goddess: lamps, miniature altars, palm
branches, serpent staves, an open hand, and several vessels
of peculiar form. Others carried the gods themselves, the
image of Anubis with its dog's head half black and half
gold, a cow standing erect, a mystic chest. Finally there
came the chief priest pressing to his bosom the golden urn
with serpent hooks which represented the goddess herself.
In this order the procession moved out of the city of Corinth—where the novelist had laid his scene—down to the
sea. Here the colorful "Isis boat" decorated with hieroglyphs was filled with incense and votive offerings amid
much ceremony, and in sight of sanctuaries set up on shore
the ship was launched on the waves. The inscription upon
the sail, "For a happy voyage in the new year," and the
date, known from other sources of the widely celebrated
Roman *navigium Isidis,* which was March 5, supply an explanation for the entire festival, which was to celebrate the
opening of the sea which had been closed during the winter. For it was precisely in her latest, non-Egyptian character as ruler of the sea that Isis received specific worship
in the Mediterranean, and the Corinthians, with a gulf on
their either side, must have been especially devoted to her.
The procession returned to the temple, and a priest standing upon a high pulpit before the gate pronounced a blessing for the Emperor, the Senate, the knights, the Roman
people, seafaring, and the entire Empire; he closed with
the formula λαοτς ἄφεσις, which has the same significance as the *Ite, missa est* of Christian worship. At this en-

tire celebration there was a distinction between the gay crowd of worshipers and the initiates of the mysteries, concerning whom we shall have to speak in the following section.

What we are told of sacred script, partly hieroglyphic, partly of other secret character, in connection with this and other occasions, may well be factually correct; but the Roman, Greek, or Gallic priest of Isis who preserved these writings and could perhaps copy and recite them certainly knew nothing of their meaning. Indeed, far from drawing any profound science from priestly Egypt (whose strong point in any case was no longer doctrine), Rome adopted the many-named gods with no regard for theological consistency in willfully altered interpretations. This has already been noticed in the case of Isis. Another eloquent example is the figure of Harpocrates, whose gesture—index finger pointing toward mouth—is meant to indicate that he has been nursed by Isis; in the excellent Capitoline sculpture of the Hadrianic period instead of the Egyptian idol we find a young Cupid bidding silence with his fingers on his lips as a *deus silentii.* Anubis, on the other hand, although he is regarded as identical with Hermes, was required to retain his dog's head; its combination with a human body in Roman drapery is peculiarly objectionable.

A notion of the symbols of this entire cycle is supplied by the brazen hands found here and there which have been recognized as *ex votos* dedicated by women in childbirth to Isis as helper in travail. The fingers are arranged in the posture of an oath, and the inner as well as the outer surface of the hand is completely covered with attributes —mystery-vessels, small busts of the divinities Isis, Serapis, Osiris, and Anubis, the latter represented as Dionysus and Hermes. This is not the place to enumerate the symbols; perhaps their number corresponds to petitions made in time of need.

The subject of the mixture of cults is far from exhausted by the alien divinities thus far named; many who fit into the category will more appropriately receive cursory treatment in the section following. Heretofore we have spoken

only of officially recognized and generally propagated
sacra peregrina; there was nothing to prevent the individual worshiper from surrounding himself with masses of
images and symbols of all countries and religions. How different in this respect, and incidentally how significant, is
the attitude of the two dissimilar cousins, Elagabalus and
Alexander Severus! Elagabalus brought his Semitic idols,
the palladia of Rome, and the stones of Orestes from the
Temple of Diana at Laodicea together haphazardly in a
single heap. Just as the Black Stone of Emesa was married
to the image of Urania of Carthage, so the Emperor-priest
himself married the chief Vestal; he is even said to have
expressed an intention to make his central sanctuary a point
of union for the worship of Samaritans, Jews, and Christians. All gods were to be ministers of his great god, and
all mysteries concentrated in that god's priesthood. Alexander Severus, on the other hand, celebrated the founders of
all religions as ideals of humanity, and set their likenesses
up in his domestic chapel, where Abraham and Christ were
placed near Orpheus, as supposed founder of the Hellenic
mysteries, and Apollonius of Tyana, as neo-philosophic
wonder-worker. The best of the earlier Emperors were also
given place in his chapel, just as colossal statues of them
were set up in the Forum of Nerva. A second chapel contained statues of Vergil, Cicero, Achilles, and other great
men; the noble and unhappy prince sought to form a new
Olympus out of the best that he knew. But what was done
in the imperial palace at Rome on a large scale was certainly repeated manifold on a small scale. Many of the
nobler spirits would gladly have turned to Christianity in
such aspects as they could apprehend; even more eagerly
would common superstition have looked up to the Christian mysteries, which must have had a peculiar fascination
because they communicated to their devotees so remarkable an attitude in life and in death. It is difficult to imagine
the feeling of many a pagan, compounded of revulsion and
desire, and we can scarcely be said to have any direct account of the subject, if we are unwilling to reckon the story
of the Samaritan magician Simon as such. Of the philo-

sophic *rapprochement* of the two religions we shall speak in
the sequel.

Once the revulsion against alien divinities had completely vanished, once the overwhelming lure of the mysterious, especially in the Oriental cult, had made itself felt,
there was no foretelling where this appropriation of alien
elements would stop. The Roman world had already been
invaded, in the train of Neoplatonic philosophy and Manichaeism, not only by Persian but even by Indian principles
of religion. Anything that could present a mysterious aspect
and produce a claim to affinity with Roman notions of deity
was sure of a welcome.

It is precisely from this later period of Roman history
that we find numerous inscriptions dedicated to "all the
gods and goddesses," "all the heavenly ones," "the assembly
of the gods," and the like. Doubtless the inscribers included the alien gods in their intentions, so that none might
feel offended. Frequently the attributes of a number of
native and alien divinities were bestowed upon a single
figure, which was then designated *Deus Pantheus,* or All-
godly God. So *Silvanus Pantheus* and *Liber Pantheus* occur; on images of Fortuna there are to be seen, beside the
oar and cornucopia which are appropriate to her, the
breastplate of Minerva, the lotus of Isis, the thunder-
bolt of Jupiter, the fawn-skin of Bacchus, the cock of
Aesculapius, and the like. This is perhaps no more than a
compendious expression for the whole host of gods, and
so to be differentiated from philosophic monotheism, which
(as we shall see below) recognized the actual identity of
all the gods in a supreme being.

There is a well-known statement of the philosopher
Themistius, of a considerably later period, when Emperor
Valens as an Arian was bitterly persecuting orthodox Christians. "Difference in belief among Christians," says the philosopher, "is no cause for astonishment; it is quite inconsiderable in comparison with the mass and confusion of
varying pagan religious views. Here there are more than
three hundred sects, forasmuch as the Deity desires to be
glorified in diverse modes and is the more respected, the

less anyone knows about them." Themistius' figure may well be too high; furthermore, these pagan sects and dogmas were not mutually exclusive, as were the Christian, so that an individual might belong to several simultaneously. Nevertheless, three hundred various manners of worship, even if they are not mutually contradictory, indicate a fragmentation of paganism which could not have been produced merely by the introduction of the foreign gods. We shall now have to show how infinite variety was introduced into the declining religion of paganism both through tangible objects of the cult and, to a greater degree, through its inward principles, and how at the same time powerful tendencies toward simplification were operative.

VI

IMMORTALITY AND ITS MYSTERIES
THE DAIMONIZATION OF PAGANISM

ALONG WITH the ancient worship and the cults brought in
from abroad, a temper of disbelief had long pervaded the
educated classes, as has been noticed above, and in the
most favorable cases this disbelief took on a philosophic
coloring. But with the third century, under the influence
of the great calamities which had befallen the Empire, a
change of heart is perceptible among the upper classes. On
the one hand they were attracted to the miraculous and (1)
superstitious interests of the common people; on the other,
they were provided for by a new spiritual dispensation (2)
which contrived to link philosophy with the most extreme
superstition, to wit, Neoplatonism so-called.

These two tendencies were not disparate in contemporary life, and cannot be wholly separated in our account
of it. It is quite impossible to say where popular belief
ceases and where philosophic superstition begins; the latter regularly recognizes the former, in order to make place
for it in its system, specifically in its doctrine of daimons.

Every page of the history of the third century gives evidence of these individual phenomena, increasing credulity
in the matter of miracles and pagan fanaticism, mysticism
and the asceticism of enthusiasts. But the total impression
is that attitudes to the supernatural as a whole had substantially altered. The change becomes evident when we
consider the new views concerning the ultimate fate of
man himself.

Enemies of Christianity make it their constant charge

that Christianity is an other-worldly religion which regards
life on earth only as a period of preparation, grim and rich
in trials, for eternal life in the world to come. Paganism,
on the contrary, is praised as a joyous doctrine which taught
ancient man to give untrammeled expression, and in his
own particular manner, to his potentialities, his inclinations,
and his individual destiny. It might be objected at once
that even the world view of the Greek at its most powerful
was far from being as joyous as is customarily believed. But
in any case we must realize that the paganism of the third
century can certainly make no unqualified claim to this
praise, if one wishes to style it such, and that it had also
become a religion of the beyond. Christian dogma places
its doctrine of death and immortality at the end of its doctrine of man; in the present case we must begin with death
and immortality, because comprehension of late pagan religions depends entirely upon this point.

The lamentable condition of the state and society certainly contributed greatly to the development of this other-
worldliness, but it cannot explain it fully. New tendencies
such as these draw their essential strength from unplumbed
depths; they cannot be merely deduced as consequences
of antecedent conditions. The earlier pagan view granted
man a persistence after death, to be sure, but as a mere
shadowy form, as a nerveless dream life. Those who pretended to fuller wisdom spoke of a transmigration of souls,
after the Egyptian or Asiatic manner. Only a few friends of
the gods were destined to sojourn in Elysium or on the Isles
of the Blessed. When paganism reached its crisis the circle
of these favored ones was suddenly enlarged and soon everyone made claim to eternal blessedness. On numberless
sarcophagi we find trains of Tritons and Nereids, quite
tastefully executed for this late period; these signify the
journey to the Isles of the Blessed. The tomb inscriptions
leave no doubt of the matter. "Ye unhappy survivors," we
find, "bewail this death; but ye gods and goddesses, rejoice
over your new fellow citizen!"

In other cases there is formal profession that true life begins only in the world beyond. "Only now dost thou live

thy happy life, far from all earthly doom; high in the heaven thou dost enjoy nectar and ambrosia with the gods." Such happy immortality is expected even for children, for eight-year-old girls. "Ye exalted souls of the pious, lead innocent Magnilla through the Elysian fields and meadows to your dwelling-places!" A ten-month-old infant is represented as speaking: "My heavenly divine soul will not go to the shades; the universe and the stars take me in; earth has received only my body, this stone my name." A widower professes to know the constellation where his wife abides; it is the Lock of Berenice near Andromeda. More modest is the prayer of a son: "Ye gods of the underworld, open for my father the groves where eternal day shines purple." There is also expression of a specific hope to see the deceased again, but only upon a late pagan stone of the fourth century. We find another logical consequence of belief in immortality, and that is a belief in intercession for survivors. A high official speaks: "Just as I have cared for your welfare on earth, so am I concerned for it now among the gods." A Christian origin has been claimed for many of these inscriptions, but wrongly; specific mythological additions clearly refute the possibility of Christian origin.

That such ideas of immortality were widespread in the age of Diocletian is proven by the admonition which Arnobius addresses to the pagans: "Do not flatter yourselves with vain hope when inflated sages declare they were born of God and are not subject to the laws of fate, and that, if their lives were on the whole virtuous, God's court stands open to them and after their death they may ascend thither without hindrance as to their home." The best result of all of this was that henceforward at least the deeply rooted belief in an earthly predestination no longer stood in such stark opposition to an ethical order of the universe, since man's destiny in the beyond was acknowledged.

These pious-sounding beliefs seem in fact to have involved, from the pagan point of view, nothing more than an enlightened monotheism and a rigid ethic, as was maintained among the Stoics in principle and partly also in practice. But for contemporary men the problem could not be so simply stated. Between themselves and the highest problems of their existence there intervened in layers numberless gods and systems of gods, and account had to be taken of these daimonic powers. Even where the pagan of this period achieved so-called monotheism we find him remarkably attached to the idea of subordinate divine beings who had to be worshiped and conciliated each in its own manner. Far from being able to satisfy the yearning for immortality by trustfully throwing oneself upon the bosom of the Eternal by an immediate moral and religious act, the individual felt constrained to undertake a long and circuitous route. Now ancient worship had always had associated with itself certain secret rites which brought the initiate nearer to his god and at the same time involved more or less specific relations to a fairer immortality than that of the usual shadowy Hades. In the Hellenic mysteries of Demeter as of Dionysus this hope is associated with the celebration of the death and resurrection of nature, especially of grain, without its becoming prominent as the essential element of the cult. These mysteries continued to be celebrated; whenever the Emperor or other distinguished visitors came to Greece they were eager to be initiated. The famous address of the Christian Firmicus to the sons of Constantine still denounces the initiations of Eleusis, the Cretan mysteries of Dionysus, and the *sacra* of the Corybantes as things still existing. Perhaps we may go so far as to assume that the mass of mysteries, with which Greece teemed in the second century at the time of Pausanias, persisted in whole or in part, if in shrunken form, until the age of Theodosius.

But remarkable as the proceedings of the mysteries may be in themselves, their details need not detain us here, because they rather point backward to earlier Hellenism and more particularly because they were local in character, even depending upon citizen rights, and thus were incapable of further expansion. For the same reason we must pass over the Roman mysteries of Bona Dea and the like. But the situation is quite different with reference to the universal mysteries of the period of the Empire, which spread over all Roman regions and were usually devoted to foreign gods.

It is not the fault of modern scholars that essential aspects of this matter remain unknown, and much depends on mere conjecture. In the first place it must be remarked that participation in such secret worship, qualitatively as well as quantitatively, according to various regions, classes, and groups, remains largely a riddle. The number of initiates may have run into thousands, perhaps even into hundreds of thousands. It is possible that individual countries did not participate, by accident or because of some internal reason, and it is equally possible that relevant evidence—inscriptions and monuments—is still underground. But one general assumption may certainly be made: these mysteries were to be found in Rome early, partly even in the period of the Republic, but were humble and even despised. But with the third century participation in the mysteries mounts, in number as well as in the importance of the initiates. This involves a new and deeper content whose central point was the promise of immortality.

At the entrance of this labyrinth there stand the two handsome figures of Amor and Psyche, an allegory based upon Plato's concept of the human soul. It may be that these figures occur on earlier individual monuments, but it is a fact that none of the marble groups we know is earlier than the second century and that the two figures separately or in caressing union, in joy or in sorrow, are represented again and again from the second century to the end of the pagan period, especially on sarcophagi. The sole circumstantial literary treatment of the myth, in the pages of Apuleius in the age of the Antonines, is apt to lead the reader astray. Apuleius' account is a fairy story whose similarity with the allegory consists only in the fact that his lovers were made unhappy by a long separation due to the fault of one, and that a blessed reunion joined them forevermore. The author has made only partial and inconsistent use of the meaning of the allegory, the names of whose principal figures he used for his story, but he has not sufficiently adapted his poetic account to conform to the allegory. Contemporary ideas concerning the human soul persisted, untouched by Apuleius' story. Though of divine origin, the soul has fallen, and in its earthly passage is subject to error; through trials and purifications it must again be prepared for a life of blessedness. The heavenly EROS who takes its part and leads it home as his bride is a revelation of deity which draws lost humanity back to itself and unites it with itself.

We do not know whether special worship or rites were associated with this symbol in the Roman period. It is only a general indication of a certain trend of thought. In the realm of art and poetic allusion it is enlarged to take in various collateral images. Psyche is represented as a butterfly in a series of scenes: Pallas lowers her onto the head of man fashioned by Prometheus; she soars up from his body at death and is led by Hermes to the world below. Linked with this as a clear image is the final liberation of Prometheus, who has been chained to the cliff and whom Heracles frees from the eagle by a bolt from his bow; thereafter he leads a divine life on Olympus.

From this general symbol of late Roman yearning for immortality we proceed to those mysteries in which some analogous content is to be recognized.

The mysteries of BACCHUS which were still widely represented in the Empire should perhaps be excluded. Their content at this time cannot be determined; we only know that they still involved devouring the raw and bloody flesh of a kid and that the initiates in their sacred madness wound serpents about themselves.

The mysteries of the three-formed goddess of the underworld, HECATE (Luna, Diana, Proserpina), seem to be closely related to belief in immortality. Writers give us no information on the subject, but in the inscriptions this worship is placed on a footing with that of the most important mysteries, those of Mithras and of the Great Mother, and hence must have had some importance. Upon an image of this *diva triformis* at Hermannstadt in Transylvania there are bands of relief which seem to represent various scenes and grades of initiation. The resources devoted to this secret worship may be surmised from the plan of the temple of Hecate built by Diocletian at Antioch—365 steps underground, if our report is to be relied upon.

The latest form of the VENUS MYSTERIES, of which there are scattered notices, is similarly unknown. But the most important occult rites referred to certain foreign gods.

Two kinds of mysteries are connected with the PHRYGIAN CULT. The older form, occurring as early as Greece's period of bloom, is the secret worship of SABAZIUS. The ancient Thracians perhaps identified him with the sun-god, the Phrygians with Atys; but in Greece he was generally regarded as a personification of Dionysus and as such possessed a public cult. Its principal feature, after the Asiatic fashion, was noisy song with cymbal and tambourine and the wild *sikinnis* dance. Of the secret initiation as it was celebrated in the Greek period, we know only the external aspects of the ritual: draping with a fawn-skin (*nebris*), drinking or sprinkling out of mixing-bowls, purifications and the like, and finally the traditional cry of the initiates, "I fled the evil and found the good," as well as carrying a tub or a cradle around. Of the secret (according to Creuzer, cosmogonic) doctrine we know nothing and can scarcely be justified in assuming any lofty intention, for the conclusion, and for most of the participants probably the goal, of the initiation consisted in nocturnal excesses of the coarsest kind; these brought the entire worship of Sabazius into serious disfavor. Later these mysteries had considerable currency in the Roman Empire, perhaps with some new religious and philosophic content; they also entered into a kind of relationship with the Mithras cult which will be dealt with below. Now—if this was not done earlier—a golden serpent was lowered into the initiate's garment with symbolic versicles and then withdrawn below, presumably as a memorial of the love of Zeus and Demeter. Then the initiate was led into the innermost chamber of the sanctuary, pronouncing the words, "I have eaten out of the tambourine, I have drunk out of the cymbal, I am now an initiate"—to say nothing of other undecipherable formulae. We may also conjecture that at least in the third and fourth centuries these initiations of Sabazius, besides acquiring a new meaning, also achieved a more respectable attitude.

The Christian writers who see in the golden serpent an obvious unmasking of Satan, who here finally calls himself by his true name, would certainly not have been silent if the ceremony were still closed by general license. Furthermore, persons of considerable standing must have participated in these mysteries; Firmicus (about 340) speaks of some of its adherents as clothed in purple, with gold and laurel in their hair.

Much more remarkable but unfortunately not much better known is the second, newer variety of Phrygian mysteries in the Roman Empire, the TAUROBOLIA. These were directly connected with the figures of the Great Mother and of Atys and included a direct promise of immortality.

From the age of the Antonines inscriptions are found which show that a *taurobolium* (sacrifice of a bull) and a *criobolium* (sacrifice of a ram) were offered to the Great Mother and to Atys. The sacrificer declares that he is IN AETERNVM RENATVS, that is reborn to eternity. We know nothing of the doctrine which conveyed this hope, and only little of the ceremonial which was involved. The classic locale for initiations at Rome was on the Vatican hill, whence constant communication with the provinces may have been maintained. The customary hour was midnight (*mesonyctium*). A deep pit was dug in the ground, and covered with boards perforated like a colander. The candidate for initiation, garbed in a symbolic dress with gold ornaments, took his place beneath. When the sacrificial animals, bull and ram and sometimes also a goat, were slaughtered above, he sought to intercept as much of the blood as possible with his face, hair, and dress. But this repulsive solemnity was not the end; the candidate was required permanently to wear the blood-stained garments in public, and to expose himself to mockery as well as to reverence. It appears that this purification by blood was valid only for a period of twenty years, and then had to be repeated, doubtless without prejudice to the eternity mentioned above. Nevertheless this was one of the commonest forms of initiation, and was undergone not only for the individual himself, but for others also, for the welfare of the imperial house, and even, at least in the second and third centuries, for whole cities. How the ceremony was modified when whole corporations participated in it is quite unknown. There were cases where such initiations were prescribed by the Great Mother, apparently in dreams. Difficult as it may be for us to associate loftier thoughts with these crude practices, this exquisite age found comfort in the *vires aeternae,* the eternal dedicatory blood of the bull. One initiate, Proconsul of Africa and City Prefect of Rome to boot, earnestly thanks the gods for their care of his soul henceforward.

On dedicatory inscriptions, especially the later ones, Atys is frequently called Menotyrannus; this shows his original identity or later identification with Men, the Asia Minor moon-god, but is of no further service in explaining the mysteries.

More important and certainly more refined were the mysteries of Isis, which have left clearer traces in literature also. Proselytes for these mysteries were solicited by books, which appear to have been written mainly for this purpose. The *Metamorphoses* of Apuleius is of this character, as is also Xenophon of Ephesus' romance of *Anthia and Habrocomes,* which dates to the second century. Here Isis is the divinity who preserves and protects the lovers who are beset by countless adventures. Isis herself is much improved; she no longer provides occasions for unchastity as she had previously done in so many of her temples, but herself guards maidenly modesty, whose triumph is the worthy theme of several of these late romances.

We are dealing here not with the ancient and genuine Isis festivals of Egypt, in which mangled Osiris was sought and found, but with the universal occult worship of Isis of the imperial period. The meaning and content of this worship is difficult to determine with precision, because the Romans' popular belief in Isis was variable and changing in form. The only consistent account is provided by Apuleius in the last book of the *Metamorphoses,* to which we have already alluded, but we are left uncertain whether his Lucius speaks rather as a speculative philosopher or as a devout initiate. But one thing is beyond doubt: these mysteries too, colorful as they were, promised a blessed immortality. "Queen Isis," who shows herself to be Mother Nature and the basic principle of all divine being, demands of the unlucky Lucius, as the price of his transformation from an ass back to human form, that he must never forget that his entire life henceforward to his last breath belongs to her. "But you will live happy, glorious in my protection; and when you have run the course of your time and go to the world below, you will find me there also as you see me here, illuminating the gloom of Acheron, ruling over the Stygian depths, and as dweller in the Elysian Fields you will pray for my grace without cease." In the same breath, indeed, Isis promises a long life on earth, if Lucius should please her by diligent service and penance; then the chief priest promises him direct protection and security against human destiny, which is normally controlled by the stars. It appears that there was still credulity for such illusions.

The sacred teaching which was imparted to candidates for initiation, presumably out of hieroglyphic books, was probably not profound. The external, spectacular ceremonial was made much too prominent for any loftier, spiritual element, any change of heart, even any lasting abstentions, to affect the spirit of the initiates. Was it really made clear to the initiate that Isis was Nature and at the same time the sum of all divine being, or was this merely the personal expression of Apuleius' own tendentious view? We only know, as has been indicated, that these mysteries were a favorite means of assuring oneself, by means of certain ceremonies and magic arts, against misfortunes in earthly life, against an unhappy existence in the beyond, or against total annihilation after death. The only aspect of these mysteries which suggests a systematic treatment of man's spiritual nature are the constant and surely not altogether involuntary dreams, in the course of which Isis' will on matters all and sundry was apprehended. Besides simple delusion from without—for dreams could be whispered into the ears of sleepers—there is the possibility of a persistent and artificially maintained nervous excitement. The external practices, on the other hand, were either taken over, half

understood, from Egypt, or calculated to impress an easily
aroused imagination. The preparations during the course of
instruction were those customary in most of the mysteries:
abstention from wine, meat, indulgence, for ten full days; a
bath, sprinkling with sacred water, and the like; christening
gifts from friends and fellow candidates. The night of the
dedication, determined by a dream, was spent in the temple. First one wore a rough linen robe, then clothing was
changed twelve times, until at last one received a flowered
coat and the Olympian stole decorated with painted figures
of mystic animals. Of the processions and spectacles exhibited to the initiates Lucius can only hint that he had to
undergo symbolic death and then resurrection by the grace
of Isis (*precaria salus*). "I walked through the gates of
death, I trod the threshold of Proserpina, and after I had
traversed all elements I returned again. In the middle of
the night I beheld the sun in its brightest illumination. I
approached the gods below and above and supplicated
them from near at hand." These are things concerning
which we shall never be certain. Are we to assume the use
for each initiation of optic and dioramatic arts which would
be necessary, by our standards, for even an outward illusion? There were sufficient means available, to be sure, as
we shall show in another connection, to make a contemporary believe in this or that conjuration or ghostly apparition;
but the temper of the age was still sufficiently steeped in
the value of symbols to produce a deep impression upon
the imagination by the mere ritual display of effective sensual images. Our modern world, in contrast, is so utterly
alien to the symbolic and so contemptuous of it that we can
scarcely understand a different point of view and grow impatient with any formalities or ceremonies. We bring this
same attitude to bear on our judgment of the past. Rather
than admit the profound effectiveness of symbol, we prefer
to premise the costliest artifices of optical and mechanical
illusion, that is to say, actual deception.

But we return to the Isis temple at Corinth. The time is
toward dawn. Lucius, attired in his colorful garb, a burning torch in his hand, a spiked crown of palm leaves upon
his head, stands upon a wooden platform before the image

of the goddess. Suddenly the curtain parts before his eyes, and the crowd assembled without in the nave of the temple beholds him as the living image of the sun. Feast and revelry conclude the ceremony.

But the true *sacrosancta civitas* of the Isis worshiper was Rome itself, where Lucius, too, subsequently fixed his abode at the temple of Isis Campensis. In the following year he is admonished in a dream to be mindful of Osiris also, and to make his way to a certain *pastophorus,* who for his part must naturally have dreamt of Lucius also. After numerous difficulties, partly of a pecuniary nature, the pious sufferer receives the initiation of Osiris also. This "all-greatest of all-highest gods" goes so far as to promise his express blessings for the legal career upon which Lucius has entered, and designates him, again in a dream vision, as member of the college of *pastophori.* The author gives no details of this initiation. According to his own statement, he had been initiated in most of the mysteries in Greece; but he clearly sets the greatest weight upon those of the Isiac circle of gods.

By far the mightiest of the secret religions was the worship of MITHRAS, which also claimed to assure redemption and immortality.

The most ancient Persian religion knew a sun-god called Mithras, and the later teaching of Zoroaster, since it could not banish him, assigned him the position of intermediary between Ormuzd and Ahriman, Light and Darkness. Mithras became the first of the heavenly *yazatas* and (with reference to the setting sun) also protector of the realm of the dead; he judged the souls upon the bridge Djinevat. But above all he was the protector of earth, of agriculture, of fertility, whose symbol—the bull—was associated with him from hoary antiquity. Numerous invocations to him are preserved in the Zend-Avesta.

But it is a mistake to expect that the characteristics of this ancient Mithras of the orthodox Persians are to be found unchanged in the Mithras of the declining Roman Empire. The later and powerful effect of Babylonian beliefs upon Persian had already made Mithras a sun-god and the head of the planetary world. Furthermore, the tradition which reached the Romans was heretical from the outset; that is, it proceeded from a religious faction in the Persian Kingdom which was hostile to the Magi. It was finally received at second hand and apparently much confused, specifically upon the occasion of the war of annihilation which Pompey the Great waged against the pirates who were mostly natives of Cilicia. These, we are told, celebrated various secret rituals and also introduced that of Mithras, which continued in being thereafter. Somehow or other, this fragment of Persian religion in half-Assyrian transformation took hold in Asia Minor. Mithras scholarship is overrich in curious hypotheses, and we must beware of adding to the number needlessly. Yet the experts may allow us one question: Was it among the Cilician pirates that Mithras-worship first took on that aspect of a martial religion of robbers which later made it so suitable as a Roman warrior religion? In any case, the Cilicians traveled widely as slave dealers, and they took their cult with them.

Numerous reliefs, some of very large scale, found in most of the collections of antiquities in Europe, present the enigmatic myth, but without explaining it. Their artistic merit is slight, and they are at best hardly older than the Antonines. A cave is to be seen, over which the ascending and descending chariot of the sun, or the sun and moon together, is indicated. In the cave a youth in Phrygian costume—Mithras himself—kneels upon a bull into whose throat he thrusts a dagger. From the bull's tail spring ears of grain; a dog leaps upon the bull, a serpent licks his blood, a scorpion gnaws at his genitals. At either side stands a torchbearer, one with raised and the other with lowered torch. Over Mithras there appears a raven, customarily the bird of prophecy, perhaps also to be interpreted as the bird of battlefields. A lion's head, which is sometimes seen in the right-hand corner, may also be a symbol of light, of the sun. We pass over numerous other additions which occur on individual Mithras stones.

The original significance of these symbols has been demonstrated with fair certainty. In the first place it is the victory of the sun-hero over the bull, which represents the moon or the quick alternations of time in general, which must die that a new year may be born. The grain is the year's fertility, the dog indicates devouring Sirius, the scorpion the autumn (that is, the approaching death of nature). The torchbearers (sometimes explained as morning and evening star) represent the equinoxes. The reliefs on either side and above the cave, which occur on certain specially rich examples, are now explained in part as astral and elemental events; previously it was thought they represented individual stages in the secret initiations. But much is still unexplained. That all of these things retained a higher significance from the ancient Persian period is obvious.

The meaning which the late Roman period associated with these figures was a far cry from their original significance. Fortunately, inscriptions provide a plain hint; they read "To the unconquered god, Mithras," "To the unconquered sun, Mithras," "To the sun, the unconquered," and the like. The last form, incidentally, is one of the most frequent formulae on the coins of Constantine the Great, who throughout his life, perhaps, never completely detached himself from the externals of the Mithras-worship. The unconquered was doubtless at the same time the giver of victory, and thus peculiarly appropriate as a war-god; recent researches suggest that this was at least a secondary function of Mithras even in his ancient Persian form. Finally Mithras is the guide of souls which he leads from the earthly life into which they had fallen back up to the light from which they issued. This notion is taken up by the sentiment common in the later Roman world; it was not only from the religions and the wisdom of Orientals and Egyptians, even less from Christianity, that the notion that life on earth was merely a transition to a higher life was derived by the Romans. Their own anguish and the awareness of senescence made it plain enough that earthly existence was all hardship and bitterness. Mithras-worship became one, and perhaps the most significant, of the religions of redemption in declining paganism.

But ancient man experienced a feeling of misery without at the same time experiencing a sense of sin. Hence remission by words profited him little; he required redemption of a quite special character. To be able to attach himself to the savior-god, each individual must become his own redeemer through terrible voluntary suffering, which was a far more serious element here than in all other mysteries. And so the Mithraic initiations developed so-called trials, compared to which the *taurobolium* and the trials of Isis were mere child's play. What confronts us here was certainly not merely a device to discourage those not truly "called" and the masses generally; it was called "castigations," and must have cost many a candidate his life. These castigations involved eighty separate steps, such as fasting for fifty days, swimming a wide circle, touching fire, lying in snow up to twenty days, torments of all sorts, being scourged for two days, lying on a torture bench, enduring painful postures, another fast in the desert, and others. Seven various degrees of initiation are named, but their order is not certain; they include the degrees of raven, warrior, and lion, and the highest initiates were called Fathers. We do not know at which of these degrees the individual ceremonies were carried out which Christian contemporaries call simply sacraments. At the lion degree the celebrant washed his hands in honey and vowed to keep them pure of all misdeeds. Somewhere bread and a cup of water were used, and there was a bath which purified from sin. Then a garland tossed from a sword was aimed at the head of the "Mithras-warrior," which he was required to block with his hand and press down upon his shoulder, because Mithras himself was his garland and crown.

In view of the numerous Emperors, courtiers, and notable personages who participated in this cult, it has been persistently maintained that these imitations and castigations were not taken literally and that much of them had been reduced to symbolic gesture or even to mere verbal formula. Who could have bidden a Commodus, for example, to submit to those strange torments? Were not the hierophants of the various mysteries complaisant to important people generally? But our accounts of the actuality of the castigations are far too definite to be brushed aside with mere hypotheses. One thing may be freely admitted:

since there was no common hierarchy to preserve and guide the cult, ritual usages may have taken on different forms in different parts of the Empire. So far as they are known to the present writer, the Mithras stones which contain a large number of pictures and reliefs at the sides and over the cave have all been found on the Rhine, in Tyrol, and in Transylvania; they come from Heddernheim not far from Frankfurt, Neuenheim near Heidelberg, Osterburken between Neckar and Tauber, Apuleum not far from Karlsburg, Sarmizegethusa, also in Transylvania. There is a very important specimen from Mauls in the Tyrol, now in Vienna; here two registers of small pictures at the sides of the main relief contain scenes which were thought to represent the various initiatory tortures: standing in snow and in water, the bed of torment, singeing by fire, and others. Different explanations may now be offered, but it is enough for us to notice that in these regions a circumstantial language of pictures was felt to be necessary for reasons which are now completely unknown. The many stones found in Italy, on the other hand, have nothing of this character. The individual lodges of the order (if one remembers not to take the loose expression too precisely) may have differed from one another substantially in admission, doctrine, and cult. The monuments enumerated above mostly derive from the third century, a period of ferment for paganism which, sensing its internal dissolution, sought, at least partially, to restore and intensify itself and in places developed a sudden fanaticism. It may well be that beside local differentiations, differences of time were also a factor.

The Mithras stones north of the Alps and the Danube which have been mentioned derive in all probability, and partly demonstrably, from Roman soldiers. What part did the initiate take in the daily life of the camp? How was this religious service related to the military and political duties of higher officers? Did it constitute an effectual bond among them? Did the religion contribute morally to the spiritual regeneration of Roman character in the second half of the third century? All of these questions must remain unanswered as long as our only sources of knowledge are the few passages in authors who are mostly Christian. The site of the finds of Mithras stones are caves, natural or artificial, and occasionally free-standing buildings, often only a few feet square, whose rear wall was occupied by the relief. The space could accommodate only a few people at most; if a crowd attended it must be thought of as standing outside. Even the large Mithreum at Heddernheim is less than forty feet long; its width of twenty-five feet is largely obstructed by adjacent cells, so that a passage of only eight feet is left. In the small Mithreum at Neuenheim, eight feet square, the interior was blocked by altars and statues of related deities, as for example Hercules, Jupiter, Victoria, and there were also implements, lamps, and other fragments. Structural additions such as richly decorated pillars and the like show that these sanctuaries did not need to keep hidden. Who would have dared desecrate them? The soldiers who performed their secret worship there were masters of the world.

The Mithras cave at Rome (which was on the declivity of the Capitoline hill) is to be thought of as much larger and more magnificent, as were doubtless those in the other great cities of the Empire. In Alexandria the sanctuary was deep underground. When it was excavated in Christian times for the foundations of a church there were still current dark stories of many murders which had been perpetrated on the site, and in fact the "castigations" may have cost many an initiate his life. When actual skulls were found they were wrongly ascribed to victims who had been slaughtered for the sake of inspecting their entrails and for conjuring the dead. Mithras-worship had nothing to do with such proceedings, but the Egyptian imagination, as we shall presently see, had always been filled with such cruelties.

About a hundred reliefs and inscriptions show that this worship had spread over the entire Empire. Thousands of others may yet lie underground, and it is to be hoped that their excavation will be as competent as those at Heddernheim, Neuenheim, and Osterburken. The content of a single well-preserved Mithras cave may well throw conclusive light upon this most remarkable of all ancient secret cults.

But in any case this cult was not unaffected by the great stream of other contemporary superstitions. In the first place, there were many who could not get enough of mysteries and therefore sought assurance of three-formed Diana, the *taurobolium* of the Great Mother, the Bacchic cults, Isis worship, and Mithras alike—a fusion of all pagan occult worship which became the rule in the course of the fourth century, but was surely not unusual in the earlier period. As the doctrine of the unity of all divine nature became a factor, men naturally grew indifferent to sharp distinctions among individual cults, so that one freely borrowed from the others. Neoplatonic philosophy entered into the Mithras religion as into all mysteries, and to Porphyry, one of its most distinguished devotees, we owe virtually our only treatment of the subject in a pagan source. But Porphyry's essay *On the Grotto of the Nymphs* deals not so much with the contemporary state of the worship as with its original significance, and that in a one-sided and capriciously symbolizing aspect in the interests of his school. We learn that the grotto is a symbol of the cosmos or universe; therefore Zoroaster had dedicated a flowery and well-watered cave in the mountains of Persia in honor of Mithras, creator and guide of the world. In this first cave the symbols of world elements and zones were employed; and from this cave all subsequent cave mysteries issued. On the other hand the entire essay is linked to the grotto in Ithaca described by Homer (*Odyssey* 13, 102–112, 346 ff.), and Porphyry had made that the focus of his symbolism. Porphyry follows the footless manner of seeking to find identity in myths and of always associating one echo with another. But isolated individual hints are of great value, as for example when he assigns the northern and southern gate of his world cave to the souls who descend to earth for birth and ascend to the gods at death, to genesis and apogenesis, and when he refers in general to the life and the purification of souls.

Finally there was a natural relationship with Mithras in

the person of the Greco-Roman sun-god, whether he was thought of as Apollo, or as Sol or Helios apart from Apollo. We can probably never know how far Mithras was merged with this sun-god; perhaps Sol Invictus, who appears more frequently on coins and inscriptions after the middle of the third century, is everywhere to be taken as Mithras, even though he is openly represented only as the sun-god. The sun-worship of the early Emperors, as for example of Elagabalus, may have derived from a Semitic cult; in the case of Aurelian we are still completely in the dark as to the character of his religion. His mother was priestess of the sun at a place on the lower Danube, and it is not impossible that she was one of the female devotees of Mithras of whom there is scattered mention, perhaps a "lioness." On the other hand, when the Temple of the Sun at Palmyra was plundered, Aurelian commanded its restoration by one of his generals, and added, "I will write to the Senate and petition it to send a pontifex to reconsecrate the temple." This implies the customary Roman rite, though it is a sanctuary of a Semitic Baal which is involved. But in Rome itself Aurelian built a large and magnificent Temple of the Sun in which he deposited fifteen thousand pounds of gold (for surely it was to this temple and none other that the gift was made); and this building backed onto the Quirinal hill in such a fashion that the possibility of a Mithraic significance is not to be brushed aside. For Mithras was and remained "the god from the rock," and all his sacred sites must therefore have something of the character of a cave, even if the cave is not to be taken essentially as the symbol of the phenomenal world. We have already mentioned that the slaughter of the bull which appears in monuments takes place in a cave. Sol Invictus occurs on Aurelian's coin. The relationship of succeeding Emperors to the Mithras cult is a matter of uncertainty; we shall have to return to this point in our treatment of Constantine.

It may seem odd to follow our discussion of the Mithras cult with MANICHAEISM, which made its way into the Roman Empire from Persia, because Manichaeism does not belong with the mysteries. But Manichaeism is not to be

regarded merely as a Christian sect, but rather as a special
religion of redemption predominantly pagan. Whether it
assumed more of a Roman-pagan character in Roman hands
than it could have had in the Sassanid Kingdom is a matter
for further investigation, as is its subsequent invasion of the
Christian Church. Its dualism is specifically at variance with
classical belief, in that it resolves everything into pure symbols through which the two great basic principles, light and
darkness, God and matter, express themselves. The highest
concept, the Christ of this system (with patent reference to
Mithras), is world soul, son of eternal light, and redeemer,
but hardly a person; his historic manifestation was thought
of as a phantom. Consequently, redemption is not a single
act, such as an immolation, but is continuous; out of the
morally unfree state of struggle between spirit and matter
(or between the good and the evil soul) Christ constantly
helps the individual man upwards to the realm of light. It
is difficult to determine how near these ideas approach to
a strictly conceived personal immortality; the "basic epis-
tle" of the sect, in any event, speaks of an "eternal and
glorious life," and it was presumably this promise which
impressed the Roman proselyte most. Further discussion of
this remarkable system is not appropriate at this place.

Mani, the founder of Manichaeism, had himself sent
forth apostles, and despite all persecution had left the beginnings of a hierarchy in his community. Barely ten or
twenty years after his martyrdom (272–275) his doctrine
was spread abroad in the Roman Empire. An imperial re-
script (287 or 296) to Julian, Proconsul of Africa, shows
that this was the case in Africa Proconsularis. Considerable
disorders must have occurred there at the instigation of the
new sect, and it was known that its attitude, like that of
several Oriental religions, was not peaceful toward Rome
but rather exclusive, and it was moreover doubly suspicious
and despised because of its Persian origin. Diocletian's
measures were drastic; he ordered that the founders together with their books be burned and that other participants should either be put to death, or (if they had the
rank of *honorati* or held other positions of dignity) be sent
to the mines and their property confiscated. The motive for

this severity was essentially the hostility of the new religion to the old; the old felt that it possessed the most sacred right as a primordial establishment of gods and men. After this striking mention we lose sight of Manichaeism for several decades. It cannot have played any great part before the death of Constantine; at least it is not mentioned by name in the great edict of heretics. It is only in the fifth century that Manichaeism raises its head for a time as the most dangerous enemy to the Church.

The above discussion shows that the late pagans did not pray to the gods for fertility, wealth, and victory alone; gloomy anxiety concerning the beyond overpowered them and drove them to the most extraordinary doctrines and rites.

But this world, too, now appears in a different light. In connection with the Isis mysteries it was indicated how the laboriously achieved protection of a great divinity provided a hope of avoiding not only the destruction of the soul but also a troubled earthly destiny which depended upon the stars. We must now show how changed was the relationship of all supermundane elements to life on earth, how astrology, magic, and demonology obtained the upper hand over earlier sacrifices, oracles, and penances. These elements had always been present, and even Homer had depicted Circe as the archetype of all magic. Plato speaks of wandering miracle workers who claimed to bring blessings and curses by secret procedures; and we hear of magicians who claim to have control over weather and fertility, storm and calm. Thessaly was and continued until late in the Empire to be the classic land of love magic, by means of verbal spells as well as secret charms. Ancient Italy was hardly far behind Greece in this matter; the conjuring of the gods, for example, which worked such evil to Tullus Hostilius, had its place in the ancient Roman cult itself. The twenty-eighth and thirtieth books of Pliny are ample indication of the degree to which magic was involved in a mass of superstitious household remedies and the like. Especially well known was the magic of the Etruscans, Sabines, and Marsians, that is to say, of most of the inhabitants of central Italy. Aside from magic healing of every kind, the Romans believed that these arts could bewitch grain fields, control weather, arouse love and hate, transform persons into animals, and work other miracles. This belief is also reflected in very remarkable goblins, among others the blood-sucking lamias and Empusae. Happy was he who protected himself adequately with salutary counter-magic! To this end amulets were hung over the body from head to foot, and there was even an entire system of magic defense, of which certain individual details may be cursorily presented.

A view of the great host of details of that magical practice which have been recorded might well lead to a conviction that the entire ancient world was wholly fettered by it and rendered continually fearful in all phases of daily life. And yet these earlier isolated superstitions were far less harmful to the ancient religion; they disturbed the naïve relationship of man to divinity far less than the later *systematic* superstition which grew predominant in the Empire.

We must speak first of astrology, which was regarded as an old prerogative of the Orient and whose adepts were regularly called Chaldeans, although very few of them actually derived from the country on the lower Euphrates. At least the better known among them, Tiberius' Thrasyllus and Otho's Seleucus and Ptolemy, bore Greek names. Besides the Babylonian wisdom, reference was also made to the Egyptian, associated with the names of Petosiris and Necepso, who were regarded as the authors of the most familiar astrological writings.

Aside from the fact that the astrologers were not content with astrology alone but turned their hands to other and more fearful ways of searching out the future, astrology itself provided a very strong impulse to atheism. The consistent devotee of astrology would scorn all moral consideration and all religion, for these could provide neither comfort nor aid against the fate which was made manifest in the stars. It was the practice of this secret science primarily which loaded the Emperors of the first century with the grimmest curses. The Chaldeans were continually being banished because their wisdom could not be made an imperial prerogative, as all the world clamored for their prophecies; and they were as often summoned to return because men could no longer do without them. If one returned to Rome with the welts of the fetters which he had worn on some Aegean island, he could be certain that people would compete for his attention. The content of this science was briefly that a list of destinies was correlated with every possible position of the planets with relation to the signs of the zodiac. Everything was determined by the hour; horoscopes could be cast for the most commonplace activities, as for example a pleasure excursion or a walk to the baths, as well as for a man's whole life—if one only knew the constellation at the moment of his birth. Those who kept their eyes open could see the futility of the delusion and palpably prove it worthless, as St. Hippolytus, for instance, did. How could the constellations have any definite and consistent significance for a man's destiny when their configuration at any given hour was quite different for an observer in Mesopotamia than it was for one on the Danube or the Nile? Why do people born at the same hour not have the same destiny? Why should the constellation have more significance at birth than at conception? Why should the greatest diversity in hours of birth not be a protection against some common destruction, as in earthquakes, the sacking of cities, storms at sea, and the like? Was the presumably sovereign fate of the stars to be extended to flies, worms, and other vermin? Might there not be—the question was put with some intimation of the true answer—more planets than were then known? And finally all reasonable people agreed that it was no blessing to know the future, and in any case the reverse of a blessing to have false notions concerning it.

But no reasonable grounds in the world could extirpate this alleged science among a people which even during the bloom of its culture was alien to the idea of a divine world order and an all-embracing system of moral purpose, and which now more than ever was confused by uncertainty and apprehension concerning the great questions of life. The need for superstition was grown the more desperate in the degree that the natural energy with which the individual confronts fate had disappeared. In the late Empire astrology sought to acquire an ethical content in the same remarkable way as did the secret cults referred to above. We have valid evidence for this transformation in the *Eight Books of Mathesis* of the pagan Firmicus Maternus, who wrote shortly after the death of Constantine. At the end of the second book of this complete theory of the religion of the stars there is a long and solemn admonition to the astrologer, calculated to minimize the compromising, sinister, and dismal elements in its practice. The *mathematicus* (as the astrologer was called) must lead a godly life, because his converse was with the gods. He must show himself accessible, righteous, not avid. He must give his responses openly and inform the inquirer in advance that his answers would be plainly uttered in order to prevent inadmissible and immoral questions. He must have wife and children and respectable friends and acquaintances; he must have no secret associations but show himself among people. He must keep away from all quarrels and accept no inquiries which involve injury or destruction to anyone to satisfy hate or vengeance. He must always behave as a man of honor, and must not combine any usurious money transactions with his calling—which implies that many disreputable astrologers must have done so. He must neither give nor require oaths, especially in money matters. He must endeavor to exert a beneficial influence upon erring people in his environment, and in general to guide passionate people to the proper path not only formal responses from the stars but also by friendly counsel. He should avoid nocturnal sacrifices and ceremonies, public as well as private. He should also avoid the games of the Circus, so that no one should think that the victory of the Greens or the Blues was connected with his presence. Questions concerning paternity, always troublesome, and inquiries concerning the horoscope of third parties, should be answered reluctantly and hesitatingly, so that it should not appear that fault is being found with a man for actions determined by evil stars. The word *"decretum,"* decree, is a constantly recurring technical term.

For the most dangerous imposition on astrologers, which

often caused the destruction of themselves and their clients
during the first two centuries of the Empire, were inquiries
concerning the fate of the Emperor. Alexander the Great
had not taken inquiries concerning his fate amiss, but had
praised them; now the matter was far more ominous. The
throne of the Caesars, with no dynastic succession, was
besieged by ambitious people who wished to know from
the stars when and how the Emperor would die and who
would succeed him. But astrologic theory had found a way
to avoid this question. Firmicus Maternus explains that
nothing could be known about the fate of the Emperor because that matter was not subject to the stars but directly
guided by supreme divinity. As ruler of the world the Emperor held the rank of one of the many daimones who had
been set over the world by deity as creating and preserving
powers, and hence the stars, which represented a lower
potency, could say nothing concerning the Emperor. The
haruspices were in the same situation when it was a matter of determining imperial fate by inspection of entrails;
they purposely disturbed veins and fibers in order not to
be compelled to deliver a response. But in the fourth century these concessions were not of much help to astrology;
bound up as it was with all other kinds of superstitions, it
was opposed alike by the throne and by Christianity, and
along with magic and other secret arts succumbed to general prohibitions and persecutions. Space does not permit
an abstract of Firmicus' doctrinal system, nor would any
modern take the pains to read it through unless he himself
is a victim of the same delusion—or unless he means to produce a new edition of the author, which in view of the
scarcity of older editions might be timely. The secrets
proper, for whose preservation the author demands a
solemn oath before the highest God of his addressee
(Mavortius Lallianus, a high official), are contained in the
last two books. These are indices of those constellations
which determine whether a man is to be a murderer, commit incest, be a cripple, or become a gladiator, lawyer,
slave, foundling, and so forth. A logical consequence of
this odious delusion would be the disappearance of any
moral considerations, and doubtless that was the intention

of the earlier unscrupulous Chaldeans. But the newly aroused morality had become so far effective that the author of the Constantinian period must endeavor to find some moral reconciliation, which might indeed have been for him more than a mere manner of speech. He expresses the belief (Book I, Chapter 3) that even the most fearful decrees of the stars may be countered by much prayer and diligent worship of the gods; Socrates, for example, was doomed by the stars to endure all passions and bore his fate visibly in his countenance, yet by his virtues he mastered them all. "For that which we suffer and which pricks us with burning torches [that is, the passions], belongs to the stars; but our own powers of resistance belong to the godliness of the spirit." The misfortunes of the good and the good fortune of the evil are primarily the effect of the stars. But this solace still seems to be merely an external attachment to the system, of little force in comparison to the precisely systematized theory of nonsense presented in several hundred folio pages. The system begins by distributing individual temperaments and bodily members among the seven planets, and complexions, tastes, climates, regions, positions in life, and illnesses among the twelve heavenly signs. The Crab, for example, signifies sharp salty taste, light and whitish color, water animals and creeping things, the seventh zone, still or flowing water, mediocrity, and all diseases of the heart and the diaphragm. On the other hand, the astrologer is not concerned with races and national characters; it is enough for him that individuals are conditioned by the stars. The numerous other curiosities which occur here and there in the book need not detain us here.

At various points in this system there is mention of a supreme god to whom all other superhuman beings are subject as mere intermediary powers. Could not philosophy grasp the concept of this god once and for all and present a reasonable theism?

It is a humbling testimony to the human spirit's want of freedom in the face of great historical forces that, precisely here, contemporary philosophy, represented in part by truly noble personalities and equipped with all the science of the ancient world, lost itself in shadowy byways, and that we can find no other classification for it, at least at the beginning of the fourth century, than as an intermediate between two kinds of superstition, though it does mark an advance in questions of ethics.

Parallel to the spiritual transformation noticeable after the end of the second century is the dying out of the ancient philosophical schools. Epicureans, Cynics, Peripatetics, and the others disappear—even the Stoics, whose temper was so closely allied to the best aspects of Roman character. Along with a highly developed theoretical skepticism, the open mockery of a Lucian proclaimed the meaninglessness of sectarian distinction. At the same time, as a reaction, a new doctrine, more dogmatic than all earlier philosophies and hence in certain respects in harmony with the new religious movement, waited at the door. This was NEOPLATONISM. Neoplatonism was preceded by an extraordinary affection for Oriental superstitions and by diligent investigations of the records of the ancient school of Pythagoras, which had long fallen into desuetude and whose wisdom was likewise believed to be of Oriental origin; otherwise the essential elements for the new structure were borrowed from the Platonic system itself. Plotinus, the protagonist of the school in the middle period of the third century, stands forth as a significant thinker, and offers the system with its impulse to mysticism as a possible advance over the old skepticism which had previously held the field. There is something of truth and even more of poetry in the doctrine of the emergence of all things from God in determined descending degrees of being, according to greater or lesser admixture of the material. No system assigned a higher position to the human soul; it is an immediate emanation from Divine Being and may at times completely unite with Divine Being and thus become exalted above all commonplace life and thought. Here, however, we are not so much interested in the doctrine of the school as in the practical attitude, moral as well as specifically religious, which Neoplatonism conferred upon or permitted its disciples. We see repeated here a phenomenon old and new, in which a speculative system, contrary to opinion, becomes only the bond, the accidental cohesive force, but in no sense the dominant central point for tendencies and forces which would have been present even without its contribution.

This latest philosophic sect of antiquity, it must be noticed at once, shows no advance whatever in the direction of monotheism, which was far more developed in many earlier thinkers than in the "One," the "absolute One," or whatever other novel designation was given to the supreme deity or prime being which was conceived as having consciousness, but in a pantheistic manner, as immanent in the world. All of polytheism, furthermore, was included in the system in the form of a belief in daimones who, as subordinate deities, held dominion over individual countries, nature, and conditions of life. Daimones had always been present in Greek religions, but in varying form, more or less distinguished from the gods at different periods, and early woven into a theological system, not without some violence, by philosophers. Later popular belief regularly attributed to them a sinister and ghostly character and considered them at times as avengers of evil and as protectors, but predominantly as senders of sickness. Neoplatonic philosophy, as we shall see, conceived of them as demiurgic intermediary beings.

The ancient gods thus became superfluous, unless they were daimonized and included in the ranks of these lesser powers. Of the popular mythology, naturally, no more use could be made, and so the myths were interpreted as shells for physical, religious, and moral truths. Some of the explanations were fantastically involved, as was the case with Euhemerism, of which this tendency is the obverse. In its teaching concerning the human soul the system, though it places the soul high as a divine emanation, does not go as far as eternal blessedness but only to migration of souls. In the case of the best souls, however, this belief is modified to allocation to definite stars; we have seen that survivors sometimes thought they could determine the star appropriate to the departed. Indeed, glimpses of blessedness were sometimes vouchsafed to the initiates, but only very rarely to the earlier and better among them, who believed they had visions of God.

More essential than this theosophy, indeed a significant sign of the country, is the confluence of Neoplatonism with the tendency toward morality and asceticism characteristic of the period. This is sometimes contrasted, as something specifically Christian, with the free morality of antiquity, just as Christian other-worldliness is contrasted with the ancient concern with this world; but there is little justification for such contrast when one examines the paganism of the third century. Here, too, we recognize a remarkable premonition or reflection of what the following century would bring.

Specifically Neoplatonism sets up pagan ideals, the biographies of favored friends of the gods who, practicing absolute abstinence, traveled about among all of the famous peoples of antiquity, studied their wisdom and their mysteries, and through their constant intercourse with the deity developed into miracle-workers and superhuman beings. The career of the divine Plato was too well and precisely known for such treatment to be given him, though the school always regarded him with the veneration due a daimon; a certain Nicagoras of Athens, for example, who visited the wonders of Egypt in the age of Constantine, wrote his name in the crypts at Thebes with the prayer, "Be gracious to me here also, Plato!" But Pythagoras was remote enough in the mythical distance to invite a reworking of his career. Such a reworking was undertaken by Iamblichus (in the age of Constantine), after his immediate predecessor Porphyry had described Pythagoras in a more reasonable historical manner. On the other hand, the life of the miracle-worker Apollonius of Tyana, though it fell in the first century after Christ, was sufficiently mysterious and extraordinary to be worked into a tendentious romance; that task was undertaken by Philostratus in the reign of Septimius Severus. This is not the place to analyze this very remarkable book; we can only call attention to the peculiar compromise concluded between ancient Greek subjectivity and Oriental taste for miracles and abstinence. The same Apollonius who goes about barefoot in a linen

garment, enjoys no animal food or wine, touches no woman,
gives away his possessions, knows all and understands all—
even the language of animals—appears in the midst of famine and insurrection like a god, works miracle upon miracle,
exorcises demons, and raises the dead—this same Apollonius practices without restraint the Greek cult of personality and occasionally shows the self-conscious vanity of
an affected sophist. He is of good family and handsome
figure, speaks pure Attic, and had mastered all systems as
a boy. He receives homage of all sorts with the greatest
dignity. He realizes very early that he has reached the
point where he need no longer investigate but only com-
municate the results of his investigations to others. There
is as yet no trace of humility; on the contrary, the holy
man endeavors to humble others, and anyone who laughs
at his discourses is declared to be possessed and is accordingly exorcised. Many details of this picture were borrowed by Iamblichus a century later to enrich his ideal
portrait of Pythagoras, which otherwise rests upon more or
less genuine ancient tradition. In order to show himself as
"a soul guided by Apollo" or even as Apollo incarnate in
human form, Pythagoras is now made not only to lead an
ascetic life but to perform miracles, to swoop down from
Carmel to the seacoast, to conjure animals, to be in several
places simultaneously, and much else of the same character.

The models for these personified ideals of conspicuous asceticism must obviously be sought in the penitents of various Oriental religions, from the Jewish Nazarites and
Therapeutae to the abstaining Magi of Persia and the fakirs
of India, who were quite well known to the Greeks as gym-
nosophists. But the doctrine of the fall of the human soul,
which might theoretically lead to morality, of its being
rendered impure by matter and of the necessity of its purification, is likewise Oriental and indeed most likely of Indian origin. However, neither penitence nor its speculative
basis could have found entry from the East if the popular
mood had not already been affected by a similar movement. Certain remarkable contacts of this system with

Christianity, indeed reciprocal influence of one upon the other, were inevitable.

And now this school which called itself by Plato's name was drawn into the mustiest of all superstitions and at times completely reduced to actual magic and theurgy. In the great hierarchy of being emanating from God, spirit works upon spirit and spirit upon nature by ways of magic, and the initiate possessed the key to this magic. Works of this nature credited to half-mythical thaumaturgists, to a Pythagoras or an Apollonius, were henceforward believed to be within the scope of contemporary practitioners. Neoplatonists functioned as rhetors, sophists, educators, secretaries, as the philosophers had done in the early Empire; but in the midst of such activity they sometimes suddenly arose to conjure gods, daimones, and souls, to work miraculous cures, and to perpetrate occult impostures of various sorts.

In the Egyptian Plotinus (205–270), the noblest of the school, this aspect was not especially prominent. His impeccable morals and his asceticism, to which he also inspired others, including many distinguished Romans, of themselves vouchsafed him the gift of clairvoyance and prophecy; he proceeded to conjuring, as it appears, only under duress. He became the object of superhuman reverence, and as long as there were pagans "his altars never grew cold." In his disciple, the Phoenician Porphyry (born 233), there is to be noticed even an express disapproval of magic; he questioned the whole daimonology of his school, which regarded him with suspicion in consequence. His objections were followed by a reply, known under the inaccurate title *Of the Mysteries of the Egyptians,* perhaps equally inaccurately ascribed to the Coelesyrian Iamblichus, who was regarded as the head of the school under Constantine, or possibly the work of the Egyptian Abammon. In ancient India and also in the Germanic Middle Ages we encounter the frequently grandiose mysticism of a more or less conscious pantheism; here, on the contrary, we have a mysticism of polytheism, even though its gods have paled to daimones of various degrees without definite personality. How these spirits are to be worshiped, to be invoked, to be differentiated, how the whole life of god-beloved sages is to be devoted to the practices of cults of this nature, is in brief the content of the whole sorry concoction, and in the fourth century the general tendency of the school is all too clearly canted to such corruption; indeed it recognized in theurgy an essential weapon in the struggle against Christianity. Henceforward the Platonic elements in its doctrine and speculation are merely an appendage.

A cursory glance at the system of exorcism is not out of place here. The possibility of exorcism rests upon the transfiguration of the soul of the exorciser into an absolutely dispassionate state and its inward union with the relevant spiritual being raised to the point of identity. It is not so much that the spirit is summoned down by conjuration or compulsion as that the soul rises upward to it. Even external objects employed in the exorcism are not merely symbols but have a mystical relationship with the relevant divine element. There is mention, indeed, of the "One," the self-sufficing supreme God, but very few may achieve union with him, and the individual may attain such union only after he has worshiped the daimones and united with them. The rungs of spiritual beings, borrowed in part from Jewish theology, are in descending sequence: God, gods, archangels, angels, daimones, dominions, heroes, lords, and souls. Souls are completely individual; as the rungs ascend, the spirits approach even closer to unity or essence. All eight rungs are classified in a large table according to form, kind, changeability, aspect, beauty, speed, size, brilliance, and the like. More important are their capacities and gifts with reference to man. The gods purify souls completely and vouchsafe health, virtue, righteousness, and long life. Archangels do the same, but not so completely or permanently. Angels free souls from the bonds of matter and bestow similar gifts, but more in special senses. Daimones draw souls downwards to natural things, burden the body, send diseases, punishments, and the like. Heroes lead souls to preoccupation with sensually perceptible things and arouse them to great and noble deeds, but otherwise behave like daimones. Dominions hold the direction of

worldly matters and bestow worldly goods and the necessities of life. Lords belong to the wholly material realm and
bestow only earthly gifts. Souls, finally, when they appear,
promote propagation, but their conduct varies greatly, according to their merit. Each spirit appears with a retinue
of the next following rung, archangels with angels, and so
on. Good daimones bring their benefactions along with
them; avenging daimones exhibit likenesses of future torments; evil daimones come with raving animals. All of these
spirits have their appropriate bodies, but are independent
of them in the degree of their position on the ladder. If an
error is committed in the ritual, evil spirits appear in the
place of those summoned, assuming their form; the priest
may recognize them by their proud ostentation. But a ritual
correctly executed has its effect even if the conjurer is not
an initiate, "for it is not knowledge that unites the sacrificer with the god, otherwise mere philosophers would
obtain this honor exclusively." There is a striking inconsistency between the sacramental indifference concerning the
celebrant and the requirement of freedom from passion and
other preparations of the soul referred to above; but there
are even greater inconsistencies elsewhere in this book.

Next we learn something of the external apparatus and
the formulae required. In contrast to other Neoplatonic
teaching, which admits only bloodless sacrifice, here, by an
obviously Egyptian addition, each god is required to have
the sacrifice of the animal over which he presides and with
which he therefore has a magical relationship. Use is also
made of stones, herbs, incense, and the like. The bad manners of certain Egyptian conjurers, their crude threats to the
gods, are expressly discouraged; such behavior is effective
only with certain slighter daimones, and was altogether
avoided by the Chaldeans. Similarly, the magic script
which some employed could at best produce only slight
and blurred appearances, and furthermore demoralized the
conjurer, who might then easily fall into the power of evil
and deceptive daimones.

Let us step out of this cloud of delusion for a moment
to ask how far objective actuality may have gone in these
appearances; for we are not dealing with purely imaginary

images. We know that exorcisms of the 18th century made
great use of the magic lantern, whose images were reflected on heavy vapors which had a narcotic effect. Something similar took place in the incantations at the time of
Porphyry. There is express mention of an art which permitted phantoms of the gods to appear in the air at favorable moments by means of certain vapors produced by fire.
Iamblichus, or Abammon, admits no deception even in this
slighter form of conjuration, although it is not without a
genuine magic effect; but he states that phantoms of this
sort which must vanish as soon as the vapor disperses were
but little regarded by priests who had ever seen authentic
divine figures; magic, then, could only touch an outward
shell, a mere shadow of the deity. But there can be no
doubt that deception was practiced over long periods and
in great volume. We shall not unqualifiedly include as pure
deception the use of a child for the interpretation of the
appearance and for prophecy, for Apuleius, whom we do
not regard as a deceiver, believed in it. Apuleius believed
that the simple childish soul was peculiarly fit to be transformed to a semi-conscious state (*sorporari*) by means of
formulae and incense, and that it could thus approach its
real—that is, divine—nature closely enough to foretell the
future. He cites Varro for the revelation of the end of the
Mithradatic war obtained by the inhabitants of Tralles by
means of a boy who saw an image of Mercury in a vessel
of water (a real image placed in the vessel or only a mi-
rage?—*puerum in aqua simulacrum Mercurii contem-
plantem*) and then described the future in one hundred
and sixty verses. But at the beginning of the third century
St. Hippolytus in his *Refutation of the Heresies* unmasks a
large number of hoaxes worked by prestidigitators. Here
again we find the use of a boy as an unhappy victim, but
lulled into a deep sleep, as was later done by Cagliostro at
Mitau, and made to rave. But mainly, what was done to
clients was pure mockery. Their inquiries to gods, written,
as they thought, in invisible ink, could be read by the
conjurers by chemical means and appropriate responses
could be prepared. When it was a matter of the appearance of a desired daimon, the conjurers clearly reckoned

on their clients' being well content, "swinging laurel and crying loud" in a dark chamber, if nothing appeared. It could not be expected, they were given to understand, that the divine should make itself visible; enough that it was present. The boy must then report what the daimones said, that is, what the conjurer whispered to him through a cleverly contrived tube. Balls of incense, in which explosive materials or materials which would produce a blood-red glow were included, and alum, which would make the embers on the altar seem to move when it liquefied, must have aided the illusion. Finally, some completely unintelligible oracle was kept in readiness for the curious. Much of what we are told has remained in the repertory not only of conjurers but of ordinary jugglers down to our own time: coloring eggs on the inside, or tricks with fire, either placing a hand in it, or walking upon it, or spitting it out of the mouth. More serious are recipes for leaving seals apparently unbroken on documents whose contents it is desired to know. Conjuring proper appears here and there among these tricks. Goats and rams drop dead by occult means; lambs even commit suicide. A house (treated with the juice of a certain sea creature) appears to be in flames. Thunder is produced artificially.* Writing appears on the liver of a sacrificial victim (because the cheat has written in reverse with strong ink on his left hand, on which the liver is placed). A skull lying on the ground speaks and then disappears—because it was made of a skin on modeled wax, which collapsed as near-by heated coals had their effect; the speaking was managed by a hidden accomplice through a tube fashioned out of a crane's esophagus. Moonlight could be kept ready unnoticed until all other lights were extinguished; a beam from a hidden light illuminated a water basin on the ground, and this was reflected in a mirror on the ceiling. At other times a hole in the ceiling was filled with a tambourine, and to this an accomplice in the upper chamber applied a light at a given signal after removing its cover. Even simpler was a lamp in a narrow

---

* Unfortunately, a recipe for an earthquake is incompletely preserved in the ms.

vessel, which would throw a round beam upon the ceiling. The star-studded heaven could be simulated by fish scales pasted on the ceiling; these would gleam if the room were even dimly lighted. We come now to the actual appearances of the gods, which the conjurers took quite lightly, for they could count on the terror and obedience of their clients. In the dark of a moonless night, in the open, the conjurer would show Hecate flying through the air, when his accomplice, as soon as the formula was pronounced, would release an unlucky chicken hawk wrapped in burning tow; the client had been bidden, the moment he saw a fiery object whirring through the air, to cover his face and fall silently to the ground. The appearances of a fiery Asclepius, for example, were more artfully contrived. A figure of Asclepius in high relief and perhaps life-size was modeled upon a wall and covered with highly inflammable material; at the instant the conjurer uttered his hexameter this was ignited and burned brightly for a few moments. To show animated gods moving about at will, finally, was more complicated and more expensive. The only solution for this problem was a cellar chamber in which costumed supers walked about. In the chamber above the believers looked through a large water basin fixed in the ground; the basin was of stone, but its bottom was glass.

Frequently, then, the appearances involved not ecstasies and hallucinations but objective actualities. Whether, besides simple charlatans, there were serious theurgists who employed delusions, but only as devout piety, remains a question; another is whether Iamblichus (or whoever wrote the treatise we have cited) intended his work for such devout practitioners.

Besides exorcisms, that author provides information on other problems in the realm of the supernatural also. In the matter of divinely sent dreams, for example, he tells us that they come not in sound sleep but that in a state of half or complete wakefulness a man will hear short whispered words, "Do this or that"; he will feel himself surrounded by a spiritual movement and sometimes see a pure and calm light. The prophetic significance of ordinary dreams, on the other hand, is reckoned very low. Individuals who are divinely inspired are said generally to live a divine, no longer animal, life, and hence feel neither fire nor pricks nor other tortures. Furthermore, the divine presence may affect only the soul or only individual members of the body, so that some dance and sing, others rise erect, hover in the air, even seem to be surrounded by fire; divine voices, sometimes clear and sometimes soft, are heard the while. Much lower stand the voluntary magic incitements induced by kinds of incense, potions, formulae, and the like, so that one perceives things hidden and things to be in water, in the clear night air, or on certain walls covered with sacred symbols. But so strong a current of premonition and prophecy runs through the entire visible world—that is, the system was so loath to forgo different popular superstitions—that it was possible to read the future in pebbles, reeds, wood, grain, even in the utterances of the insane. The flight of birds too is directed by divine powers to provide signs, so that even this proverbial freedom is rendered unfree. Ordinary astrology was looked down upon contemptuously as a futile by-way, even as error, for it was not the constellations and the elements which determined destiny but the attitude of the world-whole at the moment the soul descended to earthly life. But this did not prevent the astrologers from entering into contact with the system, as Firmicus Maternus, for example, demonstrates in many passages. One trait, it may be noticed in passing, clearly shows the un-Greek, thoroughly barbarian, origin of this theory of conjuration, and that is the undisguised pleasure it takes in the abracadabra of foreign and especially Oriental invocations. These we learn not from Iamblichus, indeed, but from other sources, and many of them have been bequeathed to the literature of magic which circulates to this day. Foreign names are preferred not merely because they are older or because they are untranslatable, but because they possess "great emphasis," that is, they sound impressive and meaningful. Newer complaints of the impotence of many incantations are based solely on the fact that the revered ancient ritual had been altered because of Greek eagerness for innovation. "The barbarians alone are serious in manner, consistent in the formulae of prayer, and therefore dear to the gods and heard by them."

This tasteless system, though it was taken literally by perhaps only a few, nevertheless more or less dominated all the philosophy of the fourth century, and no educated pagan was completely untainted by it. From the lives of the philosophers themselves, as Eunapius tells them, superstition rises to meet us like a gray fog. Iamblichus himself, for example, lets his disciples believe that in prayer he hovers ten cubits over the ground and assumes a golden-colored appearance. At the warm baths of Gadara in Syria he summons from the two springs the genii of Eros and Anteros. They appear as boys, the one with gold and the other with shining dark hair, to the great astonishment of the disciples and companions, and nestle up to Iamblichus, until he sends them back to their springs. His disciple Aedesius, who had forgotten the hexameter which a god had intoned for him in a vision, found it written in his left hand upon awakening, and therefore prayed to the hand. The woman philosopher Sosibia of Ephesus had been brought up from childhood by two daimones who had first hired themselves out to her father in the guise of field workers; her entire later life also was conditioned by magic and divination. Other stories, some very colorful, we pass over. It is obvious that the philosophers were by no means in agreement, in life as little as in doctrine. Within the Neoplatonic school itself there is a quite early example of evil magic, which the Alexandrian Olympius sought to work upon the great Plotinus. A conjurer summons Apollo in the presence of Iamblichus and several others, but Iamblichus proves that the apparition is nothing else than the phantom ($\varepsilon \emph{ι} \delta \omega \lambda o \nu$) of a newly fallen gladiator. What one produces the other regularly declares is a trifle. The philosopher Maximus was so far successful that he caused the image in the temple of Hecate at Ephesus to smile, in the presence of many persons, and the torches in its hands to ignite of themselves; but the Carian Eusebius finds that this is nothing remarkable. In the latest period, when sinking paganism mustered all its strength, such dissensions must

have diminished. There was formed that great and confused conglomerate of philosophy, magic, and all the mysteries which gives the age of Julian its physiognomy. The
more theurgy was compelled to retire into hiding under
Constantine and his sons, the more spacious was its dominance for a short period when it enveloped with its delusions the young prince who was doomed to misfortune for
all his merit. His teacher Aedesius had said to him: "If ever
you participate in the mysteries you will be ashamed of
even having been born human." It is to be wondered, indeed, that a man so preoccupied with the world of spirits
should have developed into so competent a ruler and warrior. At this quite late period elegant Canopus on the coast
of Egypt grew into a kind of teaching center for all magic,
to be the "wellhead of daimonic activity." Attendance was
extraordinary, especially when one of Sosipatra's sons, Antoninus, settled there; Antoninus himself did not practice
theurgy but enjoyed superhuman regard as prophet and
ascetic. All who came to Canopus by land or sea to perform
their religious duties, regularly visited Antoninus and heard
his prophecies. "These temples," he frequently lamented,
"will soon become tombs"—and they did indeed, when they
were transformed to monasteries and stocked with martyrs'
relics.

A remarkable twofold effect issued from this activity. On
the one hand the system demanded moral transformation
and renunciation; on the other nothing was more calculated
to destroy the remnants of true pagan morality and religiosity than this exclusive art of conjuration, aimed only
at initiates and arrogantly oblivious of the great masses,
whose belief in their old gods and heroes it only con-
founded. For while myth was denied or interpreted alle-
gorically, the gods themselves are claimed as daimones, and
even the heroes were fitted into the system at will. When
a number of temples were searched under Constantine and
the gold and silver portions of composite idols were removed for smelting, many pagans wondered that no
daimon, no prophetic being, not even a shadowy and whis-
pering apparition was to be found in the innermost parts
of the temple or of the statues themselves. Men had

learned to separate the beautiful artistic form of the god completely from its daimonic nature. The cult of Achilles in this daimonic sense, which was intensified after the third century, deserves special mention. Achilles appears to the inhabitants of the plain of Troy, significantly enough, no longer as the ideal of heroic beauty, but as a fearful apparition.

From what has been said we may deduce the fate of late pagan monotheism. Surely there continued to be pure souls and acute thinkers who clung to the oneness of God in the spirit of earlier and better times. But with the majority this belief was disturbed by daimonic additions. The paganism of an Ammianus Marcellinus, for example, is not to be lightly esteemed, for he was one of the better spirits of the fourth century and saw through the philosophic sorcerers at the court of his hero Julian; but how qualified is his monotheism! The individual gods remain, if not directly as daimones, at least as virtually personified qualities. Nemesis is a sovereign right of the deity in action, but is called daughter of Justitia. Themis is eternal law, but was thought of personally as presiding over the auspices. Mercury is called *mundi velocior sensus,* that is, approximately, the moving principle of the universe. Finally, Fortuna still directs human destiny. Among these later pagans the supreme deity must have yielded his first quality, which is personality, to the subordinate gods and daimones, to whom the cult was then almost exclusively directed. Perhaps the supreme deity retained the greatest measure of personality among the worshipers of the sun, who referred all gods to the sun and worshiped it as the physical and spiritual principle of all existence. Constantine appears to have favored this religion, at least outwardly, although he conceived it in a Mithraic form; we shall consider this further presently. His father Constantius Chlorus is expressly credited with the worship of the one true God —unless Eusebius is again misrepresenting and idealizing ordinary Mithraism as pure monotheism. In this time of mixture of all religions, elements from Judaism may here and there have entered paganism and Parseeism, as for example among the Cappadocian Hypsistarii (that is, worshipers of the Highest God) at the beginning of the fourth century. These were true monotheists, but their influence was only provincial and so need not be considered here. Finally we find a quite worthless monotheism here and there among those who were eager to sail with every wind and to avoid all offense when Constantine's edict of toleration had moved all boundaries. Of this sort is the prayer of one of those panegyrists who have been characterized above: "We beseech thee, highest author of all things, whose names are as many as thou hast given tongues to peoples, without out knowing which name thine own will demands! Whether there be in thee a divine power and intelligence, through which, poured over the entire world, thou dost mingle with all elements and dost move thyself with no force from without; or whether thou be a power over all heavens and look down upon thine handiwork from a lofty tower; we beg and beseech thee that thou preserve this our prince forever." We see that the speaker leaves a free choice between an immanent and a transcendent god, and when he later ascribes to this indefinite supreme being omnipotence and beneficence, he straightway cancels these attributes by an impertinent closing formula: "If thou deny his merits their reward, then either thy power or thy goodness has ceased." This Gallic orator doubtless represented a large number of undecided and prudent persons who wished to see what success the edict would have.

Now that we have examined philosophic belief in daimones and its influence upon pagan monotheism, we shall have to bestow another glance upon the superstitions and magic wizardry of the transition period which belong rather to popular superstition. No sharp distinction, as we have indicated, is possible.

Many of these things are merely the continuation of earlier practices. Thus, for example, the Etruscan haruspices persisted, and indeed with increased splendor, after they had nearly died out in the first century. The haruspices were the official means for consulting the gods at the imperial court, and also enjoyed considerable private practice, at least in Italy. In the narrower sense the auspices denoted determination of the future from the entrails of animals and the flight of birds, divining of the will of heaven from lightning and even drawing lightning down, the regulation of foundations for cities, and much else of the same sort; but in the course of time they had coalesced with other superstitions, particularly with Chaldean astrology, and our authors do not always differentiate them properly from other branches of theurgy.

Neither were the oracles—that is, responses to inquiries concerning the future, issued at definite sacred sites—grown mute, although they had found formidable competitors in the itinerant conjurers. The various pagan religions throughout the Empire were at one in assuming that there were favored localities and sites where the will of the gods could be apprehended more clearly than elsewhere. In all provinces, therefore, there were oracular temples, oracular fountains, sacred clefts in the earth, grottoes, and the like, some dating from high, pre-Roman antiquity, which offered responses to every possible kind of inquiry. Sleeping in the temples of Aesculapius and of Serapis for the purpose of inciting remedial dreams belonged to this category; frequently the best society foregathered on these occasions. In any case there were no longer large, official, political consultations. Such inquirers went about with great secrecy and preferred to turn to conjurers. But if no Croesus was longer counseled in hexameters to cross the Halys, still the more reputable oracles continued to be celebrated by pilgrims of various positions and interests who brought their offerings. Pausanias visited all of those in Greece, one after the other, out of motives of piety and curiosity. For Delphi we have a series of scanty notices, but never wholly interrupted for a long period, reaching down to Constantine and then resuming. There are individual notices of Hellenic and Asia Minor oracles at Abae, Delos, Miletus, Colophon, and the like, down to a quite late period; we must not be misled by Church writers, among whom it became virtually a dogma that the oracles were reduced to silence after the birth of Christ. This is most likely to have happened in the case of the very ancient oracle of Dodona. Rome retained and still inquired from time to time of the Sibylline Books, which were generally considered to be the highest authority for the fate of the state. Nevertheless it appears that against the last consultation of these books prior to Constantine, at the time of the barbarian invasions under Aurelian, an enlightened or heretical party arose in the Senate. The favorite private oracle in the vicinity of Rome, consulted even by Emperors, was that of the majestic Temple of Fortuna at Praeneste, which looked down upon the surrounding regions from its high terraces. The oracular temples at Antium and Tibur, which were highly esteemed, were only of secondary rank as compared with the "Praenestine lots." In upper Italy the warm spring of Aponus near Padua enjoyed great credit not only for its curative powers but also for its oracles, which were communicated, at least to Claudius Gothicus, in Vergilian hexameters. The spring of Clitumnus near Spoleto, with its surroundings so charming to this day, doubtless continued to be a sacred site of this sort, as it was at the time of the Younger Pliny. In early Christian times Christian emblems were introduced on the only one of the many temples and chapels that decorated this spot which has been preserved, apparently only to exorcise the prophetic daimones.

In Africa the Heavenly Goddess at Carthage continued to enjoy high esteem for its oracle down to the time of Diocletian. Even Gaul was not wholly devoid of oracles; at least the warm springs at the Temple of Apollo at Autun rendered decisions on oaths and perjury.

Of the oracles in the Eastern regions of the Empire, we have continual, individual reports concerning the Temple of Aesculapius at Aegae, the Apollo of Sarpedon at Seleucia, and the Temple of Mallos, all three in Cilicia, as well as concerning the Temple of the Paphian Venus on Cyprus, the oracle without temple on Mount Carmel, and several sanctuaries in Egypt. Of the great temples of the Asiatic interior, perhaps none was without claim to oracular authority. As late as the end of the fourth century the idol of the temple at Baalbek was periodically carried into the open, and (like the statue of Apollo at Hierapolis) indicated to its bearers the direction of the procession, which was given a prophetic interpretation. Other, ordinary, responses were issued in writing and by symbols. A remarkable feature is the diligent inquiry of the Palmyrenes, who turned to the Apollo of Sarpedon and to the Heavenly Aphrodite at Aphaka to obtain information concerning the duration of their realm.

For obvious reasons no reliable statistics concerning the extent of oracular practices in the age of Constantine can be offered. Parallel with the oracles there were constant daily inquiries concerning the future through observations of many quite external happenings which superstition had assigned to the realm of the ominous. The *sortes Vergilianae* (determined by opening a volume of Vergil at random) was one of the more intellectual devices of this kind. Bondage to more vulgar delusions has been noticed in the Introduction in Septimius Severus, who paid homage not only to omens but also to dreams, astrology, magic, the Attic mysteries, and others. With the ancient Roman superstitions there were mingled in the course of time those of the subject peoples and of the East. Men were frightened and their actions determined at every hour by omens and portents, and Chaldean or Egyptian almanacs were consulted for every step which was taken out of the house. Eusebius relates of Maximinus Daia that his fingers ventured to move nothing from its place without prophecy or oracle.

But this is not the sum of the aberration. Partly to discover the future, partly to affect it by magic means, the Roman of the early Empire often turned to repulsive methods, for which the same Chaldeans were employed who read the future out of the stars. Frequently the ends to be attained were criminal, and there were no scruples concerning the means. When Germanicus was assailed by deadly magic, and actually driven to his death by that means, no one was concerned that other murders must indubitably have been perpetrated to provide the magician with the necessary portions of the human anatomy. But even when it was not a matter of positive magic, of actual bewitching, but only of discovering the future or averting misfortune, the procedures were often of a frightful nature. Inspection of human entrails never wholly ceased as long as there was paganism. The desire for Emperor Hadrian's voluntary death cost his favorite Antinoüs his life. The fragmentation of cadavers for the sake of magic coercion, the conjuration of corpses to phantom life, and finally the invocation of souls continued to be a very familiar and by no means uncommon method of divination, to say nothing of lesser forms of sorcery, especially love potions. General terror of magicians must have been very widespread, at least to the extent that prominent and highly cultured people could be jeopardized by accusations of sorcery.

What was the relationship of these magic practices to the new third-century tendencies of pagan religiosity and morality and to Neoplatonist philosophy?

Those elements in the occult sciences which were not directly criminal or repulsive persisted unhindered and were even officially supported, for the devout Alexander Severus assigned state pensions to the haruspices and astrologers and required them to lecture on their specialties. From graver practices and such as involved crime most of the Emperors abstained, especially when continuous warfare brought a more vigorous and healthier tone to the court and Decius made the restoration of the old religion a matter of state policy. Even the superstitious Diocletian appears blameless in this respect, so far as we know; but we shall find his colleagues sunk in desolate folly.

As regards the Neoplatonists, their doctrine of daimones is too closely parallel to certain aspects of ordinary magic for us not to presume a close complicity. Indeed, their exorcism in general derives in part from popular Oriental and Occidental beliefs in magic.

Thirdly, the Christians in their belief in daimones, partly of Judaizing and partly of popular origin, run parallel with the pagans. They have not the slighest doubt that there are numerous intermediate powers which exercise a potent effect upon the life of men and can by men be exorcised; these daimones are thought of as fallen angels or as giants, that is, as sons of angels and the daughters of men. But these spirits are all evil, hostile to the Kingdom of God and the salvation of man. Many were thought of as causing evil in nature, such as earthquakes and plagues, as well as in the moral world; indeed, they are the originators of the en-

tire senseless and wicked paganism to which they have se-
duced the human species in order to retain it in their power
beyond redemption. These notions are old and in part
taken over from Judaism, but in course of time their outlines grew sharper. We may consult Lactantius as a witness
from the period shortly after the great persecution of Diocletian: "These supermundane and earthly daimones know
much of the future but not all; the genuine counsel of God
they do not know. It is they who suffer themselves to be
conjured by magicians, at whose invocation they deceive
the mind of man with blinding jugglery so that he does not
see what is but believes that he sees what is not. . . . They
produce disease, dreams, madness, in order to fetter men
more closely to themselves by terror. . . . But we need not
revere them out of fear, for they are harmful only so long
as they are feared; they must flee at the mention of the
name of God, and a pious man can even force them to
reveal their own names. . . . They have taught men to
make images of deceased kings, heroes, inventors, and the
like, and to worship them as divine; but beneath these
names they themselves lie hidden as beneath a mask. The
magicians indeed summon a daimon not by his alleged
divine name, but by his true supermundane name. . . ."
Further, Lactantius acknowledges that the daimones actually reside in temples and perform miracles, all to confirm
unhappy men in their delusive belief. Therefore knowledge
of the future, which they actually possess as being originally divine spirits, they employ for the purpose of occasionally announcing truth in oracles so that they may
thereafter acquire the reputation of having themselves
brought events to consummation. From the same period
also come the statements of Arnobius, who acknowledges
the complete objective actuality of magic in very broad
scope and finds, for example, that the chief difference between Christ and the magicians consists in the fact that
Christ performed his miracles through the power of his
name, whereas the magicians performed theirs merely by
the help of the daimones. The miracles of Simon Magus,
particularly his fiery chariot, are referred to as something
generally familiar. In all invocations and exorcisms, indeed,

it is not certain whether only one and the same figure always appears—to wit, Satan.

These preliminary observations are essential to give an indication of the prevalence of belief in magic. Perhaps even the best men of the period were not entirely free of such belief. Details will appear in examples of the different kinds of magic.

The Neoplatonic conjurers, as has been remarked above, recognized the exorcism of human souls as a separate category. Independently of their system and long anterior to it such exorcism is encountered frequently, because at all times much important information was expected of the dead, and in several ancient religious systems the deceased was regarded directly as a *genius*. In the first two centuries there is frequent mention of such evocations, carried out in part with fearful circumstances; we need only mention Nero and Horace's Canidia. The third century reveals Caracalla, who in a delirious fever believed that he was pursued by his father Severus and his murdered brother Geta, swords in hand, and who conjured a host of spirits to inquire for a means of relief. Commodus and Severus himself appeared at the summons, but the latter was accompanied by the uninvoked soul of Geta, and the horrified conjurer received no solace but only wild threats. Nothing similar, indeed, is reported of the later Emperors, but the conjuring of souls continued to be practiced, and the Christian writers often speak of it with horror as something present; accusations as well as prohibitions concerning conjuring reach far into the Christian period. But in later times they cannot always be distinguished from general charges and prohibitions concerning the crime of so-called *veneficium*, which embraced other illicit effects by external means as well as the compounding of poisons. Included, for example, were the magic means by which drivers in the Circus thought they could obtain victories. In Rome there continued to be "teachers of the evil arts," and if a man was unwilling to send his own son to school to them, he sought to compass the same end by sending a clever slave. As late as the middle of the fourth century we find a Sardinian slave who was expert in "evoking injurious little spirits and compelling ghosts to prophesy."

The true magician was able to restore life to a corpse for a short period and to cause it to speak. Greece had possessed necromantic oracles from ancient times, but in the later period which we are here dealing with the headquarters of this gruesome art was indisputably in Egypt, and even those who were not of Egyptian origin liked to assume the Egyptian tone in their incantations. In the second book of his *Metamorphoses* Apuleius places the scene of a necromancy in the forum of Larissa in Thessaly, where there was an abundance of native wizards also; nevertheless it is an Egyptian, Zachlas, who is made to appear in white linen robe and shorn head and to consummate the miracle by thrice placing certain herbs upon the mouth and breast of the corpse and by a whispered prayer to the rising sun. Another story of the same kind, told without Apuleius' humor but with stark Egyptian detail, is to be found in Heliodorus. Here a mother conjures her son, who had been slain in battle, and the corpse utters truth, whereas in the former instance we are left in doubt whether the magician may not have evoked a false and deceptive life in the body. The author, in the person of the wise priest Calasiris, disapproves of this necromancy, indeed, and upon another occasion contrasts this inferior form of mantic with higher, genuine Egyptian wisdom, which looks toward heaven, converses with the gods, and so forth. But these are excuses of the fourth century, when the power of the state no longer regarded the affairs of magic as a jesting matter; possibly also they are aftereffects of the nobler doctrine of the Plotinian-Porphyrean school which consciously avoided operative magic. But what are we to think when we encounter individual examples of necromancy among pious Christian priests, and that not in the Middle Ages, but in the fourth and fifth centuries? St. Spyridon, Bishop of Trimithunt on Cyprus, who was later present at the Council of Nicaea, had a daughter named Irene, to whom an acquaintance had entrusted a valuable object. She died, and Spyridon, who wished to restore the treasure and did not know where it was hidden, called upon his daughter by name until she supplied the desired information out of the tomb. A later teller of the tale softens it with the words, "He besought God to show him the promised resurrection before its season for an example"; in fact, what we have is an obvious example of a remnant of pagan belief. From the last years of the Western Roman Empire we have the account of a necromancy with much more important motivation, very impressive in its context. St. Severin, at a time when his congregations on the Danube were in desperate need, evoked a deceased presbyter to momentary wakefulness and asked him to consent that God should again ask him for his life. But the dead man implored that he be left in his eternal rest and sank back to earth lifeless. Here the underlying psychologic view is quite different and indeed essentially Christian; but we shall not pursue this aspect further.

Finally, mention must be made of the misuse of individual portions of cadavers as means for magic purposes. To determine the primitive forms of this special delusion, we should have to descend deep to the source of all magic; suffice it that mention of human flesh and human bones occurs in the most diverse categories of magic, for the mere investigation of the future as well as for operative magic to affect others. Originally the design may have been to conjure the shade of the person from whose body the portions were taken, but this connection is not clear for the later period. The use of the means became general, and a long list of individual examples of it from the Greek period downward may be drawn up. But a single very significant instance may spare us disagreeable wandering through this realm of darkness. The story of the treasure of Rhampsinitus in Herodotus is familiar. Perhaps the hand of the thief which was cut off has magic implications; next to the skull, the right hand was always the most highly prized portion of the corpse. Now it happens that under Constantine, and indeed again in Egypt, the native heath of stark magic, an amputated hand was said to be employed for magic arts, and by no other than the great Athanasius of Alexandria, who is charged with having hewn off the hand of a bishop of the Meletian sect in Thebais, Arsenius

by name, for magic purposes, and indeed to have had the
man murdered. At the synod at Tyre, in the presence of
the first bishop of the Empire, his opponents among the
Egyptian clergy brought forward not only the charge but
also the alleged *corpus delicti;* an actual hand—"whether
of a man murdered for the purpose or of one who died
otherwise God alone knows"—was placed before the eyes of
the holy fathers. Athanasius annihilated the charge brilliantly by producing Arsenius alive and unmutilated in the
midst of the council. But the fact that such a charge could
be ventured and indeed in such a circle provides irrefutable testimony for the extent of the delusion and for the
frequency of the practice.

Inspection of human entrails proceeds on another principle. This was practiced in antiquity and among various
peoples, especially on captives of war. It is essentially of
the character of divination, but inevitably operative magic
becomes involved in it or is assumed without explanation
by our sources, because popular belief in the magic value
of portions of the corpse was too firmly rooted to be content
with mere *extispicium.* For the persistence of this horror
again a single example will provide sufficient proof. Among
the rulers of this period, virtually all of whom were excessively superstitious, Maxentius, son of Maximianus Herculius, was particularly charged with dissecting pregnant
women and also children for the purpose of inspecting their
entrails, and of having evoked daimones by occult procedures. Although this story comes from Eusebius, whose
notions of paganism in general are not always the most precise, and whose desire for truthfulness is not always compelling, nevertheless in view of the evil and savage nature
of Maxentius there is no ground to doubt the tale. We do
not find it incredible, consequently, when another source
reports that he left his bloodstained palace two days before his end and moved to a private dwelling because the
avenging daimones would no longer allow him sleep in the
palace. Similar instances were doubtless of frequent occurrence throughout the third century. But these two categories by no means exhaust the magic use of human
corpses. Sympathetic effects were achieved, for example,

by the use of blood also, in which, according to prevalent beliefs, the essential life force was comprised. A story of this kind is even told of Marcus Aurelius, as melancholy as it is filthy, if we were compelled to regard it as true; even as a fable it casts an evil light upon a period whose educated men could believe in such things.

History's inquiries concerning the objective actualities in connection with this entire world of magic must always remain futile. Pagans, Jews, and Christians were equally convinced that spirits and the dead could be conjured up. Here we have to do not with evidence drawn by compulsion, as was the case with witchcraft in recent centuries, but with a hundred unconsidered, free, and consequently highly diverse statements given in part by writers who are very careful and of respectable morality. How much conscious deception, how much pious fraud, and how much self-deception and ecstatic exaltation was involved must remain a puzzle, as in the case of the Neoplatonic incantations. For each century has its own view of the hypersensual within and without man, and posterity can never fully enter into its beliefs.

Our account of paganism to this point was calculated to present merely the essential tendencies in contemporary belief. If all traces were to be cited individually, if all dissenting concepts of the world of gods in general could be recorded, if even all separate worship of amulets and of symbols could be enumerated, in a century when many an individual contented himself with the worship of a single little serpent as a good daimon and believed in nothing else, then it might be possible to prove at least theoretically the existence of the three hundred sects with which the philosopher Themistius was acquainted.

It was with this "polytheist madness" that Christianity was now again to enter into a decisive conflict. Fortunately, this conflict has a literary aspect also. The rational defenders of Christianity in this time of crisis, Arnobius and Lactantius, who have already been frequently cited, have an even higher value for us for their accounts of sinking paganism. To be sure, they stand upon the shoulders of their predecessors, especially Clement of Alexandria, but they contribute much that is new and that is truly significant for the decade of persecution and for contemporary attitudes. The highly respectable work of Lactantius is obviously the result of deep and many-sided studies. The writing of Arnobius, a quickly compiled outpouring of the gloomy and glowing wrath of a new convert, is the most immediate testimony of the moment. The modern reader is no longer disturbed by the constant and passionate misunderstanding of paganism with reference to its origins and development. He understands how to receive the Euhemerism of these Church writers, and is eager for valuable revelations of all sorts which they offer along with error.

If we draw the final conclusions from what has been said, we find not only that the disintegration of paganism as such was generally favorable to Christianity, but that the individual symptoms of disintegration involved a presage of Christianity and an approach to it. The mixture of gods was in itself well calculated to prepare the ground for a new religion. It denationalized the divine and made it universal; it crushed Greek and Roman pride in their old native cults. Prejudice in favor of all things Oriental must inevitably, after long wandering in the realm of illusion, also work to the advantage of Christianity. Furthermore, the essential content of late pagan beliefs was directly analogous to Christianity. The aim of existence was no longer limited to life on earth and to its pleasures and destiny, but was extended to the beyond, even to union with deity. The one group hoped to secure immortality by occult rites; the other wished to force their way to deity by steeping themselves in profound matters or by magic compulsion. But all paid homage to the new notion of conscious morality, which went as far as castigations, and which obtained at least as a theoretical ideal even if it was not carried out in life. A reflection of this tendency is to be perceived in the relegation or reinterpretation by the philosophers of the Greek myths which were not in consonance with the new viewpoint. Monotheism was approached by declining paganism, at least upon occasion, in remarkable upsurges, even though these were soon entangled in the webs of dai-monic beliefs. Whether the pagans went so far as to reach a sense of sin is very doubtful; but the prerequisites for such a sense are clearly present in the Neoplatonist teaching, which designates the soul's entry into earthly life as a fall, and its emergence from earthly life as a sort of redemption.

Christianity was bound to conquer in the end because it provided answers which were incomparably simpler, and which were articulated in an impressive and convincing whole, to all the questions for which that period of ferment was so deeply concerned to find solutions.

VII

SENESCENCE OF ANCIENT LIFE
AND ITS CULTURE

IF THE CRISIS in the life of the ancient world is anywhere
clearly revealed, it is in the twilight of paganism which
we have endeavored to present in its true colors. The question now arises whether Christianity might not have had
the force to give new life to nationalities and new vigor to
the state, whether it should not have refuted pagan complaint current as early as the third century that, after this
new religion had begun to advance, the race of man was
doomed. For the pagans were emphatic in their assertion
that since Christianity the gods had forsaken the direction
of human fate and that they had departed (*exterminatos*)
out of the wretched world, where now only pestilence, war,
famine, drought, locusts, hail, and so forth prevailed, while
barbarians were attacking the Empire from all sides. Christian apologists were constrained to undertake the circumstantial refutation of these charges. "How little credit,"
they said, "does such childish petulance do your pagan
gods! Why do they not bestow health and happiness upon
you and chastise us Christians alone? Nature has not altered; sun and moon shine as before, the harvest grows
green, trees bloom, oil and wine are pressed, and civic life
proceeds as it always has. There have always been wars
from the days of Ninus the Assyrian, and since Christ they
have in fact diminished. The undeniable evils of the present are part of the necessary world process by which
earthly things seek to renew themselves (*rerum in-
novatio*)."

But the hope of renewal, as this author understood it, was vain. Let us, for the moment, leave aside the one-sided direction taken by Christianity as soon as it became a state religion, a direction altogether unsuited for bringing new strength to the Empire. Indeed, the great advantage of the religion whose kingdom was not of this world was that it did not set itself the task of directing and guaranteeing any definite state and any definite culture, as the religions of paganism had done, and that it was rather in a position to reconcile with one another and mediate between diverse peoples and centuries, states and cultural stages. It was not Christianity, then, that could bestow a second youth upon the senescent Roman Empire; but it could so far prepare the Empire's Germanic conquerors that they did not wholly tread its culture underfoot. A century and a half later, when the decision was to be made on the Catalaunian Plains whether the Hun was to draw the death pall over Western life as later the Mongol did over Asiatic life, this preparation bore its fruit; Roman and Visigoth combined to ward off the attack.

For the senescence and corruption of conditions in the Empire, for which Christianity bears no responsibility, the entire history of this period bears eloquent testimony, and reference has been made to it on every page of the present work. But this is an appropriate place to bring together significant aspects of the old age of the ancient world. Such a collection will serve further to clarify the historic position of Christianity.

Complaints of evil times are to be found in all centuries which have left a literature behind them. But in the Roman Empire the decline is acknowledged in a manner which leaves no room for doubt. The feeling that anything in the present is trifling in comparison with a brilliantly conceived past is concomitant in growth to the colossal external expansion of the Empire and its interests; even those who depreciate the grandeur of early days do so only further to minimize the present. When Seneca in his philosophical polemic against history treats Philip and Alexander of Macedon as highwaymen, he adds, "But we regard these things as great because we ourselves are so small." More

potent though silent testimony is implied in the fact that
all philosophers and orators—and poets too, if not engaged
in begging—in a word, all the free literature of the second,
third, and fourth centuries never, except under compulsion, speaks of a man or an object posterior to the end of
the Roman Republic. It would seem as if a pledge had
been taken on the matter. For their school exercises the
Greek sophists preferred to choose themes from the flowering period of Hellenism, from the Persian Wars, the Peloponnesian War, and sometimes from the life of Alexander the Great. They represent Xenophon as offering to die
in Socrates' place, or Solon arguing against Pisistratus for
rescinding the laws, or Demosthenes advising the Athenians to flee by sea, or other such topics. Dio Chrysostom
(under Trajan) feels that he must make formal apology
for having spoken in one of his discourses of events of the
imperial period, "modern, inglorious things"; he believes
his opponent would regard him as a babbler because he
did not follow customary usage and speak of Cyrus or
Alcibiades. The declamations ascribed to Quintilian treat
either of subjects in the remote past or of imaginary cases
at law which belong to no specific period. The easy explanation that the government took an unfavorable view of
comment concerning the period of the Empire and may
even have suppressed it is altogether mistaken. Surveillance of this sort over literature and the schools was not in
the character of the Roman Empire, which was in general
not concerned with regulating cultural tendencies and su-
pervising them. In fact, the favorite subject for oratorical
practice would seem, by our scale, objectionable and dangerous. In the Rome of Domitian, Juvenal complains of the
deadly tedium of an orator who must for the hundredth
time hear "his numerous class slay the cruel tyrant." Stories
of Brutus and of Harmodius and Aristogiton were a pro-
verbially favorite theme, whereas the most notable subjects
of the imperial period, which could even be dealt with in
panegyric, as for example the Jewish War, the deeds of
Trajan, the rule of the Antonines, were never willingly
touched upon and thus were left exclusively to the official
eulogists.

And not only the orators but the peculiar category of Latin and Greek compilers who are sometimes together labeled grammarians do not readily go beyond the period of the Republic. Aulus Gellius, for example, does so only when he speaks of the education of his time and of his own studies. Aelian's *Historiae Variae* has virtually nothing of the Empire. Alciphron places his *Letters* in the earliest Macedonian period. Athenaeus in his great encyclopedia of ancient enjoyment intentionally avoids the imperial period. Even two hundred years later Macrobius in his *Saturnalia,* aside from a short incidental mention of Trajan, makes a collection of anecdotes and witty remarks of Augustus the most modern element in his work. Professional philologists who are more intimately acquainted with the relevant literature than the present author can probably confirm these observations in a much broader scope.

This age, then, which contemporaries denied and ignored and from which they constantly turned back to earlier centuries, suddenly acquired a new content by means of Christianity. A Christian literature which had long been in preparation now broke like a flood into the empty channel of the century and in a short space surpassed in volume all that has survived from the world of pagan writers.

Yet Rome as the seat and ideal of world dominion was believed to be eternal; *Roma aeterna* is a common consolation upon monuments and coins, especially during the second half of the third century. To the Christians, as long as they saw and hated Rome as paganism personified, as the Babylon of the *Book of Revelation,* this notion was folly. They regarded Rome, as Arnobius plainly declares, as the "city created for the corruption of the human race, for the sake of whose rule the entire world has undeservedly been subjugated." Only an African, indeed, could utter such sentiments; even in pagan times the distinction was drawn between Rome and the Empire, and prayers were offered for the welfare of Rome as for the pagan Emperors and the armies. Later, under the Christian Emperors, the notion of Rome's world dominion became entirely acceptable. Prudentius finds it the highest historical effect of Providence: "Lo, the whole race of mortals has come under the rule of Romulus, the most diverse habits of life and thought have become amalgamated; thus has it been foreordained so that the dignity of the name of Christian might with a single bond embrace the whole world." But the most moving utterance on the subject is the poem of a late heathen, Claudius Rutilius Numatianus (about 417), who comforts Rome bowed down like a mother in deep grief and draws new hope for eternal survival out of Rome's historical grandeur.

How far such hopes could be justified by the institutions of the state and its external condition cannot be precisely determined by mere inferences. A government like the Roman may survive for a very long while, despite growing petrification, as the Byzantine Empire has shown. If the city of Rome had been so impregnable and so easy to defend as Constantinople later was, the Western Empire might have lasted much longer; and if the capital were saved it might time and again have reconquered lost provinces. A state is as able to survive nationality as a nationality a state. Thus the idea of senescence need not signify impossibility of survival but only the gradual failure of those sources of life which once gave the nation its nobler spiritual and physical stamp.

We may begin with the physical properties of the earth itself. To people in the Roman Empire it seemed as if rivers began to grow sluggish and mountains to lose height; Aetna could not be seen so far at sea as formerly, and the same phenomenon is reported of Parnassus and Olympus. Studious natural historians were of the opinion that the cosmos itself was going into general decline.

If we look at physical man, a degeneration of the race at this time, at least in the upper classes, is undeniable. Our judgment is not limited to statements of writers—who upon occasion made similar remarks in an earlier period—art also provides irrefutable demonstrations in countless monuments, and indeed in monuments whose evidence cannot be disregarded on the grounds of the artist's want of skill. Most of the figures of this period show in part a natural ugliness and in part something diseased, scrofulous, bloated,

or sunken. Tombs, coins, mosaics, bases of drinking glasses
—all are at one in giving this impression. Diocletian's colleagues and immediate successors with their repellant traits
may not, being Illyrians, be considered average specimens. Constantine, whose outward appearance is definitely
known from statues and coins, appears sound indeed and
regularly formed, but there is something cunning in his expression; yet panegyrists and Church writers are at one in
their exclamations of delight at his beauty. This is not mere
flattery but evidence of a low standard of comparison. In
the physiognomies of his sons we observe an essentially
new species of expression which subsequently recurs frequently. The expression is what we call "priestly" in the
pejorative sense. Constantine II also has the not altogether
agreeable round head of his father; Constans' and Constantius' are rather longer drawn. Much clearer than these
Illyriot visages, clearer perhaps than portraits in general,
is the evidence of ideal figures of the period in which the
artists sought to fix universals; these demonstrate the deterioration of the human type. The Arch of Constantine
near the Colosseum is, to be sure, a hasty production, and
this is a sufficient explanation for the great crudeness of
the plastic execution, but not for the ugliness of the figures
and the meanness of expression. There are of course periods in which art makes it an object to seek its effects in
what is characteristic rather than in what is beautiful, and
even exaggerates to the point of ugliness without the artist's environment being at fault. But here there can be no
question of the artist's preference for character; rather it
is his inability to preserve classic ideals of beauty even
superficially when the world about him supplied no points
of contact with such ideals. In the fifth century the mosaics
provide a continuous scale for the same phenomenon. Here
it must be noticed that art is not yet seeking to give expression to sanctity by ascetic emaciation and moroseness,
as the Byzantine workers in mosaic later did; its figures are
not yet definitely shrunken, but the visages are always ugly
and irregular. Even excellent works in which all other fea-
tures, drapery, motion, distribution in space, and the like
are as good as can be expected in the Theodosian age—as,

for example, the Twelve Apostles in the Orthodox Baptistry at Ravenna—are no exception in this particular.

The human physique had always been singularly varied in the Roman Empire, according to individual regions and according to their state of prosperity; some populations are to be imagined as robust and some as meager. But the average as presented in classic art at this time is in general that of Italy. When and through what circumstances did outward man here and perhaps in the entire Empire change for the worse?

The answer is ready at hand. Two fearful plagues, under Marcus Aurelius (167) and then again after Gallus (252), had shattered the population of the Empire beyond repair. The latter pestilence is said to have lasted for fifteen years, to have spared no area of the Empire, and to have desolated many cities completely. If we add the unceasing wars, internal wars of succession as well as external wars against barbarians, with their inevitable consequence of neglect of agriculture, we may deduce that famine continually added to the ravages of disease. The higher classes could no longer be spared anxiety and misery. Settlements of barbarians completed the task of transforming the human type in the Empire, and rather in the direction of improvement.

In such eras of misfortune an old race dies not only in the physical sense: old customs and usages, national viewpoints, spiritual goals of all sorts, also perish. But this does not inevitably involve the decline of morality; on the contrary, there is evidence of moral improvement in the second half of the third century. For the imperial throne itself improvement is undeniable (see Chapter I). The age of Caracalla and the Maximini was past, and Carinus falls because he is a belated anomaly in his decade. With the later so-called monsters, such as Maxentius, excesses and misdeeds are petty compared to those of the earlier Emperors. Police officers for the preservation of morals seem to have been increased, and outward conduct doubtless improved. Even Diocletian was much concerned to regulate matrimonial practices, which had grown rank, and to take measures against intermarriages in the same house and in forbidden degrees of consanguinity. Great and widespread scandals become noticeably reduced. That Constantine's own private life was virtually free of such abuses is a fair deduction from the silence of hostile historians. Government was more and more concerned with general humanitarian measures and recognizes its obligation to take full thought for its subjects; though at the same time it was compelled to exert heavy pressure, and frequently overreached itself even in its measures for improvement, as for example in fixing maximum prices for foodstuffs and in barbaric criminal punishment. We have already pointed to analogies for this heightened morality in late pagan religion and in the ascetic ideals of the philosophers, but the whole matter must be examined here afresh. For perhaps reform in the direction of sobriety and moderation was specifically a symptom of senescence, which is our concern here; so much the less would it be in a position to rejuvenate the tired old world.

Now that we have confirmed the decline in man's physical beauty, we proceed to treat his outward environment, and first of all his clothing. Here plastic art does not represent actual conditions, for it regularly retained the drapery of long-departed epochs of flourishing art, which themselves employed idealizations. Even the Panathenaic Procession on the Parthenon, for example, represents not the actual costumes of Athenians contemporary with Phidias, but only beautifully simplified elements of those costumes. When we find Roman statues of the age of Constantine garbed in toga and tunic, with the chlamys for nude figures, we must not conclude that these were the ordinary wear. Here literary monuments are a safer guide, and these tell us of elaborate and overburdened costume, which might well be called Roman rococo if we may use that profane expression.

Instead of transcribing a section from available histories of costume we shall content ourselves with a few indications. A poem of the first half of the fourth century addressed by Arborius, uncle of Ausonius, "to a nymph titivated to excess," supplies a description of a Gallic maid. Her hair is braided with ribbons and built up into a large spiral (*in multiplicem orbem*); and this was surmounted by

a cap of golden material. Her neck-band appears to have
been red, perhaps of coral. Her dress was high-necked,
and was laced over the bust. Clinging dresses, and especially clinging sleeves, were becoming abundant. Such
elaborate coiffures as are described had been fashionable
for centuries, and in some marble busts are made detach-
able to accommodate changes in fashion. Before Arborius,
Arnobius complains of the bands, apparently of gold bro-
cade, with which many ladies covered their foreheads, and
of their habit of curling their hair in masculine fashion.
Facial make-up, which gave the face not only a new color
but also a new shape, was particularly distasteful. Red as
well as white applications were laid on so heavily that the
women looked "like idols," and every tear that flowed over
the cheek left a furrow behind it. Such, at least, is the
ridicule of St. Jerome, who must have been well informed
on the subject in his earlier days. A major change, perhaps to be ascribed precisely to this period, was the new
use of patterned and flowered material instead of solid-
colored, which is the only proper dress for human beings,
for it alone permits an unhampered view of masses and
folds and so indirectly of the form, attitude, and movement
of the body. From foreign ambassadors Constantine received gifts of "barbaric garments worked with gold and
flowers." Soon thereafter similar garments appear as the
usual ceremonial dress in the mosaic designs of churches,
and it was not long before priestly vestments and altar
covers had whole stories embroidered upon them. Whatever was alien and barbaric enjoyed patent preference in
late Roman fashion simply because it was dear and hard
to obtain. Under Theodosius the Great the famous Symmachus found it necessary to refuse a magnificent foreign
state coach with which the Emperor thought to make the
journeys of the city prefect more majestic.

But barbarization extended much further than merely to
clothing. The rise of German and especially of Gothic and
Frankish officers in the army and at court, and the influence
of Oriental etiquette and manners, must gradually have
fixed an un-Roman stamp upon all external forms of life.
The division of society according to position and rank,

which was effected by the bestowal of titles, was a quite new departure; nothing was more contrary to the notion of citizenship upon which the classic world had been nurtured. Christianity also, which had consumed so many elements of ancient culture with its mighty flame, contributed indirectly to barbarization, as a glance at the art and the literature of the period will make clear.

Art in the highest sense of the word was once the breath of life to the Greek people. No other nation could have ventured to date its chronicles by the development of the beautiful through poets and artists, as is done, for example, in the chronicle of the Parian marble. In the train of Alexander's victorious arms and of his successors', Greek art marched through the Orient and suppressed, as far as might be, the ancient national forms, with the single exception of the buildings and statues of Egypt, from Alexandria upwards. The Romans also willingly adopted Greek art for their service, not merely as objects of luxury, but because it answered a need for the beautiful which was inherent in them but whose active development was hindered by the predominance of war and politics. Greek art contributed magnificently to give noble expression to Rome's majesty, religious and national, though not without sacrifice of its inner character. And finally from Rome the entire West accepted Romanized art as the law of the victor, and imitated it as it imitated the victor's language. Where colonies of Italian origin persisted in the West this art may have answered a real need.

The position which art held among the Greeks of the great period, to be sure, it never retained in this age of Roman domination. Denigration of the beautiful cannot now be spoken of as blasphemy as it was when the poet Stesichorus was blinded for having reproached Helen, the pattern of all beauty. Lucian, who spares neither gods nor men, can now mock at the ancient ideals of all beauty also, though in other connections his taste in matters of art is abundantly documented. The masterly series of *Dialogues of the Dead* in which he gives free rein to his mockery under the mask of the cynic Menippus contains a scene in which Hermes of the underworld exhibits to Menippus the skeletons of famous beauties of antiquity, Narcissus, Nereis, and others. "But I see nothing but skulls and bones; show me Helen." "This skull here is Helen." "Was it for this that a thousand ships sailed, that countless men died, that cities were destroyed?" "Ah, Menippus," Hermes answers, "you never saw the woman alive!" Nevertheless, though the early Empire is inculpated by contemporary aesthetes, by Petronius and the Elder Pliny, and with some justice, as an epoch of decline in art, in Italy at least the demand for artistic surroundings for life continued unbelievably strong. Pompeii alone, in Goethe's words, shows "an appetite for art and pictures on the part of a whole people of an extent that the most ardent *amateur* of today can have neither concept nor feeling nor need of." If we apply the scale of Pompeii to contemporary Rome the implications are dizzying.

But in the third century art encountered a formidable material enemy in the derangement of the Empire by plague, war, and poverty. The fact that the Emperors, especially after Aurelian, again engaged in large-scale building, and doubtless gave proportionate support to other arts also, might have restored the balance had not increasing pressure upon the wealthy and the prosperous brought with it permanent loss.

If we assume that nature always distributes a bountiful measure of talent—and this cannot be doubted even with the deterioration of all forms—the question arises, Whence came the false directions in which talents were lost? Why, further, the anonymity which covers practically all the art of the third and fourth centuries with so deathly a pall?

It is a fact that from approximately the middle of the second century the active production of works of art which had hitherto flourished ceases and degenerates to mere repetition, and that henceforward internal impoverishment and apparent overelaboration of forms go hand in hand.

The deepest causes for this phenomenon can probably never be plumbed or comprehended in words. If the developed Greek system of forms could maintain itself for six centuries under all vicissitudes of history and always spring new shoots, why should it lose its power and its creative energy precisely from the age of the Antonines downward? Why could it not have lasted into the fourth century? Perhaps an *a priori* answer may emerge from a general philosophic consideration of the period, but it is more prudent not to seek to determine the life span of a spiritual force of such magnitude.

Collateral reasons for the phenomenon are clear enough: changes in the material and in the tasks and subjects of art, or indirectly, the changed viewpoint of the purchasers. Let us follow the fate of architecture first. Here the capital sounds the keynote for all devolution. In its travertine and peperino Rome possessed a sober and powerful material for monumental building. But when, especially after Augustus, Romans insisted on marbles from Carrara and Africa because of their plasticity and their brilliant beauty, their feelings became habituated to the idea that the brick masonry of the structure and the marble facing which covered it were two disparate things. The latter must eventually come to be regarded as a veneer to be changed at will, as mere ornament. Still the white marble always compelled the artist to give his forms the utmost refinement. But when the most expensive and exotic materials came more and more to be the rage, when all the East and Africa were ransacked for precious building stone, porphyry, jasper, agate, and marbles of all colors, when the massive use of gilt grew out of all reason, then art and the artist could only retire. Material and color monopolized attention; profiles and decorative motifs were disregarded. The extraordinary hardness of many of these stones, moreover, limited the scope of the chisel. Under these conditions, those who supplied and dressed the stones were more important than the draftsman. And where white marble or other simple material was used, it now had to compete by heaping up members and multiplying ornament; taste for simplicity was now corrupted. Despite mass, the impression is often trivial and confusing, because external architectural richness, once conceived of as the guiding principle, soon exceeds all measure and is also applied to structural members whose function makes them incapable

of receiving decorative treatment. We need not here enumerate the buildings of this style, for which the Palmyrene
temple and the palace of Diocletian at Salonae have become proverbial. Except where their arrangement and proportion are reminiscent of a better period, they belong to
the decline, and do not even compensate for the loss by
exploiting the charm of perspective, such as the degenerate
modern style has developed, for example, in the hands of a
Bernini. Bernini understood how to focus the spectator's
attention; but here everything is restless and scattered.
Bernini ignores detail and strives for total effect; here the
heaped-up individual forms pretend to significance in
themselves.

If luxury in the sense here suggested necessarily promoted the decline of beautiful form in architecture, an in-
novating advance contributed no less to the final dissolution of the structural system inherited from the Greeks. We
refer to the new requirement for large interiors, preferably
arched. In the better periods of Empire architecture, for
example in the construction of baths, the columns and their
entablature were so joined to dome, barrel vaulting, and
cross vaulting that they bypassed it, as it were, as a separate
organism. But concern for such an effect could not long
persist, especially after the Christian period brought a great
increase in the demand for such structures and the con-
current tendency toward heightened magnificence silenced
all other considerations. The Christian basilica, which is
the first great model of interiors regarded solely from the
viewpoint of perspective, carried arches and heavy, large
clerestory walls upon its rows of columns. The domed
church, with galleries above and below or accessory chapels
round about, was a complete negation of the notion of
the entablature, and employed columns virtually for their
agreeable effect alone. It was late in the Middle Ages
before Christian architecture finally exchanged ancient
forms, repeated with increased misunderstanding until they
were scarcely recognizable, for a new garb more appropriate to its principles.

Finally, Christian architecture from the beginning was
constrained to share, to its disadvantage, in a tendency of

the Church itself. That tendency was to make the entire structure and every stone in it a symbol of its power and its victory; hence the predominance of luxurious embellishment and of figured representation, in the interior as on the façades. The lavish use of mosaic, which covered every space and every surface with Biblical figures and stories, executed in the vivid and unshaded colors of glass paste, made genuine architectural articulation impossible; entablature and consoles consequently shrank to vestigial strips or were merely indicated in the mosaic ornament.

Nevertheless architecture retained a feeling for magnificently arranged and imaginatively constructed interiors and for great mechanical virtuosity. It is to the latter that we owe our knowledge of several artists of the Byzantine period, who were able to emerge from the anonymity spoken of above.

The decline of plastic art and painting resulted from the same or similar causes which determined the decline of architecture, and was aggravated by special considerations. Here too, in the first place, luxury in material surely had a corrupting effect. When it became customary to compose statues of three or even four different kinds of frequently very hard stone—to say nothing of many that were fashioned of gold and silver—the effect on style must in the long run have been adverse, for style demands primacy if it is to survive. Very mediocre style is characteristic, for example, of the colossal porphyry sarcophagi of Helena and Constantia (mother and daughter of Constantine), in the Vatican, the one with trains of horsemen, the other with genii preparing the vintage. The mere restoration of the first of these sarcophagi under Pius IV is said to have claimed the toil of twenty-five men for nine years, from which we can calculate the labor involved in the original production. There can be no question of any direct touch of artistic genius in this incredibly hard and unyielding stone; what is involved is slave labor after a given pattern. Painting must have been corrupted by mosaic in quite the same way. As long as mosaic was used only for pavement, it might be regarded as an expression of an overflowing love of art which was unwilling to leave any spot upon which the eye might fall without decoration—though there is something barbaric in treading on such a composition as the so-called Battle of Alexander at Pompeii. But after Pliny, mosaic ascended to walls and ceiling. In the baths, where ordinary painting might be damaged by dampness, there was much to be said for this change; but in other structures it needlessly deprived the artist of direct manual participation in his creation, and it also discouraged him, because the spectator would think first of a work's expense and elegance, then of its subject, and finally or not at all of the representation. With the introduction of Christianity, mosaic became the principal decoration, wherever means sufficed, for all walls and ceilings in churches.

But the decline is more decisively revealed in other symptoms, which rest upon other grounds. The small number of significant statues of gods which can be dated with certainty after the time of Alexander Severus is striking; on the other hand statues of Mithras, of the execrable Aeons, of Dei Panthei, of Ephesian Dianas, and the like increase greatly. Here clearly religion was at work. Nothing was more calculated to distract the artist completely from the ancient god-types than the admixture of amorphous alien deities and the daimonization of native deities, which deprived them of their handsome anthropomorphic personalities. In any case it was difficult for the artist to steep himself in the ancient piety even if such works were requested. Instead, his task now was to produce thousands of sacrophagi, which were the principal occupation of the sculptors of the third century. Their reliefs, to be sure, present purely Greek myths and are hence free of the monstrosities of the alien religions; but other and weightier reasons prevented the production of significant works of art. Amalgamation of plastic and dramatic laws into a pure and perfect style of relief could be achieved only in an epoch of high artistic competence; so soon as luxuriant striving for effect got the upper hand—that is, in the late Greek period, which could still produce wonderful works in other departments—relief work was also bound to lose balance. Hence even the most beautiful work of the better Roman period, which rests directly on the late Greek tradition, as for example the reliefs on the Arch of Titus, are of qualified merit. But later, when richness took the place of beauty altogether, when men had grown used to every sort of plastic extravagance by the spiral reliefs of the Column of Trajan and its imitators and by the overcrowded triumphal arches, it was inevitable that the number and confusion of the figures should crowd out any large and true effect, just as multiplication of members had done in architecture. Sarcophagus decoration was further demoralized by the fact that work was seldom done on special order, but produced for the trade, and hence had to follow the vulgar and florid taste of the average purchaser. Finally, the subject matter grew dominant in a tendentious sense, to the disadvantage of art. The relevant myths were represented as symbolic husks of general ideas, and the separation between kernel and shell could in the long run be only injurious to art. Beneath the representations of the myths of Meleager, Bacchus and Ariadne, Amor and Psyche, Luna and Endymion, Pluto and Proserpina, beneath the battles of centaurs or of Amazons, the bacchanalia, the trains of Nereids, and the like, there lie hidden abstract thoughts concerning fate, death, and immortality. Such symbolism does indeed evoke the historical and poetical participation of the spectator, but art fails in another of its obligations, and that is, to recall in each of its figures what is abiding and eternal through nobility of form alone.

In the place of the pagan figures mentioned, Christianity introduced upon the sarcophagi Christ and the Apostles or certain scenes from the Old and New Testaments, presented as parallels or singly. No advance in style can be expected here; again the "message" dominates, again symbolic expression is paramount. As skill in continuous narrative, which is essential to relief, diminished, the sarcophagus came to be divided by little columns and arches into as many fields as there were persons or stories involved. Because of its multiplicity, representation grew altogether impoverished and childish.

Another function that still remained to sculpture was the portrait, as statue or bust, and particularly as half-figure in relief. On monuments and sarcophagi we not infrequently find those comfortable representations of man and wife, hand in hand, set into a niche; it is apparently a rule, as in the coins of the second half of the third century, that the entire upper body be included. Busts properly speaking are very rare, so that we know the great Illyrian Emperors, for example, virtually only from coins. There are many references to portrait statues, but with the exception of several erected in honor of Constantine, scarcely any are preserved, and of these the ponderous and distorted forms make the losses from this period easy to bear.

Along with the material, hugeness was in many cases the object of admiration. The effect of great monoliths in themselves was considerably exaggerated. People had long been used to having Egyptian obelisks dragged to Rome; Elagabalus had dreamt of a block of stone to be brought from Thebes, and to receive a winding staircase and serve his chief idol as a pedestal; but now Diocletian had granite pillars fifteen feet in girth brought from the Orient for his baths, and Constantine transported the largest of all obelisks from Heliopolis to Alexandria, whence Constantius later brought it to Rome. The largest piece of porphyry known, a pillar of a hundred feet, was made to bear the statue of the founder of the new city of Constantinople. Sculpture too came to be gauged by sheer mass in the third and fourth centuries. Alexander Severus had a crowd of gigantic statues set up in Rome, and conscripted artists from the ends of the earth for this enterprise. Gallienus had himself represented as a sun-god, reportedly of a height of two hundred feet; the lance in his hand was to be stout enough for a child to be able to climb up its interior, chariot and horses were to be fashioned on the same scale, and the whole, erected upon a lofty podium, was to crown Rome's highest point, the Esquiline. But the work, as might be expected, was not completed. More moderate were the two marble statues of the Emperor Tacitus and his brother Florianus at Terni, each of thirty feet, which were both completely destroyed by lightning soon after they were erected. After Phidias' statues of giants, after the hundred colossi of the sun at Rhodes, gods and men

had often been represented in a scale far surpassing human
without injury to art; but at a time of decline, when drafts-
manship and modeling were no longer adequate to smaller
tasks, art on a large scale became wholly distorted and corrupted the taste of entire generations because the spectator
was everywhere overwhelmed by its gigantic figures. Extravagance in portrait statues, moreover, had a special significance which involved the fate of painting also.

Painting exhibits an internal law or at least an experience according to which periods of idealizing representation are followed by periods of realism, either because
idealism had not treated the forms of nature with sufficient
thoroughness, but had been content with the general, or
because it had traversed the circle of its legitimate creation
and hoped to discover new effects in coarse naturalism.
Related collateral categories of painting, above all genre
painting, develop this tendency into an independent existence. Something of the same sort happened in ancient
art. Even in the period of flowering there were plenty of
genre statues and genre paintings; whole schools were
characterized by close adherence to reality. But their efforts
were wholly directed toward acquiring new aspects of the
beautiful from reality, and thus interest in individual appearances was always kept at a high level. Should we not
expect the third century to be a period of genuine naturalism, carefully executed shading, study of illusions of
actuality? Analogies for such a movement are not wholly
wanting—in literature, for example, as we shall see.

But the prerequisite for perfected genre painting, exquisite and acute perception, was in process not of growth
but of rapid decline. Luxury in material and passion for
decoration had largely deprived acute perception of the
place of honor which is its due. The few wall paintings of
mythologic content which have been preserved show crude
repetition of older motifs and a stunting and ossification
of the system of arabesques which was once so decorative.
The paintings in the Christian catacombs are appealing
by reason of the simplicity and the unpretentiousness of
their representations. They are very remarkable, moreover,
as the earliest documents for the types of sacred persons;

but in composition and execution of details they exhibit great want of skill or else reminiscence of earlier work. The new Christian subjects spread a sunset glow over ancient art, but new content did not bring fresh quality. Mosaic was quickly claimed for the mighty programs of the victorious faith. It spread sacred figures and stories over all available space in the church, disregarding alike the laws of architecture as of painting. We can only wonder that so many relatively excellent works make their appearance as late as the sixth century. Ecclesiastical merit and completeness of the subject, along with magnificence of execution, were the only relevant considerations. For the artist's own joy in his work there is no room. Art had become serviceable to a symbol which lay outside itself, which had not grown up with it and through it; and the artist, even where his talent was considerable, was the nameless executor of something universally applicable, as had once been the case in Egypt. In the miniatures of manuscripts, as far as they are known directly or through late copies, we are not infrequently surprised by successful allegories and ingenious conceits, which proves that nonofficial art at least still possessed subjective vitality. Indeed, the pictures on a pagan calendar of the second half of the fourth century preserve several genuine genre figures with their baroque costume and surroundings. But the general tendency was irrevocably set in a quite different direction.

If we are to speak of a victory of realism in any aspect, we may find it in the vigorous growth of portrait painting after the third century. We have already seen how the colossal portrait statue had become a principal task of sculpture; and on sarcophagi the chief figure in the myth was regularly given the lineaments of the deceased. In painting, however, the tendency of the time was much less in the direction of lifelike representation of characters, but rather toward the so-called ceremonial picture, intended to celebrate an individual or a whole family with exact official vestments and solemn posture, frequently with symbolic accessories. Such treatment was obviously indicated in the case of rulers, and private persons followed their example. How essential costume was in such pictures is clear from the tablet in the palace of the Quintilii, which showed the Emperor Tacitus five times in different dress, with toga, chlamys, armor, pallium, and hunting garb. It is no wonder that even coins and tombstones no longer present the head alone but the entire upper body, whose dress now expresses rank and dignity. The two Tetrici had a mosaic picture made in their palace on the Caelian hill, showing Aurelian standing between them and receiving from them tokens of homage, scepter and oak wreath. On the wall of a dining hall in the palace at Aquileia there was a family portrait which celebrated the relationship of the houses of Maximian Herculius and Constantius Chlorus. Among others, the young Constantine appeared receiving a golden helmet with peacock feathers from little Fausta, who was later to be his wife. Similar family portraits can be imagined in the houses and country estates of prominent private citizens also. An echo of this category of art, which has otherwise perished, is extant in the pictures of the ivory diptychs, which usually surround the realistically conceived Emperor or official, in precisely observed official dress, with symbolic accessories.

When there were no printing presses it often became the duty of painting to make the power of the ruler known to the people, a function performed in modern times by manifestoes and proclamations. The first thing done at each accession was that the likeness of the new Emperor was sent about and everywhere received with great ceremony. Portable likenesses were carried in the field and set up at headquarters; we even find portrait figures (often of metal) used in battle standards. Victorious battles were painted upon large cloth surfaces or panels and publicly exhibited. Trains of foreign embassies, whole festivals and theatrical spectacles, triumphal processions, and solemnities of every sort received permanent monumental record as friezes in palaces. Constantine celebrated his victory over Licinius in a large encaustic picture of symbolic content which was set up before the gates of the imperial residence. He and his sons appeared, with the defeated general at their feet in the guise of a dragon, with arrows in his body and the abyss underneath; over the whole floated the sign of the cross. Later the Emperor had himself painted in the pediment of a palace gate in an attitude of prayer. And after his death a great painting was set up in his honor in Rome; this represented an allegory of heaven, with the transfigured Emperor enthroned.

Improvisations of this sort no longer had much to do with true art. But they do illustrate one aspect of the fate of art as a whole, for even in pagan times art had largely become the handmaid of propaganda, and with the victory of Christianity it could change only its master, not its position. Dominated by subject for many centuries on end, it could fulfill its internal laws not at all or only imperfectly. Actually this constitutes one of the most patent denials of the ancient outlook.

It was domination of subject over form that gave painting preference over sculpture in the realm of Christian art. Plastic expression of sacred figures, even if executed with the art of a Phidias, would have seemed a kind of idolatry; dressed in the forms of the period of decline, they were mere caricature as compared with the great works of antiquity. If it was to make any impression by means of art, therefore, Christianity required a narrative or a symbolically interrelated art, an art rich in figures; hence it must use painting primarily, or the intermediate form of relief. There is no need to speak of the prejudice against sculptors personally, who were despised as having been servants to idols.

Neither could poetry at this period supply what the fine arts were incapable of providing. Cut off from any living association with drama, surfeited to exhaustion with epic treatment of mythological material, rejecting historical subject matter along with everything modern, poetry could only withdraw to lyric and romance. Poetry continued to be composed in most categories, to be sure, in a consciously academic manner; but ever paler reminiscences of a better age, as is displayed for example in the bucolic and didactic poets of the third century, in Calpurnius Siculus, Nemesianus, Serenus, Sammoniacus, and others, cannot suffice to produce a living literature, however much talent may appear in individual cases. The lyric, on the other hand, is always capable of rejuvenation as is the human heart, and may produce individual lovely blooms even in periods of general wretchedness, though their form be imperfect. When epic and drama had lost their popular and living force, romance became the appropriate substitute form.

Unfortunately, this entire literature of the latest pagan age has reached us only in fragmentary form, and what we have lacks proper context; but romance does provide several attractive monuments. We have, for example, the *Shepherd's Tale* in Greek, ascribed to one Longus; but this name may well be the result of a misunderstanding, and in any case he cannot be dated to any definite period. But these charmingly told adventures of Daphnis and Chloë substantially determine a complete aesthetic judgment concerning the century—most likely the third—to which the doubtful author belongs. The descriptions, consistent in the naturalism of scenery and background and acute in their psychologic observation, go far beyond the bucolic characters and backgrounds inherited from Theocritus. The age capable of producing this book would appear to be not far removed from one amenable to genre and landscape painting. But *Daphnis and Chloë* stands completely isolated, and if we wish to compare it with other late Greek romances, we find that they and their authors likewise defy precise dating. Of Heliodorus (who has been several times cited), the author of the *Aethiopica*, it is doubtful whether he was the Bishop of Trikka in Thessaly of that name who flourished about 400, or whether it is not much more likely that the episcopal title was bestowed upon a pagan who lived at Emesa a century earlier (there is internal evidence for such authorship) in order to make his book eligible for preservation in Christian libraries. The author's aim, like that of Xenophon of Ephesus, is to present the greatest possible variety of adventures, and later romancers emulated this aim as well as they could. But there is no trace of the consistent and genuinely artistic character delineation of Longus or of his prudent limitations in costume and locale. Heliodorus offers diversion often not very agreeable.

Now and again (for example, at the opening of his book) Heliodorus purposely lingers over descriptions of landscapes, and similar efforts occur in Longus. I will not venture to offer a bad and abbreviated sketch of Humboldt's history of aesthetic feeling in regard to landscape; but at this point I can do no other than refer to that incomparable account which deals in masterly fashion with the subject itself and with its relations to other spiritual tendencies in late antiquity.

The true lyric of this period, if any was produced, is no longer extant. Echoes like the *Pervigilium Veneris* (about 252?) or like the *Prayer to Oceanus* can hardly date lower than the middle of the third century. Tolerable individual flights in elegiac and epigrammatic form, dating into the fifth century, are hardly adequate substitutes. These breathe too plainly of the air of the schools, especially in Ausonius, and are too consciously constructed as specimens of their respective categories to produce any living impression. The highly gifted improviser Claudian, with his panegyrics, mythical tales, and idylls (in a word, miscellaneous poetry), comes quite late. Claudian is an unworthy flatterer in a period of aesthetic decadence, and yet his brilliant colors are almost Ovidian in invention and execution. He serves as a warning to the history of literature not to fix limits between periods too rigidly. Rutilius Numatianus (about 417), who has been mentioned above, is also not without a nobler and more agreeable side, but his travel poem as a whole is quite formless.

The thing that was officially recognized as literature and admired in the age of Constantine was the most deplorable of all productions, grammatical tricks with words and verses. Great play was made with centos from Vergil, that is, partial use was made of Vergilian verses to construct new poems of quite different content. Whatever violence was done to the sense, at least these were the most melodious Roman verses in existence. Other artifices are more objectionable. Among these are epanalepsis, which repeats the beginning word of the hexameter at the end of the pentameter; figured poems, which when carefully written out take the form of an altar, a pan-pipe, an organ, or the like; the combination of all Roman meters in a single poem; enumeration of animal cries; anacylic verses, which could be read backwards or forwards; and other such aberrations. The impossible in these astonishingly laborious devices was achieved by a certain Publilius Optatianus Porphyrius. He had been banished into exile for some reason and now sought to regain Constantine's favor by quite desperate poetic leaps and vaults, and actually succeeded in so doing. He wrote twenty-six poems, most of them of twenty to forty hexameters, each containing the same number of letters, so that each poem had the appearance of a square. Certain individual letters, written in red, produced some figure, a monogram, an XP, or a flourish, and when read continuously, spelled out separate apothegms. The toil which the reader experiences is an index to the toil which the poet devoted to the most trivial content, compliments to Constantine and Crispus. At the end there follow four hexameters whose words could be arranged in eighteen different ways, each of which produced a kind of sense and meter. In a very gracious letter to Optatianus Constantine, in the attitude of a patron of the arts, accepts the surmounting of these difficulties as a genuine advance in art: "He who writes and composes in my century is followed by my favoring attention as by a gentle zephyr." The artificer of verse had already been recalled from exile; perhaps the City Prefect of Rome of the same name who is mentioned in 329 and 333 is the same Optatianus. This whole incident might have been passed over if it did not reveal the taste of the Emperor.

The advent of Christianity into ancient poetry was not as great a gain for poetry as might be imagined. Poetic treatment of Biblical history was in quite a different case from that of ancient myth. Myth was capable of manifold forms and aspects, and so with poetry and through it could serve as a continuous revelation of the beautiful. But Biblical incidents were delivered to poetry in a fixed and completed form; epic or plastic decoration might be dangerous from the point of view of dogma. Hence the dryness of the versified harmonies of the Gospels, from that of the Spaniard Juvencus (329) onwards. The declamatory element was no adequate substitute, and only betrayed the rhetorical education of contemporary Christian poets. Prudentius (about 400), also a Spaniard, the most significant of these poets, has passages of this sort that are good and almost lyrical; and in his accounts of the martyrs (*Peristephanon*) he moves with much greater epic freedom than was possible in purely Biblical material. But the total impression of his poetry is disproportionately rhetorical. Several excellent hymns of his and of his contemporary Ambrose are justly regarded as the foundation for all Christian lyric. The dominance of stress accent over quantitative, which here makes its first frank and consistent appearance, marks a transition to the poetry of the Middle Ages, only external, to be sure, but remarkable nevertheless. Later a new, medieval spirit was to be breathed into the calcified Latin.

But rhetoric still ruled as queen. Education continued to be controlled by rhetoric. Of the so-called seven liberal arts—grammar, rhetoric, dialectic, arithmetic, music, geometry, and astronomy—which once constituted the "encyclopedic" education of young men of good position, the first three had continued as such, while increase of subject matter had made the other four separate disciplines of scholarship. During the Empire all that was left alive of philosophy was attached to the three former, and the schools of rhetoric were regarded as essential to education for the practice of law. It is difficult for us to get a proper notion of the extent and importance of rhetoric during this period. Easy and rich expression was regarded as indispensable in daily life, and successful public speaking as the highest triumph. Every important city of the Empire strove to acquire one or several worthy rhetors. At Rome Greeks and natives vied for pre-eminence. There were institutions for cultivating rhetoric in Gaul at Marseilles, Narbonne, Toulouse, Bordeaux, Autun, Treves, and Rheims, in Spain at Cordova, in Africa at Carthage, Sicca, Madaura, and elsewhere. In Greece and the Near East the "sophists" were often the most important personages in a city, for besides their pedagogical functions they appeared publicly on all occasions as adherents of a given philosophic sect, as advocates, as orators on public affairs. Not infrequently very wealthy and generous men devoted themselves to this pursuit, and then cut as grand a figure as was at all possible under such a government as the Roman. Finally the state itself, which had previously left higher education to the cities and to private individuals, resolved to regard it as a public concern, gave it support here and there, and itself paid the salaries of sophists for various cities, their number depending on the rank of the city. But arrangements of this sort, which are mentioned from the time of Hadrian and Antoninus Pius downwards, can hardly have long remained in full force. Constantine still confirmed the professors appointed by the state and the similarly highly privileged physicians together with their families, at least in their immunity from burdensome offices and contributions, specifically the much-feared decurionate, and from military service. He was himself, as will be shown below, a zealous amateur of oratory; a number of his predecessors down to Numerian are praised for the same interest. But Constantine's taste in oratory can hardly have been better than his taste in poetry. Everything that issued from the imperial bureau after Diocletian, letters, edicts, and laws, all bear the same curled and bombastic character. But the Emperors customarily selected their private secretaries and many other important court officials from the class of rhetors, and accordingly must for some time have looked to aptitudes other than literary style. Eumenius, secretary of Chlorus, is probably to be regarded as a notable exception.

Did not antiquity exaggerate the importance of education in discourse and writing? Would it not have done better to fill the heads of boys and young men with useful realities? The answer is that we have no right to make a decision as long as formlessness in discourse and writing persists among us everywhere, as long as perhaps barely one of a hundred of our educated men possesses any notion of the true art of periodic structure. To the ancients, rhetoric and its collateral sciences were the indispensable complement to their norm of beautiful and free existence, to their arts and their poetry. Modern life has higher principles and aims in some respects, but it is uneven and disharmonious. What is most beautiful and delicate in it is found alongside the crudest barbarism. And our multitudinous preoccupations do not leave us leisure to take offense at the contradictions.

A glance at the school books of later Roman rhetoric which have been preserved is sufficient to fill us with shame. These writings of Rutilius Lupus, Aquila, Rufinianus, Fortunatianus, Rufinus, and others are in part not genuine Roman productions, but perhaps jejune reworkings of Greek models from the ages of Gorgias and Aristotle and later; nevertheless they show the course in which men sought to guide oratory even in the latest period of the Empire. Not only does the system give a name and treatment to every sort of sentence structure, figure of speech, and artifice of construction, which we would not know how to name without the ancients and of which our modern treatises use scarcely a tithe, but there is also circumstantial treatment of the categories of oratorical style and of the structure and execution of orations. Of the infinite refinement of the ear in those days, we may get some notion from the fact that metrical differences in words or short groups of words, to us indistinguishable, are dealt with circumstantially (in Rufinus) and assigned to appropriate positions in the sentence, whether at its beginning, end, or elsewhere. It was important to determine in what cases a sentence should open with an anapaest or a spondee. The art of delivery and of the orator's outward bearing generally (in Fortunatianus) completes this discipline, and shows us again that all our modern speech is mere naturalism and attains beautiful form only through accidental talent and unconsciously. Every gesture of the hand, every dropping or folding of the garment had its own law. The orator was no less aware than the sculptor of such laws as that arm and leg must never be extended simultaneously on the same side. It was only thus that eloquence could be raised to virtuosity of the whole spiritual and physical man.

But the obverse was that of all virtuosity—a growing indifference to content and a concomitant increase in personal vanity. The Greek sophists of the early Empire, as they are described by Philostratus, exhibited themselves

in such themes as those mentioned above in a peculiarly
arrogant manner, and offered themselves to public admiration quite like certain representatives of modern music,
whose claims are strikingly similar to those of the rhetoricians. How political oratory subsequently dissolved into
panegyric in the West, and forensic oratory sank lower and
lower, this is not the place to show. From the ages of Diocletian and Constantine we possess perhaps the best of the
kind in the eulogies on the Emperors and Caesars which
have been several times cited. These are counterbalanced
by the poor diction of contemporary edicts. Among the
Christians style had been an incidental matter; it was only
some decades later that the famous succession of pulpit
orators began. These finally reconciled the new content
with the traditional but transmuted form. A curious cleavage had to be bridged: reverence for the classical style
and horror at its pagan associations, acceptance of the language of the Bible and consciousness of its impurity. St.
Jerome had to be shaken by a fearful vision, in which the
Judge of all the World was about to condemn him as a
Ciceronianus, non Christianus.

Meanwhile, throughout the fourth century rhetoric remained a life interest for the pagans and for countless
Christians. Certain countries, like Gaul and Africa, continued to be conscious, and not without pride, of certain
peculiarities of their styles, and in these countries rhetors
were among the most highly respected persons in society.
In the Greek regions of the Empire the sophists sought by
every means possible to maintain the position they had enjoyed in the age of the Antonines. But since they functioned simultaneously as Neoplatonic philosophers and
miracle-workers also, their historian Eunapius pays far less
attention to their rhetorical activity; at most he characterizes their outward bearing and admires their pretentions.
Our final section will deal with the situation in Athens;
here we need only point to the hopeless competition the
pagan sophists offered the Christian preachers. Considered
as a matter of public partisanship on one side or the other,
the struggle was altogether too uneven. But not every
rhetor could be content with the solace with which

Themistius shielded himself: "The value of a philosopher's discourse is not diminished if it is delivered under a solitary plane tree with none but cicadas to hear."

If almost all productions of the fourth century betray decline by labored and tortured form, by heaping up of *sententiae,* by the misuse of metaphor for the simple and the commonplace, by modern turgidity and artificial archaic aridity, still a peculiar reflection of the classic period rests upon many of these writers. They still show the requirement of artistic style, which is normally alien to us; that the style emerges as something calculated and self-conscious is the fault of the sinking age, which felt quite clearly that it and its culture was something secondary and derivative, and imitated the great models painstakingly and unevenly. But it is impossible to dismiss lightly authors like Libanius and Symmachus, for example, whose every little letter was wrought into a minor work of art—even though they attached too great importance to their performance and clearly reckoned on a reading public besides the addressee—as Pliny and others had done before them. Symmachus at least knew that the Ciceronian period of epistolography was over and why it was over.

Does a formal decline in poetry and representational art always imply a people's national decline also? Are those arts not blossoms which must fall before fruit can mature? Cannot the true take the place of the beautiful, the useful of the agreeable?

The question may remain unsolved, and between such alternatives as the last there can be no solution. But anyone who has encountered classical antiquity, if only in its twilight, feels that with beauty and freedom there departed also the genuine antique life, the better part of the national genius, and that the rhetorizing orthodoxy which was left to the Greek world can only be regarded as a lifeless precipitate of a once wonderful totality of being.

VIII

THE PERSECUTION OF CHRISTIANS
CONSTANTINE AND THE SUCCESSION

FROM THE MIDST of conditions whose history is clearly and precisely known there sometimes emerges a fact of the first importance whose deeper causes stubbornly elude the eye of the student. Such an event is the great persecution of Christians under Diocletian, the last war of annihilation waged by paganism against Christianity. At first glance there is nothing strange in these persecutions; Diocletian had all too many predecessors upon the throne of the world who similarly wished to extirpate the Christians, and scarcely any other course was to be expected of so zealous and confirmed a pagan as he was. But the question takes on a quite different aspect when we consider the circumstances in detail. From the time of Gallienus—that is, for more than forty years—the Christians had remained unmolested, and to this period belong the first eighteen years of Diocletian's own reign. Even after he had ordered the Manichaeans to be burnt at the stake (296), he left the Christians in peace for seven years. His wife Prisca and his daughter Valeria are said to have been not unfavorably disposed to the Christians; Diocletian himself even tolerated about his sacred person Christian chamberlains and pages to whom he was devoted as a father. Courtiers and their wives and children might practice the Christian religion under his very eyes. Christians who were dispatched to the provinces as governors were graciously excused from the solemn sacrifices which their position entailed. Christian congregations felt perfectly secure and were so greatly strengthened that their old meeting places nowhere sufficed. New buildings were constructed everywhere; in the large cities very handsome churches arose, and there was no fear.

If the government had any thought of persecution in the future it should not have suffered the Christians to expand to such power in the state without resistance. It may be said that the state became aware gradually and late that Christianity, if completely tolerated, would strive for predominance; but Diocletian cannot have been so heedless. The persecution cannot possibly have resulted, as it seems to me, either from his original or from his gradually formed conviction without special occasion. Judgment in this case must be conditioned by the fact that we have to do with one of the greatest of the Roman Emperors, with the savior of the Empire and of civilization, with the shrewdest judge of his time, whose political memory would be quite different if he had died in 302. "He was an outstanding man, clever, zealous for the state, zealous for those under his protection, prepared for any task that might come to his hand, always unfathomable in his thoughts, sometimes foolhardy but otherwise prudent; the stirrings of his restless spirit he suppressed with inflexible perseverance."* What we have to determine, then, is whether the thing which darkens this great memory was merely an outbreak of inherent cruelty and brutality, or a consequence of the superstition which has been described above, or an unfortunate concession to colleagues who were of much less stature, or finally whether the historian is not here confronted with an obligation to seek an explanation beyond that to be derived from the letter of the records. The Christians heaped the name of Diocletian with curses, and neither could pagans of Greek or Roman education favor him because he introduced Orientalism into political and social life. The only historians who might possibly present a true nexus of events—Ammianus and Zosimus—are mangled, and perhaps for the very reason that they treated Diocletian fairly. Un-

---

* *Historia Augusta Numerian.*, ch. 13.

der such circumstances it is quite futile to look to extant
sources directly for what is essential and conclusive.

The account which is usually regarded as basic—namely,
Lactantius' *Of the Deaths of the Persecutors*—begins
straightway with a demonstrable untruth. An important inspection of entrails in the presence of the Emperor was disturbed by the fact that Christian courtiers who were present crossed themselves and so expelled the daimones; the
sacrifice was several times repeated in vain, until the chief
of the haruspices surmised and declared the cause. Thereupon Diocletian in a fury of rage is said to have demanded
idolatrous sacrifice of all the courtiers and even to have
extended this command to the army under threat of dismissal; and there, for a time, the matter rested. This story
rests upon a belief, adequately refuted by Eusebius, that
the Emperor did not know that the Christians at his court
were such and would not have tolerated Christians. The
probability is that Christian chamberlains and pages either
were not required to be present at sacrifices at all or, if they
happened to be present, that they conducted themselves
in a manner the Emperor thought seemly. Such a scene as
that described either must have taken place much earlier,
at Diocletian's accession, or was altogether unthinkable.
The Emperor's pagan convictions, which accommodated
themselves to the existence and power of the Christians for
eighteen years, cannot have been the decisive motive for
the persecutions, earnest and zealous as those convictions
were.

The second untruth in Lactantius' account is Diocletian's timorous yielding to Galerius, who had arrived at
Nicomedia (apparently from the Danube) in order to win
the Emperor over for the persecution; Galerius for his part
is said to have been incited by his mother Romula. Romula
was a zealous devotee of the great Magna Mater (who
is here designated a mountain goddess), and took it very
ill that the Christians in her place of residence refused to
participate, as the pagans did, in her daily sacrificial feasts.
All of this gossip, which places ultimate responsibility upon
the whim of a fanatical woman, is reduced to nothing when
we understand that Diocletian was not afraid of Galerius

and that Lactantius is culpable of very serious error concerning the whole character of Diocletian. No weight is to be attached to the alleged conversations said to have taken place at Nicomedia in the winter of 302–303, for the author elsewhere reveals himself as an amateur of dramatic fictions. He seeks to characterize Diocletian as more reluctant and more reasonable in order to heap greater hatred upon the monster Galerius. "When they were taking counsel throughout the winter, and no one was admitted, and everyone believed that they were dealing with matters of state, the elder long opposed the fury of his colleague and represented to him how dangerous it was to disturb the world and to shed streams of blood. The Christians would die gladly. It would be enough if courtiers and soldiers were required to renounce this religion. But Galerius persisted in his intention stubbornly, and Diocletian thereupon convoked a secret council of jurists and officers to decide on the question of the persecution. For it was in his character to draw many persons into his counsel for hateful measures in order to be able to shift the blame for evil; good things, on the other hand, he did without counsel in order to obtain the credit for himself." Such dealing is unthinkable, in view of all our other information concerning Diocletian. The concept of the ruler by which he was inspired took no account of what the people might find welcome or hateful, and took full responsibility for whatever was carried out through others, whether good or bad. For any measure which was allowed without the ruler's authority would be tantamount to a breach in his power, which must be his first and last consideration. But let us hear further. Upon the affirmative decision of the secret council Diocletian made an altogether superfluous inquiry of the Milesian Apollo, and naturally received the same response. Even now he gave his consent with the condition that no blood must flow, while Galerius is said to have been very eager to burn the Christians alive. But we have just heard from the senior Emperor's own mouth that he foresaw numerous martyrdoms of Christians! He was in better position than anyone to know that the Christians must either be left in peace or combated with extreme measures, and that the stipulation of a bloodless procedure was folly.

This is the nature of the only consecutive account of the great catastrophe. And Lactantius was in Nicomedia at the time, and might have recorded, not, to be sure, the secret negotiations, but the essential course of events, and perhaps with great exactness. For many details his treatise is as indispensable as so partisan a document can well be.

Eusebius finds it convenient to say nothing at all of special reasons for the persecution. Aurelius Victor, Rufus, Festus, Eutropius, and the rest do not even mention the persecution.

Diocletian himself can offer no defense. His edicts have perished, and his secret designs may have been the exact opposite of those imagined.

Hence the field is open to conjecture, so long as conjecture does not soar in the air but follows the true tracks that survive and is in keeping with the character of the times and of the persons involved.

The readiest conjecture is that the rulers, like many of their predecessors, were compelled to yield to popular fury against the Christians. But such yielding does not appear in the course of the events, and the power of the state was fully adequate to suppress such fury. It did indeed happen that the crowds at the games in the Circus Maximus shouted in rhythmic chant some ten or a dozen times: *"Christiani tollantur, Christiani non sint"*—"Out with the Christians, let there be no Christians"—but this apparently happened after the persecution had been in progress for some time, and in any case cries of this sort meant little.

Or it might be assumed that the pagan priests demanded the persecution suddenly and unconditionally, and the Emperors were convinced of the need of it on some grounds of superstition. With all his acumen, Diocletian was sufficiently steeped in superstition to make such conjectures plausible; at least there is no proof to the contrary. But in that case we should have had the names of such powerful priests recorded; the mere mention of Hierocles, Governor of Bithynia (known from other sources as a zealous Neoplatonist), among the supporters and instigators is not sufficient.

Could Diocletian's sense of private morality have been involved? He was not indifferent to morality; the female haruspex who was constantly employed to foretell the future and its fate had not carried him beyond moral considerations. If this involves a logical inconsistency, it is all to his credit; a similar disharmony, as we have seen, characterized the better men of the third century generally, in whom belief in immortality, if it did not reconcile fatalism and morality, at least enforced an accommodation between them. The private life of the Emperor afforded no grounds of criticism even to the most censorious Christian, and he therefore could justly stand forth as the guardian of general morality in the state. He did so, among other instances, in the marriage law of 295 (which has already been cited), in which he laid down high principles: "The immortal gods will be favorably and kindly disposed to the Roman name as they have been in the past if we take care that all our subjects lead a pious, calm, and pure life. . . . Rome's majesty has attained its great height, by grace of all the gods, only because a pious and chaste life constitutes the keystone of all legislation. . . ." Can it be that the Christians gave moral offense?

We know that in the first and second centuries the Romans bandied about rumors of horrible cruelties which were supposed to take place at the worship of the Christians. But these rumors are not relevant here; they had long been silenced, and Diocletian, who saw a great many Christians at his court daily, cannot have given the slightest credit to gossip of this sort.

The case is apparently different with Eusebius' complaints concerning the internal demoralization of the Christian communities immediately before the persecution. A host of unworthy persons had invaded the Church and even forced their way to the episcopal thrones. Among these evils Eusebius mentions in particular the bitter feuds between bishops and between individual congregations, the hypocrisy and deception, beliefs well-nigh atheistic, wicked deeds (κακίας), and again, quarrel, envy, hatred, and the violent rule of the clergy.

But these are not transgressions of a sort the state would feel bound to persecute for the sake of morality. Similar things occurred among the pagans, and in more abundant measure. But remarkably enough, one of the few official documents of the pagan side which has been preserved, Galerius' edict of revocation of 311, appears to designate the serious and multiform cleavages among the Christians themselves as the principal cause of the persecution. They had backslid from the faith of their fathers and had formed sects, they had been bidden to return to the institutions of their elders, and so on. Every word in this passage, indeed, is so oblique and equivocal that most interpreters could as well understand "fathers" and "elders" to mean pagans. Yet several expressions seem rather to charge the Christians with backsliding from their own principles. Further along we read: "We saw that they neither paid due worship to the gods, nor honored the God of the Christians." This is somewhat reminiscent of the principles of the Catholic party in the Thirty Years' War; they felt on equal legal ground with the Lutherans only, and abhorred the Calvinists as a by-sect.

But neither can this track well be the correct one. Disagreements and cleavages among the Christians can never have been so significant that the state would feel compelled to do away with the entire community for their sake. Zealous pagans, if they gave the matter any thought, could have wished for nothing more earnestly than that the process of decay should continue undisturbed, for it must eventually have delivered the Christians into their hands.

What explanation, then, is left us? I believe that some important personal occurrence is involved, and that its traces were subsequently most carefully obliterated. An inscription in honor of Diocletian accuses the Christians of wishing to overthrow the state—*rem publicam evertebant;* in this form the statement is without value, but it may conceal a nucleus of truth. Could it be that the Christians, sensible of their growth and expansion, sought to gain control of the imperial office?

This could have been achieved quite peaceably, by converting Diocletian. That something of the sort was at least intended can be virtually demonstrated. There is extant a letter of a Bishop Theonas to a Christian chief chamberlain named Lucianus, containing instructions for conduct at the court of a pagan Emperor; it is generally agreed that the Emperor can only have been Diocletian. Lucianus had already been working as effectively as he could among his associates and had converted many who had entered court service as pagans. The superintendents of the imperial privy purse, the treasure, and the wardrobe had already gone over to Christianity. Now Theonas finds that it would be highly useful if a Christian chamberlain, for example, would receive charge of the imperial library and on the occasion of literary conversations could prudently and gradually convince the Emperor of the truth of the Christian religion. Probably the Christians were impressed by the seriousness and moral bent of the great ruler and realized that his conversion would be more important and decisive than ever, now that the imperial authority had been raised to unprecedented heights by victories over barbarians and usurpers and by the reform of the whole internal machinery of state. It hardly needs to be said that all attempts of this sort were bound to be futile with a pagan like Diocletian.

We must notice carefully how the persecution began. Eusebius and Lactantius are agreed that some time before the large general measures the Christians had been expelled from the army. Perhaps as early as 298 or even earlier a muster took place at which the Christian soldiers were given the choice of becoming pagans and retaining their service or losing it. The majority unhesitatingly preferred the latter alternative, and it is said that a few lost their lives on that account. It is patent that such a step would be taken only reluctantly and perforce, for good soldiers and officers were the Empire's most valuable resource at the time. We may venture the further conclusion that this purge of the army was based not on religious but on political reasons, for otherwise it might have begun with any other class, for example, with the sudden arrest of all bishops, a step that was actually taken later. Either the

Emperors no longer felt personally secure among Christian troops or they believed they could not rely on their obedience, in war as in peace. Refusal to participate in pagan sacrifice, if that were alleged as reason for discharge, could only have been a pretext, for the military service of Christians had been looked upon as a matter of course for a decade and a half. It might indeed be said that the Emperors purged the army out of diabolic wickedness, so that it might be employed in the imminent persecution without objection on the part of Christians. The contrary cannot be proved, for we do not know what period elapsed between the purge and the persecution. If the intervening period ran to several years, the probability of this explanation vanishes utterly. Great deeds of blood may be planned and prepared far in advance, but so striking a preparation as this, if the persecution were the sole object of the purge, would be expected to be exhibited only a moment before the actual execution. The transitions are hard to distinguish. If Diocletian desired a purely pagan army, he desired it for the sake of obedience generally, without calculating how he might eventually employ it in extreme cases. Remarkably enough, Diocletian kept his entire Christian court about him until after the persecution had started, perhaps because he wished to retain the personal trust to which he had grown used as long as possible.

In connection with all of this we recall what Eusebius half admits and half conceals, that at the beginning of the persecution insurrections broke out at two places, in the Cappadocian region of Melitene and in Syria. Eusebius is not entirely reliable for the chronology of events, but we have no other resource here. He tells of the publication of the edict first, and then the beginning of the persecution in Nicomedia and indeed in the royal palace, and he describes the heroic deaths of the Christian pages and chamberlains. Then he speaks of the conflagrations in the palace and of the Christians put to death on that occasion, and also of the exhumation of the executed pages. Then he proceeds: "Forasmuch as not long thereafter some in the region called Melitene and again others in Syria sought to seize the rule for themselves, an imperial command was

issued that the heads of congregations everywhere should
be arrested and thrown into chains." Rightly or wrongly,
then, the attempt at usurpation was ascribed to Christians,
and in consequence the bishops were seized. But the immediate agents must have been in part soldiers, for at this
time no usurpation was conceivable without soldiers, and
if they were Christians they must have been retired soldiers. It may be objected that these usurpations arose out
of despair at the persecution which had already been ordered, but it is equally probable that the Emperors had
already had notice of unrest among the retired soldiers. If
Eusebius' statements on chronology and incidents are correct, and we were indifferent to the implications and concerned only for the scientific interest, criticism would acknowledge without difficulty that the Emperors found an
opposition ready armed against them and suppressed it.

Finally, the content of the edict itself, so far as it is
known, is calculated not to annihilate the Christians directly
but to degrade them consistently, as a means toward effecting their conversion. Their gatherings for worship were
to be forbidden, their churches to be pulled down, their
sacred scriptures burned. Those who possessed offices of
honor and other dignities were to lose them. In judicial
investigations torture might be employed against Christians
of every class. The benefits of ordinary law were to be
withdrawn from them; Christian slaves might never be
manumitted as long as they remained Christian. Such, approximately, were the prescriptions which were published
abroad 24 February 303 first in Nicomedia, at the time
the residence of Diocletian and Galerius, and then throughout the Empire.

In Nicomedia itself the persecution began on the preceding day, on which the festival of the Terminalia fell,
when a Prefect of the Guard accompanied by officers and
officials had the great church plundered and demolished
by his Praetorians.

After the edict was posted its first victim was a respected
Christian who pulled it down and tore it into bits, with the
scornful remark that victories over Goths and Sarmatae had
again been posted up. The man was burned to death. Defi-

ance such as this would be quite inexplicable unless we assume that even at that critical moment there was some secret hope for general resistance.

Next we are told of the cruel torture and execution of a number of palace officials and pages, of whom Peter, Dorotheus, and Gorgonius are mentioned by name. Eusebius, to be sure, informs us quite briefly only that they suffered for the sake of their piety; but if only piety were involved the law would have been content with their degradation. Why such cruelty against those who had previously been treated by the Emperors as "children of the household" despite their known Christianity? Clearly the Emperors believed they were on the track of a plot.

In the meanwhile fire twice broke out in the palace at Nicomedia. According to Lactantius, Galerius caused the fires to be set, in order to place the blame on the Christians, who were said to have agreed on the crime with the court eunuchs; and Diocletian, who always thought himself so clever, failed to realize the true situation but immediately fell into a boundless fury against the Christians. On this point it is impossible to plead with a partisan writer; but anyone who has studied the history of Diocletian will grant him sufficient intelligence to see through so clumsy a trick as that posited by Lactantius. The fire broke out in the portion of the palace inhabited by Diocletian himself. But Galerius would have been the last man to set his house afire over his head. The highest probability suggests that Christian courtiers whose safety was imperiled were the guilty parties; their intention may have been to intimidate the Emperor through superstition, not to cause his death. On a later ceremonial occasion Constantine, who had been present at Nicomedia at the time, sought to exculpate all and sundry by maintaining that the palace had been fired by a bolt of lightning, as if it were not easy to distinguish lightning from other causes of fire. Both Emperors, indeed, were convinced that the Christians were guilty, and the criminal investigation in the palace took a bloody course. "Even the mightiest eunuchs, who once ruled palace and Emperor, were put to death." It is not to be wondered that under the impress of this bitterness the general edict was carried out with drastic severity and supplemented by further orders.

Soon there followed the Christian uprisings in the East, which have been mentioned above, and these provoked the second edict, which ordered the arrest of all heads of communities.

Perhaps the reader will take exception to this investigation. Is it not altogether unjust to make the persecution a cause for incrimination? So had the fanatic party done in France in 1572, and so in Valtelline in 1620; to justify their frightful shedding of blood they subsequently charged that their subdued opponents had engineered a bloody plot, which they were compelled to forestall.

In the first place, no one can here speak of a general Christian conspiracy against the rulers or against pagans generally. Our more limited concept of the outline of the incident is somewhat as follows: Certain Christian courtiers, perhaps very few in number, and certain Christian commanders in the provinces thought they could put the Empire into Christian hands or hands favorable to Christians by a hasty *coup*, perhaps intending to spare the persons of the Emperors. It is possible that Galerius actually discovered traces of the affair before Diocletian, and that the latter could only with difficulty be persuaded.

In the second place no one will deny that among the Christians of the time there were persons whose conscience would not scruple at such a *coup*. Eusebius' characterization is sufficiently explicit. On the other hand, earthly power has never shown itself lenient when its existence has been threatened.

The great misfortune was comprised in the fact that the rulers generalized what had taken place and proceeded against all Christians as being implicated in the guilt, and in the fact that contemporary law was so quick with torture and with gruesome death penalties. But to be in a position to judge individual cases correctly we must have better sources than the *Acts of the Martyrs* usually are. In any case a very great majority accommodated themselves to participation in sacrifice in the course of time, and Diocletian's last edicts, of which we shall speak below, perhaps rest on the premise that success had been achieved, by and large, and that only a remnant of opposition was left to be overcome. The surrender of their sacred scriptures was further calculated to deprive the community permanently of a spiritual support.

But there was more than enough of struggle left to maintain a state of high tension. It is not the task of this book to follow the frightful course of events in detail. Of Diocletian's colleagues, the Augustus Maximian proceeded to the persecution with zeal, whereas the gentle and monotheistic Caesar, Constantius Chlorus, is said to have contented himself, in his area of Gaul and Britian, with merely pulling down the churches. In any case he retained Christians at his court at Treves or York, and even for military employment. But in other parts of the Empire the persecution was all the harder. From the many cases of torture and martyrdom it appears that the investigation had fallen in part into the worst hands; but we must also consider the possibility that the judges thought they were dealing with a political investigation, in which the extortion of confessions is important. The attitudes of officials varied greatly. In Africa, where political suspicions were perhaps wholly out of the question and where substantially all that was involved was surrender of the sacred scriptures, the Christians were frequently given to understand that even that requirement would not be too rigidly enforced. But many purposely declared that they had sacred scriptures in their keeping which they would not surrender, and suffered death for their defiance. Others immediately heeded the general order and delivered all that they had; these were later branded with the name *traditores,* "surrenderers." In general a varied range of tempers was revealed, from the most cowardly weakness to fanatic provocation, and in between there were not wanting splendid examples of calm and reasonable fortitude. Here we learn something about the lower strata of the Christian community also. There were people who wished to expiate some crime of which they were guilty by a Christian martyr's death, quite like the thousands of robbers and murderers who joined in the First Crusade. Others were indebted to the state for taxes

they could never pay or were burdened by private indebtedness, and sought to escape their troubles by death,
or hoped to move rich Christians to help them by their
endurance under torture and in imprisonment. Finally,
there were destitute people who enjoyed a better life in
prison than outside, because Christians fearlessly supplied
their captive brethren with more than bare necessities. In
the face of such abuses Bishop Mensurius of Carthage had
the courage and consistency to demand that those who had
needlessly invited martyrdom must not be revered as
martyrs.

Meanwhile, in the course of little more than a year, the
investigation had sharpened into an actual, general persecution of Christians. The second edict, which ordered the
arrest of the clergy, was followed by a third, according to
which the prisoners were to be released if they offered
sacrifice, otherwise they were to be forced to do so by any
means. In 304 a fourth decree extended the latter provision
to all Christians generally, and by construction implied the
death penalty. In the East the persecution continued at
this pitch of rigor for some four years, and then with certain deviations for five more; in the West it came to an
end earlier.

Church history has long regarded it a sacred duty to preserve the memory of the noblest and most edifying of the
martyrdoms of this period. We must be content to refer to
Eusebius and the collections of legends for details. Despite
the exceptions which historical criticism may justly take to
individual circumstances and especially to the miracles
which have become attached to them, the sight of this
new society with its new religion and philosophy struggling against the most powerful of all states with its paganism and its millennium-old culture, and eventually prevailing by its very suppression, is nevertheless a historical
spectacle of the greatest magnitude.

Apparently the persecutors became thoroughly demoralized when Diocletian and his colleagues laid down their
dignities (305), Galerius and Constantius advanced to the
rank of Augustus, and Severus and Maximinus Daia took
their place as Caesars. Henceforth the campaign degen-

erated, especially in the latter's realm—the southeastern portion of the Empire—to a true war of extermination; the reader may be spared the gruesome scenes of horror.

We now return to political history, which underwent highly important developments at this same time.

Soon after the beginning of the persecution, as early as the spring of 303, Diocletian journeyed to the West, and in the autumn arrived at Rome, there to celebrate, jointly with Maximian, the triumph for so many victories which had been saved up, and at the same time the vicennalia of his reign. In comparison with the luxury of a Carinus, the expense of the triumph and the duration of the festival were very moderate; and when the Romans murmured the Emperor replied jestingly that in the presence of the censors the games could not be so extravagant. He revealed his opinion of Roman gossip by leaving the city on 20 December, without awaiting the new year and the ceremonies incident to the change of consuls. This had been his first visit to Rome since his accession. That he had built (after 298) the most colossal of all baths appears to have earned him no gratitude; that he had even now presented the Romans with a greater gift in money (a congiary of 310 million denarii, equivalent to some sixty-two million talers) than had any of his predecessors did not improve the popular temper: the people had expected more sumptuous games, and they had been disappointed.

Diocletian greeted the new year (304) at Ravenna. He fell gravely ill on the wintry journey to Nicomedia, and from then till his abdication (1 May 305) he was scarcely seen in public. Of the great ceremony of abdication itself Lactantius gives a circumstantial description, vitiated only by Lactantius' essential unreliability. The hill three thousand paces from Nicomedia, the column with the statue of Jupiter, the tears of the old Emperor at his address to the soldiers, the traveling-carriage which stood ready for him —all this is doubtless true. But that everyone expected that Constantine, who was present, would be raised instead of Severus or Maximinus, that the sudden advance of the hitherto unknown Maximinus aroused the greatest astonishment, and that the procedure had been expressly designed to take the soldiers by surprise—this we may venture to doubt. What did the populace of Nicomedia know of the senior Emperor's system of adoptions, or even of his intention to proclaim new adoptions on the spot? But there may well have been persons who wished to see the rise of Constantine; whether there were such in the army is questionable, for as a mere tribune of the first rank he can hardly have acquired wide popularity. What Diocletian thought of him at this time we do not know; earlier he had been favorably disposed to him, from the period of the campaigns—and Constantine subsequently repaid him by deprociatory remarks and cunning plots.

The motives for the abdication we have endeavored to present in their true light in an earlier context. Unless our conclusions are wrong, the imperial office was to be limited to a fixed period of twenty years, in order to regularize, as far as possible, the wonderful dynasty which had no hereditary rights, and to make a calm and undisturbed succession of adoptions possible. It is not unlikely that superstition had its word in this business also, at least in the matter of Diocletian's firm reliance on the obedience of his co-rulers. Here we can only suppose that Diocletian had secret fatalistic grounds for hoping to convince all his successors of the necessity of his measures.

However that may be, Diocletian was content and happy, at least for some time, in his camp-palace at Salonae. It is high testimony in his favor that after long years of war and a dream of rule that lasted for twenty years he sought out the sites and the occupations of his youth and delved and planted his vegetable garden with his own hands. May we not conclude that he had always inwardly risen above the Oriental court ceremonies which he introduced and that at Nicomedia he had often longed for his Dalmatian home? In the case of this remarkable man it will always remain impossible to distinguish what belongs to ordinary ambition, to a belief in destiny, and to the force of political genius. He understood how to give the Roman Empire what it needed for its preservation, namely, permanence of rule; and he must have been driven to the throne inexorably in order to give his thoughts realization. Now his task was absolved, and he could retire to silence.

Maximian, who was obliged to carry out the same official act in Italy, but much against his will, retired to a beautifully situated estate in Lucania, while his son Maxentius chose despised Rome or its vicinity for his seat. Himself despised and reckoned unworthy to rule, he had a correct appreciation of the situation, and it is hard to believe that Galerius willingly allowed him to reside in this region. Perhaps objection was made at once, but he was not to be moved by fair means. One consequence of Diocletian's system, as has been noted above, was not provided for: sons of Emperors had either to be promoted or executed. But for reasons which we have sought to determine above, a hereditary dynasty was avoided, and of pure sultanism, as it appears, Diocletian would have no part, as previously, after the fall of Carinus, he would have no part of proscriptions. Furthermore, Maxentius had married Galerius' daughter, possibly against his own and Galerius' will and only for the sake of following an arrangement of the aged senior Emperor.

For several months the entire succession seemed to follow its prescribed course. But at the beginning of the year following (306), a new character appears in this remarkable drama. Constantine, whom history justly styles the Great, spirited himself away from the court at Nicomedia and suddenly appeared with his father Constantius Chlorus as the latter was on the point of sailing from the harbor of Gessoriacum (Boulogne) for Britain.

Constantine's historical memory has suffered the greatest misfortune conceivable. That pagan writers must be hostile to him is obvious and would do him no damage in the eyes of posterity. But he has fallen into the hands of the most objectionable of all eulogists, who has utterly falsified his likeness. The man is Eusebius of Caesarea and the book his *Life of Constantine*. The man who with all his faults was always significant and always powerful is here presented in the guise of a sanctimonious devotee; in point of fact his numerous misdeeds are amply documented in a number of passages. Eusebius' equivocal praise is basically insincere. He speaks of the man but really means a cause, and that cause is the hierarchy, so strongly and richly established by Constantine. Furthermore, to say nothing of the contemptible style, there is a consciously furtive mode of expression, so that the reader finds himself treading concealed traps and bogs at the most vital passages. The reader who notices these hazards in time may be easily misled into putting the worst possible construction upon what has been withheld from him.

The introduction of this biography is ecstatic enough: "When I gaze in spirit upon this thrice-blessed soul, united with God, free of all mortal dross, in robes gleaming like lightning and in ever radiant diadem, speech and reason stand mute, and I would willingly leave it to a better man to devise a worthy hymn of praise." Would that had been the case! If we only possessed instead the description of a reasonable pagan like Ammianus, we should come infinitely closer to the great historical phenomenon which was the man Constantine, even though his moral character might not have emerged unsullied. Then we could perhaps see clearly what we can now only surmise, namely, that virtually throughout his life Constantine never assumed the guise of or gave himself out as a Christian but kept his free personal convictions quite unconcealed to his very last days. That Eusebius is fully capable of ignoring and concealing such a fact he himself reveals by his earlier characterization of Licinius, whom he claims straightway as a Christian Emperor beloved of God as long as the war against Maximinus Daia is involved, though he must have known that Licinius was nothing else than a tolerant pagan. It is highly probable that his treatment of Constantine is of a similar character. Then at least the odious hypocrisy which disfigures his character would disappear, and we should have instead a calculating politician who shrewdly employed all available physical resources and spiritual powers to the one end of maintaining himself and his rule without surrendering himself wholly to any party. It is true that the picture of such an egoist is not very edifying either, but history has had ample opportunity to grow accustomed

to his like. Moreover, with a little latitude we can easily
be persuaded that from his first political appearance Constantine consistently acted according to the principle which
energetic ambition, as long as the world has endured, has
called "necessity." It is that remarkable concatenation of
deeds and destiny to which ambitious men who are highly
gifted are drawn as by some mysterious power. In vain
does the sense of righteousness enter its protest, in vain do
millions of prayers of the oppressed rise to Nemesis; the
great man, frequently unconsciously, consummates higher
decrees, and an epoch is expressed in his person, while he
believes that he himself is ruling his age and determining
its character.

With Constantine our judgment of his very first step is
decisive. Galerius, it is said, planned his certain destruction
in the war against the Sarmatae and then in a "gymnastic"
contest with wild beasts, but the fearless hero prevailed
over barbarians and lions alike, and laid them at the feet
of the new senior Emperor. Then, despite frequent requests
of Constantius Chlorus to send him his son, Galerius in a
quite hostile spirit retained Constantine near his person like
a prisoner, and only yielded when it was no longer possible for him to refuse. Provided then with permission,
Constantine departed in greatest secrecy before the time
fixed, and at the first stage lamed the horses of the imperial
post so that no one could pursue him. From all of this we
may probably accept so much—that he seriously thought
he was threatened. Galerius must have hated him, as a
rejected and yet ambitiously striving son of an Emperor,
but he *did* release him, though it is highly probable that
Constantine was deeply involved in court intrigues after
the persecution. In any case Constantius had the right to
summon his son to himself.

After he joined his father, he participated in his father's
victorious campaign against the Picts in Scotland. Chlorus
was by no means at the point of death, as Eusebius and
Lactantius say to make their account more moving, and had
not summoned his son for that reason. But shortly after his
return from the war he did die (at York, 25 July 306).
According to the arrangements of Diocletian, to whom all

concerned owed their positions, Galerius was now to nominate a new Augustus and to provide him with a new
Caesar. But if the law of heredity were to be held a factor
along with this imperial law, then the sons of Constantius
by his marriage with Flavia Maximiana Theodora, the stepdaughter of the old Maximian—to wit, Dalmatius, Han-
niballianus, and Julius Constantius—would have unquestioned precedence. They were all very young, however,
the eldest being barely thirteen.

Instead, Constantine succeeded. It may be too much to
spring to the defence of the wonderfully contrived Diocletianic ordinances for the succession; but by their strict
letter Constantine was a usurper. He was born to Constantius of his concubine Helena at Nissa in Serbia in 274,
and thus, strictly speaking, was ineligible even according to
the laws of inheritance. The panegyrist Eumenius, to be
sure, makes him out to be legitimate and thinks he would
have willingly asked permission of the retired Emperors,
but these are mere words. Aside from this, the panegyric
in question is not without interest, because the sanctity of
the right of inheritance is there defended with genuine
warmth. With reference to his descent from the house of
the great Claudius Gothicus, Constantine is thus addressed: "So exalted is the nobility of thy origin that the
Empire can bestow no higher dignity upon thee. . . . It
was no accidental agreement on the part of others, no sudden favor that made thee emperor; by thy birth didst thou
merit rule, as a gift of the gods."

But the agreement and favor of others was not so trifling
a matter for Constantine's accession to the throne. Whether
his father directly empowered him to become his successor we cannot determine, because of the partisan nature of
our sources. Perhaps the father summoned his thirty-two-
year-old son, who was vigorous and experienced in war,
only to protect his helpless family. Later authors, as for example Zonaras, have a convenient explanation: "Constantius Chlorus lay sick, and was troubled by the thought that
his other children had turned out so badly. Thereupon an
angel appeared to him and bade him leave the rule to Constantine." Others, like Eusebius, Lactantius, and Orosius,

do not take the trouble to find a motivation, but write as if Constantine's succession was altogether self-evident. The fact is that the soldiers of his father raised him to be Imperator Augustus. The principal voice was that of a chieftain of the Alemanni named Crocus (or Erocus) whom Constantius had recruited, together with his followers, for service in the war against the Picts. Hope for a rich donative was naturally a contributory motive. The panegyrist cited above provides a sentimental account of the transaction: "Upon your first riding forth the warriors cast the purple over you as you wept. . . . You wished to flee this demonstration of zealous devotion, and put spurs to your horse; but that, to speak plainly, was a youthful error. What steed could have proven fleet enough to withdraw you from the rule which pursued you?" To divine the details of the intrigue here enacted is futile.

When Galerius learned what had happened he did what he could; since Constantine could be disposed of only by a very dangerous internal war, he accorded him recognition, but only as second Caesar; he named Severus as Augustus, and Maximinus Daia as first Caesar. His true consecration as ruler Constantine procured in his campaigns against the Germans over a period of several years, which have been treated above. Gaul could be ruled at the time only by the man who was its defender and savior, and upon that field the father had left the son at least gleanings.

The immediate and inevitable consequence of Constantine's usurpation was the usurpation of Maxentius. What one Emperor's son had been permitted to do could hardly be denied to another's. Out of regard for Diocletian's prescriptions, Maxentius' father Maximian long opposed the usurpation, but he eventually proved unable to resist his own temptations and acceded to it. Although Maxentius was perhaps already known as profligate and vicious, he found natural allies in the ill will of the Romans, who had been deserted by the Emperors, and in the Praetorians, whose prestige had been so greatly reduced. It is also possible that Diocletian's last angry departure from Rome in 303 was somehow connected with the first beginnings of a plot of this character. Galerius had finally transgressed all limits by making the ancient world metropolis equally liable for his new imposts. Maxentius won over a few officers, a large contractor, and the Praetorians, who straightway proclaimed him Emperor. The city prefect, who was minded to oppose them, had already been put to death. It appears that all Italy quickly fell into the power of the usurper.

Now Galerius could no longer merely look on. He dispatched his colleague Severus (307), who as heir to the dominions of Maximian was presumably master of Italy. But Severus' army, consisting largely of Maximian's veterans, could not be used against Maxentius. There followed treason, retreat, and personal surrender in or near Ravenna; but this did not protect the lamentable Severus from a treacherous murder subsequently. Galerius marched to avenge his death, but his army proved no more reliable and he was compelled to turn back in haste.

In the meanwhile old Maximian, as has been stated, joined his son—if indeed Maxentius was born of him and the Syrian Eutropia and was not a changeling, as was maintained by certain pagans and Christians, whose evidence of the value which was again suddenly placed upon the law of inheritance must here be noticed. The relations between father and son, indeed, were so lacking in filial piety that such rumors must inevitably have arisen. Neither were the soldiers pleased with the old man, probably because they feared his discipline; at least he met with no response when he shortly thereafter sought to win them over against his son. They replied with defiant scorn, whereupon he is said to have declared that he was only testing their temper. Zonaras, who gives this account, even has him visit the Senate beforehand and there declare his son unfit for rule. In any event this is a remarkable decline from Diocletianic principles of rule, particularly so in view of Maximian's hostility to the senators (as mentioned in Chapter II, above).

When the restless old man saw that his hopes for supreme rule were deceived, he proceeded to Gaul to endeavor to obtain of Constantine what he had failed to obtain of Maxentius. He still had one pledge of rule with him, his younger daughter Fausta; her he married to Constantine, and in addition bestowed upon him the title of Augustus. It was his intention to wait until Maxentius was involved in war with Falerius, who was again ready for conflict, and then to intervene with superior force. But Constantine accepted the daughter and the title, and refused Maximian any further participation, whereupon nothing was left to Maximian but to return to Rome and procure some tolerable footing with his son.

We still possess a festive oration delivered on the occasion of the marriage. Perhaps no occasional orator has ever had a worse assignment than the unnamed Gallic rhetor who was to veil everything in silence and yet to declare everything; and we must acknowledge that he discharged his duty with talent and with tact. Of particular interest to us are the felicitations for the final establishment of a dynasty: "May the world dominion of Rome and the posterity of the Emperors alike be eternal and deathless!" Remarkably enough, the existence of Constantine's son Crispus by a previous marriage with Minervina was ignored, while the marriage itself was expressly mentioned and cited in praise of Constantine's high moral standards. In compensation the speaker praises Constantine's good fortune in acquiring Herculians, that is, sons of Fausta, for his house.

While Galerius was making his preparations against Italy, Maximian again fell to quarreling with Maxentius. Things came to a public scene in which the father sought to tear the purple robe from his son. Again he had to leave Rome.

In this general confusion Galerius resorted to the sagacity of the aged Diocletian, who upon his request (307) came to a meeting at Carnuntum (St. Petronell, not far from Haimburg). Lactantius has the senior Emperor go mad some years previously, but his colleagues appear not to have lost their faith in the energy of his mind when they met together on the Danube. Here, first of all, a tried old military comrade and friend of Galerius, the Illyrian Licinius, was named Augustus in place of the murdered Severus. Old Maximian also appeared but, instead of obtaining encouragement and help, was again persuaded to

abdicate. Licinius was to be sole legal Emperor for the
West. But Maximian could no longer endure rest or repose,
and as soon as he was out of sight of his former colleagues
and again with Constantine in Gaul, he could not resist
the temptation to practice at the expense of his son-in-law
what he had twice failed to do at the expense of his son.
While Constantine was on a campaign against the Franks,
Maximian assumed the purple for the third time, got possession of the treasury and the arsenal, and threw himself
into the stronghold of Arelatum (Arles), whence he fled
to Massilia when Constantine hastily turned in pursuit.
Here, it appears, his men delivered him to his son-in-law,
who is again said to have granted him life and liberty. But
Maximian employed them only for new and dangerous intrigues, of which Constantine was informed by Fausta herself. There was nothing left but to remove the sinister old
man from the world. He was permitted to choose the manner of his death, and chose to be strangled (310). At the
beginning of the eleventh century his grave was discovered
at Marseilles. The well-preserved body, richly embalmed
and decked, was found in a lead coffin inserted in a marble
sarcophagus. Archbishop Raimbald of Arles had the enemy
of God and of Constantine with all his appurtenances
thrown into the sea, which was said to seethe violently
at that spot, night and day.

How these events must have embittered Diocletian's last
years! Ambition, supported by the law of inheritance, had
already overthrown half his system, and he was destined
to experience the grief of seeing usurpation again raise its
head outside the imperial families in the style of the third
century, when an Aelianus and an Amandus, a Carausius
and an Allectus, an Achilleus and a Julian, and their followers, paid for their presumptions to rule by streams of
blood. A Governor of Africa, the Phrygian Alexander,
whose homage had been foolishly solicited by Maxentius,
suffered himself to be clothed with the purple by his soldiers half reluctantly (308). We cannot blame the aged
gardener of Salonae, trying to fathom the future, for believing that he saw the most frightful calamities, the fall of
the Empire itself, before his very eyes. Naturally, all of

these civil wars were constantly reflected in the progress of the persecutions; the recurrences of frightful severity which took place from 308 to 313, in the intervals of relative calm, are intimately connected with questions of the succession. Of Maxentius, Eusebius tells us that he spared the Christians over a considerable period out of hostility to Galerius, and that he even posed as a Christian himself. Maximinus Daia was also alternately gentle or cruel to the Christians, according as he wished to defy or flatter Galerius.

Meanwhile the question of succession began to be simplified. Galerius died in 311, allegedly of a loathsome disease, at Sardica in Moesia. We shall allow Lactantius to revel in descriptions of the lower body, devoured by worms, to his heart's content, and affirm, in turn, that that prince, who was certainly savage and inhuman to Christians, was called by the pagans "a brave man and a mighty warrior." We must also remember to his credit that he possessed sufficient strength of character to forgo the throne for his own family in order to turn the imperial office to his friend Licinius, whom he regarded as the most worthy. Shortly before his death Galerius acknowledged the failure of the power of the state in its campaign against the Christians in a sullen edict of toleration, at the end of which he asks that those who had previously been persecuted intercede on his behalf before their God. His colleagues also subscribed to the edict; Constantine, Licinius, and even Maximinus Daia indirectly, in so far as a decree of his highest functionary could perform this office. The Christians returning home from prisons and mines were joyfully welcomed even by the pagan population, so weary had men grown of horrors. Details of regulations which followed the edict are no longer extant, and can only be surmised from a later ordinance. They appear to have been severe and to have been couched in the same surly tone as the edict itself.

A complication which threatened the succession was quite unexpectedly resolved, quickly and peacefully. Maximinus Daia, Galerius' former Caesar who had already assumed the title of Augustus on another occasion, thought he had grounds to fear that his Eastern realm would be curtailed by Licinius, who had been designated Augustus of the West. Each marched his army against the other, but they were reconciled at a conference aboard ship in the midst of the Hellespont (311), and made it and the archipelago the boundary of their dominions, so that Licinius retained the entire peninsula between that sea and the Adriatic. What Diocletian thought of such a division is not known.

At the same time Maxentius' generals subdued the revolt in Africa. The usurper Alexander was defeated, overtaken in flight, and strangled, and the unhappy province was chastised with great severity. The city of Cirta suffered such drastic punishment that it later had to be built anew under Constantine. When he celebrated his triumph in Rome, Maxentius alluded to the enmity of ancient Carthage for Rome.

And now there were again two Western and two Eastern rulers, Constantine and Maxentius, Licinius and Maximinus Daia. But their relationship was far different from that of the harmonious "tetrachord" which had once bound Diocletian to his colleagues. No subordination and no mutual obligation was recognized; each was Augustus on his own account, and measured the others with distrustful glance. Their dominions were sharply delimited; none would venture to share the rule in the realm of another, but neither would any come to the assistance of another before he had exacted selfish terms in separate treaties. The Empire lay divided in four portions, and Constantine, who had first broken the peace, now had the task of instituting some new bond to replace the earlier.

We shall now follow the course of his life with reference to the manner and means by which he fulfilled this task.

Among his three colleagues he sought out the most competent and at the same time the most legitimate, and allied himself with him: Licinius was betrothed to Constantia, Constantine's sister. Thereupon war began against Maxentius (312). Maxentius had meanwhile allied himself with Maximinus, primarily against Licinius, from whom he designed to wrest the Illyrian country. Constantine's overtures to him were in vain; Maxentius rejected "the murderer of his father" and armed himself against him. Which of the two was responsible for the overt breach remains questionable. Eusebius claims this merit for Constantine, expressly praises him for it, and speaks of his great sympathy for poor and oppressed Rome: "He could no longer take pleasure in life if he should be compelled to see the sufferings of the metropolis continue." This is hardly a correct indication of Constantine's motive, but it is a correct indication of Eusebius' approach. Now Maxentius had assembled huge military forces, which did not betray him at the critical moment and would certainly have helped him to victory if he had not been so incompetent strategically and had not been sunk in cowardly indolence. Constantine's military strength, on the other hand, was comprised not in the heavenly legions under the leadership of the deceased Constantius Chlorus, with which writers of both religions honor him, nor yet in the sympathy of the Christians, perhaps not even in the despair of Italy, which had been trodden to earth, for the voice of the people is hardly to be heard in this conflict—but rather in the warlike energy of his some one hundred thousand men (Britons, Gauls, and barbarians) and in his own personality. If praise of this war did not derive from so suspicious a source we should perhaps find it as admirable as the Italian campaign of the youthful Napoleon, with which it has more than one battlefield in common. The storming of Susa, the battle at Turin where the enemy's heavy cavalry—men and horses alike armored—was struck down by iron clubs, the entry into Milan, the cavalry engagement at Brescia, all correspond to the opening of the campaign of 1796, and then we might balance Constantine's frightful battle for Verona with the forcing of Mantua. The enemy too is not unworthy of comparison with Napoleon's enemies. They fought with courage and perseverance and did not go over to Constantine's side, so that he was compelled, for example, to throw the entire captive garrison of Verona into chains to prevent them from making their way back to Maxentius. To put them to death was not in accord with the advanced ideas of humanity nor with the well-understood interests of the state, and their parole, it appears, was not to be relied upon; their swords therefore had to be forged into fetters. Verona yielded, however, only after another part of Constantine's army had taken Aquileia and Modena by storm.

Thus a solid base was won for the conquest of all Italy. Maxentius and his generals were taken by surprise. What they might have achieved at slight cost by timely occupation of the Alpine passes, even streams of blood could not compass at the foot of the Alps and in the plain. Strategists may determine whether Maxentius may not have had reasons for allowing the enemy to advance almost to Rome. Our authors describe him now as a cowardly stay-at-home and now as a superstitious conjurer, and both descriptions may have elements of truth. That the inhabitants of Rome hated the tyrant there can be no doubt. In a dispute with his soldiers six thousand persons were slain, and his dissolute life and his exactions could only win him enemies. But all this was not a decisive factor. He still had a large army on his side, and Rome itself was provided with enormous supplies for the event of a siege and had been newly fortified with trenches, so that the enemy might have been halted and perhaps suddenly enveloped. But if the famous battle which began at Saxa Rubra nine miles from Rome and ended at the Milvian Bridge was actually fought as our authors say, there can be no question of strategic justification. Maxentius' army, to wit, was arranged in a long line, in such a manner that it had the Tiber at its back. But this torrential stream seems to have had no bridge other than the Milvian and a bridge of boats near by. The first reverse must prove irremediable. All who escaped the sword drowned. The Praetorians resisted longest about the person of Maxentius, who was their creature. But he too fled and sank in the river, while the Praetorians suffered themselves to be cut down, as Catiline's Troop had once done at Pistoia, on the spot where they had stood at the beginning of the battle. Their destruction was of great advantage to the victor, for otherwise he would still have had to reckon with them one day. Now it was easy for him to destroy the Praetorian camp.

With this battle the entire West found its master; Africa and the islands also fell to the conqueror. Between two illegitimate claimants, greater talent and determination, as was fitting, decided the victory. Constantine, who had previously been known only through border wars, suddenly stood forth in the public eye with the radiance of a hero's glory. Now the problem was to base his new power, wherever possible, on foundations other than mere military strength.

If we listen only to the ceremonial orators, Constantine made it his first business, after removing the worst Maxentian abuses and persecutions, to pay honor to the Senate and raise its prestige by additions from the provinces. But it wants no special acuteness to perceive that after the events of the last three years there was no possibility of senatorial participation in rule. To please the Romans Constantine might well restore its external honors to that body, but he could hope for no substantial support from it, and he must therefore have remained indifferent to it. Indeed, he may already have cherished plans which would involve a cleavage between himself and the Senate. Nine years later a panegyrist who can call the Senate a blossom of the whole world and Rome the citadel of all peoples and queen of all lands, nevertheless allows the truth to appear between the lines: "This honored soul of the Roman people [i.e., the Senate], restored as it was of old, shows neither bold frowardness nor sorrowful humility. The constant admonition of the divine prince has brought it into such a path that, following his every gesture, it willingly heeds not his awefulness but his kindliness." In other words, the Senate, largely composed of pagans and with no influence upon the government, finds itself in an exposed position with regard to the Emperor. It still met regularly, and its sessions are even marked in the calendar —senatus legitimus, "lawful meeting of the Senate"—but with the exception of January these occur at most once a month.

In the meanwhile the Emperor had proclaimed himself protector of Christianity. The question of his personal beliefs may be disregarded for the moment; let us ask what

political grounds might have moved a Roman Emperor to
such a step. The Christians were still only a small minority,
which did not require to be spared; how could toleration
of them now seem a means of power to an ambitious man,
or at least a profitable thing?

The puzzle is resolved if we assume that the majority of
pagans whose opinion was to be considered disapproved of
further persecution, that they looked with dissatisfaction
upon the interruption of civic life and with anxiety upon
the bloodthirstiness aroused in the mob, that in recent years
ominous comparisons had been drawn between Gaul,
which was not flourishing, to be sure, but nevertheless
peaceful, and the disgraceful police methods of the east
and south. Every terrorism falls lame when the mass of
average persons has stilled its passion and itself begins to
realize the untoward consequences. Fanatics who wish to
perpetuate it are either destroyed by their own logic or are
thrust aside. Even the persecuting Emperors had upon occasion allowed periods of toleration, either as a political device or only to annoy Galerius, and in his last terrible illness (311) Galerius himself had issued a very remarkable
edict of toleration. With his two edicts of toleration at
Rome and Milan (312 and 313) Constantine introduced
nothing altogether new, nor did he use the question of
toleration as a weapon against the other Emperors, but
rather persuaded Licinius, who had in the meanwhile married into his family, to participate in the decrees at Milan
(winter of 312–313), and both together negotiated with
Maximinus Daia to join in the obligation and obtained his
qualified consent. The toleration of the Christians would
then be simply a matter of necessity, and require no further explanation. The edict of Milan which Licinius joined
in signing went very far indeed. It granted unqualified
freedom to all cults, including, in effect, the numerous
Christian sects. As regards recognition by the state, Christianity was made fully equal to belief in the old gods; it
received the character of a corporation, and recovered
churches and other corporate property which had passed
over to the imperial treasury or to private ownership.

But there was one occasion upon which the new master

of the Occident indicated that his actual attitude to the Roman state religion was one of indifference. After the battle at the Milvian Bridge, in addition to other tokens of honor, Senate and people awarded him a triumphal arch. The arch was put together hastily, in part out of handsome fragments from an arch of Trajan. Perhaps it was known that Constantine habitually referred to Trajan as "the weed on the walls" because of the many inscriptions which perpetuated his memory; all the less need for scruples, then, in using Trajan's stones. The inscription which is to be read on the arch states that Flavius Constantinus Maximus had prevailed over the tyrant and his entire party "by the impulse of the divine" (*instinctu divinitatis*); but underneath these words an earlier reading is to be distinguished, "by the nod of Jupiter Optimus Maximus" (*nutu I.O.M.*).* Probably the change was introduced for the occasion of the Emperor's first inspection of the inscription (which had been composed without his previous knowledge), that is, at his visit to Rome in 315, when his religious position had been more definitely determined. The original reading can only show that immediately after the victory nothing else was known than that the Emperor was a Roman pagan. The correction does not deny this, and even less does it represent the Emperor as a Christian; it only separates him from any direct profession of faith, and in any case leaves him free for monotheism. Some of the sculptures on the arch, as is well known, show pagan sacrifices, to Apollo, Diana, Mars, and Sylvanus, and also the combined sacrifices called *suovetaurilia*.

Not Eusebius alone, then, but the highest official quarters called Maxentius "tyrant," that is, according to contemporary usage, "unlawful ruler," "usurper." The term was equally applicable to Constantine, but men persuaded themselves that Maxentius was only a suppositious child and that his mother had admitted the fact. So soon as men can choose and are no longer compelled to content themselves with evil princes of the blood, they long for hereditary succession and yearn for a dynasty. Henceforth pane-

---

* This "earlier reading" is in fact erroneous.—Translator.

gyric makes it a rule to speak of Constantine as the sole
lawful ruler and of all others as tyrants.

In the face of such great ambition Diocletian's system of
adoptions, which depended on so large a measure of renunciation, proved wrong. He procured his own death at this
time (313), either through starvation or through poison.
Constantine and the inexplicably blinded Licinius had intended to set a pitfall for him and had invited him to Constantia's marriage at Milan—which he would doubtless
never have left a free man or a live one. He did not give
them the satisfaction, but excused himself on the ground
of his sixty-eight years. Thereupon they sent him threatening letters in which they charged that he sided with Maximinus Daia and had sided with Maxentius before his
death. Diocletian was too weary of life or too convinced
that his destiny had run out actually to throw himself into
the arms of Daia, and he relished being strangled by the
others as little. Although he died as a private citizen, the
honor of apotheosis was granted him (probably by the Senate), for the last time in the ancient pagan sense. The
decorative little temple in the palace at Salonae which
previously passed for a sanctuary of Aesculapius is probably
nothing other than the tomb of the great Emperor erected
during his lifetime, and the sarcophagus bearing the reliefs of the Caledonian hunt which still lies near by once
contained his corpse. But the Meleager who here confronts
the boar is Diocletian himself at a decisive moment of his
life (see above, pages 27–28). Not everyone could see the
sculpture; as late as a generation afterwards a purple pall
covered the coffin.

What would the rulers of the period have been without
him? At most, generals with more or less distant prospects
for the imperial throne—and for assassination at the hands
of soldiers or conspirators. Only through the constancy
which he introduced into the imperial office, through the
decisive period which he put to unbounded Caesarism, had
it again become possible to speak of a right of succession
and soon also of a hereditary right even if, in specific cases,
such claims were of rather doubtful worth. Without Diocletian there could have been no Constantine, that is, no

power strong enough to carry the Empire unshattered out of its old condition into the new and to remove the center of gravity of imperial power to new locations in accordance with the requirements of the new century.

The next victim bound to fall was Maximinus Daia. Debauched and uncommonly superstitious, he still possessed that bold decisiveness which is so essential an ornament to a ruler and which had probably moved Galerius to adopt him. Otherwise his reign, as appears from his conduct toward the Christians, seems to have been heartless and malicious; but he can hardly be judged from individual instances because, like Julian after him, he had in effect accepted priests and Magi as co-rulers. He had indeed yielded to the solicitations of the two other Emperors in the matter of participating in the measures of toleration, but obviously only under duress, so that the Christians, mindful of his earlier equivocations, were unwilling to venture into the light.

For years he had had a premonition that he would one day have to struggle for his existence, and for that reason he had once entered into secret alliance with the usurper Maxentius, as Licinius had done with the usurper Constantine. But Maxentius was of no help to him in his hour of peril, perhaps because he knew that Daia was beyond help; instead, he saved his strength for a new and sudden attack upon Licinius (313). With lightning speed he moved out of Syria through Asia Minor to Europe, and seized the stronghold of Byzantium as well as Heraclea, in the territory of his opponent. A battle with his surprised adversary took place between Heraclea and Adrianople. Contrary to the wishes of the two leaders, what was involved was patently a struggle between Christianity and paganism, for men knew that a victorious Maximinus would renew the persecution of Christians in the most frightful fashion. But it is very questionable whether the fighting armies were in any sense aware of this, although Lactantius has the Licinian army learn by heart a whole prayer which an angel is said to have communicated to the Emperor in a dream. Maximinus succumbed probably to the greater military skill or the warlike reputation of his opponent, to whom a portion of his own army went over. On his flight he mustered his forces again in Cappadocia and sought to bar the passes of the Taurus by fortifications, but he died, apparently of natural causes, at Tarsus in Cilicia. Licinius, who had already taken Nicomedia and had there issued a new edict of toleration, now entered without further opposition into the inheritance of Asia and Egypt.

Constantine doubtless took great pleasure in the spectacle of the two legitimate rulers fighting among themselves and in their number being reduced by one. Licinius obliged him, moreover, by doing away with the families of Galerius, Severus, and Maximinus Daia, including their innocent children; even Prisca and Valeria, the widow and daughter of Diocletian, were later seized at Thessalonica and beheaded. Cruelties of this sort would have been rendered useless—nay, impossible—under the Diocletianic system. But as soon as men again began to think of a sort of hereditary right, such princes and princesses might become dangerous. The new master of the Orient found a natural solution in ordinary sultanism, which continues to murder until no possible pretender remains. As ruler, Licinius is said to have done meritorious service on behalf of the peasantry, from whom he himself derived, and also on behalf of the prosperity of the cities; if he speaks of literary education as a poison and plague to the state, he might rightly have wished, in that period of the Empire's need, that there were fewer orators (to wit, lawyers) and more industrious and vigorous hands. The most gruesome deed told of him —he is said to have had two thousand Antiochenes shot down in their circus because they mocked him—has been recognized by modern criticism as a fable; but he never hesitated at deeds of blood that might be useful, and among these may be reckoned the executions of wealthy men of which we hear. Besides their property, their women too are said to have fallen into the hands of the elderly libertine.

Meanwhile it was recalled from the age of Diocletian that designated successors or Caesars might still contribute to the security of the throne. Constantine made the first venture, and designated a certain Bassianus, who had one of his sisters, Anastasia, to wife. But his brother Senecio, a relative of Licinius, incited Bassianus against Constantine himself. Constantine found it necessary to put his own brother-in-law out of the way, and to demand of Licinius, his other brother-in-law, the surrender of Senecio. Licinius boldly denied the request; indeed, in one of the western border cities in the Licinian domain, at Aemona (Ljubljana), the statues of Constantine had already been pulled down. Upon these events, which presume some irreconcilable family intrigue, there blazed out a mighty war, in which Constantine must have been the aggressor. At least he marched into the realm of his brother-in-law, defeated him (8 October 314) at Cibalis on the Sava (modern Sevlievo), and pursued him to Thrace, where a second, apparently less decisive battle took place on the Mardian plain. Licinius for his own part had nominated a border commander named Valens to be Caesar. The first condition of the peace now negotiated was Valens' retirement to a private station, so that no third dynasty should arise. Besides, Licinius was forced to cede all his European holdings, that is the land south of the Danube, together with all Greece except Thrace and the coast of the Pontus.

Thus far had the legitimate Emperor been brought by his earlier alliance with the usurper who was so far his superior in spirit, and against whom, after the death of Galerius, all of the others would have had to unite if they hoped to maintain themselves. The less certain a power is of the legitimacy of its origin, the more inevitably is it forced to do away with everything legitimate in its orbit. To destroy Licinius utterly still appeared too difficult, but Constantine now clearly had the upper hand. As far as appearances went, complete equality subsisted between the two rulers. After some time (317), both nominated their sons as Caesars, Constantine naming Crispus and the younger Constantine, and Licinius naming Licinianus. But a glance at the ages of these Caesars betrays the unequal position of the Emperors; Crispus was a vigorous youth, soon to be able to command an army, whereas Licinianus was an infant of twenty months, and furthermore the only son of an elderly father, at whose death he would surely be helpless and easy to dispose of. It was for that reason that the legitimate Emperor, in keeping with the Diocletianic system, was eager to adopt comrades-in-arms, such as Valens and later Martinian, as Caesars; but Constantine would not allow it. Himself he permitted a second nomination; in addition to Crispus, his elder son by his first marriage, he placed in reserve his very young son by Fausta, who was his namesake.

Then Constantine waited patiently until 323 before he incorporated the domain of Licinius under his rule. He allowed the fruit to ripen until it fell into his hands virtually of its own accord.

These were the decisive years during which Constantine attentively observed how Christianity might contribute and be useful to a clever ruler. When he became convinced by the significant growth of the community, by the clearly developed character of its hierarchy, by the peculiar form of its synodic organization, and by the entire character of contemporary Christianity that a support for the throne might be contrived out of this enormous power—and that he must assure himself of it betimes because this power had already begun to assure itself of the Emperor—he realized that he had found an infallible lever against Licinius. Licinius during this same period had been so foolish as to divert his righteous anger against Constantine to the Christians (after 319), as if they were to blame for his opponent's ruthless lust for power. If he had still possessed or wished to use the means for a renewal of the persecution, he would at least have made an ally of terrorism, and the conflict of principles would then have had to be fought out on a grand scale. But he limited himself to dismissing Christians from his court, and to petty vexations, which then in any case grew to a sort of half-persecution by reason of the refractoriness of the greatly augmented numbers of Christians. Christians of every rank, from bishops down to the lowliest, now formed a natural propaganda against Licinius and in favor of Constantine, who furthered the tendency by patent provocations. The incomparably greater favor which he had always shown Christians in his domains must have embittered the Christians of the Licinian realm. Every synod, every meeting of bishops, was now grown actually dangerous, and Licinius forbade them. Every service was suspect as a gathering of subversives, and Licinius caused men and women to assemble separately, and then banished the entire cult from the cities to the open fields, on the ground that the open air was more salubrious than that of the prayer-houses. The clergy sought to influence the men through the women, and Licinius ordered that women should henceforth receive religious instruction only from women teachers. He degraded Christian officers; certain apparently especially suspicious bishops were put to death, certain churches were pulled down or closed. "He did not know," Eusebius sighs, "that prayers used to be offered for him in these churches. He believed that we prayed only for Constantine." Licinius indeed issued no general order which might have contravened the edict of toleration of his earlier period, and Arians like Bishop Eusebius of Nicomedia could remain in his favor and on his side to the end, but he did go as far as confiscations, exile to desolate islands, condemnation to the mines, deprivation of various civic privileges, sales into slavery, and all this in the case of highly respected and highly educated persons. The prince who was once tolerant, who once found it advantageous to keep his subjects in some doubt about his personal faith, finally turned altogether pagan and surrounded himself with Egyptian magicians, thaumaturgists, and sacrificers. He consulted interpreters of dreams and oracles, among others the Milesian Apollo, who replied in two threatening hexameters. Finally Eusebius represents him as assembling his most faithful friends and bodyguards in a sacred grove studded with statues of the gods. After solemn sacrifice he delivered a discourse of which the substance in brief was that the struggle which impended would constitute a decision between the old gods and the new alien God.

What could have moved Licinius to these desperate and foolish steps? The simplest reflection must have suggested that he vie with Constantine in favoring the Christians. Apparently his patience and his reason were exhausted when he became aware of his opponent's fearful malignancy, and he cursed his earlier yielding to the Christians who were represented by such a merciless leader. An attack upon Constantine's dominions was as much out of the question as it had been in 314. Eusebius thinks that he is again doing his hero great honor by having him take up arms purely out of sympathy for the unhappy subjects of Licinius, that is, without Licinius having given him the slightest political occasion.

Of a sudden, Goths swarmed across the Danube into the territory of Licinius. Without being asked, Constantine marched against them, thrust them back, and forced them to give up the captives they had carried off. But Licinius complained of this intervention in his own domain—so far the notice of a monosyllabic and late but nevertheless important excerptor, the so-called Anonymous Valesianus. In this connection we must notice what Jornandes, the well-known historian of the Goths, has to say: "It often happened that the Goths were invited (by the Roman Emperors), as they were summoned by Constantine to immigration and bore arms against his brother-in-law Licinius, and when he was shut up in Thessalonica and robbed of his realm, murdered him with the sword of the conqueror." Anyone who has observed Constantine attentively knows or surmises how these bits are to be fitted together. At least the alleged invasion of the Goths was one of the immediate harbingers of war.

We pass over the individual events of this last struggle for world dominion, this second war of Actium. With Thessalonica and the other harbors of Greece, Constantine acquired, after 314, significant additions to his sea power and assembled two hundred warships; Licinius, who controlled the shores of the East, had three hundred and fifty. The same scale obtained in other arms of service, so that Constantine had one hundred and thirty thousand men altogether, and Licinius one hundred and sixty-five thousand. Such enormous forces had never been put into the field for a civil war since the time of Septimius Severus. But Constantine had a great advantage in the fact that the men of the Illyrian provinces were under his standards. At Adrianople, where Constantine won the first victory, thirty-four thousand men fell. Then his fleet under Crispus defeated Licinius' under Abantus (Amandus) not far from the entrance to the Hellespont, and a storm then destroyed Licinius' fleet utterly. Licinius could no longer remain in Europe and crossed over from Byzantium to Chalcedon, where he named Martinianus, one of his court officials, Caesar. At the beginning of the campaign this step might have had decisive value. By timely adoptions in the Diocletianic pattern, disregarding the protests of the usurper, the legitimate Emperor might have secured the three or four most reliable generals of his realm for his cause. But now, in the midst of discouragement and treason, it was too late.

After a pause the struggle was renewed. Martinianus, who was stationed at Lampsacus to prevent a landing of the enemy at the Hellespont, was hastily recalled by Licinius to the principal army at the Bosporus, where Constantine had succeeded in effecting a crossing. Finally a great and decisive land battle took place at Chrysopolis near Chalcedon, from which barely thirty thousand of Licinius' one hundred and thirty thousand soldiers (Goths among them) are said to have survived. The unhappy Emperor himself fled to Nicomedia, where he was promptly besieged, while Byzantium and Chalcedon opened their gates to the victor. Constantia, wife of Licinius and sister of Constantine, who came to the camp to negotiate, received assurances under oath that her husband's life would be spared. Thereupon the old comrade-in-arms of a Probus and a Diocletian strode forth out of the city, bent his knee to the conqueror, and laid his purple aside. He was sent to Thessalonica, and Martinian to Cappadocia. But in the following year (324) Constantine found it more expedient to put them to death; "he was instructed by the example of his father-in-law Maximianus Herculius and feared that Licinius might resume the purple to the discomfiture of the Empire." With this motive of undeniable expediency posterity should be content in the case of a character like Constantine's, but instead a fable was later spun of a military conspiracy in Thessalonica in favor of the deposed King—of which Eusebius would certainly have had some-

thing to say if it were true. But in his magisterial way he
passes over Constantine's perjury and all the other circumstances with the bald remark that the enemy of God and
his evil counselors were condemned and punished according to military law. So much is certain, that the old Emperor was throttled and the Caesar cut down by bodyguards. Of the equally dismal fate of Licinianus we shall
speak shortly.

Eusebius idealizes this war as the purest contest of principles. Licinius is the enemy of God and wars against God.
Constantine, on the other hand, wages war under the most
direct divine protection, which takes on visible form in the
semeion, the familiar ornamental fetish which was carried
into battle. There is no lack of heavenly apparitions and of
hosts of spirits, which move through Licinius' cities and
perform other wonders. Eusebius is no fanatic; he understands Constantine's secular spirit and his cold and terrible
lust for power well enough and doubtless knows the true
causes of the war quite precisely. But he is the first thoroughly dishonest historian of antiquity. His tactic, which
enjoyed a brilliant success in his own day and throughout
the Middle Ages, consisted in making the first great protector of the Church at all costs an ideal of humanity according to his lights, and above all an ideal for future rulers.
Hence we have lost the picture of a genius in stature who
knew no moral scruple in politics and regarded the religious
question exclusively from the point of view of political expediency. We shall see that he found it advisable to attach
himself more closely to the Christians after this war, and
that the elevation of Christianity to the position of state
religion was thus consummated. But Constantine was a
more honorable man than Eusebius; he rather allowed
these events to transpire than intervened actively on their
behalf, and as regards his own personal conviction, he enjoined definite beliefs upon his subjects as little as did Napoleon in his concordat.

To pass for a Christian would, indeed, have been a great
presumption on his part. Not long after the Council of
Nicaea he suddenly had Crispus, his excellent son by his
first marriage and a pupil of Lactantius, put to death at

Pola in Istria (326), and soon thereafter he had his wife Fausta, daughter of Maximian, drowned in her bath. The eleven-year-old Licinianus was also murdered, apparently at the same time as Crispus. Whether Fausta played Phaedra to her stepson, or by what device she maligned him to his father, or whether she was merely concerned for the elevation of her own sons, or whether it were the representations of the aged Helena who bewailed her grandson, that moved Constantine to murder his wife—all these questions may be mooted. But that the horror was not merely a family affair but possessed political implications can be deduced from the fact that Licinianus was included among the victims. In connection with this tale mention is often made of Philip II and of Peter the Great; but the true parallel is offered by Suleiman the Magnificent and his noble son Mustafa, who succumbed to the plots of Roxalana. With hereditary rule it was inevitable that sultanism should enter in as its complement, that is, that rulers should never for an instant feel safe in the midst of brothers, sons, uncles, nephews, and cousins who might one day be in line of succession, unless they were at any moment ready to resort to convenient throttlings and the like. Here Constantine took the lead; we shall see how his sons followed.

These sons, Constantine II, Constantius II, and Constans had meanwhile been advanced to the dignity of Caesar. The breed of the Herculians was multiplying claimants for the throne after the father had done away with the mother, the maternal grandfather, the uncle Maxentius, and the stepbrother. The seed of so abundant a curse was destined to grow rank.

For the moment we pass over the elevation of Byzantium to be Constantine's city and the capital of the world. Logically, Constantine required a residence and a populace that should be without previous commitments, that should owe everything to him and depend upon him for everything, and that should serve as center and instrument for so much that was new in state and society. Without these definite requirements he might have remained quietly in

Nicomedia. The removal is the most conscious and pur-
poseful act of his entire reign.

It is incomparably more difficult to explain Constantine's
last great political decision, namely, his division of the Empire.

Of Constantine's brothers, Dalmatius had two sons,
Dalmatius and Hannibalian, and Julius Constantius also
had two, then still in their infancy, Gallus and Julian, whom
posterity later called the Apostate. Of these four nephews
Constantine, two years before his death, elevated Dalmatius, who had already held the consulship (333), to be
Caesar (335). Previously Constantine had conferred distinction upon Dalmatius' father, the elder Dalmatius, and
had relegated him, under the ambiguous title of censor, to
the important and perhaps dangerous post of Antioch
(332), as a generation later Constantius was to station
Gallus in the same post, to watch as well as pacify the old
and supplanted capital of the East. Later the elder Dalmatius was even entrusted with a kind of kingship over
Cappadocia. The occasion for his like-named son being
made Caesar in the same year may have been the successful suppression of an insurrection on Cyprus, where
Calocerus, superintendent of the imperial dromedaries,
came forward as usurper. The younger Dalmatius laid
hands upon him and had him burned alive at Tarsus "as
a slave and thief."

Soon afterwards, still in 335 and so two years before
Constantine's death, there followed a regular division of
the Empire, by which Constantine II received the lands
of his grandfather Chlorus, namely, Britain and Gaul together with Spain; Constantius II received Asia, Syria,
and Egypt; and Constans Italy and Africa. On the other
hand the entire land mass between the Black, Aegean, and
Adriatic Seas, that is, Thrace, Macedonia, Illyricum, and
Achaia (with Greece), fell to Constantine's nephew Dalmatius. Even Dalmatius' brother Hannibalian, who is otherwise known for no special achievement or merit, received
rule—we do not know whether unqualified or under the
authority of Constantius II—over Roman Armenia, Pontus,
and the surrounding territory, and was married, then or

previously, to Constantia, daughter of Constantine and sister of his co-heirs. This testament of empire was doubtless public and generally known. But its contents are correctly given only in the second Aurelius Victor, while other writers distort it or, like Eusebius, have good reason to pass over it in silence.

The first question which cries out for answer is this: Why did Constantine divide the Empire at all, after hundreds of thousands had shed their blood for its unification? Next, it is a matter for astonishment that the central area, including the new capital, was given to his nephew and not to his sons. The answer probably lies in the character of the sons. Eusebius has a moving chapter on their education in the fear of God and in all the virtues of rulers, of which we shall speak again presently. Actually they were an abandoned lot, with neither scruple nor faith. If their father named one of them sole heir, then as soon as his eyes were shut the murder of the other brothers and kinsmen would inevitably follow; and what would happen to the Empire if there were suddenly no more Herculians or Constantinians? Constantine was compelled to divide, in order to preserve the dynasty. Without doubt he foresaw the imperial wars of his sons, but he could still hope that out of three to five princely houses one heir of his race would survive, if only they would have time to multiply by begetting new princes. It was not for nothing that he dispersed his sons to their assigned provinces far and wide while he was still alive.

His bestowing the entire Illyrian-Greek peninsula together with Constantinople upon his nephew is perhaps to be explained by the fact that this pearl of the Empire must inevitably become the object of intense jealousy if it were placed in the hands of one of the three sons—as indeed happened in the sequel. It may be objected that Dalmatius was now thrust into a very difficult and dangerous position. But resources for defense were proportionate to the danger. Whoever held the Illyrian country with its generals and soldiers could defy all the rest of the Empire.

The endowment of Hannibalian, finally, seems to be a

simple consequence of that of his brother. We cannot judge
his special assignment at the northern border of Asia Minor
more precisely.

This attempted explanation and motivation of the darkest
point in Constantine's history may well not find acceptance,
because it assumes such unnatural enmities in the imperial
house. But I believe that I have not gone beyond prob-
abilities.

Perhaps the only decent relationship in the circle of this
great Constantine, "who persecuted what was nearest him
and slew first his son and nephew, then his wife, then a
crowd of friends," was that with his mother Helena. Whatever her position with reference to Chlorus may have been,
in the Oriental view she was sufficiently legitimized by having given birth to the ruler. He is said to have been accessible to her counsel always. Purposely clothed with official honors, she spent her last years in charitable works,
pious pilgrimages, and Church foundations. She died at
an age past eighty, apparently not long before her son.
Drepanum in Bithynia was named Helenopolis for her.

Constantine himself was smitten by a fatal illness while
making preparations for a defensive war against Shapur II
of Persia. It was now that he had himself enrolled among
the catechumens of the martyr-church of Helenopolis, and
then taken to the Villa Achyrona near Nicomedia, where
he received baptism and died on the last day of the Whit-
sun holiday, 337.

About his corpse, which the soldiers brought to Constantinople and laid out in a hall of the palace with great
ceremony, the most curious events took place, and continued on into the year following.

The story begins with violent wailing on the part of the
soldiers. Privates tore their garments and wept, officers lamented that they had been orphaned. This sorrow was
surely deep and genuine, especially among the Germans
of the bodyguard, who regarded their relationship to the
Emperor as one of personal loyalty. The deceased had been
a great general and had cared for his soldiers like a father: what else mattered to them? But these grieving soldiers were also, in the absence of the heirs, the authorities

responsible for immediate arrangements; for example, it was they who determined that the burial of the Emperor must await the arrival of one of his sons. "In the meanwhile the officers (and in especial the taxiarchs or tribunes) dispatched trustworthy and devoted men out of the number to the Caesars with the sorrowful news. And as if by inspiration from above all the army was of a single mind, namely, to recognize none other than his sons as heirs. Thereupon they considered it right that these should no longer be called Caesars but Augusti. The armies sent one another their opinions in writing, and everywhere the harmony of the armies was made known at the same time." That is all Eusebius finds it necessary to say.

But where was Dalmatius? It was in his portion of the Empire and in his capital that the corpse lay and the soldiers ruled; why is he not even named when the soldiers deny him the Empire? Instead, Constantius hastens to the city and then leads the solemn military cortege from the palace to the Church of the Apostles. Had Constantine credited his nephew with greater determination than he actually possessed? Or were the intrigues set on foot against him too powerful? We do not know. Perhaps he was arrested straightway, perhaps he was cajoled for some time with a shadow of participation in government. But after a few months the coup was struck (338), from which certain authors vainly seek to absolve Constantius on the grounds that he rather condoned than commanded it. The soldiers or other assassins first disposed of Julius Constantius, brother of the great Constantine; his children Gallus and Julian were spared, the former because he was dangerously sick, the latter because of his extreme youth. Next, Dalmatius and Patricius Optatus were murdered, then Ablavius, formerly an all-powerful Prefect of the Guard, and finally Hannibalian also. It is a mere quibble to assert that the soldiers would recognize none other than the sons; to be sure, direct inheritance would be most comprehensible to them, especially to the Germans, but they would never have gone to such extremes without considerable instigation. For the credulous a story was contrived that the great Constantine was actually poisoned by the

agency of his brothers but had become aware of the misdeed and in his last will called upon that one of his sons
who should first appear on the scene to exact vengeance.
Nothing simpler could be imagined.

To deal with the further destiny and the divisions of the
supreme imperial power in greater detail lies outside our
present purview. Constantine had strengthened that power
greatly by his new organization of state and Church, and
his sons could therefore use great license until they had
entirely consumed the capital which they inherited, just
as the sons of Louis the Pious, of whose history so much
here is reminiscent, could carry on their fraternal wars for
more than a generation until Charlemagne's shadow had
quite lost its magic. The occasion for the first quarrel was
naturally the legacy of Dalmatius, and particularly the possession of Thrace and Constantinople. The questions of
compensation connected with the disposition of that legacy,
specifically Constans' demand for a share in the rule of
Africa and Italy, then led to war (340), in which Constantine II perished without leaving a dynasty. The victorious Constans would now have had to share with Constantius, if the latter were not detained in the East by his
Persian war. But this was also evident to Constans' retinue,
mostly hireling Germans, among whom because of his misdeeds he felt more secure than among Romans. In the
presumption that the Emperor of the East could not lift a
sword for intervention in the West and in Africa, whatever
happened, the Frank Magnentius, at the time commander
of the Jovians and Herculians, ventured to appear suddenly at a banquet in Autun clad in imperial purple (350).
Constans was to be seized while hunting, but received
word in time. Nevertheless he found himself suddenly deserted by soldiers and populace, so that nothing was left
him but flight. Assassins, the Frank Gaiso at their head,
overtook him in the Pyrenees.

While the entire West was now falling into the hands of
Magnentius, the garrisons on the Danube thought they had
the same right of usurpation, and elevated Vetranio, an old
general. To give the story its element of comedy, a nephew
of the great Constantine by his sister Eutropia, Nepotianus

by name, proclaimed himself Emperor in Rome; but this unhappy collateral prince, who wished to re-enact the role of Maxentius, no longer had a Praetorian camp on his side, as Maxentius had had, but only the gladiators' barracks at Rome, and so the army dispatched by Magnentius disposed of him easily. But about Constantius, men had been wrong; he interrupted the Persian War and bent every effort toward suppressing opposition within the Empire. There is a remarkable report in Zosimus, according to which Constantius was able to inspire his soldiers for the dynasty as such, so that they shouted out that the false Emperors must be erased from the earth. In any event, Constantius showed skill and determination at this period. After he had held Vetranio off for some time, he subdued him with great presence of mind in the sight of his own army. Then he overcame Magnentius in a war which is among the most frightful in these internal struggles for the Empire. In consequence of this war a despicable horde of spies and informers was let loose over the entire West to persecute the adherents of the usurper. But despite all his success, the victor must have been inwardly tormented by the most disconsolate reflections concerning the future of the Empire. While the army would no longer have any "false" ruler, Constantius suspected his genuine kinsmen, as many as he had not yet put out of the way, or hated them with a deadly hatred. His marriage with Eusebia was barren, and so in the end the son of Constantine the Great, in consequence of the unbounded sultanism of two generations, had arrived at the point from which Diocletian had departed—he was forced to resort to adoption. He had a sister worthy of himself, Constantia (or Constantina), widow of the murdered Hannibalian, who had subsequently allowed herself to be used to win Vetranio's confidence by giving him her hand. Then when it was a question of destroying the last surviving branch of the family, the sons of Julius Constantius, who was murdered in 338, Constantia married Gallus, the elder of these sons, and although she died before he was murdered we need have no doubt that she was somehow responsible for his destruction immediately thereafter. Now only Julian, Gallus' younger brother, survived, and when the Empire looked to him with respect as the savior of Gaul and victor over the Germans, his shameful cousin left him no choice but death or usurpation of the imperial throne. But Constantius died as the civil war was on the point of breaking out, whereupon Julian was generally recognized. With his memorable two-year reign the line of Constantine comes to an end, for Julian's marriage was childless.

The next successions, those of Jovian and Valentinian, were the concern of the armies, as most of those in the third century had been. But the principle of heredity had impressed the minds of men so strongly that it was hence-forward reverted to and maintained at all costs. There followed the Valentinian dynasty and the Theodosian, which was related to it by marriage, both free at least of sultanic family murders. From the middle of the fourth to the middle of the fifth century the possession of the throne was indeed many times contested by pretenders and pressure of all sorts, but never for a moment was the succession doubtful from the point of view of law. The conviction of the generals, who were mostly German, and the view of the Christians, based on the Old Testament, combined to give the right of heredity this late triumph. It retained its value throughout the Byzantine period, and despite interruptions due to sultanism and praetorianism, ever and again produced new and sometimes enduring dynasties.

IX

CONSTANTINE AND THE CHURCH

ATTEMPTS have often been made to penetrate into the religious consciousness of Constantine and to construct a hypothetical picture of changes in his religious convictions. Such efforts are futile. In a genius driven without surcease by ambition and lust for power there can be no question of Christianity and paganism, of conscious religiosity or irreligiosity; such a man is essentially unreligious, even if he pictures himself standing in the midst of a churchly community. Holiness he understands only as a reminiscence or as a superstitious vagary. Moments of inward reflection, which for a religious man are in the nature of worship, he consumes in a different sort of fire. World-embracing plans and mighty dreams lead him by an easy road to the streams of blood of slaughtered armies. He thinks that he will be at peace when he has achieved this or the other goal, whatever it may be that is wanting to make his possessions complete. But in the meantime all of his energies, spiritual as well as physical, are devoted to the great goal of dominion, and if he ever pauses to think of his convictions, he finds they are pure fatalism. In the present instance men find it hard to believe that an important theologian, a scholar weak in criticism, to be sure, but of great industry, a contemporary as close as was Eusebius of Caesarea, should through four books repeat one and the same untruth a hundred times. Men argue from Constantine's zealous Christian edicts, even from an address of the Emperor "to the assembly of the saints," an expression impossible on the lips of a non-Christian. But this address, it may be remarked in passing, was neither composed by Constantine nor ever delivered; and in writing the edicts Constantine often gave the priests a free hand. And Eusebius, though all historians have followed him, has been proven guilty of so many distortions, dissimulations, and inventions that he has forfeited all claim to figure as a decisive source. It is a melancholy but very understandable fact that none of the other spokesmen of the Church, as far as we know, revealed Constantine's true position, that they uttered no word of displeasure against the murderous egoist who possessed the great merit of having conceived of Christianity as a world power and of having acted accordingly. We can easily imagine the joy of the Christians in having finally obtained a firm guarantee against persecution, but we are not obliged to share that elation after a millennium and a half.

Tolerant monotheism Constantine appears to have derived as a memory from the house of Chlorus, who was devoted to it. The first definite notice of a religious act on the part of Constantine is his visit to the temple of Apollo at Autun (308) before his renewed attack upon the Franks. He appears to have consulted the oracle and to have made rich offerings. But this worship of Apollo does not necessarily contravene the monotheism of his parental home, for Chlorus conceived of the highest being as a sun-god. Constantine's nephew Julian speaks of Constantine's connection with a special cult of Helios. From a familiar obverse on coins of Constantine, representing the sun-god with the inscription SOLI. INVICTO. COMITI, we deduce that the personification of the sun as Mithras is here implied. Anyone who has dealt with ancient coins knows that out of five Constantinian pieces probably four will bear this obverse, so that there is high probability that this device was retained until the Emperor's death. Other devices which are frequent are Victories, the Genius Populi Romani, Mars and Jupiter with various epithets, and a number of female personifications. But the coins with unequivocal Christian emblems which he is said to have struck are yet to be found. In the period during which he ruled with Licinius the figure of the sun-god appears with the inscription COMITI. AVGG. NN., that is, "To the comrade of our two Augusti"; and many coins of Crispus and of Licinius himself bear the same obverse. On inscriptions and coins Constantine continually calls himself Pontifex Maximus, and has himself represented as such with head veiled. In the laws of 319 and 321 he still recognizes the pagan cult as existing as of right; he forbids only occult and dangerous practices of magicians and of haruspices, but he admits conjurers of rain and hail, and on the occasion of public buildings being struck by lightning he expressly requests the responses of the haruspices. Zosimus, if we may credit that fifth-century pagan, confirms Constantine's consultation of pagan priests and sacrificers in even larger scope, and has them continue to the murder of Crispus (326), which, in his view, is the correct period of Constantine's supposed conversion.

Opposed to all this is the fact that after the war with Maxentius (312) Constantine not only permitted the toleration of Christianity as a lawful religion, but spread abroad in the army an emblem which every man could interpret as he pleased but which the Christians would refer to themselves. The interlocked letters X and P, which form the beginning of the word Christ (ΧΡΙΣΤΟΣ), were introduced on the shields of the soldiers, we are told, even before the war. At the same time or later the same emblem, surrounded by gold and jewels, was attached to a large battle standard, whereupon the sign received a special and remarkable cult and the soldiers were inspired with the greatest assurance of victory. Soon similar standards (*labarum, semeion*) were prepared for all armies, and a special guard was entrusted with the preservation of the emblem on the field of battle. The emblem even had its own tent, into which the Emperor mysteriously retired before any important affair. Should not all this signify an open profession?

First of all it is to be noticed that Constantine employed this sign not among the populace but in the army. The army knew him as a mighty and successful general from the time of the Frankish wars; it had descended to him largely from his father; and it was ready to accept any symbols or emblems he chose. Among the Gauls and Britons in the army there were certainly many Christians and indifferent pagans, and to the Germans the religion of their leader was a matter of no consequence. On his part it was an experiment that obliged him to nothing more than toleration, which was already in fact the rule in his previous domains and which he now extended to his conquests also. For him Christ may have rated as a god along with other gods, and the professors of Christ's religion along with the servants of the pagan deities. We shall not deny the possibility that Constantine developed a kind of superstition in favor of Christ, and that he may even have brought that name into some kind of confused relationship with the sun-god. But without doubt he was concerned exclusively with success; if he had met with a powerful resistance against *XP* in Italy, the symbol would quickly have disappeared from shields and standards. Instead, he could now apparently be fully convinced that the great mass of pagans was displeased with the persecution and that he incurred no danger in setting up his statue, *labarum* in hand, in the midst of Rome and inscribing underneath it that this saving sign was the true proof of all courage. If he had wished to make a proper profession of Christianity, surely a very different sort of declaration would have been in place. A glance at the year 312 would make everything clear if we were better informed concerning general conditions. Nothing is more difficult to prove, and yet nothing is more probable, than that the temper of the pagans was more yielding and milder at the critical moment at the end of the persecution than either before or after. They did not know, or they forgot, that Christianity, once tolerated, must inevitably become the predominant religion.

Neither, perhaps, did Constantine know it, but he allowed it to come about, and he kept his eyes open. As soon as his lucid, empiric logic informed him that the Christians were good subjects, that they were numerous, and that the persecution could no longer have meaning in a reasonably governed state, his decision was taken. From the political point of view, the practical execution of his decision is wholly admirable. In his victorious hands the *labarum* was a physical representation at once of rule, of warlike power, and of the new religion. The *esprit de corps* of his army, which had been victorious over one of the greatest armies of ancient history, hallowed the new symbol with the aura of the irresistible.

But the familiar miracle which Eusebius and those who copy him represent as taking place on the march against Maxentius must finally be eliminated from the pages of history. It has not even the value of a myth, indeed is not of popular origin, but was told to Eusebius by Constantine long afterwards, and by Eusebius written up with intentionally vague bombast. The Emperor indeed swore a great oath to the bishop that the thing was not imagined, but that he actually saw in heaven the cross with the inscription "In this sign thou shalt conquer," and that Christ actually appeared to him in a dream, and the rest; but history cannot take an oath of Constantine the Great too seriously, because, among other things, he had his brother-in-law murdered despite assurances given under oath. Nor is Eusebius beyond having himself invented two-thirds of the story.

A great inconsistency in Constantine's outward bearing persists; he accepts the monogram of Christ as the emblem of his army and has the name of Jupiter on his triumphal arch erased, but at the same time he retains the old gods on his coins, and especially the sun-god as his unconquerable companion, and on important occasions his outward conduct is entirely pagan. This cleavage rather increases than decreases in his latter years. But he wished to give direct guarantees to both religions, and he was powerful enough to maintain a twofold position.

His edicts of toleration, of which the second, issued at Milan (313) in common with Licinius, is extant, confer nothing more than freedom of conscience and of religion; the latter granted freedom of worship without limitation and qualification. The notion of a state religion was thus abolished, until Christianity clothed itself with the shell which paganism had discarded. One regulation soon followed upon the heels of another, especially when Maximinus Daia in hostility to Licinius and then Licinius himself in hostility to Constantine provoked the enmity of Christendom. The places of assembly and other landed property of the Christian communities which had been confiscated during the persecution were restored; the Christians were openly favored and their proselytization actively supported. A moment of anxiety because of the displeasure of the pagans is revealed in the laws of 319, cited above, in which the private practice of haruspices and home sacrifices are strictly forbidden, apparently because the secret consultation of haruspices and sacrificial feasts behind closed doors might be subversive politically. With the edict to the provincials of Palestine and with that to the peoples of the East after the last victory over Licinius (324), there follows an apparently quite unqualified personal devotion of the Emperor to Christianity, whose professors are freed of the consequences of the persecution with all possible indulgence, and are restored to their former position and property. These official decrees show a specifically polemic tone against polytheism; they speak of sanctuaries of falsehood, of darkness, and of miserable error which must still be suffered, and the like. But it is not Constantine's pen that wrote these things, though Eusebius maintains that he saw the autograph. The draftsman betrays himself at least in the second document, in which he has the Emperor say that he was "only a boy" at the beginning of the persecution, whereas in fact Constantine was almost thirty in 303. But indirectly the content is substantially the work of the Emperor, who, as is noticeable upon closer examination, does not once represent himself as a Christian. What personal tones are perceptible are those of the dreary deism of a conquerer who requires a god in order to justify his acts of violence by an appeal to something outside himself. "I, proceeding from the Britannic Sea and from the regions prescribed for the setting of the sun, dispersing and destroying through a higher power the evil which everywhere prevails, so that the race of men raised by my assistance might be recalled to the service of the loftiest law . . . I have arrived in the regions of the East which summoned me for help greater in the degree that their misery was more profound . . . you all see the quality of that power and grace which has caused an entire race of the most godless and troublesome men to disappear. . . ." These are things which a conquering caliph might as well have signed. Napoleon resorted to similar turns of expression in his Arabic proclamations in Egypt.

It is not impossible that in his deism, originally derived from the sun and Mithras, Constantine believed that he possessed a more general and hence presumably a loftier basic configuration of all religions. At times he tried to find basically neutral expressions for religious practices which Christians and pagans alike should observe. Of this character is the common Sunday and the common Pater Noster. "He taught all armies zealously to honor the Lord's Day, which is also called the day of light and of the sun. . . . The pagans too were required to go forth into an open field on Sunday, and together to raise their hands, and recite a prayer learned by heart to God as giver of all victory: 'Thee alone we acknowledge as God and King, Thee we invoke as our helper. From Thee have we obtained our victories, through Thee conquered our enemies. Thee we thank for past favors, of Thee we hope for future favors. Thee we all beseech, and we pray Thee that Thou long preserve to us unharmed and victorious our Emperor Constantine and his God-loving sons.'" Christians would be content with this formula, and the pagans who might have taken offense at such outspoken monotheism were before all else soldiers. That special thought was taken for believers in Mithras also Eusebius indicates quite clearly with his "day of light and of the sun." How significant is this so-called prayer! Emperor, army, victory—and nothing else; not a word for moral man, not a syllable for the Romans.

Before we proceed further we may briefly dispose of Eusebius' other reports of the alleged Christianity of his hero. After the war with Maxentius Christian priests always attended him, even on journeys, as "assessors" and "table companions." At the synods he took his seat in the midst of them. These facts are easily explained. It was essential for Constantine to have intelligence of the viewpoints of the contemporary Church; he had his own informants who delivered reports on the individual sects. With the eloquent reports of one of them, Strategius by name, he was so pleased that he gave him the cognomen Musonianus. No clever and energetic ruler could let the praesidium of the synods out of his hands, for they were a new power in public life which it was unwise to ignore. One may deplore and contemn such egoism, but an intelligent power, whose origin is ambiguous, must of necessity act in this manner. When we are told further how frequently divine manifestations were vouchsafed the Emperor, how he secretly fasted and prayed in the tent of the *labarum*, how he daily shut himself in to converse with God on his knees, how he filled the watches of the night with thoughts on divine matters—on the lips of a Eusebius, who knew the truth, these things are contemptible inventions. In the later period Constantine was patently even more attentive to the bishops and gave them the first word at his court, apparently because he realized that it was to their greatest interest to support the throne in every way possible, and in the end because he could not do otherwise. In his encyclicals bishops are addressed as "beloved brother," and he himself affected to comport himself as one of them, "as a common bishop." He put the education of his sons, at least in part, in their hands, and in general so ordered matters that these sons should be regarded as unqualified Christians. Their personal environment, their court, consisted exclusively of Christians, whereas their father, by Eusebius' indirect admissions, did not hesitate to keep pagans in high positions about his person and as *praesides* in the provinces, along with the clergy, until the last period of his life. The prohibition of gladiatorial games was doubtless a concession to his clerical environment, although the relevant law speaks only of "peace in the land and domestic quiet" for which bloody spectacles were not appropriate. In any case this was one of those laws which were promulgated only to fall straightway into oblivion, for Constantine himself later paid no attention to it.

The sermons which Constantine delivered from time to time in the presence of the court and "many thousands of auditors" are a complete puzzle. He wished, it is said, to prevail over his subjects "by discourses with edifying purpose" and "to make the reign one of discourse." Assemblies were convoked for this purpose, and the master of the world nonchalantly stepped forward and spoke. If he touched upon religion his gestures and voice took on an expression of deep humility. Applause he deprecated with a gesture toward heaven. His themes were usually refutation of polytheism, monotheism, providence, redemption, and divine judgment. In this section (the court bishop continues) he scored his auditors most directly, for he spoke of robbers, and men of violence, and the avaricious; the scourge of his words smote certain of his confidants who stood in attendance, so that they cast their eyes to the ground. . . . His intention was righteous, but they remained deaf and stubborn. They clamored their approval, but their insatiability suffered no emotion to stir within them. Constantine wrote these discourses in Latin, and interpreters turned them into Greek.—What are we to think of this account? Would Constantine, who preserved the Diocletianic fashion of imperial appearance so zealously, and who set such great store by his personal majesty, condescend to show himself before the crowds in the capital? The criticism to which he would thus subject himself is the least of the problem, and perhaps his auditors would forgo criticism on very good grounds. But why speeches, when the Emperor possessed the fullest power to act? Perhaps one reason may be divined. In this period of religious crisis the spoken word, previously confined to rhetorical exercises and eulogies, now delivered from the preacher's pulpit, must have won so enormous an influence that Constantine could not entirely forgo it as an adjunct of power, just as the most powerful governments today must be represented in the periodical press. If it could occur to this unbaptized non-catechumen to give himself out as "a common bishop," he could equally well present himself as a Christian preacher. How he dealt with Christian dogma in these discourses we do not know; that he presented himself as an unqualified Christian is not even probable. Eusebius clearly indicates a collateral purpose of these discourses; they were

a welcome occasion to express favor and disfavor, to inspire
fear, and to present in an artfully ambiguous form things
he could not well bring before people even in the most
elaborate edicts. They were, in fact, the senatorial speeches
of Tiberius in another form. We must not forget that among
other things Constantine "put a great many of his friends to
death," as the unsuspicious Eutropius says, and the more
than suspicious Eusebius finds it well to pass over in silence.

A glimmer of edification still clings to Constantine because so many admirable Christians of all centuries have
claimed him for their own. But this last glimmer must also
vanish. The Christian Church has nothing to lose in this
terrible though politically grandiose figure, just as paganism would have had nothing to gain by him. In any case
the pagans fell into the same error of assuming that his
conversion was genuine and not merely for outward show.
Zosimus recounts the familiar hostile version. Because of
the execution of Crispus and Fausta and the violation of
his oath (to Licinius) the Emperor's conscience pricked
him, and he turned to pagan priests (according to
Sozomen, to the famous Neoplatonist Sopater) for absolu-
tion. When they told him that there was no expiation for
such malefaction, an Egyptian (apparently Hosius) who
had come to Rome from Spain succeeded in making his
way to the Emperor through the ladies of the court and
in convincing the Emperor that Christianity was able to
wash every misdeed away. Thereupon he made his conversion known, first by his measures against pagan prog-
nostications of the future, and then by building a new
capital. It is possible that this account contains a kernel of
truth, but the version before us is surely not authentic.
Events so gruesome transpiring in his own house must have
awakened whatever remained of Roman belief in the soul
of Constantine, and despite his education in other respects
he may have been crude enough to expect some alleviation,
some washing away of the ugly impression, by means of
powerful pagan exoricisms; but the causal nexus in the
remainder of the account is demonstrably false.

It is precisely in the last decade of his life that Constantine gives certain very plain indications of un-Christian, even of directly pagan, sympathies. While he and his mother were ornamenting Palestine and the large cities of the Empire with magnificent churches, he was also building pagan temples in the new Constantinople. Two of these, of the Mother of the Gods and of the Dioscuri, may have been merely ornamental structures to house the idols which were preserved in them as works of art; but the temple and image of Tyche, the deified personification of the city, was intended to receive an actual cult. At the consecration of the city certain occult pagan practices were demonstrably celebrated; the solemnities involved superstitions of all sorts, which later writers vainly seek to identify with Christian worship.

To others also Constantine granted permission to build pagan temples. An inscription of the Umbrian village of Spello (between Foligno and Assisi), which was long regarded as spurious because of its strange content, a judgment seemingly justified by its careless and barbaric script, is most probably a perfectly genuine monument of this indulgence to the pagans, and dates, indeed, from the last two years of the Emperor's life. He permits the Hispellati to build a sumptuous temple to his own family, which he calls the Gens Flavia, and his only condition is that the temple should not be tainted "by the delusion of contagious superstition"—a prescription that every man might interpret as he would. He issues binding decisions also concerning the pagan priesthood of the place and concerning the removal of the games from Bolsena to Spello, naming the gladiators expressly. During these same years he releases certain priestly colleges of the pagans, the Sacerdotes and the Flamines, who held life tenure, from burdensome local offices, in which the Christians, especially in Africa, wished to compel them to serve. It was indubitably with his knowledge that the Senate procured the restoration of the Temple of Concord as late as 331, to say nothing of the restoration of individual altars of the gods in the years immediately preceding.

Paganism approached the Emperor very closely during these last years through personal contacts. The Neoplato-

nist Sopater, a disciple of Iamblichus, appears with all the
claims of a proud Greek sophist. "For him other people
were too insignificant; he hastened to the imperial court
in order to exert in the most direct manner a dominant influence over all of Constantine's deeds and thoughts. And
the Emperor was in fact soon completely won over by
him, and caused him to sit at his right hand, to the general
envy and displeasure of the courtiers." So far Eunapius,
who, however, deserves as little unqualified credit as
Philostratus when he brags of the noble connections of the
philosophers. But there is some truth at the bottom of this
account; Sopater did stand in close relation to Constantine.
That it was he who refused expiation for the execution of
Crispus we may leave out of account; but he was undeniably employed at the ceremonial consecration of Constantinople. Later, in any case after 330, Ablavius, the Prefect
of the Guard, caused his fall. During the famine in the new
capital Ablavius is said to have imposed upon the Emperor
the opinion that Sopater, by means of his extraordinary science, was holding bound the winds that were to move the
Egyptian grain vessels over the sea. In any event Constantine had the sophist executed. That this was caused merely
by an intrigue of Ablavius may however well be doubted,
on the basis of a notice in Suidas. "Constantine put
Sopater to death," says Suidas, "to show that he was no
longer a pagan in religion. For previously he had been on
terms of intimacy with him." We shall have to repeat in
another connection (that of the story of Athanasius) the
conjecture that the Christian priests had become somehow
frightening to the aging Emperor and that he was unable,
in his last years, to maintain consistently the personal freedom he had so long guarded. Many even feel justified in
assuming that sometime toward the end of his life Constantine prohibited pagan sacrifices entirely, and if Eusebius
merits consideration, that not only sacrifices, but also consultation of oracles, erection of idols, and celebration of
mysteries were completely abolished. That a law against
consulting oracles was issued some time after 326 is confirmed by Zosimus. But for all this, a blind eye must have
been turned toward infractions. Even if the decree of

Spello is spurious, there is still enough other evidence. Our chief source for the large-scale persistence of sacrifices and mysteries, the treatise of the Christian Firmicus, derives precisely from the years following the death of Constantine. His sons are admonished in the most vigorous language to do what their father is presumed already to have done: "Hew them down, hew them down with an ax, these temple ornaments! To the smeltry, to the mint, with these gods! All votive offerings are yours: take and use them!"

Even under Constantine, to be sure, temples were pulled down and destroyed and images melted down. A sanctuary like that of the Heavenly Goddess at Aphaka in the Lebanon deserved no better than that soldiers should be dispatched to raze it to the ground (about 330); the spot was in fact "unworthy that the sun shine upon it." More questionable was the razing of the famous Temple of Asclepius at Aegae in Cilicia, whither crowds of people had until that time resorted for the sake of curative dreams. Apparently the god ("the false guide of souls," Eusebius calls him) had become involved in political questions. At Heliopolis, whose cult was hardly less debauched than that of Aphaka, there was merely a prohibition and the enforced establishment of a bishopric, for which a congregation was then engaged for pay. Elsewhere it happened that converted populations pulled down local pagan sanctuaries of their own volition and then received official imperial approval. Probably as reward for such merits Majuma, the harbor city of Gaza, received the name of Constantia, and another Phoenician locality received the name of Constantina.

Constantine caused many temples to be plundered moreover, as it seems, out of desire for booty or need of pelf. Here too Eusebius dissembles the cause and the true extent of such spoliation, but he betrays himself unwittingly. For he does not speak of marble statues at all, but only of such whose interior consisted of some special material; Eusebius implies skulls, skeletons, old rags, hay, straw, and the like, but what is obviously intended are the wooden or other armatures that supported the hollow interiors of the so-called chryselephantine statues, that is, statues of gold and ivory, like that of the Zeus of Olympia. In his panegyric of Constantine this is fully avowed: "The valuable portions were melted down, and the amorphous remainder was left to the pagans as a memorial of their reproach." What and how many statues (perhaps the finest in Greek art) met a fate inextricably involved in the value of their material we cannot know. For the decoration of his new capital, in any case, Constantine was very willing to use images whose material was of no great value, as we shall see. Of the brazen statues the same passage continues, "They were haled forth like captives, these gods of antiquated myth, they were dragged forth with ropes." Confiscation was in the hands of trusted commissioners, who came directly from the court. They encountered no resistance; priests were compelled to open their most secret crypts to them. But it is conceivable and not improbable that Constantine ventured such measures only in thoroughly reliable, predominantly Christian cities in the near vicinity of the imperial residence. He might have left the statues of gold and silver untouched, but they were too convenient and the temptation was too great in the face of pressing financial need, which must take precedence over any other consideration in rulers of this sort. In the same category, doubtless, falls the removal of doors and beams, which is said to have taken place in the case of several temples; these members were often of massive bronze, and well worth the trouble of smelting. If this made a beginning of destruction and the interior was then injured by partial collapse and inclement weather, the inhabitants could hardly be prevented from venturing on columns and other structural members, if only for burning lime. We have official confirmation that such things happened after 333, at least to pagan grave monuments. Even earlier a law put a period to the repair of dilapidated or incompleted temples. How the temple properties fared is not precisely known; in individual cases they were certainly confiscated, but it was only under Constantine's successors that this was done in volume and systematically. It is out of the question that Constantine could have issued a law enjoining the general destruction of temples, as the *Chronicle* of Jerome reports for the year 335. What Constantine did or suffered to come about happened intermittently, out of frivolous desire for plunder and through the influence of the clergy, and hence his measures are not consistent. It is futile to seek for a logical system in a man who was intentionally illogical in this respect.

Of Constantine's profession of Christianity and his death-bed baptism, every man must judge according to his own criteria.

The great outward changes which the position and hence constitution of the Christian Church assumed through Constantine are sufficiently familiar and can be repeated here only briefly. Simultaneously with the first edict of toleration the clergy (*clerici*) were recognized as constituting a class or corporation; the effect of this recognition was of immeasurable importance for the whole development of the Church. The clergy had long been prepared for their new position; on the one hand they had isolated themselves from the laity, and on the other they had acquired the character of a corporation by community of official functions, especially in the institution of synods. But was it necessary for the state which had barely declared toleration to yield so fully on this point? Could it not have ignored the clergy as a class and addressed itself directly to the communities? Constantine found the clergy already so suitably organized for power and so elevated by the persecution that he must either rule through this corporation and its high credit or acquire its irreconcilable enmity. He therefore gave the clergy every possible guarantee of favor, even as far as a sort of participation in rule, and in return the clergy were the most devoted agents for spreading his power, and completely ignored the fact that he still stood with one foot in paganism and that his hands were over and again stained with blood.

The new position of the clergy involved a grave obverse. Out of the persecution, along with its noble moral consequences, there had arisen an evil spirit of strife. The party of enthusiastic devotion came to oppose fanatically not only those who had denied their faith during the persecution or had delivered up the sacred scriptures, but even those who had saved themselves by permissible means of Christian prudence. Hence there arose the Donatist schism in Africa and the Meletian in Egypt, almost while the persecution was still in progress. These were the first occasions for the Emperor, who had been merely tolerant, to intervene actively in Church quarrels, for of neutrality, once he had concerned himself with Church affairs, there could naturally be no question. Here, as later in the much more comprehensive Arian schism, Constantine usually showed great tact; he declared for one party, to be sure, but gave it no sort of power to penalize the other. Church unity would doubtless have been a desirable thing in his sight, for it seemed to be a parallel to unity of power, but he understood how to accommodate himself to a Church rent by strife and was far from compromising the imperial power itself by stubbornness or rigor on behalf of or against persons and things which could inspire no fanaticism in him. He had observed the Christian reaction to persecution of every sort thoroughly; just such schisms as the two named would inevitably have been exacerbated by nothing so much as new martyrdom. He must indeed have realized that not all of his successors would maintain similar independence; once called Christians, it was to be foreseen that their personal zeal must be involved for or against conflicting practices of the Church. But the sequel proved that the imperial power was strongly enough founded in other respects not to permit its course to be disrupted by even the most extreme trials, as for example the iconoclastic controversy of the eighth century.

As a corporation or class the clergy first received from Constantine release from all public obligations (*munera;* 313 and 319), which were comprised partly in burdensome offices and partly in imposts, or in the execrable decurionate which united both. (The immediate rush to clerical standing on the part of wealthy people eager for immunity had to be met in the year following [320] by a blunt general prohibition, which was then apparently not infrequently circumvented.) The next significant mark of corporate recognition accorded to the Church was permission to accept legacies (321), numbers of which it then received. Later, apparently after the victory over Licinius, the state accorded the Church regular revenues, chiefly in landed property and crop shares. An ample income and the foundation of great wealth was thus assured the Church, and in addition the state relinquished also a portion of its prerogative of power. Previously the Christians had preferred to settle their quarrels through bishops as a sort of court of arbitration before they resorted to the worldly, pagan judges, to whom the sentence of the bishops could in any case be appealed; this right of appeal Constantine abolished and made the decisions of the bishops, once they were referred to, binding. Thus rivalry between the secular and clerical judges was obviated, as was also opportunity for strife between the two, which might now have been very dangerous whether the secular judge were still a pagan or already a Christian. This consideration alone is sufficient to explain the extraordinary concession, obviously dangerous to any vigorous state organization. Here, as in his handling of Church matters in general, Constantine did not introduce innovation of his own choice, but merely confirmed and regulated what had transpired without his agency. It is easy to reproach him, from the standpoint of modern theory, for not maintaining a sharper distinction between Church and state; but what was he to do when, by the general tendency of the age, the Church had turned into the state under his hands and the state into the Church, when every Christian official in his sphere of duty and every judge upon his tribunal might stray in his function by the confusion of religious and civic points of view, when the intercession of a bishop or of a sanctified eremite for or against any individual or any condition might throw everything into confusion? The theocracy which here developed was not the work of a single Emperor who favored the Church, and as little the conscious foundation of single especially clever bishops, but the large and necessary result of a process of world history. Considered from a higher point of view, it may well be deplored that the Gospel was made into law for those who did not believe in it, and specifically by a ruler who was not inwardly moved by the substance of the religion which he imposed upon others. "Christianity grows alien to its essence when it is made into law for those born instead of for those reborn." (Zahn, *Konstantin der Grosse und die Kirche*.) Constantine desired an imperial Church, and on political grounds; but it is difficult to determine whether another in his place, pure in character and a convinced Christian, might not have been compelled to follow the same path.

Once the clergy was raised above society, its theoretical claims upon itself and others increased with remarkable rapidity. Celibacy had already been an issue; now the penalties which the state had previously imposed upon the unmarried had to be rescinded. And if a man who was himself an ascetic, a confessor, and an unrivaled exorciser, the old and blind Paphnutius, had not spoken against it at the Council of Nicaea, celibacy might even then have been decreed binding upon all clergy. Ordination or consecration was given an increasingly mystical value, and came to be regarded, in relation to men and things, as something magical, as a communication of supernatural powers. Within the priestly caste itself old distinctions were accentuated and new ones formed. Presbyter was separated from deacon, and bishop from presbyter; among the bishops themselves there were very diverse degrees of influence according to the rank of their cities. This influence came to be concentrated chiefly in the five (later) patriarchal seats—Rome, Alexandria, Antioch, Constantinople, and Jerusalem. To maintain the episcopal office as such in its higher prestige, the lowest grade of bishops, the so-called rural bishops (χωσεπίδκοποι), that is bishops of localities without the rank of city, were completely abolished not long after Constantine. According to the importance of the see, the ambition of the persons involved, and already existing partisanship, the election of a bishop was sometimes the subject of vigorous campaigns, which in individual cases might rock the entire Church. The candidate who thrust himself forward and succeeded was seldom the best man; rhetorical and political and especially financial talents, even personal influence of a most intimate nature, frequently bore off the victory over a man with a true vocation. The hierarchy was extended downward not only, as previously, through the classes of doorkeepers and acolytes, but also through a large and sturdy company of servitors, the so-called *parabolani* and *fossores*, that is, sick nurses and gravediggers, of whom in Constantinople alone there were about a thousand, and in Alexandria about half that number.

This rich and mighty Church was not long wanting in brilliant outward show. The cult was made majestic by sumptuous church buildings and an imposing ritual; the life of the higher clergy, at least in the large cities, was princely. But these natural developments became clearly apparent only under the sons of Constantine and later. In one aspect in particular it is easy to perceive the means of power which the state had surrendered; the whole huge apparatus of public benefits with its influence upon the masses now devolved upon the clergy, who established shelters for the poor, hostels, almshouses, orphanages, hospitals, and other philanthropic foundations in many places, partly through gifts of the state, whereas the state came into contact with the individual only through its soldiers and its brutal tax collectors.

Who could prevent this clergy from constituting itself the state government after it had converted the pagan majority? What means were left to the ruler to remain master, or at least not servant or even pensioner of its priests? Emperor and local bishops alike now had their burial place in the Church of the Apostles at Constantinople, "forasmuch as the priesthood is the equal of the ruler in honor, and in holy sites even takes precedence."

Upon closer consideration we find that every care was nevertheless taken for the Emperor and his power. In the first place it was a piece of good fortune for the Emperor that the Old Testament, often as it depicts cleavage between the Kings and the high priests of Israel, still reports no theocratic revolution against the kingdom as such, but leaves the abolition of the kingdom to God and the King of Babylon. Appeal was made to the Old Testament theory of government at every turn as the only non-pagan precedent. As in the period of the English Puritans men overlooked the

fact that the Old Testament referred to a particular and
now vanished polity; the New Testament, however, to
which men would surely have preferred to take recourse,
concerns itself, as is well known, neither with forms of government nor with nationalities, because its compass is universal.

As long as the Emperor professed orthodoxy, he could
not be impugned; what he might otherwise be as man and
ruler did not enter into consideration. To the position of
Constantine himself, who became the object of boundless
flattery, history need no longer refer; but for subsequent
Emperors there survived a theory of divine right which did
not fall short of the deifications of pagan Emperors and in
sincerity far surpassed them. "When the Emperor has received the name of Augustus," we read in Vegetius, at the
end of the fourth century, "loyalty and obedience and
ceaseless service are due him as to a present and incarnate
deity. For in peace and in war it is a service to God to ad-
here loyally to him who rules at God's ordinance."

But materially also the imperial power with its military
force, barbarized and in religious matters neutral, and its
administrative system was far too well established to have
to give way to a purely priestly government. And finally
Constantine was clever or lucky enough to make himself
head and center of the Church and to leave this position,
in addition to his legacy of power, well established for his
successors.

We have already noticed his claim to comport himself
"as a common bishop." This was not merely a manner of
speaking; actually the Church had no other central point.
This appeared first of all in episcopal elections, in which, in
all important cases, the court could exert paramount influence, for the bishops of the province in question who foregathered to choose a new shepherd for the orphaned
community took the Emperor's wishes into consideration,
because they themselves hoped to rise higher by imperial
favor. To exploit its position fully the Church would, above
all, have required higher principles. In the great imperial
synods, furthermore, the Emperor was at an advantage, inasmuch as he determined time and place, and, more im-

portant, inasmuch as many sought to discover his desires so that they might vote accordingly. If he himself was not present he sent commissioners with plenipotentiary powers, and finally he reserved for himself the right of approval, without which no conciliar decree was valid, but with which it was raised to imperial law. In the end the synods with their equal right of voting proved an excellent means to counter the excessive power of the more important bishoprics when the court found them in any way troublesome.

The idea of a council, as it was developed in the early centuries of Christianity, was a lofty one, namely, that the spirit of God rested upon an assembly of the representatives of Christian communities when they had reverently prepared themselves to take counsel on important communal affairs. A feeling of this sort would pervade any assembly whose business concerned the highest matters and every one of whose members had perhaps ventured or would venture his life for the cause. But the period of the Church triumphant and grown worldly, whose councils became increasingly frequent and brilliant, quickly reveals a sad picture of essential devolution.

The first great occasion was the Council of Nicaea (325), whose chief purpose was to be the disposition of the Arian conflicts. It is one of the most intolerable spectacles of all history to see the Church, barely saved from persecution, particularly in the Eastern countries of the Empire, wholly consumed in strenuous conflict over the relations of the three Persons of the Trinity. Oriental rigidity and Greek sophistry, equally represented in the episcopal thrones, tormented themselves and the letter of Scripture to produce some symbol which would make the incomprehensible comprehensible and to give general validity to some expression of the idea. From *homoousios* and *homoiousios* ("equal" and "similar") the conflict proceeded through a hundred metamorphoses and several hundred years and split the Eastern Church into sects, of which one, in the form of the Greek Orthodox Church, remained to support the Byzantine Empire. A host of other interests, in part very worldly, attached themselves to the conflict and were concealed in it, so that it assumes the aspect of a merely

hypocritical pretext. For the sake of this quarrel the Church
made itself inwardly hollow; for the sake of orthodox
dogma it suffered the inward man to be famished, and, itself demoralized, it completely forfeited its higher moral
effect upon the individual. And yet this business, so distasteful in itself, was of supreme importance in world history. This Church with its collateral sects, grown rigid and
cut off from all development, was for another millennium
and a half to hold nationalities together against the pressure of alien barbarians, even to take the place of nationalities, for it was stronger than state or culture, and therefore survived them both. In it alone there persisted the
quintessence of Byzantinism, which is not without its future; and of Byzantinism, the soul is orthodoxy.

It must be admitted, therefore, that strife over the Second Person of the Trinity had far-reaching historical justification. But we shall beware of pursuing the dogmatic
aspects of the question further, and limit ourselves to a few
notes concerning the relations of government and clergy as
they appeared in the Council of Nicaea and in the events
following.

When the Alexandrian Presbyter Arius stepped forward
with his doctrine of the subordination of the Son to the
Father, there arose against him the Alexandrian Deacon
Athanasius and the Bishop himself, whose name was Alexander. As early as 321 Alexander had convoked a synod of
the bishops of Egypt and Libya, who deposed Arius and
excommunicated him. Thus his doctrine and position assumed an importance which they would not in themselves
have had. Attention and partisanship on both sides grew
immeasurably through preaching, solicitation, and correspondence. When Bishop Eusebius of Nicomedia took the
part of the vain and peculiar but not impractical Arius, the
struggle took on the aspect of a conflict between the sees of
Alexandria and Nicomedia. In or near Nicomedia another
synod was held, which declared in favor of Arius. At this
time Eusebius of Caesarea was also inclined to this position;
later, in his *Life of Constantine*, he presents an account of
the conflict which is unique in its kind for dishonesty and
intentional meagerness.

This was the state of affairs (323) when Constantine, in consequence of his last war against Licinius, assumed control of the East. He inherited the cleavage in its full bloom. His interest and inclination must certainly have tended to pacification, either by adjusting differences, or by a declaration for the stronger or more intelligent party, or by a shrewd balance between the two parties.

One of the most distinguished bishops of the Licinian realm, the same Eusebius of Nicomedia who had had such great influence over Constantia, sister of the Emperor and wife of Licinius, now half won Constantine over to the Arian side. But a court theologian of the West, Bishop Hosius of Cordova, who saw his own influence on Constantine imperiled, reached an understanding with the Bishop of Alexandria, and so confused matters that the Emperor saw that the only solution was the convocation of a general council. He must incidentally have welcomed an occasion to become personally acquainted with the clergy of his new realm and personally to impress them, and also to put an end to the dangerous abuse of provincial synods. Of the 318 bishops who assembled at Nicaea in June 325, barely a half dozen were Westerners. Bishop Sylvester of Rome did not appear in person but sent two presbyters, in accordance with a correct discretion which restrained his successors also from visiting Eastern synods. Moreover, of the perhaps thousand bishops of the East only those received invitations from the imperial secretariat whose opinions could be swayed or overborne.

And now when "the great priestly garland woven of colorful flowers," "the image of the apostolic roundelay," "the repetition of the first Whitsuntide," was assembled, when, beside the bishops, a numerous priestly retinue and a throng of "laymen expert in dialectic" had forgathered, Constantine in person opened the synod. He was stiff with purple, gold, and precious stones, and in this pomp Eusebius compares him to an angel of the Lord of Heaven. But an impressive personal appearance was not the sum. In the course of the proceedings it became evident that Hosius had influenced the Emperor against the Arians and that he and his party were using every means to persuade the great

mass of those undecided to the same view, pointing especially to the fact that it enjoyed imperial favor. It was neither the speeches of Arius, then, nor the counter-arguments
of Athanasius in honor of the eternity of the Son that determined the issue. A period was finally put to the debate by
the exercise of imperial authority; Constantine insisted
upon the questionable expression *homoousios* against the
will of the majority, whereupon the majority patiently submitted. Only two bishops refused their signature, and so
deserve to be mentioned, even if their action derived from
irreligious stubbornness; they were Theonas of Marmarica
and Secundus of Ptolemais. Their reward was deposition
and excommunication. Eusebius of Nicomedia signed, but
since his fall was predetermined, he and others were required to sign a supplementary article execrating his own
former opinion. Upon his refusal to do so he was banished
to Gaul, as was also Theognis, Bishop of Nicaea. Arius himself was dispatched to Illyria. Constantine had now learned
to know, and largely to despise, his Eastern clergy. How
these men, who could successfully have disjointed the Empire, had cringed before him! Many had secretly sent him
letters incriminating their fellows; these libels he caused to
be burned and he admonished them to harmony. Before
the departure a great banquet was held at the court; "the
gates of the palace were surrounded by bodyguards with
bared swords, but the men of God strode fearlessly by and
reached the inner chamber." The Emperor presented them
with gifts and admonitions to peace for their journey. To
the community of Alexandria he caused to be written,
"What has pleased three hundred bishops is nothing other
than the will of God."

But now the struggle began in real earnest. Three years
later (328) Constantine, who had no real convictions on
the theological question, found, allegedly upon the instigation of an Arian presbyter recommended to him by the
dying Constantia, that a new turn was suitable or perhaps
that it was just. Arius and the others who had been deposed
were recalled from exile; Hosius was overthrown or at least
vanished from his office for a very long time; the see of
Antioch was taken, so to speak, by storm and occupied by

an Arian—an affair which involved outrageous incidents
and aroused the city's populace, which was in any case
menacing. Eusebius of Nicomedia, who played the principal role in these events, now directed an attack against the
hated see of Alexandria. But he found it occupied by a
formidable antagonist, Athanasius. Athanasius is the first
thoroughly consistent exponent of the hierarchical personages of the medieval Church. He was steeped from childhood in the dignity of the priestly office, filled with large
ideas and aims, as for example the conversion of Abyssinia,
had no fear of man or regard for circumstances which might
stand in the way of his principles, was ready for any sacrifice the cause might demand, but as unyielding to others
as to himself and incapable of appreciating their viewpoint,
and not always scrupulous in regard to means. The fate of
orthodoxy in the period immediately following, so far as we
can judge, unmistakably depended on Athanasius. Constantine demanded his rehabilitation of Arius; he refused,
and had his way. Thereupon his opponents adduced absurd political slanders, because Constantine could not be
embittered on the religious score; Athanasius hurried to the
court and won the Emperor over personally. Finally his opponents thought they had found a proper device; they
accused the bishop to Constantine as being intolerant, as
persecuting the Meletian sect, which had received the
peace of the Church at Nicaea. Here Athanasius was actually not wholly guiltless, but the Meletians had purposely
been provoked against him. The Emperor decided that the
matter should be examined in a synod, which was to meet
at Caesarea in Palestine; Athanasius, however, declared
(334) that he would never stand before an authority which
consisted wholly of his deadly enemies. And Constantine
again yielded! But the incessant charges finally prevailed,
and in the following year (335) an assembly was actually
convoked, and in Tyre, whence the assembled fathers
were to go directly to Jerusalem to be present at the dedication of the Church of the Holy Sepulcher. The proceedings were presided over by a high court official, named
Dionysius. The most serious charge (p. 199, above) Athanasius brilliantly annihilated; for the lesser charges a parti-

san investigating commission proceeded to Alexandria, and
their report was eventually followed by a decision. The
Arians triumphed here, as the orthodox party had done at
Nicaea. But at almost the same instant Athanasius was
again at court. "As soon as I rode into Constantinople," the
Emperor wrote, "he and his party suddenly met me; God is
my witness that I did not even recognize him on the spot,
and at the beginning would have nothing to do with him."
The result of this encounter was that Constantine summoned the fathers of Tyre to the capital for a prompt justification of their conduct and their decisions. Here they
ventured their first disobedience; instead of all the party,
only its six chiefs appeared, and Constantine yielded,
though not unconditionally. He banished Athanasius to
Treves, but stipulated that the see of Alexandria should
not be occupied, obviously with the intention that Athanasius should be restored at a suitable time. It is not easy to
decide whether Constantine was frightened by the bishops'
defiance, or what other considerations might have guided
his decision. The plaintiffs charged that Athanasius had
threatened to restrain the sailing of the Egyptian grain
fleet, but probably the Emperor disbelieved this charge,
even if he pretended to believe it. Thereupon he ordered
Arius to Constantinople, apparently with the friendliest intentions. After a visit at the imperial palace Arius suddenly
fell ill on the street, and died immediately (336) in a
near-by public latrine, which was shown as a remarkable
sight a century later. Whether he was given poison, and by
whom, is doubtful; his death was of no advantage to Constantine.

Constantine would doubtless have been pleased to have
a firm and harmonious Church, but now wide fluctuations
had set in. In view of his own inward neutrality it was not
difficult for him to keep the Church parties in suspense and
not attach himself to any permanently. And so he allowed
them to conquer in turn, and by energetic interventions
provided only that he and his power should not be forgotten. He probably saw from the beginning that the conflict
was waged largely for the sake of conflict, and that con-
ciliation would be out of place. This attitude his successors

failed to understand, because they were themselves seriously concerned with the theological questions involved, and they left the party which they supported free to use violence and vengeance against its opposition.

Living testimony of Constantine's impartiality is extant in the familiar edict on heresies, dating from the last years of his life. The clerical draftsman assails the heretics vigorously, Novatians, Valentinians, Marcionites, Cataphrygians, and all the rest; but after all the reproaches heaped upon them the conclusion is only that they are deprived of their places of assembly. Eusebius exults, "They were driven away, like animals were they driven out"—it is easy to see, however, that this far from satisfies Eusebius. Of the Novatians, it is specifically noted that Constantine only wished to frighten them a little. Persecution proper, it appears, was visited only upon the Montanists or Cataphrygians, who, as fanatics, might become dangerous, and even they were not molested in Phrygia, the home of the sect. In any case Constantine's regulations display certain remarkable inconsistencies. After the condemnation of Arius an order was issued to all the churches to burn Arius' writings, concluding with the words, "Whoso conceals a book shall be put to death. God preserve you!"—and Arius himself was allowed to live in exile in peace and subsequently restored to honor.

Immediately after Constantine's death his sons personally immersed themselves in Church partisanship. Their education was of that nature, and their disgraceful characters were no deterrents. Socrates Scholasticus tells how Constantius, for example, was won to Arianism. An unnamed presbyter, who is said to have delivered his father's will to Constantius and thus to have established himself at court, first brought the Grand Chamberlain Eusebius, a eunuch, over to the Arian side, and then the other eunuchs; these and the presbyter then won the Empress over, and finally Constantius himself made his decision. Thereupon the entire court staff, the military suite, and the city of Constantinople took sides. In the palace eunuchs and women disputed, and in the city every house became the scene of "dialectic battle." This situation spread over the whole

East, while in the West Constantine II and then Constans were convinced Athanasians. Frightful persecution, exile, murder, came in due course. All the tortures and hangman's arts of the Maximinian period were on occasion restored. Holy communion and baptism became objects of police enforcement, and strident factionalism beset the occupation of bishoprics.

These further crises are not part of our task. Along with the Church, rent by incurable obstinacy and ambition and by fantastic dialectic, there grew up the boy Julian, barely saved from the general murder which Constantine visited upon his own family. He and his brother Gallus were educated for the priesthood in the Villa Macellum in remote Cappadocia; their recreation consisted in building a chapel to the sainted martyr Mamas. It was under such impressions that the mind of the future pagan reactionary was formed.

We must not forget, however, that alongside a Church rapidly disintegrating in victory, there also was a religion. The lofty moral consequences of the introduction of Christianity disappear from view all too easily while dogmatic hierarchical quarrels wax huge. The great men of this and the following decades, Athanasius, Basil, Gregory Nazianzen, Jerome, Chrysostom, carried a more or less definite stamp of outward churchliness in addition to their religiosity, and hence seem more one-sided and less agreeable than the great, complete, and harmonious figures of antiquity; but their life principle is loftier, and indeed incommensurable.

The moral consequences of Christianity in profounder natures must not be measured according to the outlook of a Eusebius, who simply postulates earthly happiness and dominion as the divine reward for conversion to Christianity. What is involved is rather a new attitude to earthly matters, sometimes more consciously adopted and sometimes less consciously. The great mass sought as pleasurable a life in Christianity as could be managed and as the state's morals police permitted; but more serious people abstained from many pleasures entirely, and by the end of the third century even a Christian teacher found it necessary to express apprehension lest separation between man and wife

might work injury to marriage. In respect to their worldly
goods many felt themselves obliged to share with the poor
and the churches, and some denied themselves use of their
property altogether. The two great expressions of contemporary practical Christianity are charity and asceticism, if
we may pass over a third, namely, the mission to the
heathen peoples, as an almost exclusively clerical prerogative.

As for charity, the Christian, following the familiar prov-
erb, could begin in his own home and with his slaves, partly
by milder treatment, and partly by manumission. Slavery
in itself was not regarded as wrong; even much later the
very monasteries might possess slaves. But it was early recognized as a good work to manumit them, and under
Diocletian Chromatius, the City Prefect of Rome, liberated
fourteen hundred slaves. At the end of the fourth century
much more extensive liberations took place in the devout
circle of St. Jerome, but only among people who renounced
the world entirely; even so, the contemporary Chrysostom
demanded the unqualified abolition of slavery. As a soldier
in his youth Martin of Tours retained his single slave, to be
sure, tending him, however, with great humility, often
drawing his shoes off and serving him at table. Constantine
had already endeavored to abolish by law the right of the
master over the life and death of the slave, although the
legalistic distinction between the death of a slave *after* mistreatment and *in consequence of* mistreatment always provided the master an easy refuge. It is even posited that a
slave might die a natural death under blows "through the
necessity of fate." Theoretically the pagans abided by their
old view of slavery; Themistius would grant the born slave
no capacity for higher human rationality, and Macrobius
deals seriously with the question whether slaves possess human standing and whether the gods concerned themselves
with slaves. In point of fact the treatment of slaves by most
pagans was not bad.

Charity in the narrower sense, which rested partly on the
belief in worthlessness of earthly goods and partly on the
obligation to alleviate poverty and misery, involved, in the
manner of its expression, serious problems in national econ-

omy. In the beginning, charity had been entrusted to a special office within the Church, that of the deacons; it had been abused by many unworthy of charity, but in the state of war of the *ecclesia pressa* there was something of the magnificent in not observing these things too narrowly. This was the result of a mood of exaltation, prepared for the very worst. The deacons, since the character of their task was local, were better able to test and become acquainted with individuals. But now alms were distributed lavishly under all forms and without restrictions. It is difficult for our own age, with its insistence upon work, to understand or approve; but it is questionable whether, apart from an agrarian law, any other solution was possible in an Empire which was almost exclusively agricultural and in which the distribution of landed property had been suffered to grow so unequal—in an Empire, moreover, whose cities were largely filled with propertyless proletariat and whose rural population had so diminished that it had everywhere to be supplemented by barbarian colonies. For centuries the urban population had received huge doles which were, however, not regarded as such; namely, the distribution of provisions, at first limited to the populace of Rome, who were presumed to be the masters of the Empire, and then extended, in the guise of imperial beneficence, to a large number of more important, and eventually to lesser, cities. The Empire, whose revenues were for the most part delivered in kind, fed the cities with the produce of the countryside. Certain grants of this sort were newly made in the age of Constantine.

When Christianity was introduced, the Church acquired very large means by gifts, in addition to the endowments of the state; henceforward it was more or less obliged to meet requirements for alms from these two sources. Above we have enumerated the institutions established by benevolent bishops and congregations out of these funds—*xenodochia* (hostels), *ptochotrophia* (poorhouses), *gerokomia* (homes for the aged), *nosokomia* (hospitals), and *orphanotrophia* (orphanages); the Basilicas founded and built by Basil the Great at the end of the fourth century may be regarded as the ideal and model of such institutions. For the larger part these were foundations for people actually helpless, and as such comprised a truly magnificent advance over the old pagan world, although the ancient world had long ago made a beginning of state activity in this direction.

The state itself, as has been remarked above, granted the Church these functions, and with them a means of influence. Constantine bestowed upon the church of Alexandria, for example, a special *annona* (grain supply) for distribution to the poor, besides which the general *annona*, confirmed to the city by Diocletian, doubtless continued in force. The Church *annona* was patently a not entirely immaculate means of proselytization, and Constantine's endowments generally have the aspect of conversionist treasuries. When he founded a bishopric at Heliopolis, for example, and the city nevertheless remained almost entirely pagan, he contributed generously to the support of the Christian poor, "so that so many the more might be converted to the Word." His personal benevolences and stipends were certainly of a predominantly political character, and only apparently planless; later he probably permitted himself to be guided by priests in this respect also. When he wished to make himself popular in Rome after his victory over Maxentius, he distributed to rich and poor alike large sums of money that he brought with him or found in Rome. People of social standing in reduced circumstances received money and dignities; girls of good family were given husbands from his retinue and provided with a dowry; and the ragged beggars of the Forum got alms, food, and decent clothing, the latter apparently because nakedness gave offense.

In later years Easter morning was the great occasion for gifts. If the court bishop gives way to bathos on such occasions, the incisive words of Ammianus may serve as a corrective: "As our sources have clearly shown, Constantine first opened the jaws of the people about him, and then Constantius stuffed them full with the marrow of the provinces." The gifts of an Emperor can never provide a criterion, for it can seldom be shown why he gives them or from what source he obtains them. There is something political and equivocal about even the charities of old Helena.

When she traveled through the East she gave large sums to the inhabitants of individual cities, and additional amounts personally to those who approached her. She also distributed large sums to the soldiers; the poor, moreover, received money and clothing, and others were helped out of imprisonment for debt, exile, and oppression of every sort. Obviously Constantine regarded such an excursion by the only completely trustworthy member of his family as appropriate and as consonant with the spirit of the East. Of the financial system upon which this generosity was based we shall have to speak briefly in the sequel.

Let us now turn from the egoist robed in purple who measures and calculates all that he does or suffers to be done by the aggrandisement of his own power. Contrasted with this essentially frivolous authority of the state is the great and selfless devotion of many who gave away all of their possessions during their lifetime in order to "dedicate themselves to God"; here charity and asceticism merged completely. Men and women, in part of the upper classes which were used to all the pleasures of life, took Christ's command to the rich young man with strict literalness; they sold all their possessions and gave the proceeds to the poor, so that, in the midst of the world and surrounded by the clamor of great cities, they might live in voluntary poverty, free for the contemplation of the sublime. Even this did not content some; they fled out of the world and out of civilization as "men escaped," as anchorites.

History is wont to conceal the origins of great things, but it does provide a quite exact account of the rise of eremitism and its development into monachism. No other tendency or event characterizes the later third and the fourth century more sharply.

It is in the nature of man, when he feels lost in the large and busy external world, that he should seek to find his proper self in solitude. And the more deeply he has felt the inward cleavage and rending, the more absolute is the solitude required. If religion adds to this a feeling of sin and a need for abiding and uninterrupted union with God, then every earthly consideration vanishes and the recluse be-

comes an ascetic, partly to do penance, partly to owe the
world without nothing more than the barest existence, but
partly also to keep the soul capable of constant intercourse
with the sublime. Quite of his own accord the recluse
sought to bind himself from a return to his previous state by
taking vows. If several inspired by the same striving were
met together in their retirement, their vows and their general manner of life took on the character of a community,
of a rule.

The anchorite way of life premises a not wholly healthy
state of society and the individual, but belongs rather to
periods of crisis, when many crushed spirits seek quiet, and
at the same time many strong hearts are puzzled by the
whole apparatus of life and must wage their struggle with
God remote from the world. But if any man possessed by
the modern preoccupation with activity and its immoder-
ately subjective view of life would therefore wish to place
the anchorites in some institution for enforced labor, let
him not regard himself as particularly healthy-minded; he
is no more so than the multitudes in the fourth century who
were too weak or too superficial to have any comprehension of the spiritual forces which drove those towering personalities into the desert. Even if we disregard the question
of profit or loss which accrued to the ascetic in the Thebaid
or in the hills of Gaza, there remains an enormous effect
upon history, which the student must evaluate after his
own manner. It was these anchorites who communicated to
the clerical order of succeeding centuries the higher ascetic
attitude toward life, or at least the claim to such an attitude; without their pattern the Church, which was the sole
pillar of all spiritual interests, would have become entirely
secularized and have necessarily succumbed to crass material power. Our own age, in its enjoyment of free work of
the mind and free interchange of intellectual endeavor, too
readily forgets that in this it still profits from the halo of the
supermundane which the medieval Church imparted to
science.

The earliest Christian anchorites were Egyptians and
Palestinians who led a solitary or at least a retired life in the
vicinity of their homes and permitted younger men to join

them in a kind of apprenticeship. But this half-eremite existence did not satisfy the natures of a Paul (235–341), an Anthony (252–357), or a Hilarion (292–373). To be entirely secure against the seductions of the world and to dedicate themselves wholly to God, they disappeared from the world and lived for sixty or eighty years in the literal desert. Some happened into solitude in their flight from the persecuting Romans; but more sought solitude for its own sake, and would never again leave it because it had become home to them, and because they could no longer think of life in the secular world and in corrupt society without horror. Furthermore, "when the world took on its Christian coloring, those were not the unworthiest members of Christian society who felt driven, for a time or permanently, into the desert, there to find the freedom which appeared to have vanished out of the victorious Church. This monachism in the first century of its existence bears venerable testimony against the lie of Constantine's creation" (Zahn, *Konstantin der Grosse und die Kirche*).

Paul the Hermit lived in a secluded mountain retreat where counterfeiters had plied their business in the days of Cleopatra. They had burrowed caves into the rockfaces, in which Paul still found rusty anvils, hammers, and mint blocks. An ancient palm shaded the secure spot, and a little spring watered it. Anthony first prepared for the anchorite life in the country not far from his home (at Heracleopolis in Middle Egypt), then he lived for a long while in a tomb, later in a deserted fort full of snakes, and finally escaped the devout in an oasis shielded by rocks, of which we shall speak below. Hilarion of Tabatha near Gaza sought out the worst robber-infested beat of his region, between the swamp and the sea, there to serve God at first with no shelter, then in a small reed hut, and then in a stone cell five feet high. The deprivations to which these men who had been brought up in abundance subjected themselves are so drastic that only an extraordinary constitution could face them. More trying than the inadequacy of the food, in quantity and quality, was, to our way of thinking, the repulsive filth and insects, to the endurance of which these men believed they were obligated, as did Friar Amandus

(Suso) and others in the fourteenth century. A reaction of this sort was in any case quite natural, after preceding generations had surrendered to every manner of carnal indulgence in the sumptuous baths. The greatest deprivation, that of human society, need not enter into the reckoning; the only cultural resource of the eremites was that they knew the Bible by heart. But this did not shield them from violent inward trials, which manifested themselves in part by seemingly external daimonic temptations. Here one might think of the personification of all spiritual forces which is peculiar to antiquity, but no such explanation is required. Sometimes it is their own sensuality, sometimes memories of their former life, sometimes the reaction to the desert and its natural terrors, which inflict these torturing visions upon the recluses. The appearance of the hellish host in the tomb which served Anthony as a dwelling is world-famous, though it has been forever relegated to the realm of the burlesque by Jacques Callot: "Then the walls opened, and the daimones appeared as serpents, lions, bulls, wolves, scorpions, leopards, and bears, all roaring and threatening"; at other times they appeared in human guise, clamoring, whistling, and dancing, and they smote the saint half dead. Even more colorful are the visions of Hilarion. Each night there arose about him ghostly noises of every description, the wailing of infants, the bleating of flocks, the bellowing of bulls, the tramp of armies. In the clear moonlight a chariot drawn by wild horses rushed upon him, but was swallowed up by the earth at his anguished cry of "Jesus." Naked women and richly laden tables appeared, or wolves and foxes leapt by as the saint was at prayer. Once a duel of gladiators rose before his eyes, and a dying gladiator fell at his feet and with beseeching look begged for burial. The evil spirit even takes on the harrowing character which makes the ghost in Sindbad's voyages so unforgettable; he leaps upon the kneeling but somewhat distracted Hilarion, mounts his back like a rider, mockingly kicks his heels into his flanks, and refuses to be shaken off.

These eremites dispose most easily of certain daimones who appear honorably in their true shape as satyrs and centaurs and sometimes desire conversion and intercession. On the question of centaurs, the great Jerome refuses to decide whether they are merely disguises of the devil or whether the desert actually produces such creatures, but he insists on the genuineness of the satyr who showed Anthony on his journey the way to St. Paul and besought him for intercession. Under Constantius such a creature is said to have been found in the desert, brought to Alexandria alive, to have there straightway died, been salted, and sent to Antioch, so that the Emperor who resided there might have a look at him. St. Anthony's satyr, moreover, retained goat feet and horns, and thus was a Paniscus; he had also kept the crooked nose of the wanton old days.

After a period of such torments there followed in the life of the ascetic another stage, which he must have regarded with mixed feelings. The world which needed help discovered him, saw in him something lofty and unusual, and sought him out in the wilderness. He becomes a wonderworker, not through mysteries and phantasmagoria, but through sheer prayer. Did his soul profit thereby? Must spiritual pride not have been aroused? Admirers gathered about him and built cells near his; gradually he must recognize them as disciples, and in view of the volume of visitors he soon required assistants. Half against his will he soon became a "Father," a master. Anthony, who endured this new life for several decades, fled to the interior of the desert about 310 and discovered, parallel to Aphroditopolis, a rocky mountain whose rustling rills nourished a stand of palms. But here too the brethren searched him out, and he was compelled to allow two of them, Pelusian and the interpreter Isaac, to live with him. Again he was made the object of a large and uninterrupted pilgrimage; heretics and the orthodox, high Roman officials and pagan priests, the healthy and the sick, came in such numbers that it was found profitable to establish a regular camel post from Aphroditopolis through the desert to his dwelling. He had no choice but to build a quite inaccessible cell high upon a hill with a steep ascent, where he could withdraw at least periodically. The last concern of his life was that his burial place should be kept secret, for a rich property owner of the neighborhood was already lying in wait for his corpse, in order to install a *martyrium,* that is, a church containing the grave of the saint, at his country estate, perhaps for business reasons. The two disciples did in fact hold their counsel, apparently in the face of Hilarion himself.

For Hilarion had undertaken a journey to Egypt, which was also nothing other than a flight from the enormous concourse of visitors and from the growing care of the thousands of fellow eremites who had joined him in the desert of Gaza. His biography, one of the most interesting of Jerome's works, describes the origin and manner of this concourse quite vividly. It gradually became known in Gaza and its harbor city of Majuma that a holy anchorite was living in the desert. An important Roman lady, whose three children had fallen ill of fever on her travels, went on a pilgrimage to him with her maidservants and eunuchs, and by tears and lamentations moved him to come to Gaza, where he cured the children. Thereupon pilgrimages to him from Syria and Egypt went on incessantly, but in his immediate neighborhood paganism defended itself most vigorously. The great god Marnas in his temple at Gaza entered into direct competition with St. Hilarion, and in the pleasure-seeking commercial city there developed a cleavage, which requires some trouble to understand. The cleavage finds essential expression in the crowds of possessed persons who were constantly being dragged out to the saint in the desert, and who were for the most part surely nothing other than people morbidly divided and broken between two religions, both really daimonic. Theoretically, the victim was not conscious that he was possessed; according to the older, more generalizing view, the daimon might seek out its own people or its own animals at will, or it might be conjured into victims by the malice of magicians. Hilarion, for example, once had to cure a camel that was possessed. The daimon is always conceived of as a second person, distinct from the man possessed, and may for example speak Syrian or Greek when his victim understands only Latin or Frankish. He is a personification of the evil pagan gods, and in this case, of course, usually of Marnas. In his contest with the idol, the saint for once departed from his principle, and opposed the pagan magic with Christian magic. Of the Circus entrepreneurs at Gaza, one, a pagan city official, was a devotee of Marnas, and kept a magician who caused his patron's horses to win and slowed his opponent's horses. The latter, a Christian called Italicus, applied to Hilarion, who first ridiculed him and asked him why he did not sell his horses and give the proceeds to the poor. But Hilarion was softened by the man's conscientiousness in preferring to seek help of a servant of God rather than from magicians, and by the consideration that a triumph of Gaza's whole Christendom was involved. He gave Italicus a basin of water with which to sprinkle horses, chariot, stall, driver, and barriers. The spectators watched the beginning of the race with tense interest, the Christian's horses won easily, and even the pagans shouted, "Marnas is beaten by Christ," so that the day caused many to be converted. And yet on one occasion Hilarion cured a circus driver who was deathly sick only on condition that he give up his previous occupation entirely.

Just as the anchorite became a wonder-worker half against his will, so he became a monk also. The cells of those who followed him into the desert gradually formed a monastery, which then submitted to his leadership with the greatest devotion.

In Egypt there was a precedent not only in the Jewish Therapeutae, who led a life of this sort by Lake Mareotis, but also in those who were walled into cells at the temples of Serapis (see p. 139, above); this was the hardest of all forms of asceticism, but it was to find followers, though few in number, throughout the Christian world. The climate, moreover, made great moderation not only possible but necessary, and, as we shall see, even the industrial character of the country rendered existence easy for an unmarried proletariat with little or no landed property. Innumerable fellow anchorites had gathered at the various stations of Anthony, and he enlightened them by prayer, example, and admonition; but he never considered it his goal in life to give them a fixed constitution and direct them according to a set plan. This was rather the function of Pachomius, whose life embraces approximately the first half of the fourth century. As a young man he had learned the value of a closed discipline in a short career as soldier, and he put his lesson into effect in the famous monachist district of Tabenna in Upper Egypt, between Tentyris and Thebes. Several thousand monks were gathered here even during his lifetime, and the rules which he set them obtained validity in other monastic colonies which arose at the same time or later. Of these the most important are: that at Arsinoë in the region of Lake Moeris (ten thousand strong in Valens' day); the great settlement in the Nitrian or Scetian Desert, west of the Delta; the so-called Eremica not far from Alexandria; and finally the scattered monasteries and cells along the entire coast of the Mediterranean and Lake Mareotis, including some on the Red Sea and the Sinai peninsula. But all these were surpassed by Tabenna, where in Jerome's day no fewer than fifty thousand monks were wont to celebrate Easter; not all of these lived in the central monastery (*monasterium maius*), but they came from all the monasteries belonging to the congregation of Tabenna. We can see that not all these colonies were situated in the desert; even before the end of the fourth century there were city monasteries, as part of the campaign against pagan remains and reminiscences. Thus, for example, the temple of Canopus in the city of that name was transformed into the monastery of Metanoia ("repentance"). According to organization the Egyptian institutions were partly cenobitic or partly monastic, that is, larger structures for many monks; and partly *lauras,* groups of cells which were at a specified distance from one another and thus were still in a manner hermitages. At the time mentioned there were at least one hundred thousand men in Egypt dedicated to this form of life. Along with these monasteries we begin to hear of nunneries also; of these one, under Pachomius' sister, counted four hundred nuns as early as 320.

A historical phenomenon of such magnitude has a profound basis in national history, and if it should cause a nation to perish, that would only be the necessary form of its fall. In Egypt it was natural for the question of religion to oscillate to extremes. Having emerged from fanatical

paganism after a hard struggle, the Egyptian knew no
bounds in his reaction, and believed that he must dedicate
his life to the new religion in a manner analogous to his
forebears' bondage to symbols. Thus there arose this remarkable fakir existence, the last product of the ancient
Egyptian spirit to affect world history; for future centuries
that spirit now falls passive.

The rule which Pachomius laid down for this host was
a thing of the most urgent necessity, but at the same time
it was the first step toward externalization and untruth;
asceticism is now no longer the result of free individual
inspiration but a common law to fetter many thousands of
unequal persons permanently to an equal practice. And if
one give truth its due he must confess that Pachomius assumed a low average and that his constitution presupposes
a great number of persons without the proper vocation who
must above all be kept in bounds. This was usefully done
by means of work by which the monasteries lived. With the
rise of monasticism a great change must have taken place
in Egyptian industry. Now that the monasteries were very
far from producing merely baskets and mats out of Nile
sedge, but engaged in the important trades of weaving linen
and tanning hides (to say nothing of their other products),
many factories in the country found themselves at a disadvantage, for the monasteries could offer goods at much
lower prices in the open market of Alexandria. The man-
ager of a large monastery who distributed the tasks and
arranged delivery was the equivalent of a great industri-
alist. Monks who lived alone could sell their work directly
and sometimes accumulated a private fortune, the rule
notwithstanding. Otherwise it was a guiding principle that
the work of the monks was intended rather for the benefit
of their souls than to supply necessities, and any excess
must be distributed to the poor. Little is said of agriculture;
on the other hand monasteries situated on the Nile maintained large boats, apparently also for the sake of profit.

Along with work, the monk was occupied with prayer,
worship, and continuous castigations of every sort, which
were the essential element in a life purposely contrived to
be one-sided. In view of the origin and the tendency of the

institution, literary occupation is not to be expected; what, indeed, had erudite Alexandria with all its Greek and Oriental scholarship achieved? The monk pursued aims and ideals which were at the opposite pole from pagan over-education and immorality, and if elsewhere there were points of accommodation, even of *rapprochement*, between the two moral worlds called paganism and Christianity, here at least the essential and principal relationship between them was one of permanent and basic hostility. Every line that had come down from previous ages, from hieroglyphs to Greek cursive, was tainted with paganism, idolatry, or magic; all that was left to read, therefore (in so far as reading was allowed), was devotional Christian literature which had in part to be created by these very monks or translated into Egyptian from other languages. The relations to ancient art were the same as to ancient literature; Ammonius is expressly praised, for example, because on his visit to Rome he had looked at nothing more than the Basilicas of St. Peter and St. Paul.

In its narrower sense, furthermore, the discipline was systematically calculated to cut the monk off from all his previous connections, especially from his family, and then to guard him strictly and keep him at his work. By its predominantly negative content the rule conveys a dreary, police-like impression, and is thus not remotely comparable to the Rule of St. Benedict. The articles dealing with mockery and loose talk from monastery to monastery, and with angry rivalries between them, clearly recall the character of the country in which they flourished. Similarly, the rule of no Western order required that the monks should sleep separately in locked wooden stalls as in a sheath. Thoroughly Egyptian, moreover, is the secret and mysterious language, which an angel is said to have suggested to Pachomius and his disciples Cornelius and Syrus, and which (to judge by extant examples) consisted in nothing other than a conventional designation of individual objects and persons by letters of the alphabet. Along with such designations, Pachomius is said to have employed the device of dividing his monks into twenty-four classes according to their capacities and character and calling them *alpha, beta, gamma,* and so forth. But it is hard to believe that a man so practical in other respects was so at fault in his psychology.

Surely the ideal Christian life is not to be sought in the Egyptian monastic colonies. Along with these colonies, however, there persisted genuine anchorite practices, and to these, in view of conditions in the contemporary world, we must grant a high degree of justification. Most of the famous recluses of the fourth century spent part of their lives in the monasteries or at least in the *laura;* either previously or subsequently they retired to deeper solitude, to which the monastery sent them only bread and salt. Here too they were not always secure from spiritual pride, fearful temptations, and fantastic enthusiasms. Their penances were in part truly murderous in character; however, they not only usually regarded themselves as fortunate and their lives as worthily spent, but they left behind many a profound and beautiful saying which proves that their happiness was no mere delusion but derived from constant preoccupation with the sublime. The names of an Ammonius, an Arsenius, an Elias, the two Macarii, and a number of others will always belong among the memorable records of the Church.

A third form of Egyptian monachism were the somewhat disreputable Remoboth, who lived in twos or threes in cities and castles, and had no rule but followed their own inclinations, and hence frequently fell into bitter strife. They lived by trades, and were better paid than others because of their apparent sanctity. Their fasting is criticized as being vainglorious, and on festive days they are said to have indulged in gluttony.

The later development of Egyptian monachism, its sects, and its participation in the general dissensions of the Church do not belong in this place.

In Palestine monachism under St. Hilarion took on a different form in its economic relationships and hence received a physiognomy quite different from the Egyptian. Agriculture and viticulture predominated. Many monks even retained their personal property and are scarcely to be differentiated from unmarried farmers with paid servants. The founder himself continued to live in the uncultivated desert, and was greatly displeased that the desert had become populated on his account. But the "villas" of many of his comrades, where vines and grain flourished, must have been better situated. About Hilarion's cell a monastery proper seems to have developed in the course of time; otherwise the Palestinian monks constituted a large, widely dispersed, and loosely connected *laura*. In Egypt Pachomius was able to summon all the monks of his congregation to the Easter festival at Tabenna and all of its superiors and officials to the festival of forgiveness in the month of Mesore (August), whereas in Palestine Hilarion was forced to make periodic journeys over his entire domain in order to oversee his people. On these journeys he was accompanied by an army of two thousand monks, who at first carried their provisions with them but later were fed by landholders along the way. Since the saint did not wish to overlook the most remote and simplest cell, his travels often took him to Saracen villages, where he worked as a proselytizer.

Beyond Palestine through all of Roman Asia and into the kingdom of the Sassanids we have evidence of individual anchorites from the beginning of the fourth century, and not long thereafter also of monasteries as well as scattered institutions corresponding to the Egyptian *laura*. Of the latter sort was the monastic association at Mount Sigoron near Nisibis; these are called the grazing monks because at mealtime they went out with sickles to cut herbs, which were their only sustenance. Among these Syrian monks, those at Edessa early became famous, especially by reason of their great exorciser of daimones, Julian. For Armenia, Paphlagonia, and Pontus, Eustathius, the strict Bishop of Sebastia, was a principal founder of monachism; for Cappadocia and Galatia, somewhat later, Basil the Great, who was destined to give Eastern asceticism in general its permanent form. In these colder regions where life in scattered cells could not so easily be managed, the monks formed monasteries, mostly, indeed, in cities or villages.

In the more moderate countries of the West this tremendous example found imitators only gradually. It was not till the second half of the fourth century that monasteries arose in or near cities and that the little rocky islands of the Mediterranean which had previously served only as places of exile became filled with eremites. Enthusiastic Westerners traveled to the East in order to learn the ascetic practice or even to stay there, for life. Even in the midst of the activity of cities men, virgins, and widows devoted themselves continuously to a life so rigorous and devout as could only be led in a cloister. This is the epoch of St. Martin of Tours, St. Ambrose, and St. Jerome, who knew and portrayed both the dark and the bright side of this entire movement. We shall have to refer to this briefly in our treatment of Rome and Palestine. Gaul soon had the victorious feeling of having equaled if not surpassed the East.

General discussion concerning the moral and religious value and the historical necessity of monachism and the entire ascetic movement is superfluous in this place. Views on the subject must always remain diametrically opposed. One frame of thought will always abhor these things in life as in history and oppose them, another will love and praise them. But if a man wish to dispute with those ancient heroes of the desert from a Christian standpoint, he must take care that his reasoning should not prove the less consistent. The doctrine of vicarious penitence is not yet present, and the ascetic therefore represents none but himself. Penitence was still regarded as giving him no more claim to salvation than any other good work; nevertheless he strove for absolute denial of everything sensual and everything worldly. Wherefore such rigor? Because there can be no connection with the outer world whatever if one takes certain words of the New Testament seriously and refuses to compromise their literal meaning. And as long as there is a Christianity there will be communities, sects, and individuals who will be unable to evade such strict interpretation.

X

COURT, ADMINISTRATION, AND ARMY
CONSTANTINOPLE, ROME, ATHENS,
AND JERUSALEM

CONSTANTINE used to say: "To become Emperor is a matter of destiny; but if the power of fate has imposed the necessity of rule upon a man, he must strive to appear worthy of the imperium."

All things considered, Constantine was in fact worthier of rule than all his contemporaries and colleagues, frightfully as he may at times have abused his power. None has contested his right to the title "Great," which despite all flatterers has adhered to so few men. The measureless praise of Christian writers has not been the decisive factor in this point; rather it was the powerful impression which Constantine made upon the Roman world. That world was first conquered by him, then reconciled to a new religion, and newly organized in highly important aspects. Such demonstrations of capacity justified the Romans in calling him "Great" even if all that he did would have proved injurious. In an age less unusual Constantine similarly endowed would hardly have attained such historical importance; he would have had to be content with the reputation of a Probus or of an Aurelian. But since "the power of fate," as he expresses it, placed him at the border of two world epochs and in addition granted him a long reign, it was possible for his qualities as ruler to manifest themselves in much greater variety.

But it is not our task to recount his biography; we shall also pass over the whole imaginary picture of the hero current in the Middle Ages, his alleged baptism by Pope

Sylvester at Rome, his gift of Italy to the Pope, and the like. Just as our earlier pages have given only an indispensable sketch of his relation to throne and Church, so other aspects of his reign can be treated only briefly. Concerning most of the questions involved, historical judgment is in any case not uniform, and even the facts themselves are often in dispute.

This is the case, first of all, in the matter of the completed development of court ceremonial and court dignities. The so-called *Notitia Dignitatum*, a calendar of court and state deriving from the beginning of the fifth century, enumerates an elaborately graded hierarchy of officials of court and state which must have received its form largely through Constantine, even though the fact is not demonstrable. Many of the court dignities, however, must have existed under Diocletian and even far earlier, perhaps under Hadrian. As we have no detailed account of the procedures, one aspect of the list appears startling: the solemnity with which despotism surrounds its display of pomp. The adjective *sacer*, "sacred," occurs where we should expect simply "imperial"; several titles, for example, refer to the *sacrum cubiculum*, "the imperial chamber," and the like. But in order to reach a definite conclusion and to determine court procedure precisely we should have to know which of the many offices involved actual attendance and which were merely titular. Even today there are courts which are in fact moderately and economically organized but which distribute an inordinate number of honorary titles.

How accustomed the contemporary Roman world must have been to titles as symbols of rank we learn from the usual honorific epithets *illuster, spectabilis, honoratus, clarissimus, perfectissimus, egregius,* and the addresses *amplitudo, celsitudo, magnitudo, magnificentia, prudentia tua,* and the like, which were in part obligatory prerogatives of certain offices. The significance of these innovations has been briefly indicated in connection with Diocletian; here also we may conjecture that the rulers involved did not so much institute novelties out of caprice as confirm usages which had arisen out of the spirit of the age and reduce them to form and rule. Constantine indeed was perfectly aware of the character of the innovations; "he devised various titles of honor," says Eusebius, "in order to bestow distinctions upon as many as possible."

The prerogatives of the courtiers, consistently applied and extended, must moreover have gradually produced a new hereditary aristocracy. Not only were they raised above the entire oppressive tax structure and the distress of the municipalities into a loftier, transfigured sphere, but they were also protected against *calumnias,* the fate of ordinary mortals. Their privileges applied not only to themselves but also to their children and grandchildren, and continued in the case of retirement. There was already an aristocracy which rested upon hereditary immunity to taxation, namely, the senatorial families; now everything pointed toward the creation of a second aristocracy, comprising courtiers (*palatini*) and higher officials.

But as far as his own person was concerned, at least, Constantine was able to hold these things in proper balance. His court was very slippery ground, and anyone standing there must beware of a fall. In his immediate environment the Emperor had a crowd of "friends," "intimates," "confidants," and others, whatever their title might be; he was not one of the reserved, taciturn tyrants. Along with his constant "reading, writing, and reflection," he felt the needs of an expansive nature. But this does not exclude great inconsistency and duplicity. There are characters which are a peculiar mixture, in this respect, of loyalty and falseness, of gregariousness and cunning egoism; in an authoritarian ruler of Constantine's sort the latter is customarily swathed in the garb of "reasons of state." Thus we see how Constantine first raises his "friends" and makes them wealthy, even allowing them to wallow in the imperial treasury—abuses which extort profound sighs even from a Eusebius and which are recognized by Ammianus as a cancer in the Empire. But suddenly there followed catastrophes which must surely have frequently made the entire court tremble; the "friends" are executed and (we venture to assert) their possessions are confiscated. Perhaps those sermons of the Emperor of which we have spoken above

were harbingers of warning, perhaps even immediate an-
nunciations of doom; a careful man could take warning.
Even in his conversation Constantine was rather sneering
than amiable, *irrisor potius quam blandus*. The law of the
year 325 was promulgated in an especially menacing mood:
"Whoever, of whatever place, condition, or rank he may
be, is confident that he can prove truthfully any impropri-
ety or injustice against any of my judges, higher officials,
friends, or courtiers may come and apply to me without
fear; I shall hear and investigate his claim in person and
if its truth is demonstrated I shall myself take vengeance
. . . ; I shall avenge myself upon the man who had previously deceived me with hypocritical innocence. But the
man who furnishes information and proof I shall reward by
dignities and by property. So may the Supreme Divinity
ever be gracious unto me and preserve me for the happiness
and prosperity of the state." Whether anyone heeded this
vehement invitation we do not know, for the entire internal
history of the court lies in darkness. In any case there was
no improvement; even in the last decade of his life, Constantine was mocked, because of his immoderate extrava-
gances, as being a *pupillus*, that is, requiring a legal guardian. There is something very puzzling about the entire
situation. Here we have a tirelessly energetic autocrat who
is very far from allowing a professed regime of favorites to
arise and yet tolerates and provokes such a state of affairs,
only suddenly to put a period to it by terrible penalties—
and then occasionally ruing his haste and setting up statues
to the men he had executed, as was the case with the
murdered Crispus. In this conduct we may perceive either
a calculated plan or an impulsive and inconstant nature;
we know too little of Constantine to decide upon one or the
other alternative, and, as has been indicated above, prefer
to assume a mixture of motives. With a certain quantity of
pragmatism and a certain quantity of imagination one might
easily construct a court romance out of the scattered notices concerning Crispus, Helena, the Prefect Ablavius, the
usurper Calocerus, and the heir apparent Dalmatius; such
a romance might well be very interesting and at the same
time totally untrue from beginning to end. In any case there

was a general conviction that in his last decade Constantine was no longer the ruler he had been in his vigorous years. Of the complete corruption of the court under his sons, Ammianus provides very adequate testimony.

The state of the finances, which must have been closely interrelated with the other court affairs, we here pass over, because essential data are wanting; we do not, for example, know whether the new taxes introduced by Constantine were on the whole a benefit or a burden. The true balance sheet of the Roman Empire, also for this time, remains an enigma. There was much amiss, as we have noted, in the system which Constantine inherited; of the elements probably added or expanded by Constantine, the monopoly on numerous branches of industry, which the state retained for itself and exploited through its serfs, was thoroughly bad, but we must not forget that modern economic theory has only recently rejected these and similar incubuses. The manner of collection, in particular the responsibility of the decurions for the taxes of their district (see p. 65), was perhaps worse than the greed of the state in itself. A series of laws of Constantine shows us by what desperate means men sought to evade the decurionate—marriage with slave women, escape into the army, promotion to the Senate, removal to cities less pressed, going into hiding and living incognito, later even flight to the barbarians. For a short period entry into the class of clergy provided safety; but this sudden rush produced as sudden a prohibition. The state was fully occupied in making evasions of tax responsibility impossible. Local distress became all the greater when local Christian churches were endowed by municipal property, as must have happened in at least certain instances.

Neither can the new division of the Empire be touched upon here with more than a word. Now the twelve dioceses and more than hundred provinces of Diocletian were grouped together in four large prefectures. Considered superficially, many reasons may be adduced both for and against this division. Whether these reasons actually correspond to Constantine's motives in individual cases is another question; surely he would not have introduced so

great a change out of mere idle desire for innovation. It is
to be assumed that the division involved a great increase
in the number of officials; but we cannot easily discern how
far the increase was useless and oppressive. Judgment on
this matter can have no adequate basis as long as we are
partly or wholly ignorant of the duties, activity, and pay
of these officials, and as long as we have no notion of their
number in relation to the population. Many and powerful
officials were probably evil and corrupt in the days of
Constantine, as they were in the days of his predecessors
and successors.

Very clear, however, and of the highest importance, is
the separation between civil and military powers. The
former *Praefecti Praetorio,* who previously also had been
prime ministers and frequently rulers of the Emperor, retained their title, it is true, but are henceforward only the
highest administrative officials of the four great prefectures
—Oriens, Illyricum, Italia, and Gallia; the significance of
the name had wholly changed. For military affairs there
were now two high generals, the *magister equitum* and the
magister peditum. The fact that there were two and that
their business was divided not according to regions but according to cavalry and infantry shows the deeper purpose
which underlay the change; any thought of usurpation was
rendered difficult or futile as long as the one could initiate
nothing without the other. The general separation of civil
and military administration was carried through consistently; those dangerous high provincial officials who as proconsuls, propraetors, rectors, and the like, had in the past
held military command in their region, shared only with the
legates who were subaltern to them, could now no longer
render the throne anxious. The consequences of this separation for the fate of the Empire would be even more striking if the house of Constantine had not substituted domestic
atrocities for the disused usurpation by generals.

In military matters considered in themselves, it is the general assumption that Constantine's reign marks rather a
recession than an advance, in spite of the Emperor's military genius. The dissolution of the Praetorians which had
been begun under Diocletian and consummated after the

victory over Maxentius does not belong in this place; it was a matter of political necessity and the Empire suffered no great loss in that force, which was personally brave but politically evil. Naturally, a new bodyguard was formed, the *palatini*. The rest of the army, under the old names of legions, auxiliaries, and so forth, was divided, as it appears, according to their barracks into *comitatenses*, which were situated in the cities of the interior, and *pseudocomitatenses*, to which the troops on the frontier and in the frontier fortresses chiefly belonged. In the large reckoning of faults with which the pagan Zosimus concludes the biography of Constantine, the quartering of the *comitatenses* in large cities is sharply rebuked, on the grounds that the frontiers were half denuded and laid open to the barbarians and the cities needlessly subjected to distressing oppression, while the soldiers themselves learned the pleasures of the theater and of luxury. Under Diocletian, he continues, the Empire had been guarded very differently; all the troops were quartered on the frontier, so that any barbarian attack could be repulsed at once. The justice of this accusation can neither be assumed nor rejected without qualification. Perhaps the large cities also required guarding. Whether Constantine had actually grown so indolent toward the end of his life that he and his army took to flight before a few hundred Taifales, as the same author reports, is very doubtful. At least he made considerable preparations for a war against the Persians shortly before his death.

The increasing barbarization of the Roman army was a necessary consequence of depopulation in the interior and of the settlements of barbarians, which was undertaken as a remedy. Furthermore, the free peoples beyond the frontiers were safely stripped of their most warlike young men by recruiting them for hire. The Franks in particular must have occupied an important position in the army; at least later, under the dynasty of Constantine, Frankish officers made themselves heard at court. Preservation of the state took precedence over preservation of the Roman nationality; and even in regard to nationality it might still have been hoped that the incorporated barbaric elements would gradually be mastered and assimilated, as had been the case in the early conquests during the Republic and the first centuries of the Empire.

Whether Constantine actually showed preference for barbarians, and in what sense, cannot be determined. It is charged against him that he was the first Emperor to make consuls of barbarians, but there is no detailed evidence. The records of the consuls of his period show almost exclusively names of the native Roman nobility—except for the frequent recurrence of imperial personages. Other state dignities he did bestow upon barbarians, and these may well have been by no means his worst appointments. Captive barbarian soldiers of his opponents he ransomed on the field of battle from his own victorious soldiers, by the thousands. It is conceivable that he had in view the bold possibility of supplying the depleted Roman Empire with barbarians, even of making them a ruling caste, and still controlling the imperium from above; specific declarations on this point are naturally not to be expected. But the strongest negation of the essential Roman character is comprised not in this relationship to non-Romans but in the establishment of the New Rome on the Bosporus. Of this New Rome we must now speak.

What could have been the purpose of establishing a new capital under conditions then prevailing?

Much more than the mere change in the residence of the prince was involved. It was to be foreseen that the dwelling of the Emperor would be frequently changed, and for considerable periods, according to the state of peace or war on the several frontiers. Even though a remarkable truce prevailed under Constantine himself, his successors in the fourth century could in fact make little use of the new capital and its splendors. A mere change of residence, furthermore, would have had a quite different aspect; Constantine might have built a new palace in Byzantium as Diocletian had done in Nicomedia and have embellished the city, even have fortified it if circumstances required, and then have left it to his successors to do something similar elsewhere. In this case the greatest gain was the military security of the central government by reason of the incomparable situation of the city.

The entire question concerning the choice of place is made extremely difficult, however, by our uncertainty concerning Constantine's deepest political plans. He shed streams of blood to restore the unity of the Empire, and then himself mysteriously divided it. Had his decision already been taken when he founded the new capital? We shall never know. The ruler of the world was in no position to direct and secure the fate of his own dynasty, because they were an atrocious breed. He had to trust to chance regarding the heir to whom the Empire and Constantinople would ultimately fall.

Geographical considerations, which are usually regarded as paramount, must not be overrated. Byzantium, it is true, lay much nearer the threatened frontiers than Rome; the Goths of the Danube and the Pontus and the Persians could be far better observed here. But despite all victories over them, the affairs of the Franks and the Alemanni were not yet so settled that the remote Rhine frontier could be regarded as indubitably secure. It is a question, furthermore, whether the capital properly belonged in one of the most perilous regions of the Empire, where only a few decades before Gothic pirate fleets had plied their business. Now, it is true, the city was so fortified that for nine centuries the storms of invaders raged against its walls in vain.

But Byzantium has another geographic significance besides its impregnable military location. Let us recall the role which the so-called Illyrian triangle—that is, the land mass between the Black, Aegean, and Adriatic Seas—played in the third century. Its generals and soldiers, among them the family of Constantine himself, had saved and ruled the Empire. That triangle could now demand the imperial residence for itself, and so Constantinople is in the first instance the affirmation and the crowning honor of Illyricum. This interpretation is justified by a statement in Zonaras, who tells us that Constantine had originally thought of a city deep in the interior, namely, Sardica (modern Sofia, in Bulgaria); only consideration for a privileged people within the Empire could have suggested such a choice.

But Constantinople, wherever it was to be situated, was to be not merely the imperial residence but the expression of new conditions in the state, in religion, and in life. Its founder was doubtless perfectly conscious of this fact; he must needs choose a neutral location, unhampered by traditions. Deservedly or not, history has endowed his deed with the stamp of greatness; in the City of Constantine history developed a peculiar spirit compounded of Church and politics, and a separate category of culture, to wit the Byzantine, which, whether a man love or hate it, must nevertheless be recognized as a world force. At its summit was despotism, infinitely strengthened by the union of churchly and secular dominion; in the place of morality it imposed orthodoxy; in the place of unbridled and demoralized expression of the natural instincts, hypocrisy and pretence; in the face of despotism there was developed greed masquerading as poverty, and deep cunning; in religious art and literature there was an incredible stubbornness in the constant repetition of obsolete motives—altogether its character had much that was reminiscent of the Egyptian, and with the Egyptian it shared one of its highest properties, namely, tenacity. But we have to do not with the later historical perspectives, but rather with their beginnings.

It has been assumed that Constantine conceived a decided dislike of Rome, and that the Romans had occasioned or requited this dislike by their objection to Constantine's neglect of pagan ceremonies. But there is no need for such an explanation. Since the time of Diocletian Rome's unfitness for the imperial residence had been clearly recognized, along with the necessity for the division of the Empire. The intermediate rule of a Maxentius had demonstrated, to the great injury of Rome, how dangerously the noble old name of the mistress of the world might be misused when the Emperors were far away in the East and the North; but after the dissolution of the Praetorians Constantine knew that nothing serious was to be apprehended from that quarter. No one longer seriously expected that he should reside in Rome. The center for highest imperial affairs had for a long while been situated in Diocletian's bureau, hence usually at Nicomedia. Later Constantine as ruler of the West, along with Licinius, visited Rome only periodically, but sojourned mostly in Gaul and in the army posts. But perhaps after the victory over Licinius he was in no position to deny the East (aside from the special claims of Illyricum) the privilege of harboring the capital, just as in other serious affairs also he appears to have let matters take their course. Perhaps the secret personal developments which accompanied the fall of Licinius might also have been a factor in the choice.

And finally the urge for building, one of the strongest in the natures of mighty princes, grew to a passion in Constantine. There can be no more solid external symbol of power than buildings of impressive character. Furthermore, building itself quickly executed with massive resources provides a similitude of the creative ruler, and in times of peace a substitute for other activity. For its founder a new city serves as image and pattern for a new world.

The new foundation was preceded by remarkable decisions and trials. Besides Sardica, the Emperor had his eye also upon Thessalonica, and then Chalcedon, on the Asiatic side of the Bosporus. But the first fixed decision involved a place no other than the region of ancient Troy, whence once through Aeneas the migration to Latium and hence the foundation of Rome issued. There is no more question of historic sentimentality in the case of Constantine than in the case of Caesar and Augustus, who cherished a similar plan. Certainly definite grounds of pagan superstition were a consideration, and we have seen that the Emperor was not above such considerations. Ilium was the sacred and ancient seat of the Romans; by some oracular utterance, of which we no longer have knowledge, they were instructed one day to remove the seat of their rule back to Ilium, whence their origin derived. Constantine in person proceeded to the famous fields where for a thousand years sacrifices had been offered at the sepulchral mounds of Homer's heroes; at the grave of Ajax, on the spot of the Greek encampment, Constantine himself began to mark the

outlines of the future city. The gates had already been built
when one night God appeared to him and admonished him
to select another site; and thereupon he determined upon
Byzantium. A century later voyagers passing Troy could
see the structure which Constantine had left unfinished. If
a reader wishes to see in this story a conflict between the
pagan and Christian elements in the Emperor's suite, none
can gainsay him. It is conceivable that the court clergy set
every means of opposition in motion when Constantine occupied himself with essentially pagan ceremonies and oracles.

But neither did the foundation of Constantinople proceed without similar interventions. For the eagles which
seized measuring tapes and building stones from Chalcedon
and carried them across the Bosporus for the new building
at Byzantium, Zonaras and Cedrenus may answer; several
similar details express the need of contemporaries for some
superhuman connotations for great events. Constantine was
compelled to indulge in superstition for the sake of the pagan population of the Empire, and apparently he himself
was not wholly free of it. His own utterance upon the event
was monotheistic, but in an indefinite and enigmatic sense:
"We have endowed the city with an eternal name at God's
bidding." What is this eternal name? Apparently not Constantinople, perhaps not even New Rome, but Flora or
Anthusa, "the Flourishing," which was the priestly occult
name of Rome. But the god who prescribed this name was
hardly the God of the Christians. Neither has the dream
vision which later chronicles ascribe to the Emperor—a
ragged woman asking him for clothing—any Christian character whatever.

The ceremonial foundation of the western wall took
place on 4 November of the first year of the 276th Olym-
piad, that is, the year 326, when the sun was in the sign of
Sagittarius but the Crab ruled the hour. Shortly before, the
heir apparent and perhaps also the Empress had been executed. It was the period when Constantine had become
intimate with the Neoplatonist Sopater (see p. 292), and
we find Sopater present at the foundation, acting as
telestes; that is, he carried out certain symbolic actions

which were to secure the fate of the new city by magic means. Besides Sopater, the hierophant Praetextatus, apparently a Roman pontifex, is named. Later a legend was in circulation that under the porphyry pillar in the Forum of Constantinople which supported the statue of the new founder there lay the Palladium which he had secretly abstracted from Rome. This would be a true *telesma*, such as was frequently carried out in antiquity for averting plagues and conjuring fortune; Apollonius of Tyana, for example, had employed such means in Byzantium itself to avert floods of the river Lycus, pestilential fleas and gnats, the fright of horses, and other such evils.

Now the city of Byzas was no longer concerned with such trifles, but with the fate of the world, which was to be linked to this spot. The ancient history of the city, which was now regarded with heightened interest, the old myths and oracles which could be interpreted as referring to it, everything seemed full of presage of a great future nearing fulfillment. Byzantium had drawn the attention of the world to itself by its energetic recovery from the catastrophe it suffered under Septimius Severus and Gallienus, particularly by its heroic defense against the former; now it was appointed to be the world's mistress.

We shall not attempt to describe the ancient city or the new. Only such details of the great enterprise as are characteristic for Constantine himself may be briefly mentioned.

He himself, spear in hand, indicated the outlines of the encircling wall. A legend relating to this circumstance may have a kernel of truth. His attendants found that he was walking in too wide a sweep, and one ventured the question, "How much further, Sire?" Thereupon he replied, "Until he who walks before me stops walking," as if he saw some superhuman being moving before him. It is quite conceivable that he found such a reply useful, if the others believed or pretended to believe in such apparitions. We cannot determine whether the remaining ceremonies were actually nothing but a repetition of those that took place at the foundation of Rome, as they are described by Plutarch in the eleventh chapter of his *Life of Romulus*.

Almost four years later, on 11 May 330, there followed

with renewed great solemnities and sumptuous circus
games the dedication of the new foundation and its naming
as Constantinople. That Constantine dedicated the city to
the Virgin Mary is surely a later invention. In all reason,
he dedicated it above all to himself and his glory. It was
not enough for him that the name of the city and its every
stone recalled his name and that a number of magnificent
monuments were expressly dedicated to him; annually
upon the day of dedication a large gilded statue representing him with Tyche, that is, the tutelary genius of the city,
upon his outstretched right hand, was to be carried in a
solemn torch procession through the Circus, upon which
the current Caesar was required to arise from his place and
prostrate himself before the image of Constantine and of
Tyche. Who could prevent people from gradually bestowing a kind of cult upon the porphyry pillar with its colossal
statue of Constantine, mentioned above, and from burning
candles and incense before it and making vows to it? The
Arian Philostorgius blames the Christians for this development, and despite all protests may well be right; for where
the ruler of the world points the way with such an example, Christians and pagans alike need not hesitate to deify
him, even while he is still alive.

The same spirit finds expression in the manner in which
the new city received its population under compulsion and
was endowed with special privileges. Its equality with
Rome was conceived in a quite literal sense, and accordingly it received the same institutions, officials, and prerogatives; it even possessed seven hills like the Rome on the
Tiber. Above all, it had to have a Senate, even if no one
knew why; at most the court required figurants for its processions. A small number of Roman senators did settle in
Constantinople, moved by material advantages such as
mansions and estates; and if a later legend is correct, this
was done with a very delicate courtesy, for the Emperor
surprised them with facsimiles of their Roman villas and
palaces on the shore of the Bosporus. He also built them
a magnificent Senate House; but neither the statues of the
Muses, which had once stood upon the sacred hill of Hel-
icon, nor the statues of Zeus of Dodona and Pallas of Lindos,

which now decorated the doors of the building, could avail to make the new body more than a cipher.

Besides courtiers, officers, officials, and senators, the new city also required a population worthy of itself. On the year of dedication St. Jerome notes: "Constantinople is dedicated, while almost all other cities are denuded." This refers primarily to population. Whether it was that Constantine used the collapse in the conquered East of Licinius to enforce migration, or that he assembled a populace for the imperial residence by enticements of another sort, in any case he achieved his wish. This wish, in the realistic and unfriendly language of the pagan Eunapius, is expressed as follows: "From the subjugated cities he brought a populace together at Byzantium, so that many drunkards might alternately applaud him in the theater and spew forth their wine. He was pleased with the acclamations of persons who were not in control of their senses, and he rejoiced to hear his name called by men who were mindful of no name at all had it not been thrust upon them by daily usage." The vanity of great men and their thirst for praise is always a matter difficult to judge if we do not have first-rate sources. In the case of Constantine the strikingly vain and pompous appearances which a number of writers notice may well have had a consciously political purpose. There can be no question that he inwardly despised the Constantinopolitans.

But Jerome's remarks have still another significance. The Empire must have been more or less oppressed to produce the charges for the new establishment. Constantine is said to have expended sixty millions of francs of our money—an estimate which is clearly too low rather than too high, if we consider the volume and expense of the new buildings. The distribution of grain, wine, and oil, which became regular after 332 and without which the large population could not have survived, constituted a heavy and continuous drain. Eunapius complains that all the grain fleets of Egypt, Asia Minor, and Syria could not suffice to satisfy the mob. In the fifth century, when Eunapius wrote, the city was already more populous than Rome.

Finally, many cities of the Empire were robbed of their art treasures, which was always a grievous experience for

men of Greek education. We have already spoken of the
plunder and smelting of statues made of precious materials; in addition the most disgraceful and extensive thefts
of art in all history were committed for the purpose of
decorating the new capital. Here Constantine is neither pagan nor Christian—for he affronted both religions by carrying images of the gods off to Byzantium—but a self-seeking plunderer for the sake of glorifying his own name.
There is no sadder reading for the amateur of ancient art
than the inventory of art works set up in Byzantium by and
after Constantine, especially if one remembers their even-
tual destruction on the occasion of the fourth crusade.
When Eusebius, for example, speaks of the Pythian and
the Sminthian Apollo and when we read elsewhere of the
Samian Hera, the Olympian Zeus, and the like, it is not
necessarily the actual original of the statue in question that
is involved; but the loss of any Greek work of art is ir-
replaceable, and the originals of the statues named have
in any case vanished. The heaping up of incompatible
works, for example the 427 statues in front of Saint Sophia,
must have produced a crude and repellent effect; in certain cases elements of the statues were altered in quite
barbaric fashion, as when Constantine set his own plump
portrait-head upon a colossal statue of Apollo, for display
upon the great porphyry pillar of which we have spoken.
From Rome there was brought, among other things, a number of statues of Emperors; it was perhaps accidental that
one of Maxentius was included, and when the pagans of the
new capital paid it reverence, perhaps for political reasons,
Constantine is said to have caused the image to be removed
and its worshipers to be put to death. But far the greater
number of works came from Greece and western Asia
Minor. Once Roman proconsuls and Emperors had plundered the same regions, and they may be forgiven because
Rome and its culture historically depended upon Greek art
for its completion and transfiguration; but Byzantium
wished to swallow up all that was beautiful only in order
that the provinces might not possess it. It knew no other
means of paying honor to its statues than by contriving

superstitious explanations and anecdotes and lame imitations of ancient epigrams for them.

We can have no conception, despite relatively abundant sources on the subject, of the buildings of Constantinople which were similarly erected in part of plunder, specifically of the columns of older buildings in the vicinity. At the time architecture was in a period of crisis. Arched construction with its relatively new static organism was engaged in its decisive struggle with the vestigial and ineffective forms of earlier Greek temple architecture. The prevailing character of Constantinian building must have been a colorful and odd sumptuousness. Cupolas, niches, round halls, precious incrustations, gold plating, and mosaic are the essential elements of this rich and restless complex. Constantine's own impatience was clearly expressed in the hasty and structurally imperfect execution, which brought its own punishment in the rapid ruin of several buildings and in the need for extensive repairs.

In addition to many and magnificent churches, Constantine's building includes two undeniably pagan temples. The one, belonging to the Circus, was dedicated to the Dioscuri, Castor and Pollux; the other was the Tycheion, the sanctuary of Tyche, or the tutelary divinity of the city. We have already encountered the annual dedicatory procession in the Circus in which the statue of Constantine with a small Tyche on its outstretched right hand was carried. Several other statues of this goddess are mentioned besides, of which one had been brought from Rome. Obviously this theft of the goddess was more than a mere symbol; it was intended to put a magic seal upon the transfer of world dominion to its new site. The Emperor, indeed, made remarkable efforts to remove her purely pagan significance from Tyche. For example, a cross was affixed to her forehead, and indeed at the great dedicatory festival in 330 there is a curious intermingling of prayer to Tyche and the *kyrie eleison;* but the basic pagan sentiment was and continued to be predominant. A fortune-amulet was even affixed to a publicly displayed cross. Over the ornamental structure of the Miliarium there were to be seen the statues of Constantine and Helena, together bearing a cross at the center of which a chain was to be observed. This chain was said to possess the magic virtue of assuring the New Rome victory over all peoples and security from all hostile attacks; and it, too, was called the Tyche of the city. It is possible that this whole ornament is of more recent origin and that the significance of the chain existed only in the imagination of the Byzantines, but Constantine had surely given occasion for the rise of such legends by his own magic procedures.

The reaction on the part of the Christian courtiers and clergy is to be recognized, as we have suggested, in the fall and execution of Sopater. From the period immediately preceding the dedication the fall of another pagan philosopher, Canonaris by name, is reported. Canonaris appeared in public and cried out to the Emperor: "Do not raise yourself above our ancestors, because you have made our ancestors [that is, their customs and religion] nought!" Constantine had the philosopher approach him and admonished him to desist from his pagan sermon, but Canonaris shouted that he would die for his ancestors, and was thereupon decapitated.

We now turn our glance from the proud new cosmopolis back to the old.

Rome had retained one advantage, which appeared perhaps not of particularly great weight at that moment, to wit, the acknowledged precedence of its bishop over all the clergy of the Empire. Men of the time could not yet surmise that at a distance from the imperial throne of Byzantium there would arise the throne of a Western high priest and that the hierarchy, overshadowed in Constantinople by worldly dominion, and weakened in Antioch, Jerusalem, and Alexandria by heresy and by the sword of Islam, would at Rome one day become the center of a new spiritual world. Constantine's personal relationships to the Roman community are very ambiguous. His alleged donation is a fiction; the fabulous sumptuousness of his church building and offerings as it is depicted by Anastasius Bibliothecarius is in fact to be reduced to relatively small compass, which induces some doubt concerning the Emperor's generosity in general. Finally his alleged baptism by Bishop Sylvester in the Baptistry of the Lateran is a mere legend, born of the wish to supplant the Arian Eusebius of Nicomedia by an orthodox baptizing priest. In the Arian conflict the Roman bishopric was not able to avoid involvement and maintain the position of a mere observer and arbiter. Later also it found itself deeply implicated in the political storms of the Church, and only gradually did it rise to the position of a world power.

For the time being, the great pagan majority in Rome itself was a significant hindrance to the Church. All through the fourth century the physiognomy of the ancient cosmopolis continued to be predominantly pagan.

This was true even externally, as regards architecture. A long period of destruction and persistent rebuilding was subsequently required before Christian Rome with its basilicas, patriarchies, and monasteries arose out of the Rome of the Empire. Even the buildings of the third century were largely calculated to serve the glorification of paganism, its culture and its pleasures. The Baths of Caracalla, of Alexander Severus, of Decius, and of Philip, and later those of Diocletian and of Constantine, the elaborate decorations of the Forum of Trajan, the magnificent villa of the Gordians, the Temple of the Sun of Aurelian, the Basilica and the Circus of Maxentius, and finally the project cherished by the younger Gordian, enlarged by Gallienus, but never carried out, of erecting a sumptuous colonnade with terraces to traverse the entire Campus Martius and then flank the Via Flaminia as far as the Milvian Bridge—all of these things characterize the spirit of building in that epoch. From the second half of the fourth century we still possess the *Regionary Catalogues* (poorer in their genuine form, to be sure, than with the interpolations which were formerly regarded as authentic and which enumerated, among other structures, more than one hundred and fifty temples by name). But even conservative calculation on this basis leads to enormous figures. The *Regionary Catalogues* (the so-called *Curiosum Urbis* as well as the *Notitia*) present specifically not the structural content of the fourteen regions of the city but only their boundaries; even in defining the

boundaries they name an extraordinarily large number of
temples, forums, basilicas, baths, gardens, halls, buildings
for games, statues, and the like, though no single church.
This omission was probably intentional, for in the age of
Constantius and of Theodosius there must have been many
very considerable churches which only a pagan would ignore. Though we may imagine these churches as magnificent and extensive as we will, in keeping with the wealth
and power of Rome's Christian community, they could
nevertheless not compare with the ancient pagan magnificence. The summary of important items at the end of the
two books named is unreliable precisely in the matter of
numbers, but we shall still perhaps fall short of the truth
if to the twenty-eight libraries, the eleven forums, the ten
large basilicas, the eleven colossal baths, we add only two
amphitheaters, three theaters, two circuses, and the like,
for these additions still fall short of extant remains. Besides these and other colossal and handsome buildings we
must imagine—and it is not easy to do—an endless abundance of majestic monumental decoration, such as the
thirty-four (or thirty-six) marble triumphal arches and
countless public statues and groups; all of this pictur-
esquely distributed over valley and hill, enlivened and interrupted by gardens and groves (*luci*), accompanied by
the gay murmur of springing waters which descended to
the city from the surrounding hills upon nineteen lofty
arched aqueducts to keep man and beast, air and foliage
in the mighty city fresh. Many peoples, ancient and modern, have known how to build upon a colossal scale; but the
aspect of ancient Rome will remain unique in history, because never again will the delight in the beautiful aroused
by Greek art be coupled with such resources for its outward execution and with such a desire for magnificent environment. One who came to Rome fresh from the impressions of Constantinople, as Constantius did, for example, in
356, when he celebrated his triumph over conquered
Magnentius, could only fall mute with astonishment and
believe, each time he saw something new, that he was look-
ing upon the most beautiful of all. The Forum of Trajan

with its Basilica Ulpia was regarded, as we learn on this occasion, as the apex of the marvelous.

And all of this magnificence was available to a population whose number is equaled or exceeded by several of our modern capitals. The queen of the world Empire, whose population under Vespasian can be estimated at 120 million souls, probably never had more than a million and a half in population. Modern research has receded from earlier estimates, some unconscionably exaggerated, when calculations were made of the area of Rome and its suburbs and the large extent of the uninhabited area on the basis of the relationship between the density of population in modern capitals and the space devoted only to traffic and ornament. One may well ask whence in fact came the people who were to use and enjoy all of these temples, theaters, circuses, baths, and parks. The Colosseum itself could perhaps contain a fifteenth of the entire population, the Circus Maximus more than a tenth. To fill such structures required a people which had been educated by its rulers to such amusement for centuries, which lived on bounties, and knew and demanded nothing other than ceaseless and constantly accentuated pleasure. The considerable numbers of unmarried persons with little or no occupation, the migration of rich provincials, the concentration of luxury and corruption, and finally the confluence of large governmental and financial affairs must have made of the Roman a type whose like is not easily to be imagined elsewhere.

In this colorful mixture and through all its classes there were two separate societies, a pagan and a Christian. How the latter developed and comported itself in the first three centuries of the faith and during the age of persecution is not our present business. From the critical period of Constantine, when it certainly increased and underwent internal change, we have no adequate sources; but descriptions from the second half of the fourth century, specifically those of St. Jerome, show the community as degenerated. The world with its pleasures had thrust itself into the upper as well as the lower classes of the Roman community; one could be zealously devout and at the same time quite immoral. At times the entire community was stirred by ter-

rible crises; from Ammianus we learn that upon the occasion of the conflict of Damasus and Ursinus over the
bishopric (366) one hundred thirty-seven casualties lay in
the Sicinian basilica. Jerome, who became secretary to the
victorious Bishop Damasus, came in contact with high and
low in his new position. He knew how general the practice
of abortion was; he saw two persons of the populace marry,
of whom the man had already buried twenty wives and
the woman twenty-two husbands; nowhere does he make a
secret of the general corruption. The greatest detail he de-
votes to his description of the upper classes and certain of
the clergy, and indeed on their reciprocal influences. The
grand lady, the rich widow, moves about royally with full
cheeks brightly rouged; her sedan chair is surrounded by
eunuchs. With this retinue she appears regularly in the
churches, and strides majestically through a gantlet of beggars, dispensing alms. At home she has Bibles written in
gold upon purple parchment and set with precious stones,
but she will allow the needy to starve if her vanity is not
served. A crier makes the rounds of the city when the lady
deigns to entertain at an *agape* or love-feast. On other occasions also she is free with her board; among other flatterers the clergy appear, kiss their hostess, and make a
gesture with their hands—for a blessing, one would think?
—no, but to receive a gift; nothing makes the lady so proud
as the dependence of the priests. The widow's freedom is
much more delicious than the rule of a husband, and moreover presents an appearance of abstinence, for which many
found compensation in wine and gourmandizing. Others
who go about in haircloth cowls like night owls, sighing
continuously, and secretly indulging in coarse voluptuousness are no better. The austere churchly teacher is wholly
suspicious of artificial relationships based on so-called spiritual bonds, which were injurious to normal family life.
There were men who deserted their wives and formed alliances with others under some pious pretext; women who
adopted lads as their spiritual sons and eventually indulged
in carnal intercourse with them, and many similar abuses,
particularly of certain Tartuffes who attached themselves
to women as a sort of confessor and then lived with them.

The clergy proper, as has been indicated, was not spared either. Jerome condemns unqualifiedly their habit of living with spiritual sisters, the so-called *agapetes* (otherwise *syneisactes*), and even more vigorously their haunting prominent houses for the sake of procuring legacies, power, and luxury. Some masqueraded as ascetics with long hair, goatees, black cloaks, and bare feet; they deceived sinful women by apparent fasting, for which they compensated by gluttony at night. Others—somewhat like the abbés of the last century—had themselves consecrated as presbyters and deacons only to be able to associate with women more freely. This sort was elegantly attired, with elaborate hairdress, breathing of perfumes, all their fingers glittering with stones; because of their chic footwear they tiptoed mincingly; their aspect was rather of a bridegroom than of a priest. Such, likely, was the bearing of Jovinian, "in silk robe of the fine stuff of Arras and Laodicea, red-cheeked, with shining skin, his hair falling partly over his shoulders and partly curled over his forehead." Some devoted themselves wholly to discovering names, addresses, and tempers of women. Jerome knows of one such cleric who had made himself dreaded by carrying wicked gossip about from one house to another. From morning to night he rode about the city with fast and handsome horses, so that he was generally called the city postillion (*veredarius urbis*). Frequently he surprised people while they were still in their bedchambers; whatever stuff or vessels took his fancy he praised in such a tone that anyone who was clever at once made him a present of it. We even have the portrait of a clerical wastrel of the interesting type. Jerome tells with ardent displeasure of the wolf who broke into the sheepfold; but we should not relate a secret love story to expand an episode which has already carried us down to the second generation after Constantine.

Clearly the institution of monasteries with a rule of confinement which would separate ascetics from the temptations of city life once and for all was a genuine contemporary need. Asceticism was an inevitable urge of the times, because of the number of those who were rent in two by the clash of the old religion and old habits with the new

ones, and sought salvation in an extreme resolve; they
could not, however, wholly protect themselves against
backsliding. Jerome devoted all of his efforts, at least in
the devout circle which hearkened to him, to raise complete abstinence to a life-principle. The precept and example of this one-sided but mighty man may have dominated
the outlook and the thoughts of his Paula, Marcella, and
Eustochium throughout their lives and made them insen-
sitive to all earthly happiness. Celibacy seemed to him the
indispensable condition of all higher life; because of celibacy higher secrets were revealed to the virgin apostle
John than to the others who had been married.

The invasion of the Empire by German tribes, and the
threatening collapse of all institutions—*orbis ruit!*—doubtless
accentuated the mood of resignation in him and in others
to an enormous degree. There were already in Rome and
in the entire West many men and women who with a deep
and abiding resolution had espoused asceticism. The rocky
cliffs of the Mediterranean and the desolate shores of Italy
began to be populated with anchorites and soon with monasteries; certain islands were visited as the burial places
of martyrs, as, for example, one of the Ponza islands. It was
possible to live in complete seclusion in the midst of Rome
itself, as was done, for example, by the wealthy Asella, who
sold her jewels, lived in a narrow cell on bread, salt, and
water, addressed no man, and only went out to visit the
graves of the Apostles. She was completely separated from
her family and rejoiced that no one any longer knew her.
Jerome was confident of his rare ability to discern between
the genuine city nuns and those who simulated.

A thing which must certainly have existed but is not to
be found in the descriptions of the zealous Church Father
is the picture of simple and sound-thinking Christian families without asceticism and without debauchery. He is more
concerned to present the extraordinary and the extreme.

Between this Christian society and the more educated
and nobler pagans of the fourth century we insert the description of the great masses of Rome as it is presented to

us, to be sure not without artful illumination, by Ammianus Marcellinus.

Ammianus begins on the occasion of a commotion because of a shortage of wine, and teaches us, incidentally,
that the Roman populace was very bibulous; even today
there is somewhat more drinking in Rome than in Florence
or Naples. The distributions of wine instituted in the time
of Constantine did not suffice; anyone with money to spend
passed whole nights in the taverns. When it was rumored
of the City Prefect Symmachus that he would rather use
wine to slake lime than reduce its price his house was set
afire. When Rome was mentioned anywhere, there was
at once talk of riotous drinking-houses. Like *morra* today,
dice was the pastime inside and outside the inn and filled
all leisure; this was accompanied by jarring cries which
penetrated the marrow of all within earshot. If games with
tesserae were considered more respectable than those with
aleae, Ammianus is of the opinion that the difference is no
greater than that between a thief and a highwayman. Unfortunately, he says, gambling companionship was the only
bond which still held people together. The ordinary Romans were moreover still a defiant people filled with conscious pride; despite accretions of half a millennium from
all lands, there were still many ancient citizen families who
prided themselves on such names as Cimessor, Statarius,
Cicimbricus, Pordaca, Salsula, and the like, even if they
went barefoot. From time to time, at least in the theater,
the wild and menacing cry was heard, "Out with the foreigners!"—these foreigners, says Ammianus, who were their
sole support and salvation. But the chief cry of Rome was
still *panem et circenses*. As regards bread, there was no
more anxious moment than when the corn fleets from Africa
were held back by war or adverse winds. On one such occasion the City Prefect Tertullus (359) presented his children to the raging mob as a pledge, and thereby so far
calmed them that it was possible to proceed to the ever-
green Tiber Island near Ostia, fragrant with roses and
adorned with the temple of the Dioscuri, where the Roman people were accustomed to celebrate a gay festival
annually; there Tertullus offered sacrifice to Castor and

Pollux, and the sea became calm and a gentle south wind wafted the corn-laden fleet to the shore. That part of the holiday crowd which was not content with the bread, wine, oil, and pork which had been distributed took places at the vents of cookshops and enjoyed at least the aroma of roasts and other food.

The Romans were altogether insatiable for anything that might be called a spectacle. In the fourth century state subsidies for the purpose were far from sufficient, and the want was supplied by the munificence of newly nominated higher officials and of senators. This obligation constituted a very heavy burden upon these persons, who were not necessarily wealthy, for everyone must seek to outdo his predecessors, not merely out of ambition but even more because of the insatiability of the populace. A great part of the correspondence of Symmachus is devoted to the anxiety which the necessity of providing entertainment, at the time of his own promotion and that of his relatives and on other occasions, caused him. Since Diocletian there was no longer such imperial extravagance in entertainment as had suggested to Carinus the notion of covering half a quarter in the region of the Capitol with a wooden amphitheater, decorating it most sumptuously with precious stones, gold, and ivory, and then displaying, among other rarities, mountain goats and hippopotamuses, and presenting fights between bears and seals. The Emperor still provided for the buildings, as for example when Constantine carried out a magnificent restoration of the Circus Maximus; but the spectacles themselves had become predominantly the affair of wealthy dignitaries who were required to compensate the state in this fashion and to expend their incomes in return for their immunity from taxation. It was of no avail to leave Rome; the registrars of taxes, as it appears, presented the games in the name of the absent donor in such cases. A man was lucky if he could import the exotic beasts dutyfree. The most important item was always the choice of horses for the Circus; it was in the horse races that the distinguished like the ordinary Roman satisfied his superstitious passion for wagering, and where a jockey could acquire the greatest personal glory and even a kind of inviolability. Roman taste in these matters had grown so refined that breeds had to be constantly changed; commissioners traversed half the known world to find something new and extraordinary and to transport it carefully to Rome. Symmachus' letters to these agents could not be more obsequious. For the beast fights in the theaters and the Colosseum and for the hunts (*sylvae*) in the Circus Maximus there were required gladiators, "a band of fighters worse than those of Spartacus." Captive barbarians, as for example Saxons, occasionally appeared, but by now, in keeping with the spirit of the time, fights between animals probably predominated. Here we find the givers of the games in constant embarrassment as to how the requisite animals were to be provided—the bears, which sometimes arrived in an emaciated state and sometimes were exchanged in transit, the Libyan lions, the crowds of leopards, Scottish hounds, crocodiles, and even animals whose identity cannot now certainly be determined, such as *addaces*, *pygargi*, and the like. There is mention of the Emperor's helping out with a few elephants after a Persian victory, but this was an exception.

To this same category belongs the scenic decoration of the Circus or a specific theater, for which Symmachus once summoned artists from Sicily. Of Symmachus, we can assume that he did only what his office required and was himself above such interests; but there were as fanatic admirers of individual gladiators in his day as ever there had been in the earlier Empire. The very extensive but somewhat barbarized mosaics in the Villa Borghese representing gladiatorial games and beast fights probably derive from the fourth century; the persons who appear in these mosaics have their names inscribed by their figures. Art now had often to reconcile itself to perpetuating such displays and to decorating entire halls and façades with them. The theater proper still had its ardent admirers also, among them persons bearing great names, like that Junius Messala who, in the age of Constantine, bestowed upon the mimes his entire wealth, including the valuable clothing of his parents. "Comedy" at least still enjoyed a certain interest in Rome, but more among ordinary people, whose greatest

pleasure was said to be in hissing the actors off the stage,
a fate which the actors are said to have sought to avoid by
bribery. We may presume that the "comedy" in question
is the farce (*mimus*). Much more important was the
pantomime, that is, the ballet, which, according to a perhaps hyperbolic statement, still employed three thousand
dancing girls and a large number of musicians.

If our sources are adequate on the subject of bread and
circuses, we are left wholly in the dark concerning a thousand other details which are necessary for a complete picture of contemporary Rome. For example, the prime
question of the numerical relationship of slaves to freemen
cannot be answered even approximately, and attempted estimates vary widely. Here and there a chasm opens before
the eyes of the researcher and provides a glimpse into that
cross between state factory and slave galley where work
was done for the public need. This is the case with the
great bakeries which provided for the general distribution
of bread. In the course of time the superintendent of these
bakeries (*mancipes*) built taverns and brothels near by,
from which many an imprudent man was suddenly shang-
haied into the factory to spend the rest of his life in slave
labor; he disappeared completely, and his family regarded
him as dead. The Romans must have known of the practice,
and the victims were usually foreigners. The officials were
informed about it as surely as certain modern governments
are informed concerning the impressing of sailors; and if
Theodosius put an end to the cruelty on a specific occasion,
we may not therefore infer that it was first discovered at
that time.

Ammianus' account of the life and conduct of the upper
classes raises a strong suspicion that that proud and spirited
man was unduly irked by a feeling of offended pride. As an
Antiochene he had no special justification for depreciating
the Romans; but as a courtier of Constantius and Julian
his reception in the great Roman families was probably not
very cordial. Many of his complaints are directed against
the vices which are ascribed to rich and prominent people
at all times and in all places; others refer to his own age in
general. Ammianus deplores the prodigious passion for

gilded honorific statues on the part of a class immersed in
trivial novelties and complete effeminacy. He scores the
habit of refusing to know strangers who have been presented after their first visit, and of making it plain that
persons who are seen again after a long absence have not
been missed. He describes the unfortunate practice of giving dinner parties only to discharge social obligations—dinner parties at which the *nomenclatores* (a sort of master
of ceremonies of the slave class) sometimes provide substitutes from the common people for a gratuity. Even in
Juvenal's day vanity frequently found an outlet in riding
at breakneck speed and in showing fanatical enthusiasm
for one's own and for the circus horses; this fashion also continued. Many would appear in public only if they were
surrounded by a whole procession of servants and domestics; "under the command of the majordomos with their
staves there marched by the carriage first a company of
slave weavers, then the kitchen slaves in black dress, then
the other servants of the household, mingled with idle
folk from the neighborhood; the procession is closed by an
army of eunuchs of every age, from old men to mere lads,
all sickly and deformed." At home even in the better families, as presently among ourselves, music concealed numerous social gaps. Song and harp sounded continuously;
"instead of the philosopher, the singer was employed; instead of the rhetor, the teacher of the arts of enjoyment;
while the libraries were closed tight like a tomb, hydraulés
were constructed and lyres as big as stagecoaches." Rage
for the theater was characteristic of the higher classes also,
and the coquetry of many a lady was comprised in imitat-
ing theatrical poses with slight variations. Gestures and
bearing continued to be of studied artifice; Ammianus knew
a city prefect named Lampadius who took it amiss when
the sense of style he displayed in spitting was not properly
appreciated. The practice of maintaining clients and para-
sites was probably not much changed since Juvenal's day;
neither was legacy-hunting among the childless rich and
many other similar abuses of the early Empire. But it must
be emphasized that despite his sour mood Ammianus has
almost nothing to say of the iniquities and enormities which

Juvenal excoriates. Christianity contributed little to this improvement; the transformation which caused the new moral standard had already made its appearance in the third century.

This fashionable society is plainly pagan, as can be observed in the first instance by its superstitions. Whenever there was a question of wills and legacies, for example, the haruspices were summoned, to seek a decision in the entrails of animals. Even unbelievers would refuse to walk in the street, take their place at table, or go to the bath without consulting the *ephemeris*, or astrological calendar, for the position of the planets. We know from other sources that the majority of the Senate was pagan until the times of Theodosius. Everything possible was done to maintain the priesthoods and the ceremonies in their complete forms; this endeavor cost Symmachus enormous effort and anxiety. But along with the public *sacra*, the most respectable Romans of the fourth century addressed themselves with great enthusiasm to occult worship, and indeed, as we have observed above, in a peculiar amalgamation. By taking practically all available secret initiations, the individual sought to secure and strengthen himself against the inroads of Christianity.

All things considered, Rome's pagan Senate may still have been the Empire's most respectable assembly and society. Despite Ammianus' slanders, the Senate must still have contained many men—provincials as well as Romans—of the old stalwart Roman spirit, in whose families traditions were cherished which would be sought in vain in Alexandria and Antioch and certainly in Constantinople. Above all, the senators themselves revered the Senate, the *asylum mundi totius*. They still demanded a specific simple and serious style of eloquence, which should display nothing of the theatrical; always the effort was made to maintain at least the fiction that Rome was still its ancient self and that the Romans were still citizens. These are merely big words, to be sure, but there were men of stature among the senators and it was not their fault if big things did not issue from them. In Symmachus himself the courage of his advocacy for persons oppressed arouses high admiration

and, like the patriotism of Eumenius (p. 62), balances the
inevitable flatteries in which he elsewhere indulges. As a
gentleman of large and independent stature he was personally above the titles of dignity which were the ambition
of so many others.

The higher education which prevailed in these circles
can no more be judged according to the literal words of
Ammianus than can other matters. He allows the Romans
no other reading than Juvenal and the imperial history of
Marius Maximus, of which we know that the first half of
the *Historia Augusta* is a jejune reworking. Of the literary
rendezvous at the Temple of Peace (where one of the
twenty-eight public libraries was located) there is not much
to say, for even a Trebellius Pollio could display his wares
there. But the circle of friends which Macrobius gathered
about himself, the environment in which Symmachus himself moved, shows how much true education still survived
in the upper classes. We must not be misled by the ped-
antry of the former (very useful to us) or by the Plinian
preciosity of the latter. The literary age is indeed one of
decline, more appropriate for collection and criticism than
for creation. The epigone betrays himself by his wavering
between Plautine archaisms and the most modern abstract
substantives. We may even be tempted to recognize in pre-
figuration the one-sidedness of the Romance peoples, who
would keep a literature alive by the use of a dictionary;
the dainty affectation of Symmachus' letters and notes is
certainly conscious artifice. But the reverence for the ancient literature, to which indeed we may owe its preservation, was of as great importance for contemporary cultural
life as is the cult of Ariosto and Tasso for modern Italy. The
finest gift which Symmachus can make to a friend is a copy
of Livy. Vergil was virtually worshiped; he was incessantly
analyzed, expounded, learned by heart, worked into centos,
and even consulted for fortune telling. It may well have
been in this age that the life of the great poet began to
be transformed into something miraculous and magical.

And finally the rural life of these upper-class Romans
deserves a fleeting glance. The same man who accounts it
a great praise for his daughter that she is an industrious

spinster or at least supervises the maidservants engaged in
spinning, possessed dozens of villas whose enormous mé-
nage required the services of an army of superintendents,
notaries, collectors, builders, carriers, and messengers, to
say nothing of thousands of farm slaves and share farmers.
As many of the great families died out, the *latifundia*,
which had long been "the ruin of Italy," were concentrated
in fewer and fewer hands. No one denies that this was on
the whole an evil, and Italy's dependence upon the African
grain fleets demonstrates the fact. The owners themselves
were not always happy; they were looked upon by the
government with suspicion, burdened with honorific obligations, annoyed by billeting requirements, perhaps frequently pressed by a complicated financial economy, and
could thus derive only qualified satisfaction from their well-
nigh princely position. But those who could still take pleasure in their possessions enjoyed their sojourns at their country estates, moving from one to the other according to the
season of the year; of these estates at least the older might
still have recalled the spacious elegance of Pliny's villas.
Symmachus' holdings included—to begin in the vicinity of
Rome—country houses on the Via Appia and on the Vatican, at Ostia, Praeneste, Lavinium, and cool Tibur, then an
estate at Formiae, a house at Capua, as well as estates in
Samnium, Apulia, and even in Mauretania. The inventory
includes as a matter of course properties on the heavenly
coast of Naples as well. The Romans had always given the
Gulf of Baiae a preference, unintelligible to us, over the
Bay of Naples. To sail on gaily colored boats from Lake
Avernus out to sea to Puteoli was still looked upon as a
blissful excursion; over the quiet waters songs echoed from
all the boats, from the villas built out over the sea there
came the sounds of gay parties, and far from the shore the
splashing of bold swimmers. Lucullan luxury was the paramount pattern, and the solitude which visitors pretended
to seek was hardly to be found in the row of villas and
palaces which extended for miles; genuine Roman country
life flourished rather upon estates which were actually op-
erated as farms. Here the Roman delighted to celebrate his
harvest-home: "The new wine has been pressed and stowed

in kegs; ladders reach to the tops of the fruit trees; now is the olive pressed; now the hunt takes us to the woodland, and keen-scented hounds follow the tracks of the boar." As regards the hunting, which we may conjecture to have been excellent, Ammianus is of opinion that the effeminacy of many made them content to be mere spectators; but for those whose limbs were vigorous the hunt, in the fullest sense of the word, was surely as important an activity as it is for the modern Italian. Even for this occupation a poem rather than a handbook divided into sections was required. Just as the *Georgics* provided artistic representation of country life in general, so the *Cynegetica* and *Halieutica*, some of which may go down to the fourth century, glorified hunting and fishing. A few verses of Rufus Festus Avienus, of the end of the fourth century, are our last reflection of the mood which inspired the country life of the Roman pagan. "At dawn I pray to the gods, then I go over my estate with the servants and show each his appropriate task. Then I read and I call upon Phoebus and the Muses, until it is time to anoint myself and to exercise in the sand-strewn palaestra. In happy mood, remote from money affairs, I eat, drink, sing, play, bathe, and rest after supper. While the small lamp consumes its modest measure of oil these lines are indited to the nocturnal Camenae."

The number of those who were able to enjoy life so fully must, however, have grown scant, for the crisis of the Empire, the belief in daimones, and anxiety concerning the beyond had shattered the pagan spirits also. That peculiar view of the world which combined nobler Epicureanism with Stoicism and made the earthly life of better men into so admirable and amiable a whole was dying out. A late echo of this spirit, from the age of Constantine, is provided, among others, by Pentadius' little poem, *On the Happy Life*. But his lines are mere reminiscences of Horace and need not be repeated here, because one can never know whether their author was in true earnest.

There was another city in the ancient world Empire, a city which was perhaps never named under Constantine, but concerning whose life and survival our sympathetic curiosity may well be aroused.

The position of ATHENS had been greatly diminished after the Peloponnesian war, and after the conquest of Sulla it had grown more and more deserted and was reduced to small compass. But the aura of glory which surrounded the city, its easy and pleasant life, the majestic monuments, the reverence for the Attic mysteries, and the awareness of the whole Hellenic world of its debt to Athens —all of this drew a continual stream of free and educated spirits to the city; philosophers and rhetors appeared, and numerous disciples followed. From the time of Hadrian— the new founder of Athens, as gratitude styled him—study burgeoned into a sort of university, which was in a way made secure by imperial endowments and later became the most important source of livelihood for the impoverished city.

All who cherished antiquity in these late ages must needs love the Athenians. Lucian has his Nigrinus utter beautiful and moving words concerning this people, among whom philosophy and poverty were equally at home, and who were not ashamed of their poverty but regarded themselves rich and happy in their freedom, the moderation of their life, and in their golden leisure. "The climate there is altogether philosophical, the fairest for fair-thinking men; indeed, one who wishes luxury, power, flattery, lies, servitude, must live in Rome." But not only the Syrian of Samosata, who is otherwise so seldom serious, but also an Alciphron, a Maximus of Tyre, a Libanius of Antioch, and other even later figures burst into flame whenever the Athenians are mentioned; we can never be certain whether in a given case ancient Athens of the period of bloom is thought of or whether the virtues of ancient Athens are discovered or assumed in the contemporary population. Speaking of forgiveness for insults which might be avenged, Libanius says, for example, that such conduct is "worthy of the Greeks, the Athenians, and godlike men." Heliodorus of Emesa has an Athenian girl who has been captured by Egyptian robbers write: "Barbarian love is not of so much worth as Athenian hatred." These later pagans, who could not be at ease either in the organized life of Rome or in the Christian Church, adhered to the most sacred site of ancient Greek life with a genuine tenderness. Anyone who could spend his life in that environment counted himself happy.

But the studies for which sophists and their disciples assembled in Athens bore the stamp of their age all too plainly. Just as Philostratus and Gellius are copious sources for the school of Athens in the early Empire, so are Libanius and Eunapius for its condition in the fourth century, and it cannot be said that it had improved in the interval. The one-sided predominance of rhetorical education and the extravagance and mysterious airs of individual Neoplatonists, the vanity of the teachers and the partisanship of their devotees—all of this disrupted the calm of Athens with a peculiar kind of rivalry. The very arrival of the student was a perilous affair; at the Piraeus, if he had not already been encountered at the headland of Sunium, men stood ready to watch for new students in order to recruit them for one or another lecture hall (*didascaleion*), even employing threats to change a decision which the student might already have taken at home. Teachers suddenly appeared at the harbor to make sure of their prey. If a man got safely to Athens, perhaps under the protection of the ship's captain, he found himself exposed to actual violence; not infrequently there were assault, murder, and consequent criminal investigations, and all because of the rivalry of teachers. The student's country of origin was a matter of great importance; when Eunapius was a student in Athens the Easterners mostly adhered to Epiphanius, the Arabs to Diophantus, the men of Pontus to their divine countryman Proaeresius, who also attracted many from Asia Minor, Egypt, and Libya. But no student was bound to follow this practice, and moreover the incessant transfers from school to school kept enmities constantly aflame. The students were divided into armed "choruses" with *prostates* at their head; their bloody brawls appeared to them "of equal value with battles for the fatherland." If things went so far that two parties, comprised of teachers and auditors, were required to answer for their deeds before the proconsul of

Achaia at Corinth, a regular ceremonious rhetorical contest
was staged in the presence of the proconsul, especially
when it was worth while, when the official was "quite well
educated for a mere Roman." There was no sort of com-
radely feeling. It had long been imprudent to venture an
appearance in public theaters and halls, which might immediately arouse bloody riots. The more prosperous sophists built themselves small theaters in their homes. Eunapius
gives us a description of the house of Julianus, which was
so equipped: "It was a small, modest house, but it breathed
of Hermes and the Muses, so like was it to a sanctuary,
with statues of its owner's friends; the theater was of stone
masonry, an imitation of the public theater on a small
scale." But a teacher who was as poor as Proaeresius, who
at first shared only a robe, a cloak, and a few carpets with
his friend Hephaestion, had to help himself as best he
could.

In the "choruses" of the students there were great and
deeply rooted abuses. At his first arrival the new student
was pledged to a costly and elaborate initiation and permanent obligations under oath, and this not infrequently
led to acquaintanceship with usurers. By day there was a
great deal of ball playing; by night wanderings and visits
to "the sweet-singing sirens." Crude and unscrupulous elements thought it a prank to attack unprotected houses in
robberly fashion. When Libanius finally disentangled himself from these "fraternities"—not without some difficulty—
he took pleasure in peaceful excursions, especially to Corinth. Apparently many still journeyed, as they had done at
the time of Philostratus, to the Olympian, Isthmian, and
other national festivals, which were even then held in great
esteem. But the greatest prize which a zealous pagan could
take with him from Athens was the Eleusinian initiation.

All of this colorful activity took place among the most
majestic monuments of the world, in which the noblest of
forms and the most significant of historical reminiscences
united to produce an inexpressible effect. We no longer
know what these works meant to the sophist of the fourth
century and his pupils. It was the period during which one
mainspring after another of the Greek genius died, until

only hair-splitting dialectic and lifeless compilation remained. The Parthenon of Pallas Athene and the Propylaea looked down upon the city in their ancient and virtually undisturbed majesty; despite the Gothic incursion under Decius and despite the plunder under Constantine, perhaps most of what Pausanias had seen and described in the second century still survived. But the pure harmony of architectural forms, the untrammeled grandeur of the images of the gods, uttered a language that was no longer wholly intelligible to the spirit of this age.

The century was eager to find a new home for its thoughts and aspirations. For zealous Christians their earthly-heavenly fatherland existed, and its name was Palestine.

We shall not here repeat what Eusebius, Socrates, Sozomen, and others relate of the official glorification of the country by Constantine and Helena, of the magnificent church buildings of Jerusalem, Bethlehem, Mamre, on Mount Olivet, and elsewhere. In the case of Constantine the motive which impelled him to such expenditures was quite superficial. The highest spiritual value which he could perceive in reverence for holy objects was a sort of belief in amulets; he had the nails of the True Cross worked into a bit for his horse and a helmet for use in battle.

But in countless numbers of the faithful there arose the natural and irresistible urge to visit in person the localities which they held sacred. It is true enough that a thoroughly spiritual man can forgo such pilgrimages, indeed that pilgrimages make what is essentially sacred superficial and dependent upon a given locality. Nevertheless a man who is not wholly unfeeling will visit at least once the sites which are for him hallowed by associations of love or of worship. In the course of time, when passion has become habit, the mood of the pilgrim will be reduced to a sort of superstitious "good works," but this by no means impugns its pure and beautiful origin.

From the apostolic age downward there must always have been visitors to the sites in Palestine which so strikingly combined memories of the ancient covenant between

God and man with those of the new. Perhaps the earliest
pilgrimage to remote parts was that of the Cappadocian
Bishop Alexander, who visited Jerusalem—at the time called
Aelia Capitolina—under Caracalla "for the sake of prayer
and of the history of the spot." Origen also came "to seek out
the paths of Christ, the disciples, and the prophets." But
at the time of Constantine longing for Palestine was remarkably interwoven with the growing cult of the burial
places of martyrs and of relics. Jerusalem itself was at once
the greatest and holiest of all relics, and it was surrounded
by a series of sacred sites of the first importance, involving
journeys of many days. From the itinerary of a pilgrim of
Bordeaux who visited the Holy Land in 333, we can see
how pious legend, and perhaps profit interest also, had
filled the whole country with classic sites, whose authen-
ticity continued unquestioned in the Middle Ages. Visitors
were shown the chamber in which Solomon wrote the Book
of Proverbs, the bloodstains of the priest Zacharias on the
floor of the former temple, the house of Caiaphas and
that of Pilate, the sycamore of Zacchaeus, and many other
objects which might afford historical criticism amusement.
Some decades later, in his description of Paula's journey,
Jerome enumerates the sacred sites from Dan to Beersheba
in much greater detail. Though otherwise very levelheaded
in his views concerning relics, Jerome himself settled in
Bethlehem for the remainder of his life, and drew after him
all those who were devoted to him. Toward the end of the
fourth century there lived in Jerusalem and its vicinity, with
great self-denial, a large colony of devout persons from all
quarters of the Empire; "there were almost as many chant-
ing choirs as there are diverse peoples." Among them were
Westerners of high rank and great wealth who had left everything behind them in order to live their lives out in
purer contemplation than was possible elsewhere. Those
whom circumstances prevented from so doing were deeply
grieved; Jerome wrote more than one letter to pacify such
persons and to assure them that eternal blessedness did not
depend upon a visit to Jerusalem.

But this much envied existence was by no means ideal.
Aside from external danger because of plundering Saracens

whose raids reached the very gates of Jerusalem, paganism persisted with desperate stubbornness in the near vicinity, in Arabia Petraea and in Coele-Syria; furthermore, daimonic activity, which had so long been native to Palestine, was as vigorous as ever. We have already seen St. Hilarion as an exorciser of daimones (p. 317). Jerome himself takes us to the tombs of the prophets not far from Samaria, where a large number of possessed persons waited for relief; they could be heard at a distance, howling with the cries of various animals. These were the stray spirits who hovered over the battlefield of all religion, the land between the Jordan, the desert, and the sea.

A strange providence brought it about that even in what Constantine did for Palestine there was an effect upon world history which endured for many centuries. If it had not been for the splendor which he bestowed upon Jerusalem and its vicinity, the reverence of the Roman world and consequently that of the Middle Ages would not have been so ardently fixed upon these sites, and the land would not have been wrested back after half a millennium of bondage under Islam.

ADDENDA ET CORRIGENDA

(Under this heading Burckhardt appended a number of notes written in the light of later research, partly bibliographical and partly expanding certain points made in the text. Of the latter category two are especially noteworthy as revealing Burckhardt's mind more fully, and are included here.)

Page 286: In the *résumé* of the edict of 324 A.D. it should have been emphasised (as I now realize from Brieger's work*) that, despite all expressions of contempt, continued toleration of paganism is specifically enjoined. Constantine desiderates a kind of parity, which was in fact bound to work out in favor of Christianity. But he had no intention to make his calculations explicit, and it is difficult to reduce him to a hard and fast principle.

This affords occasion for an additional word on Constantine's historical achievement in general. He ventured one of the boldest strokes imaginable, a stroke before which perhaps more than one Emperor had doubtless retreated in dismay, to wit, the separation of the empire from the old religion, which, in its dilapidated condition, could be of no further help to the authority of the state, despite the cult of the Emperor which it imposed. This implies that even in his youth, even before the persecution, Constantine must have reached a decision concerning the Christian Church also: small as was the minority it comprised in the face of the entire pagan world, it was nevertheless the only organized force in the Empire—aside from the army—when all else was crumbling dust. His perspicacity in perceiving in this force a future support for the Empire and in acting

* Brieger, *Konstantin d.Gr. als Religionspolitiker,* Brieger's Zeitschrift fuer Kirchengeschichte IV, 2. Gotha 1880.

accordingly constitutes Constantine's enduring claim to
fame. Along with an intelligence as cold and hard as it was
lofty, along with complete inner independence of any Christian sentiment, this implies extraordinary determination and
resourcefulness. Like Henry VIII of England, Constantine
understood how to accommodate his individual measures
to prevalent trends at every turn, and almost until the end
he was fearless enough to offer paganism at once defiance
and a degree of favor.

Page 312 ff.: The entire concept of the actual and chrono-
logical development of monachism has newly been considerably modified by Weingarten's work on "The Origin of
Monachism in the Post-Constantinian Era" (*Der Ursprung
des Mönchtums im nachkonstantinischen Zeitalter*, Jena,
1877). Here, to say nothing of numerous other critical
conclusions, the *Life of Paul* is declared to be a romance
by Jerome, and the *Life of Anthony* not of Athanasian authorship. If, these arguments notwithstanding, I fail to alter
my previous account substantially, I may justify my course
by the consideration that such pieces of fiction—if that is
what they are—were nevertheless fashioned in the spirit of
their time and place, and may hence claim truth from the
viewpoint of cultural history. (In the case of Anthony I
regard a combination of extreme asceticism and previously
acquired theological and philosophical education as quite
possible.) But I feel constrained to lay much greater weight
than Weingarten does on the anchorite as preparation to
the cenobite stage. Furthermore, the *argumentum ex
silentio* as applied to Eusebius and other bishops seems to
me somewhat questionable; perhaps they had little regard
for monachism, and were preoccupied with matters which
seemed to them very much more important. Finally, I regard asceticism generally, even in its fearful stages, as a
quite possible consequence of rigorous Christian doctrine
and Christian views. That the very remarkable recluses of
the temple of Serapis survived in those of the Christian
period I do not deny; but a recluse—however austere his
life might be—and an eremite living in the open differ much
more than our author assumes.

ON THE ANCIENT SOURCES

For his historical reconstructions Burckhardt made full use of ancient sources—numismatic and epigraphic as well as literary, and *belles lettres* as well as professed history—and of modern authorities. The latter are now largely antiquated, in a measure by Burckhardt's own work. Among the ancients the authors most frequently referred to, as is inevitable in any treatment of the subject, are Eusebius (mainly the *Life of Constantine*) and Lactantius (mainly the *On the Deaths of the Persecutors*) among the Christians, and among the pagans, the *Scriptures Historiae Augusta*, Ammianus Marcellinus, Aurelius Victor, and the *Panegyrici*. On the historical worth of all these sources widely differing opinions have been held, and it may serve the reader's convenience to have a brief statement concerning them.

Eusebius of Caesarea (*ca.* 265–340) was a prolific writer on Biblical exegesis, apologetics, and church history. His work on the Bible included, besides regular commentaries, such helps as an *Onomasticon* of Biblical place names; his principal 'apologetic' works are the *Preparation for the Gospel* in fifteen books and the *Demonstration of the Gospel* in twenty (of which more than half are extant); his *Church History* in ten books (aside from a briefer work on chronology) is a pioneer work in its field and was widely used by subsequent historians. All of his longer works are especially valuable for their copious extracts from earlier writers. Eusebius wrote after Christianity had become an established religion, and he is the first writer to apply to church scholarship generally the techniques of the objective secular researcher. Considered from the viewpoint of objective historiography the *Life of Constantine* is in fact clearly liable to the stricture Burckhardt pronounced upon it (see pp. 272 ff.). But it is not altogether just to regard it from that point of view, for it really belongs to the genus of panegyric, in which it was universally recognized that objective truth must yield to fulsome adulation. But if such exculpation saves the character of Eusebius, it does not establish the veracity of the *Life*.

Lactantius (born *ca.* 250) marks the same transition in Latin patristic writing as Eusebius does in Greek. His doctrinal works include *On the Creation, The Divine Institutes,* and *On the Wrath of God,* but it is *On the Deaths of the Persecutors* which contains historical data. This treatise relates the horrible deaths suffered by all earlier Emperors who persecuted Christians—the abdication of Diocletian and Maximian is interpreted as a divine chastisement—with a view to demonstrating God's care for His elect, possibly in order to deter Licinius from hostile measures against the Christians. After Burckhardt's day there was a tendency among scholars to deny the genuineness of this treatise, but latterly the pendulum has swung in the direction of regarding it as a work of Lactantius. The author, whoever he may have been, gives every indication of having been an eyewitness, however biased, of the persecutions in Nicomedia.

The *Historia Augusta* presents biographies of Emperors, Caesars, and usurpers from Hadrian to Numerian (117–284), with a lacuna for the period 244–253. It purports to be the work of six authors—Aelius Spartianus, Vulcacius Gallicanus, Aelius Lampridius, Julius Capitolinus, Trebellius Pollio, and Flavius Vopiscus—and to have been written between the reigns of Diocletian and Constantine, or about 330. Some scholars accept this genesis as true, but others hold that the work was written by a single hand almost a century later, and that the names of the six authors were attached to give it credit. As history the book rates low in any case, being chiefly concerned with petty gossip and sprinkled with palpable untruths.

Ammianus Marcellinus (born *ca.* 325) wrote a history of the period from Nerva to Valens in thirty-one books, of which the first thirteen are lost; what remains covers the years 353–378. Historians generally agree with Gibbon's judgment that Ammianus is "judicious and candid" and that his testimony is "unexceptionable." But such passing remarks as that "the enmity of the Christians towards each other surpassed the fury of savage beasts against man" (22.5) has been taken in some quarters to imply a general anti-Christian bias on the part of Ammianus.

Aurelius Victor was personally acquainted with Ammianus Marcellinus, was Prefect of Rome in 389, and assembled his tripartite history in 360. The first two parts, *Origin of the Roman Race* (on the Aeneas legend) and *On Illustrious Men* (on the early monarchy and the republic) are irrelevant here; the third part, called *Caesars*, deals with the Empire and has much the same merits as Ammianus' work. What Burckhardt refers to as the "Second Victor" is an epitome, ostensibly of Victor but really an independent work, attached to the *Caesars*.

The *Panegyrici* is a corpus of twelve cloyingly fulsome orations addressed to various emperors on special occasions. They are indubitably genuine and, cautiously used, a valuable historical source. Eight refer to our period: II, to Maximian, on 21 April (the birthday of Rome) 289, in some northerly city of the Empire; III, to Maximian, for his birthday; IV, a petition of Eumenius to rebuild the schools of Autun; V, to Constantius, 1 March 297, on the subjugation of Britain; VI, for the marriage of Constantine and Fausta, 307; VII, for Constantius, on the birthday of Treves, 310; VIII, gratitude to Constantine in the name of Treves, 311; IX, felicitation to Constantine for his victory over Maxentius, at Treves, 313; X, Nazarius' panegyric of Constantine for the fifth year of his accession, 321.

Among other writers frequently cited by Burckhardt mention may be made of the historians Dio Cassius, Zonaras, Eutropius, Herodian; the church historians Socrates, Sozomen, Moses of Chorene; the church writers Tertullian, Jerome, Athanasius, Arnobius; the biographers of the rhetoricians Philostratus and Eunapius; the novelists Apuleius, Heliodorus, Longus.

MOSES HADAS

CHRONOLOGY OF THE EMPERORS

98–117	Trajan
117–138	Hadrian
138–161	Antoninus Pius
161–169	Marcus Aurelius Lucius Verus
169–177	Marcus Aurelius
177–180	Marcus Aurelius Commodus
180–193	Commodus
193	Pertinax
193	Didius Julianus
193–198	Septimius Severus
198–208	Septimius Severus Caracalla
208–211	Septimius Severus Caracalla Geta
211–212	Caracalla Geta
212–217	Caracalla
217–218	Macrinus
218	Macrinus Diadumenianus
218–222	Elagabalus
222–235	Alexander Severus
235–238	Maximinus
238	Balbinus Maximus
238–244	The Gordians
244–248	Philip the Arab
248–249	Philip the Arab and son
249–251	Decius
251–253	Gallus and son
253	Aemilianus
253–260	Valerian Gallienus
260–268	Gallienus
268–270	Claudius Gothicus
270	Quintillus
270–275	Aurelian
275	Interregnum of about one month
275–276	Tacitus
276	Florianus
276–282	Probus
282–283	Carus
283–284	Carinus Numerianus
284–286	Diocletian
286–305	Diocletian Maximian
305–306	Constantius Chlorus Galerius
306–307	Galerius Severus
307–308	Galerius Constantine [Maximian Maxentius]
308–310	Galerius Licinius
310–311	Galerius Licinius Maximinus Daia Constantine
311–313	Licinius Maximinus Daia Constantine
313–324	Constantine Licinius
324–337	Constantine
337–340	Constans Constantius II Constantine II
340–350	Constans Constantius II
350–361	Constantius II
361–363	Julian

(Numbers in parentheses refer to dates)